Japanese Society and Lay Participation in Criminal Justice

Masahiro Fujita

Japanese Society and Lay Participation in Criminal Justice

Social Attitudes, Trust, and Mass Media

Springer

Masahiro Fujita
Kansai University
Suita, Osaka, Japan

ISBN 978-981-10-0337-0 ISBN 978-981-10-0338-7 (eBook)
https://doi.org/10.1007/978-981-10-0338-7

Library of Congress Control Number: 2018946107

Printed on acid-free paper

This Springer imprint is published by the registered company Springer Nature Singapore Pte Ltd.
The registered company address is: 152 Beach Road, #21-01/04 Gateway East, Singapore 189721, Singapore

Preface

"This system itself is an adventure and a type of decision, and there are many areas for which we can't see outcomes, or which require further consideration, or on which we need to enlighten the public much much more. However, this is an attempt which will place us on a new track vis-à-vis the traditional judicial system, that is, uh, a sort of, umm, a revolution in the judiciary, according to my fellow Giichi Tsunoda[1], director of this committee." (comment made by Satsuki Eda, a member of House of Councilors, taken from the minute of Committee on Judicial Affairs at House of Councilors, the National Diet of Japan, May 20, 2004)

This book is dedicated to those who are interested in Japanese mixed jury system which was introduced in May 2004 and was taken effect in May 2009. The system is called as "saiban-in seido" in Japanese. This book describes the social attitudes of Japanese citizens toward the system, what appears in deliberation from mock juries, the issue of trust in the justice system, the society's concern which can be observed through statistical analyses on newspaper articles.

Within the combined term "saiban-in seido," the separated term "saiban" means trial(s) in law courts, "in" here means member(s), and "seido" means the system(s). Together with all these three words, "saiban-in seido" literally means "trial member system."

This system has been introduced to establish "the popular base of the justice system" (Justice System Reform Council, 2001). This policy was drawn from one of the fundamental philosophies of the recommendation of the Justice System Reform Council. This council was established temporarily in the Cabinet Office of Japan in 1999. In the recommendation, JSRC reviewed that Japan experienced a series of reforms in many parts of its society in the second half of the twentieth

[1]Giichi Tsunoda, Democratic Party member of the House of Councilors at the time. Tsunoda served as the chairman of the House of Councilors Budget Committee and Committee on Rules and Administration. With a prior career as an attorney, Eda was queried as to his perspective as a lawyer regarding the saiban-in system. Tsunoda acted as secretary-general of the Shin-ryokufûkai in the House of Councilors for the Democratic Party in 2000, and the vice chairman of the House of Councilors in 2004, retiring from politics in 2007.

century. The reforms included political reforms, administrative reforms, decentralization of governing systems, and economic reforms including regulatory reforms. And "what commonly underlies these reforms is the will that *each and every person will break out of the consciousness of being a governed object and will become a governing subject, with autonomy and bear social responsibility*, and that *the people will participate in building a free and fair society in mutual cooperation* and will work to restore rich creativity and vitality to this country." (Justice System Reform Council 2001 in Chapter 1, italicized by the author.)

The saiban-in system was introduced to realize the philosophy shown above. But why didn't the JSRC recommend to revive the Japanese pure jury system which was conducted in Showa era (1925–) or just recommend to develop a new pure or mixed jury system, instead of starting a novel system? Why did the JSRC invent the somewhat awkward term "saiban-in seido"?

The author assumes that the reason why the JSRC coined a new word should be that there were conflicts between a group of people who actively support for reviving Japanese pure jury system exercised in the twentieth century and another group of people who would like to introduce a mixed jury system in which the citizens have less influence compared to the pure jury system. The JSRC included both groups of people in order to reflect either side of opinions to their final outcome. The JSRC didn't like to set it as one of the significant issues in their deliberation whether they adopt pure jury system or mixed jury system, they may thereby be stuck on a somewhat political conflict rather than how do they realize one of their philosophy, promoting popular base of the justice system. After they decided to introduce a public participatory system in the primary trial procedure, they wouldn't like to have a real political clash just about how do they label the new system as "jury" or something different. If they had a discussion like that, the discussion might lead to serious political conflict in the council, and they might have run out of their time before they reached discussion on the substance of civic participation to the justice system.

Coining a new word was a smart solution for avoiding the ineffectual political arguments. But at the same time, the JSRC was obliged to seek a new system which is suitable for Japanese society.

The Justice System Reform Council (JSRC) referred to other jury and mixed jury systems which were run in other countries, and they proposed "saiban-in seido," in some extent a mixture of the pure jury system and mixed jury systems. In *saiban-in seido*, the civic participants are randomly selected from the pools of the sound adults with Japanese nationality for each case as like a jury system, but the judicial panels consist both of professional judges *and* the civic participants. That's the reason why the author calls the system as "mixed" jury system. In the system like that, different from jury systems, the professional judges can advise the citizens on legal matters at any time throughout the criminal procedures and deliberations. The professional judges might also advise the citizens how to find the facts from the presented evidence, how to question the witnesses at the stand in the law court, and even how to decide the case including the sentencing which will be imposed on the defendant as well. This can give rise to a serious doubt on the independence of judgments of the civic participants. If we put on the most substantial significance on the independence of the citizens, the system like Japanese mixed jury system is imperfect because the professional judges can intervene in the lay people's decision-making at any time.

Some scholars call *saiban-in seido* as "quasi-jury system" in English. It means that the "saiban-in seido" is apparently like a jury system, but it is substantially not a satisfactory jury system. That's supposed because the independence of the lay participants' judgments can be easily impaired by professional judges as the lay persons are always with professional judges throughout the trial procedure, while in a pure jury system, jurors can make decisions out of the influence of professional judges. But even "saiban-in seido" is not a perfect system, like other social or legal systems, when we look at the fact that "saiban-in seido" was invented in the process of pursuing the Japanese ways of justice with civic participation, "saiban-in seido" should be estimated from the viewpoint whether the system promotes the popular base of the Japanese justice system, civic participants have better consciousness of ruling subject of their society rather than governed objects, rather than the extent how the system completely replicate a pure jury system. The important thing is whether the aim has been accomplished by implementing the "saiban-in seido," not whether the system is a sound jury system.

To approach the state of the system and the Japanese society which accept the saiban-in system, this book begins with some short descriptions of the outlines of lay participation in the Japanese criminal justice system. Then this book deals with the questions of what the lay participants think about the system after their participation, and how the general public evaluate the system. With these data, we are going to obtain some pictures of how Japanese people think about the system. Then we continue to the question whether the introduction of lay participation has promoted trust in the justice system in Japan. This would deal with the question whether "saiban-in seido" accomplish the aim of its introduction. The next part is showing the foci of Japanese society's interest in the lay participation system by analyzing the database of newspaper articles. With those data, the author describes the foci of interest concerning the saiban-in system and positive or negative evaluations of the system in Japan.

Unfortunately, attempts like this book – discuss whether the fundamental philosophy and the aim of the JSRC raised in their recommendation are realized through implementing saiban-in seido with somewhat objective data – are hard to be adequately or straightforwardly understood as a scientific issue in Japan. The issues about *saiban-in seido* are interpreted as too much political. Typically, in those debates, the starting question is "are you pro for or con against saiban-in seido?" (e.g., Aoki, 2009; "Saiban-in seido ni hantai suru kai no ikensho [The opinion paper of the opposing party against the saiban-in system]," 2004; Takayama, 2010). Writers or thinkers are forced to choose one of the two positions. Discussions on "saiban-in seido" are just understood as battles of the pro group versus the con group for the system. After choosing one position, the writer is expected to develop his or her opinion entirely consistent with the position. This style of discussion can be a political entertainment, but would never be productive nor scientific, and the questions like this do not lead us to the depth of the aim or philosophies of the introduction of *saiban-in seido*. But a significant part of arguments on the saiban-in system in Japan has been made in this framing.

Instead, this book would like to contribute to the discussion in the saiban-in system in more productive ways. For doing that, the author thought that the first problem should be whether we should accept the fundamental philosophy in the JSRC recommendation. This could be an issue of values or policy, not entirely science. If we refuse to accept the philosophy, the discussion and this book end here. And once we decide to accept the philosophy, the next problem is that the philosophy is well realized by implementing a specific legal system, to date, the saiban-in system. We should test whether the saiban-in system works well for realizing the aim of the introduction of the system. This issue can be scientific, with which this book aims to deal. We can decide whether we should keep implementing the saiban-in system, whether we should change the system, or whether we should abolish the system, based on the results of the research. The decision may also be political, not scientific.

This book is a compilation of the essence of significant parts of the studies which have been carried out since the author was a master's course student. Some parts of this book are brand new results of the studies which have not ever been published. The works which were previously (or simultaneously in Japanese) published are specified by the footnotes in the parts. Because of this, some parts of the contents of the chapter in this book are repeatedly appeared – for example, the explanation of introduction of the saiban-in system and the meaning of the system – the author asks to pardon it in consideration of the history of the composition of this book.

More than 15 years have passed since the author intended to study on the new civic participation system in Japan. The system has grown from its infancy to the adolescence in the 15 years. But it is not mature yet, and the system needs to be cared for working satisfactorily.

The time that the author started to study the saiban-in system just fell on the infancy of revival period of "law and psychology" in Japan. Law and psychology is an academic field in which the researchers study on human behavior in legal context. This field has been long forgotten since finishing its height which came in the first half of the twentieth century until the Japanese Society for Law Psychology was established in 2000 (Sato, 2013). Every time the author explained his job when he met new people, they requested him to explain what the law and psychology are like, why and how those two disciplines are interconnected, even they were experts in law or psychology. The author struggled for demonstrating the meaning of the existence of the studies like presented in this book in Japan. In that situation, the advancement of the studies has been much slower than if the field was widely recognized at the time of the beginning of the series of the studies. But time has passed, people's and the academic's recognition evolved in this 15 years. This phenomenon has progressed under the influence of many factors and incidents in the society. And studies of *saiban-in seido* are recognized as one of the major industries in psychology or sociology of law. This must be a better situation to promote studies of public participation system, and better for those who are involved in the studies on lay participation system in Japan. In these circumstances, the author decided to publish the results of the studies concerning saiban-in seido as a compilation to contribute the discussion whether the saiban-in seido does a satisfactory job for implementation of the aims and philosophy proposed by the JSRC.

The author profoundly thanks all persons who have helped to carry the studies forward. From the time when the author started the series of studies on the saiban-in system, many persons have supported to proceed studies combined in this book. The author apologizes for not including all persons here, but especially thanks (in alphabetical order of the surnames) Hisashi Aizawa, Malcolm M. Feeley, Daniel H. Foote, Hiroshi Fukurai, Akira Goto, Nahoko Hayashi, Valerie P. Hans, Marianne Hegeman, Syûgo Hotta, Makoto Ibusuki, Yasuyo Ikari, Hiroshi Kawatsu, Manako Kinoshita, Mika Kudo, Tadahiko Maeda, Nancy S. Marder, Takashi Maruta, Yoshiyuki Matsumura, Setsuo Miyazawa, Makiko Naka, Hiroyuki Nakayama, Takeshi Nishimura, Yoshinori Okada, Shozo Ota, Victoria Plaut, Miyuki Sakai, Satoru Shinomiya, Tadahi Shibayama, Yuji Shiratori, Takashi Takano, Dimitri Vanoverbeke, Matthew J. Wilson, and Arinori Yosano and as an organization, the author thanks to Osaka Judicial Colloquium of Representatives of Every Sector of Society. Juno Kawakami at Springer Japan arranged everything and helped to realize this publication. Finally, Yumiko Fujita, Akari, and Satsuki Fujita who have become the fellow passengers of my voyage of life during advancement of my studies.

It is a great pleasure for the author if this book contributes to understand the state of the saiban-in system and to spur on the discussion of whether the system has done excellent work for improving the justice system with scientific methods and the society of Japan.

References

Aoki, S. (2009). Anata wa shikei wo senkoku dekimasuka (Saiban-in seido ni hantai suru) [Can you sentence death penalty? (Opposing the saiban-in system)]. *Kin'yôbi [Friday]*, *17*(3), 10–13 [in Japanese].

Justice System Reform Council. (2001). *Recommendations of the justice system reform council: For a justice system to support Japan in the 21st century*. Tokyo: Justice System Reform Council. Retrieved from https://japan.kantei.go.jp/judiciary/2001/0612report.html

Saiban-in seido ni hantai suru kai no ikensho [The opinion paper of the opposing party against the saiban-in system]. (2004). *Hanrei Jihô [Precedents Reporter]*, (1844), 3–7 [in Japanese].

Sato, T. (2013). Hôshinrigaku no rekishi: Ôbei to nihon ni okeru sokuseki [The history of legal psychology: The trajetory in Europe, America, and Japan]. In M. Fujita (Ed.), *Hô to Shinrigaku [Law and Psychology]* (pp. 221–234). Kyoto: Hôritsu Bunka Sha [in Japanese].

Takayama, M. (2010). Nihon no jikenbo (29) Saiban-in seido e no hantai wa hijoushiki [Case file in Japan (29): It is lack of common sense to oppose the saiban-in system]. *Boisu [Voice]*, (389), 19–22 [in Japanese].

Contents

Chapter 1
Introduction: Lay Participation to Criminal Justice System in Japan

Introduction of the System and the Interest of This Book

As we saw in the preface of this book, the Japanese Government introduced the all-new lay participation system in the Japanese criminal procedure in May 2004. The system was named "*saiban-in seido*," from now on the author calls it "saiban-in system." The Act on Criminal Trials with Participation of Saiban-in ("*Saiban-in* Act")[1] came into effect in May 2004.[2] After a five-year preparation, trials by the system started in May 2009. Actual public hearings began in the August of 2009[3]("Saiban-in saiban kyô kaitei [The trial by saiban-in starts today]" 2009). As of May 2018, a full 9 years' period has passed since the trials by the system have begun.

Introducing this system has been one of the most significant, and revolutionary changes in the criminal, or in the whole Japanese justice system since after WWII. The impact of the system on the Japanese justice system and the society has been tremendous, and the author has come to realize it along with the operation carried out. The author has studied the system since 2000. Under that concern, this book is wholly dedicated to explaining the state of the system, people's behavior concerning the system, and discuss social issues on the system. In some parts of this book, the author discusses based on data obtained with psychological, sociological, or behavioral science's methods.

[1] Precisely speaking, the name of the law is "the act concerning criminal trials in which saiban-in participate" (裁判員の参加する刑事裁判に関する法律 *saiban-in no sanka suru keiji saiban ni kansuru hôritsu*) act no. 63 in 2004 (平成16年法律第63号).

[2] Saiban-in Act Supplementary Provisions, art. 1.

[3] The very first trial by saiban-in system began on August 3 after its pretrial conferences, and finished on August 6, 2009, at the Tokyo District Court.

M. Fujita, *Japanese Society and Lay Participation in Criminal Justice*, https://doi.org/10.1007/978-981-10-0338-7_1

About This Chapter

The purpose of this introduction part is to give an overview of changes in the public and criminal trials in the eight years since the start of public hearings with the saiban-in system. In other words, this introduction examines expectations, criticisms, and what impact the system may have had on Japanese society while presenting issues in validating future empirical research. In the next section, we are going to review the outline of the system with a description of Japanese criminal justice system.

The General Outline of Japanese Criminal Justice System

The saiban-in system was put in practice as a special law for criminal trials. Some of the readers of this book may not be familiar with the criminal justice system in Japan. To deepen the understanding of future issues, the author would like to make a brief introduction of the criminal justice system in Japan.

The criminal justice system in Japan consists of three stages; the stages are investigation stage, trial stage, and correction stage. While the investigation part covers the period from the occurrence of a crime to the indictment, the trial part related to the process from indictment to judgment and dealt with emergency relief procedures such as appeals and retrials. The saiban-in system is based on the Saiban-in Act, that regulates the procedure of the trial part as one of the special laws of the Criminal Procedure Law.

From Investigation to Indictment

An investigation starts once the investigation agency acknowledges it. The police may acknowledge crimes through police patrols; there are also reports from individuals or organizations other than the police. The reports may come from the public, shops, or reports from security companies. The police[4] or the prosecutor's office[5] can initiate an investigation. The investigation agency collects evidence related to the incident.[6] The police or the prosecutors use arbitrary execution and compulsory execution for collecting evidence.

The arrest is compulsory execution for restraining a suspect.[7] Arrest becomes legally possible only in the case that the agency has enough reasons to presume the

---

[4] Criminal Procedure Law (The act no.131 in 1948), art. 189.

[5] Criminal Procedure Law, art. 191.

[6] Criminal Procedure Law, art. 197.

[7] Criminal Procedure Law, art. 199.

suspect commits a crime. Before the police arrest the suspect, they should obtain an arrest warrant from the court. In case of emergency, anyone who acknowledges the crime can arrest the suspect without a warrant.[8] This type of arrest is called the flagrant offender arrest.

After an investigation has started and the police have gathered evidence to some extent, they have some understanding of the details and the outline of the incident. As a rule, the police should send the case with full evidence to the prosecutor's office.[9] If the investigating office arrests the suspect, the agency can request the court to allow them to put the suspect into custody.[10] In principle, the police should send to the prosecution all cases which the police complete their investigations. However, in some minor cases which the police consider the suspect not to send to the prosecution (minor punishment for misdemeanor), suspects are not sent to prosecution authorities.[11]

When the police send the case to the prosecution, the prosecutor's office should decide whether they should prosecute it or not. If they need additional evidence to make their decision, they hold an investigation and collect additional evidence. In case the suspect is not in custody, the police and the prosecution should decide whether they request a warrant to the court within a reasonable period. On the other hand, if the investigation already arrests the suspect, the prosecution should decide whether they request detention warrant within 24 h of their reception of the suspect and within 72 h from the time of arrest.[12] If the warrant judge accepts the request after questioning the suspect, the suspect will be in detention for ten days. Moreover, if the warrant judge acknowledges the extension of the detention upon the prosecution's request, the suspect will be in detention ten more days. If the warrant judge denies the investigation's request for a warrant, they release the suspect right away.

Occasionally, some scholars call the criminal justice system in Japan as "hostage justice." "Hostage justice" implies that the investigation put the suspects in custody as long as possible, they conduct interrogations as much as possible to get confessions, especially in case of serious crimes. The places of the detention should be the detention centers in principle, but the reality is that the suspects stay in the jails in the police buildings. They are notorious "代用監獄*daiyô kangoku* (substitute jails)." As long as the suspects stay in the substitute jails, the police can interrogate as they wish. The practice of investigation is very efficient for the investigation, but the substitute jails make fertile grounds for violating human rights under common circumstances that the investigation does not allow the defense attorneys to attend interrogations.

---

[8] Criminal Procedure Law, art. 213.

[9] Criminal Procedure Law, art. 246. If the suspect is arrested, the case should be sent to the prosecution within 48 hours from the time of arrest. (Criminal Procedure Law, art. 203.)

[10] Criminal Procedure Law, art. 204.

[11] Criminal Procedure Law, the proviso of art. 246.

[12] Criminal Procedure Law, art. 205.

The confinement upon arrest can last up to 72 h,[13] and one detention period is ten days.[14] The ten-day detention can be renewed for once with a warrant.[15] Consequently, the detention can last for a total of 23 days for one crime.[16] If the prosecutors' office indicts the case, the court should decide whether the defendant should be in detention. The warrant judge needs to find that there is a possibility of escaping or destroying the evidence if they release the defendant to issue a warrant. The defendant, the defense attorneys, agents, or family members can request a bail when the defendant is in detention.[17] The warrant judge needs to admit a bail unless the defendant committed serious crimes, the defendant has a prior record of serious crimes, there is a risk of escape, destruction of evidence, threating witnesses, or the court cannot know the defendant's name or address.[18] The defendant needs to pay the bail money upon the release.[19] The court confiscates the bail money when the suspect escapes or the bail is canceled.

The prosecution has the entire discretion of whether to prosecute or not,[20] in principle. The discretion is called "起訴便宜主義 (*Kiso bengi shugi*; indictment opportunism)." Prosecutors also have a high authority as they are the only agencies which are in principle authorized to make decisions on whether to prosecute or not[21] (起訴独占主義 *Kiso dokusen shugi*: monopolization of prosecution). In deciding whether the prosecution indict or not, it considers the strength of the evidence, whether the prosecution has indicted similar cases, precedents, and other related factors.

Regarding indictment, the grand jury system does not currently exist in Japan. One of the exceptions of monopolization of prosecution is the Committee for Inquest of Prosecution.[22] The Committee for Inquest of Prosecution consists of eleven randomly selected citizens.[23] The Committee is set up in correspond to every

[13] Criminal Procedure Law, art. 205, para. 2.

[14] Criminal Procedure Law, art. 208, para. 1.

[15] Criminal Procedure Law, art. 208, para. 2.

[16] For particular categories of serious offenses, the detention can be extended for another five days, totaling 28 days. Criminal Procedure Law, art. 208–2.

[17] Criminal Procedure Law, art. 88, para. 1.

[18] Criminal Procedure Law, art. 94.

[19] Criminal Procedure Law, art. 87.

[20] Criminal Procedure Law, art. 248 prescribes that the prosecutor can decide not to indict when the prosecutor finds there is no need for prosecution based upon the circumstances concerning the case.

[21] Criminal Procedure Law, art. 247.

[22] Another exception is the quasi-indictment procedures (準起訴手続 *Jun-kiso Tetsudzuki*) which is prescribed by the Criminal Procedure Act articles 262 to 269. The cases which can be processed by quasi-indictment procedures are restricted by the crime categories. The crimes are oppressions by public service personnel, assault and cruelty by special public officers, the crime prescribed article 45 in Subversive Activities Prevention Law (Act No. 240 of 1952), and the crimes prescribed in the article 42 or 43 of the Act on Regulation of Organizations Which Have Committed Indiscriminate Mass Murder (Act No.147 of 1999).

[23] Kensatsu shinsakai hô [The Committee for the Inquest of Prosecution Act, the law no. 147 in 1948], art. 4.

district prosecutor's office. The Committee initiate reviews in response to the requests made by the concerned parties or the initiation of the Committee itself.[24] The Committee reviews the cases, and the Committee can issue its opinions. The opinions may be "起訴相当 (*Kiso sôtô*) suitable for prosecuting"or "不起訴不当 (*Hukiso hutô*) unreasonable for not prosecuting," when the Committee judged the decision of the prosecutor's office was not appropriate.[25] In case the Committee decides suitable for prosecution or unreasonable for not prosecuting, the prosecutors' office reconsiders their prior decision for having not indicted. However, the Committee had not had any authority to compel prosecutor's office's indictment. The judicial reform in Heisei era (around 2001 to 2005) strengthened the power of the Committee for Inquest of Prosecution. After the judicial reform, in case the Committee judges the case to be suitable for prosecuting again after the prosecutors' office's decision for not indicting after their reconsideration, the case should be prosecuted.[26] In that case, the court appoints designated lawyers (指定弁護士 *shitei bengoshi*) who should carry out the duty of prosecutors.[27]

Trials

When the prosecutor's office decides to prosecute, the office sends a bill of indictment to the court.[28] In the bill of indictment, the prosecutor describes the outline of the case in a format by specifying the time and place of the incident occurred.[29] The law does not allow the prosecutors to attach any evidence with the letter of the indictment (起訴状一本主義 (*Kisojô ippon shugi*) bill-of-indictment-only principle).[30] The principle is a measure to prevent prejudice in judges in advance. Currently, it also helps to avoid prejudice for saiban-in.

The court to have received the bill of indictment examines whether the indictment meets legal requirements. A trial procedure starts when the court accepts the indictment. The court designates the first trial date,[31] and the trial will start.

In case there is much evidence, and the case is complicated, the court will hold pretrial conferences.[32] At the conferences, professional judges, prosecutors, defense

---

24 The Committee for the Inquest of Prosecution Act, art. 2.

25 The Committee for the Inquest of Prosecution Act, art. 39–5. The decision should be made with the approvals at least eight members of the board. Other decisions can be made with the approvals of more than half of the board.

26 The Committee for the Inquest of Prosecution Act, art. 41–6.

27 The Committee for the Inquest of Prosecution Act, art. 41–9 and 41–10.

28 Criminal Procedure Law, art. 256, para. 1.

29 Criminal Procedure Law, art. 256, para. 2.

30 Criminal Procedure Law, art. 256, para. 6.

31 Criminal Procedure Law, art. 273.

32 Criminal Procedure Law, art. 316–2.

attorneys[33] gather in one hall and create a plan of hearing. They make efforts to specify the issues of the case, what kinds of evidence they will examine in their trial. It is a system introduced separately from the saiban-in system, but it is almost always held in saiban-in trials.[34] If the case is very complicated, it can take from one to several years. The detention of suspect can last even they conduct the pretrial conferences.

In principle, the law adopts the adversarial system in conducting trials. So, the trial prosecutors and the defense lawyers are rivals who fight against each other. Also, prosecutors do not need to submit anything other than the evidence to prove the guilt of the defendant to the court. However, to secure fairness, the court can order the prosecutors to disclose the evidence in a pretrial conference.[35] The court can issue disclosure orders upon its initiative and at the request of defense attorneys. However, at the defense attorneys' request the disclosure of evidence, the attorneys need to identify the kinds of evidence that they want to request the disclosure. It is hard for the defense lawyers because they do not know that the prosecutors have what kind of evidence. In this regard, in recent years improvements have been made and it is now possible to request evidence disclosure by designating a general framework. If the prosecutors judged to be disadvantageous to disclose such evidence, the prosecution could reply that it is "inappropriate (不相当 *husoto*)" and the court will judge whether the prosecution should disclose the evidence. If the prosecutors do not have the evidence which the defense request to disclose, the prosecution replies "not being found (不見当 *hukento*)." There are doubts that the prosecution replies "not being found" when they want to refuse to disclose. There are cases that the evidence appeared after the prosecution replied: "not being found." (e.g., Nippon Hoso Kyokai 2011).

After pretrial conferences finished, the court designates the first date of the trial. The procedures are different whether the case should be tried by saiban-in or not. If the trial should be tried by saiban-in, the court will conduct saiban-in selection procedure before the first date of the trial. The later section of this chapter will describe the details of the procedure of saiban-in selection.

At the start of the trial, the presiding judge will make an identity-establishing inquiry of the defendant to confirm whether the person who is present at the court is not another person who may be mistakenly brought to the court.[36] After the question, the prosecutor reads aloud the bill of indictment.[37] Then the presiding judge asks the defendant whether he/she accept the contents of the bill. The defendant

---

[33] Prosecutors and defense attorneys must attend to hold a pretrial conference. (Criminal Procedure Act, art. 316–7.) The defendants may attend the pretrial conference. (Criminal Procedure Act., art. 316–9.)

[34] The Criminal Procedure Act art 316–2 prescribes "In case the court acknowledges the need in order for planned and prompt exercising substantial trials … (the court) can put the case on the pretrial arrangement procedures."

[35] Criminal Procedure Law, art. 316–5.

[36] Criminal Procedure Rule, art. 196.

[37] Criminal Procedure Law, art. 291, para. 1.

may answer by agreeing on all or some parts of the bill. The presiding judge then asks the defense lawyers whether they approve or not the bill.[38] The hearing after this will mainly focus on the issues with which the defendant and the defense lawyers did not agree.

Then the court starts an examination of evidence.[39] At the beginning of the evidence examination, one of the prosecutors makes an opening statement to argue what the prosecution will prove in the trial.[40] In the opening statement, the prosecutor clarifies more about the case and the prosecutors' arguments on the case. The defense lawyers make opening statement after the prosecutor's opening statement. The defense lawyer presents the defense side's theory of the case. The opening statement by the defense lawyers is not necessary.

When opening statements are over, the court starts an investigation of every piece of the evidence. Material evidence, testimonies, and expert witnesses are presented at the court. The prosecutors and defense lawyers present the material evidence so that judges and saiban-in look and hear them. The judges, saiban-in, prosecutors and defense lawyers may question witnesses at the court to find the truth of the case.

When all evidence examination is over, the prosecutors should make a closing argument.[41] After that defense lawyers can make their closing argument.[42] Then the presiding judge asks the defendant to say anything regarding the trial (defendant's final opinion statement).[43] When the defendant finishes answering the question, the presiding judge concludes the trial. After the conclusion, the saiban-ins and the professional judges deliberate over the case. If they judge the defendant as guilty, they decide the punishment. Then one of the professional judges drafts a written judgment. The first instance of the trial ends when the presiding judge pronounces the sentence in the law court where all parties are present.[44]

[38] Criminal Procedure Law, art. 291, para. 4.

[39] Criminal Procedure Law, art. 292.

[40] Criminal Procedure Law, art. 296.

[41] Criminal Procedure Law, art. 293, para. 1.

[42] Criminal Procedure Law, art. 293, para. 2.

[43] Criminal Procedure Law, art. 293, para. 2 prescribes that the defendant can also state his or her opinion after the examination of the evidence is over.

[44] Criminal Procedure Law, art. 342.

Participation of Aggrieved Parties

The aggrieved parties[45] can participate in criminal proceedings during trials.[46] This system was introduced because of strong movement by victim associations without any relation to the saiban-in system. The aggrieved parties are the victims of cases and their families.

Aggrieved parties can attend trials[47] to state their opinions[48] and ask the defendants questions.[49]

Although aggrieved parties can participate, it is an institutional inconsistency that they can give their opinions on sentences before the court find the defendant guilty. The inconsistency exists because the law does not divide criminal trial procedure into fact-finding stage and sentencing stage. If we want to solve this problem, we have to change the law to divide the trial procedure into two stages. However, the change looks to be unlikely to happen shortly.

Appeal and Retrial (Exceptional Relief Procedure)

In case of dissatisfaction with the contents of the first trial, it is also possible for the prosecution and defense to appeal.[50] The appeal is to be made within fourteen days[51] after the judgment. The party which wishes to appeal need to submit a written letter of appeal (控訴申立書 *kôso môshitatesho*) to the court where the case was tried.[52] The first instance court will send the letter of appeal the second instance court. The party that requested for appeal should explain the reason. The document explaining the reason is called the appeal brief (控訴趣意書 *kôso shuisho* in criminal cases, while 控訴理由書 *kôso riyûsho* in civil cases) to the second instance court in the designated period.[53]

In an appeal trial, based on the evidence used in the first trial, professional judges at the second instance[54] make the judgment regarding the fact of whether the

[45] The victims or the legal representatives of the victim. Criminal Procedure Law, art. 316–33. The aggrieved parties can entrust presenting trial to lawyers.

[46] Criminal Procedure Law, art. 316–33. The article 292–2 prescribes the victims' opinion statement in trials.

[47] Criminal Procedure Law, art. 316–34.

[48] Criminal Procedure Law, art. 316–38.

[49] Criminal Procedure Law, art. 316–37.

[50] Criminal Procedure Law, art. 372.

[51] Criminal Procedure Law, art. 373.

[52] Criminal Procedure Law, art. 374.

[53] Criminal Procedure Law, art. 376, para. 1. The period should be designated by the appeal court. (Criminal Procedure Rule, art. 236)

[54] The second instance court should be High Court for the cases tried at district court of its first instance. If the first instance is heard at summary court, the second instance should be at district court.

judgment of the first trial had been appropriate. There is no public participation system in the high courts or the Supreme Court. The appellate court examines the dossier and the written judgment of the first instance. However, since the appellate court can also examine the fact, evidence can be submitted by both the defense and prosecution if necessary. The court will examine the evidence. Based on them, the appellate court makes a judgment on the case.

In case of dissatisfaction with the judgment of the appellate court, either the prosecution or the defense can appeal to the Supreme Court. However, the legal requirements to appeal to the Supreme Court are very strict. It is the trial for reviewing the judgments and the evidence up to the second instance. The Supreme Court judges whether the Court need to annul the conclusions up to the second instance from the constitutional or legal point of view.[55] In case of annulment, the Court return the case to the original instance, or the Court makes a final judgment by itself.[56] Also, in some cases, the Supreme Court can make judgments or express the Court's opinion on essential points of the case. Trials in Japan are under the three-instance system. In principle, trials start from district courts and ending in the Supreme Court. For minor crimes, trials start at Summary Courts and end in High Courts. For just a handful of exceptional crimes, High Courts will be the first instance, and the Supreme Court will be the final instance at the second trial.

In several cases even after the end of trials, it may be found that the final judgment was wrong. Those are the cases of retrials.[57] Retrials can be requested in case the evidence is forged; witnesses commit perjury, the case is indicted by a false accusation, the new evidence which proves the defendant's innocence or less serious crimes, or the investigation commit crimes concerning the case. The court will consider the records of the original trial and the new evidence and decide whether the court should start a retrial. On a retrial, there will be a new hearing, and the court will judge again. Typically, the court overturns the judgment at the original trial, and in many cases, the court judged "not guilty" on the case.

The Outline of the System, *Saiban-in System*

What Is the Saiban-in System?

In short, *saiban-in seido* (裁判員制度) is the criminal trial system in which professional judges and general citizens participate in Japan. The *saiban-in*s (裁判員), who are randomly selected citizens to participate in the procedures, sit and hear

---

[55] Criminal Procedure Law, art. 405 and art. 411.

[56] Criminal Procedure Law, art. 413.

[57] Criminal Procedure Law, art. 435.

criminal trials, deliberate with professional judges, and decide the case including the sentencing if the defendant is found guilty.

The saiban-in system enables citizens along with judges to determine criminal trials of the first instance held in district courts. The rationale for the system is the *Saiban-in* Act, which is one of the special laws of the Criminal Procedure Act. The *Saiban-in* Act will, in principle, be applied to all[58] significant[59] cases. In general, cases will be conducted with a team of three judges and six citizens, though it is also possible to have teams of one judge and four citizens.[60] Reserve saiban-ins are often also selected, in case accidents arise with *saiban-in* that make their participation impossible.[61] Majority vote makes a decision. In making a decision, at least one professional judge and one saiban-in need to agree with the decision.[62]

Those who can vote in House of Representatives elections with age 20 or older are eligible to become *saiban-in*[63] in this system.[64] The people who have the voting rights are Japanese citizens 18 years old or older.[65] Even the Public Office Election Act lowered the age requirement from 20 to 18,[66] but the Saiban-in Act has kept the eligible age for saiban-in as 20. The *Saiban-in* Act sets forth terms for disqualification,[67] prohibiting employment,[68] declining,[69] and ineligibility.[70]

Both citizens and judges deal with fact-finding, application of laws and regulations, and sentencing.[71] If there are objections to the conclusions made by *saiban-in*,

---

[58] However, if there is a fear of danger to the saiban-in or a family member of the saiban-in, or if the saiban-in fears such, or if the court will likely make a decision after a long period of time, Judges can determine cases on their own (Saiban-in Act art. 3 and 3–2.

[59] The trials by saiban-in deal with the cases concerning crimes with punishments of the death penalty or indefinite imprisonment, or crimes falling under art. 26 paragraph 2 number 2 of the Court Act in which the accused intentionally put the victim into death (Court Act art. 2 paragraph 1 number 2).

[60] Saiban-in Act art. 2 paragraphs 2 and 3.

[61] Saiban-in Act art. 10 and art. 38 paragraphs 1 and 2.

[62] Saiban-in Act art. 67 paragraph 1 and 2.

[63] "In this system" because the term "saiban-in" is also used to designate those members of the Diet that are responsible for making determinations in judge impeachment courts as stipulated in the constitution. Of course, the constitution stakes precedent as a matter of course, since "saiban—in" in the "saiban-in system" came later.

[64] Saiban-in Act art. 13.

[65] Public Office Election Law art. 9.

[66] Act to Revise Portions of the Public Office Election Law (Law 43 of 2015, announced June 19, 2015).

[67] Saiban-in Act art. 14.

[68] Saiban-in Act art. 15.

[69] Saiban-in Act art. 16.

[70] Saiban-in Act art. 17 and 18.

[71] Saiban-in Act art. 6 paragraph 1. Judges have the sole authority to interpret law, make determinations on court proceedings, and other determinations that do not involve saiban-in (art. 6 paragraph 2).

appeals from both prosecutors and the accused are allowed,[72] and appeals to the Supreme Court are also possible.[73] In these cases of the second and third instance, only judges determine cases.

The Meaning of the Term "saiban-in seido"

Before we look further into the system, we examine the meaning of the term "saiban-in seido." The term *saiban-in seido* is a new word which was invented by Justice System Reform Council (JSRC) in 2000. "Saiban" means trials in law courts, and "in" here means persons with some roles or as members of a certain group. Combining those two words, "saiban-in" literally means members who belong to a group which carries out trial procedures, or persons who have a role in conducting trial procedures. Compared to a fairly common word "saiban-kan" (裁判官), which means professional judge(s) since "kan" (官) here means "public officials," Japanese speaking people who hear the word "saiban-'in'" may think that "saiban-in" might be not a public official because the term avoids using "kan."

The last part of the term, "seido" (制度) means that "the norm in the society which is established to regulate human behaviors and human relations in the society. Alternatively, the norm that is established to govern or manage nations or groups."[74] This definition of *seido* can include rather abstract social construct in its broadest meaning. However, since we think here about a concrete legal system, and the meaning of *seido* should be restricted accordingly. We can interpret *seido* as system(s) or institution(s)[75] which is formed by a set of human behaviors and interactions under a specific aim which the planner of the system intended to realize. The term *seido* is commonly used in the context that people do something in their societies. The whole term "saiban-in seido" consequently means "trial member system." The literal translation is somewhat awkward, or even it gives us some impressions that the term does not contain proper meaning[76] if we scrutinize it.

The reason why the JSRC coined the term *saiban-in seido* would avoid severe political conflict in JSRC, and they knew that they should establish a better-fitting system to the state of the Japanese society no matter how we call the system. In its

---

[72] Criminal Procedure Act art. 372.

[73] Criminal Procedure Act art. 405.

[74] This is taken from Digital Daijisen, online version of one of major Japanese dictionaries. In Japanese, it explains *seido* as 「社会における人間の行動や関係を規制するために確立されているきまり。また、国家・団体などを統治・運営するために定められたきまり。」

[75] Since nouns in Japanese do not have distinctions between singular form and plural form in principle, the term *seido* can have singular and plural meaning.

[76] The trials by *saiban-in seido* are not carried out solely by *saiban-in*. Professional judges are also involved in the trials. Strictly speaking, the term *saiban-in seido* overlooks this feature of the system. Or, we should take it that this term indicates only the most remarkable characteristic of the system.

31st meeting,[77] one of the committee members argued that it was not proper to assume that the Council had to have debated whether Japan should introduce pure jury system or mixed jury system. The member continued that the Council should discuss flexibly the system which fit better to the Japanese society. Otherwise, the introduction of a new system with great efforts would result in its failure to take root in our society. It was important that the member showed a recognition that they had better not to decide the introduction of pure jury system or mixed jury system. The opinion issued by the JSRC did not refer to the political conflict overtly. However, some members argued to introduce pure jury system while other members insisted that they should consider the matter carefully[78] or introduce a mixed jury system without citizen's verdict power. It was sound that the JSRC involved the members of both sides in discussing the matter thoroughly and reflecting both sides of opinions in their final recommendation. At the same time, they had a risk to be stuck their discussion due to the conflict. Once they decided to introduce some citizens participation system to the justice system in their early stage,[79] the mainstream of their discussion went along according to the idea that they had to recommend some citizen participation system in the significant process of trials.

Before the introduction of *saiban-in seido*, the word "saiban-in" has been used to call the members of the Court of Impeachment (弾劾裁判所 *dangai saibansho*), which is provided by the article 64 in the Japanese Constitution.[80] The Court tries cases on the misdeeds which are committed by professional judges, which are indicted by the Judge Indictment Committee. The National Diet Act[81] legislates accordingly on the Court of Impeachment in its chapter 16. For example, its article 125 prescribes that impeachment of judges should be done by the Court of Impeachment which consists of the same numbers of *saiban-in* who are elected from Diet members in each House.[82] The fact that *saiban-in* has been used before

[77] The summary of the discussions in the 31st JSRC meeting is available in Japanese at http://www.kantei.go.jp/jp/sihouseido/dai31/31gaiyou.html. (Last acceess: September 5, 2016)

[78] To "consider the matter carefully" is one of the stereotyped phrases which is often used by whom have objections to a certain idea. People who use this phrase usually expect that realization of the matter will be postponed, the time runs out during the careful consideration, or the objection to the matter gets more powerful in the course of the consideration, since they find disadvantages of the matter.

[79] The JSRC decided that they should recommend to introduce civic participation system in their 9th meeting, in which they decided their "organization of the issues" (論点整理).

[80] "Article 64. The Diet shall set up an impeachment court from among the members of both Houses for the purpose of trying those judges against whom removal proceedings have been instituted.

Matters relating to impeachment shall be provided by law." (http://japan.kantei.go.jp/constitution_and_government/frame_01.html, last access: September 2, 2016) 「第六十四条 国会は、罷免の訴追を受けた裁判官を裁判するため、両議院の議員で組織する弾劾裁判所を設ける。/2 弾劾に関する事項は、法律でこれを定める。」

[81] The act no. 79, in 1947. 「国会法」

[82] In Japanese, 「裁判官の弾劾は、各議院においてその議員の中から選挙された同数の裁判員で組織する弾劾裁判所がこれを行う。」As of March 2018, the Court consists of fourteen members, Seven of them are selected from the House of Representative, the rest are selected from the House of Councilors.

the introduction of *saiban-in seido* does not seem to be much well-known in Japan, since the Court of Impeachment may not be famous for general citizens.

We can realize according to the usage of the term *saiban-in* in the provisions concerning the Court of Impeachment that *saiban-in* can mean the people who are involved main trial procedures as significant decision makers even they are not professional judges. Since "*in*" means just members, its meaning is not restricted to public officials, it can refer both to people who work for the government and to people who do not. As a result, the term *saiban-in* can be used in both contexts in discussing the Court of Impeachment and civic participation in the justice system.

After the saiban-in system has got popularity in Japan, jury system (陪審制度 *baishin seido*) is often mistakenly called as "*baishin-in seido*" (陪審員制度). The reason why people started to use this word would be that "something-in seido" word sound also has got popular in Japanese citizens including mass media along with the popularity of saiban-in seido. "陪審" has come from the short form of "聴坐陪審 *chôza baishin*," that means "to sit(坐)and hear(聴), and deliberate (審)with accompanying (陪)somebody (in this case professional judges)."

Why Was This System Introduced?

The Government introduced the saiban-in system as one means of establishing a democratic foundation for the judiciary as part of twenty-first-century justice system reform (Justice System Reform Council 2001). The Justice System Reform Council expressed the reason for the introduction of the system as "to establish a popular base of the justice system."

If we want to know the reason of the introduction of the saiban-in system with its background, we need to refer the opinion letter published by the Justice System Reform Council, records of proceedings by the Justice System Reform Council and the article 1 of the Saiban-in Act. The minutes of some committees in the Diet are also meaningful if we would like to know what was discussed in the process of legislation. Below, the author briefly reviews the significance of system is the introduction with relying mainly on the opinion letter by the Justice System Reform Council and law provisions.

The opinion report of the Justice System Reform Council states the meaning of introduction the system is to "to establish a popular base of the justice system." The original Japanese phrase states it is the "司法の国民的基盤の確立 establishment of a national foundation for the administration of justice." We can find the statement of the necessity in the first part of the opinion letter. We can seldom find in Japan arguments which cite the JSRC opinion properly, and we can find that misleading arguments have been spreading which is neglecting the original meaning of introduction of the system. In order not to pass on such misunderstandings to the international readers, the author would like to cite relevant parts from the opinion letter by the Justice System Reform Council.

In the opinion letter by the Justice System Reform Council, it is brought up from the basic idea and direction as to why citizens need to support the justice system. The Council reviewed the 100-year history since the times of compilation of the Civil Code and the 50-year history since the establishment of the Constitution of Japan. They determined their fundamental task for the reform is "what must be done to transform both the spirit of the law and the rule of law into the flesh and blood of the country, so that they become 'the shape of the country'" and "what is necessary to realize, in the true sense, the respect for individuals (Article 13 of the Constitution) and popular sovereignty (Article 1), on which the Constitution of Japan is based." (p. 3). Also, the issue of how to transform the spirit of law and the rule of law into the "flesh and blood of this country", namely, "to make the law (order), which serves as the core of freedom and fairness on which 'our country' should be based, broadly penetrate the entire state and all of society and become alive in the people's daily life? How can we deepen the public understanding of the significance of the justice system and set the justice system on a more solid popular base? These are fundamental issues that the Council asked itself." (p.3).

It has been proclaimed that what revolves around " various reforms, including political reform, administrative reform, promotion of decentralization, and reforms of the economic structure such as deregulation" in Japan before the Justice System Reform. Those previous reforms are in line that "each and every person will break out of the consciousness of being a governed object and will become a governing subject, with autonomy and bear social responsibility, and that the people will participate in building a free and fair society in mutual cooperation and will work to restore rich creativity and vitality to this country." (p. 3).

Further, " the role of the justice system will become dramatically more important in the Japanese society of the 21st century. In order for the people to easily secure and realize their own rights and interests, and in order to prevent those in a weak position from suffering unfair disadvantage in connection with the abolition or deregulation of advanced control, a system must be coordinated to properly and promptly resolve various disputes between the people based on fair and clear legal rules. " (p.8).

The Council established the three pillars of the Justice System Reform. The first one is " a justice system that meets public expectations," the second is reforming "the legal profession supporting the justice system," and the third one is "establishment of the popular base." The Council set their goal as "public trust in the justice system shall be enhanced by introducing a system in which the people participate in legal proceedings and through other measures." (p. 9).

Consequently, as a means for that, the JSRC proposed to introduce broad citizen participation in criminal trials in serious criminal cases. They chose severe cases because they put significance on the viewpoint of raising the public's confidence in trials by entrusting important work to citizens. The Committee thought that entrusting the punishment serious criminal offenders is vital to work in the society. As the Committee request the people to "break out of the consciousness of being a governed object and will become a governing subject," the Committee proposed involvement from the wide range of the population. They chose the method of random selections from a wide range of citizens to be saiban-ins for each new trial instead of participating in trials for extended periods of time as amateur judges. In this regard, translating "saiban-in" into "lay judge" is not ideal because if the citizens become judges, the intention of the introduction of the system would not be accomplished.

Furthermore, the purpose of having citizens participate in trials is not for the Government to use citizens conveniently to carry out the trials. Contrary, this is a means for the citizens to get out of the feeling that they are "being governed" by the state, and nurture a sense of themselves forming a society and participating in the actions of the state.

In the opinion letter by the Justice System Reform Council mentioned above, the Council summarized the notion into the slogan to "break out of the consciousness of being a governed object and will become a governing subject, ".

Also, in the opinion letter by the Justice System Reform Council, the Council said about the history of the Japanese judicial system after the World War II. GHQ (General Headquarters) performed a substantial reform of the justice system including an introduction of the American-style criminal procedure law immediately after the war. There also came up new trends for doing things among professional judges. However, as bureaucratization of the judicial system progressed in nearly 70 years since then. It brought the situation that the citizens became distanced from the trial system and trial results. Since the Justice System Reform Council does not show concrete data regarding this statement, but it seemed that it was one of the driving forces for the reform.[83]

After the office term of the Justice System Reform Council, the Government established the Justice System Reform Promotion Headquarters. The Headquarters prepared for detailed drafts of the Saiban-in Act. They were submitted to the Diet, and the Diet discussed at both the House of Representatives and the House of Councilors. When looking up minutes of the Diet, the members of the Diet made remarks confirming the significance of the saiban-in system in the process of discussion. In these remarks, the members referred to the viewpoints of ensuring confidence in the justice system and the viewpoint of people having an opportunity to consider the security of the society. For example, on May 20, 2004, in a meeting of the Legal Committee of the House of Councilors just before completion of the Saiban-in Act, a Diet member Ryuji Matsumura made a question.[84] He said that "I think that there is also a need for citizens' consciousness to change for this introduction of the saiban-in system to be accepted and established in our society. Also, at public hearings in Osaka and from the experience of neighborhood associations, there are lots of people who just live their own lives and are not concerned about public matters. However, there have been voices of people who say that it was

[83] In fact, regarding the discussion on the introduction of the saiban-in system, representative judges had expressed their opinions by stating their position that there had been no problem with trial practices up till then and some members of the Council argued against the statements.

[84] The text from here is based on the minute of the Committee. The translation is not official, made by the author.

perfect that they started having public consciousness after having experienced being saiban-ins. So, I would like to ask the minister: as the government, do you think that the citizens' consciousness should be changed along with the introduction of the saiban-in system? If so, I would like to hear your opinion on what kind of activities will be carried out with such point of view by the government?" In response to that, the minister Daizou Nozawa said, "About the saiban-in system, we believe that they will for the first time be able to fulfill the role as the foundation of our justice system with the people's awareness and cooperation. Also, we believe that it is a significant opportunity for people participating in the process of criminal trials. It is a good chance for each citizen to think about problems concerning social order and security, the problems of damage caused by crimes, and the problems of human rights. Those problems relate to each citizen. From this point of view, from now on, we will deepen the understanding of and interest towards the significance of the saiban-in system and its details. We believe that it is necessary to sufficiently conducting public advertising the system so that citizens can continue to participate in criminal trials. We think that a national mentality of being proud to be appointed or nominated as saiban-ins is necessary". Also, the deputy minister Yukio Jitsukawa said, "Although it is just introduction of the saiban-in system, there is no doubt that it is a reform related to the very stem of our justice system. Moreover, in the sense of contributing to deepening the citizens' understanding of the system of justice, the promotion and increasing of trust in the justice system will be of vital importance." During discussions in the Diet, the members mentioned to the importance of public understanding of the justice system and the increase in trust. Also, the Diet member Matsumura mentioned the change in citizens' consciousness in a very similar way which the Justice System Reform Council had proposed in the opinion report. The interesting point was that Miniter of Justice added the viewpoint of social security to the JSRC'a argument as a head of the organization which holds the prosecutors' offices.

It is essential to understand the purpose of introduction of the saiban-in system correctly. If we misunderstand the fundamental purpose, it is hard to understand the saiban-in system correctly, and it is also hard to understand what the Japanese society has been trying to do since the beginning of the twenty-first century in the justice system reform.

In Japan, the mass media often state that "the purpose of introducing the saiban-in system is to introduce 'the citizens' perspective' in criminal trials." However, a statement like this does not exist in official views on the purpose of introducing the saiban-in system covered above. To state that the purpose of introducing the saiban-in system is like that is often misleading. The misleading argument might be based on ignorance or insufficient research on the issue. We need to consider this issue to grasp the purpose and background correctly, as we are dealing with this issue in the latter part of this chapter again.

Who Does What in the System?

In the saiban-in system, citizens and judges will conduct trials, but here we will explain it more in detail. What we are about to describe here is an outline of court trials to be conducted under the saiban-in system as of March 2018.

According to Article 2 of the Saiban-in Act, the judicial panels with saiban-ins try the following kinds of cases. (1) Cases of crimes to which death penalty or infinite imprisonment with hard labor or infinite imprisonment without labor are applicable. (2) Cases listed in Clause 2 of Paragraph 2 of Article 26 of the Court Act (裁判所法 *saiban-sho hô*), relating to crimes of causing the victim's death by intentional criminal actions. The following crimes in the Criminal Law are included in the coverage of saiban-in trials. They are arson, infringement, capsizing of trains, water poisoning, currency counterfeiting and its use, official document counterfeiting, burglary with bodily harm and burglary with murder, crimes involving causing death such as indecent assault, murder, kidnapping for ransom, less frequent cases of criminal insurrection, instigation of foreign aggression, and assistance in foreign aggression.

Regarding this point, in the JSRC's 32nd meeting,[85] they discussed what kinds of cases should the saiban-in system try. In the discussion, there were opinions that the cases should be restricted to some sorts of criminal cases at the start of the system. They said there were practical problems to introduce public participation system to civil cases.[86] One of the members referred that England and Wales ceased civil juries due to the cost. The significant parts of the members of the Council thought that it is hard to introduce the new civic participation system[87] in civil trials though they acknowledged the significance of citizen participation. Another member said that we should start in the range that we can manage at the time of introduction.

However, the court may decide to try only by professional judges for some types of the cases which can be tried by saiban-in. The cases are in which the defendant is related organized crime groups when there is a saiban-in's risk or threat of harm.[88] They are also cases when it is difficult to appoint saiban-ins or to secure the performance of their duties due to the trial being expected to become excessively long.[89] Also, the lengthy trial process can be divided into several sections which can be heard by different trial bodies of saiban-ins. In that case, the court holds interim discussions (中間評議 *chûkan hyôgi*).

There are six saiban-in in one trial body and three professional judges. Also, two reserve saiban-ins are selected. However, when the defendant admits the crime and

[85] The summary of their discussion can be reached at http://www.kantei.go.jp/jp/sihouseido/dai32/32gaiyou.html. (Last access: March 9, 2018)

[86] In civil procedures, they discussed the system of special member participation to the trials (専門参審制), which was not adopted in the justice system reform.

[87] At that time, the term *saiban-in seido* was not invented.

[88] Saiban-in Act, art. 3.

[89] Saiban-in Act, art. 3.

the court confirm it in the decision, the case will be heard by a panel of four saiban-ins and one professional judge. In that case, the court will select one reserve saiban-in. Reserve saiban-ins are present at all hearings and get to hear the discussion which is kept the secret to the outside.

Saiban-ins can hear the cases along with professional judges and can ask the defendants and victims questions after informing the presiding judge.[90] Prosecutors and defense lawyers often distribute handouts with information related to the case.

Saiban-ins decide together with professional judges, whether the defendant is guilty or not, and if found guilty, what crime the guilt falls under, and what the most appropriate punishment should be.[91] Professional judges and saiban-ins have the same voting power; the majority decision decides results.[92] However, the trial body cannot make its final decisions unless at least one professional judge and at least one saiban-in agree. For example, even when all six saiban-ins opine that the defendant is guilty, but no professional judges approve of the decision, then the defendant cannot be convicted.

When the trial body reaches a final decision, professional judges write a judgment statement. The court will pronounce the judgment the final day of the trial.[93]

The Saiban-in Act imposes confidentiality obligation on saiban-ins,[94] so they do not publicly disclose secrets regarding discussion contents during trials. In case that obligation is violated, a punishment of imprisonment for six months or less, or a fine up to 500,000 yen may be applied.[95] However, there is no problem in disclosing one's impressions after participating in trials. The information which the Act prohibits to disclose includes who had what kind of opinion during the trial. The meaning of the Act is to secure a situation in which saiban-ins and professional judges can freely speak during the deliberations.

Saiban-in trials can be only first instance trials.[96] If the prosecutor or the defendant is dissatisfied with the judgment results of the trial by saiban-in, they can appeal in the same way as other ordinary trials. The process of the appeals is the same as which we already reviewed in the section of Japanese criminal justice system. Up to the second instance, it is possible to appeal regarding unreasonable fact-finding or sentencing. However, a further appeal to the Supreme Court is only limited to cases when the punishment is significantly unfair, or the judgment up to the second instance violates the Constitution, legal rules or precedents.[97] Trials of the second and third instance are conducted only by professional judges. In some cases, the second instance judgments overturn fact-finding and sentencing given by trials by saiban-in. Sometimes this point is criticized because this system can nullify

[90] Saiban-in Act, art. 58 and art. 59.

[91] Saiban-in Act, art. 6, para. 1.

[92] Saiban-in Act, art. 67.

[93] Saiban-in Act, art. 63.

[94] Saiban-in Act, art. 9, para. 2 and art. 70, para. 1.

[95] Saiban-in Act, art. 108.

[96] Saiban-in Act, art. 2.

[97] Criminal Procedure Law, para. 405.

citizen participation in the justice system. However, there is an opinion that overturning the judgments by trials by saiban-in is an indication that judiciary works correctly (Professor Maruta's comment in "Saiban-in hanketsu hakiritsu joushou tudzuku seido shiko 8 nen [Judgments in saiban-in trials overturn rate raises: Eight years after implementation]," 2017).

There are two more essential systems of the Criminal Procedure Law which were introduced separately from the saiban-in system. Those are the pretrial conference and the victim participation system, including victim impact statement. The author referred to the system in the Japanese criminal justice system section.

A pretrial conference involves judges, prosecutors, lawyers and, in some cases, defendants gathering to arrange the points of discussion and decide in advance what kind of evidence to investigate to finish the trial as fast as possible in complicated cases. By clarifying the claims of both prosecution and defense, they deliberate to specify the points of dispute, and they talk about what kind of witnesses should be called to trials, what kind of evidence the prosecutor will show. This system is not necessarily linked with the saiban-in system.[98] However, the saiban-in system only tries the severe criminal cases, and the Criminal Procedure Law requires pretrial conferences for the cases which try severe crimes. Moreover, it is highly necessary to squeeze hearings in a short period as efficiently as possible in saiban-in trials not to request saiban-ins to be present at the trials for an extended period. The court will hold pretrial conferences in saiban-in cases with those reasons.

Professional judges who attend pretrial conferences will oversee later hearings. The judges gain information about the case in advance, whereas saiban-ins face the trial with no previous detailed information. The Criminal Procedure Law expects the judges not to have any previous knowledge at the first date of the trial. The situation in which the professional judges know of the case in advance is problematic from this viewpoint.[99]

Victims or bereaved families can participate in trials as victim participants. Because of that, they can ask defendants questions and give opinions on the sentence. Also, they can provide evidence regarding the victims and express their opinions. Also, if victims themselves cannot express their opinions directly, they can prepare a written statement and have the prosecutor read it, prosecutors or lawyers can ask questions on their behalf and present their opinions.

This is the outcome of a political movement of criminal case victims' organizations, and the victim participation system had begun just before the introduction of saiban-in trials. However, the introduction of the victim participation system also attracted attention in the media. One of the issues related to the saiban-in system was whether saiban-ins could make a reasonable judgment after hearing the victims' and their families' emotionally expressed opinions in the courtroom. Upon a study conducted in Japan, presentation of the picture of the deceased victim's

---

[98] The pretrial conference system is prescribed in Criminal Procedure Law, while the saiban-in system is prescribed in Saiban-in Act, which is one of the special law of Criminal Procedure Law.

[99] The information difference among group member can affect the power of the member during decision making. See later chapter of this book.

portrait photograph had statistically significant effects on the judgments of guiltiness and defendant's malicious intent (Naka 2009). The effects were found in the judgments made by college students and law school students. The judgments on punishments were severest made by the college students who saw the portrait and heard the recorded statements of the bereaved family. This may be problematic if the information presented on a victim can distort the results of the trials. Also, we need to think about the judgments without counting in the victim are just and fair as a trial.

Is the Purpose of Implementing the Saiban-in System to Reflect the "Sense of Citizens" ('*Shimin-kankaku*')?

Newspapers and other media have described the reason of the introduction of the saiban-in system often argue thus: "the system began with the purpose of reflecting the sense of the citizenry into major trials" (e.g. Ichikawa et al. 2008). However, neither the *Saiban-in* Act, the Justice System Reform Council opinion paper (Justice System Reform Council 2001), nor an interim report of the Justice System Reform Council (The Justice System Reform Council 2000) contains such phraseology. Thus, the understanding that the system "began with the purpose of reflecting the sense of the citizenry into major trials" does not conform to the official view. Given that, how did this alternate view come to be? An understanding of the reason behind the implementation of the saiban-in system is essential in discussing the system itself, and therefore we will briefly consider this issue.

Article 1 of the Saiban-in Act gives the purpose of the saiban-in system as "increasing citizen understanding and improving trust in the law by having saiban-in, selected from among the citizenry, and judges involved together in criminal trials." Accordingly, it is natural to view the purpose of implementing the system as being "increasing citizen understanding and improving trust in the law." We can think the passages cited here are results of rephrasing the Justice System Reform Council's phrase, "popular foundation of the justice system" in a way fitting into the terms of the law.

The Justice System Reform Council opinion paper stated the third pillar of justice reform is "establishing a popular foundation [for the justice system]," and that to do so, "citizens will deepen understanding of justice through various types of involvement, including participation in certain court proceedings, and will support justice." In this section, the purpose of establishing the saiban-in system is "to establish a popular foundation for the justice system" (Justice System Reform Council 2001, p. 12).

At the same time, this document states, "regular citizens will participate in the process of trials, while will enable a greater reflection of the healthy societal wisdom of the populace, deepening understanding and support of the justice system by the citizenry and allow the justice system to have a stronger popular foundation.

From this viewpoint, a new system should be implemented whereby a broad swath of regular citizens will take responsibility along with judges in criminal court proceedings.” (Justice System Reform Council 2001, p. 102).

A look at the earlier interim report shows that in discussions on citizen participation in the justice system, “as the court process becomes open to citizens, and with a reflection of the healthy societal wisdom of the populace in the courts, popular understanding of and support for the justice system will deepen. It is critical that we consider what type of system is ideal for bringing this about” (The Justice System Reform Council 2000). The main focus here is on popular understanding of, and support for, the justice system. “A reflection of societal awareness” is a tool for deepening this understanding and support.

From this, we see the following progression: the purpose of implementing the saiban-in system was to strengthen “the popular foundation for the justice system.” Thus, it is necessary to deepen understanding of, and support for, the justice system, and this requires a reflection of the sound societal wisdom of the populace towards the courts, which in turn requires citizen participation in the justice system. Accordingly, a “reflection of healthy societal wisdom for the courts” is one method (or one process) for achieving the goal of implementing this system. For the saiban-in system to be reflecting public sentiment, “societal awareness” and “public sentiment” must be seen as being the same.

In meeting minutes of the 45th Justice System Reform Council, council member Masahito Inouye did not use the phrase “public sentiment” in an explanation,[100] but used a phrase “reflection of societal awareness.” However, this is not given as an objective, but rather an expected effect of implementing the system. Behind the notion that citizen participation is required to strengthen the public foundation for the justice system, there is a point of view that the justice system can be a method for securing democratic legitimacy because the justice system can work as one of the political systems (Mitani 2004, 2005). And the Vice Chairman Takeshita stated, “Doesn’t democratic legitimacy come about when trials are conducted with citizens participating alongside judges, even in only certain cases, (moreover, the practice is) making the courts become a window open to the public, and (the justice system is) obtaining the understanding of the public, which allows for a broader, deeper foundation of support?”[101]

[100] “From a different perspective, in the end people wonder what we expect from citizen participation, or what we can expect, and this is nothing other than the ‘expected impact’ given in B of the ‘Interim Report Main Points’. Of these, the meaning of 2 in particular, ‘a reflection of societal awareness in the courts,’ is important.

On that point, [saiban-in] will evaluate evidence from a fresh perspective that reflects societal awareness, different from the judges who see many cases on a daily basis. This validation of the facts is perhaps the greatest merit or point of significance. I believe it is understood that the main point, more broadly speaking, is whether a healthy societal awareness of the courts in general should be reflected, including the interpretation and application of laws and sentencing.

[101] The original text is as follows: 「やはり民主的正統性というのは、一部の事件にでも国民が参加をして、裁判官と協働して裁判をやる。そのことによって、そこが一つの窓口になって国民に開かれたものになり、そこで国民の理解を得て、広い、より深い支持の基盤が得られる。そういうところにあるのではないでしょうか。」

Thus, if we explain the purpose of implementation of the saiban-in system as "reflecting public sentiment," we would understand the effect as the purpose.

The phrase "public sentiment" appears in interviews[102] with well-known researchers of the saiban-in system and Criminal Procedure Law in Japan, and the legal systems in the UK and US. The council conducted the interviews at the 43rd meeting. In an explanation given by Professor Kôya Matsuo, one of the interviewees, this phrase[103] is used as evaluation criteria for the criminal trial system.

In the media, "public sentiment" has traditionally been made an issue in discussion around criminal law reform in the Showa era, and in examination committees and government administration. Also, there have been media criticisms of previous trials departing from public sentiment. Because of this, there has long been intriguing in whether the national and local systems have reflected public sentiment.

In this context, we can well imagine that there was great interest in the saiban-in system and whether the national system of justice reflects "public sentiment." In that context, we can surmise that because the phrase "reflection of a healthy societal awareness"[104] appeared in the JSRC opinion paper in the course of discussing the implementation of the saiban-in system, the similar phrase "reflection of public sentiment" came to be seen as the reason for the implementation. People might come to believe the phrase "reflection of public sentiment" as the real purpose of introduction of the saiban-in system after repeated saying. Then we can see the articles with a leading "Saiban-in Trials Begin with Purpose of Reflecting Public Sentiment"[105] (Ichikawa et al. 2008).

The argument above is a conjecture based on Justice System Reform Council records and newspaper articles. However, we can hypothesize above to explain the gap between the phrases found in the Saiban-in Act and Justice System Reform Council opinion paper and "reflection of public sentiment."

If we understand the purpose of the introduction of the system correctly, the purpose is to increase understanding of, and support for, the justice system by the public. In actuality, members of the Council and the Diet gave explanations like that

---

[102] Professors Kochiro Fujikura, Taichiro Mitani, and Kôya Matsuo (in order of interviews).

[103] This is used in regard to current trials being seen as departing from "public sentiment" or in line with public sentiment.

[104] In considering the significance of the phrase, "societal awareness," it is understood to be different than "public sentiment". The former is an understanding in regard to society and certain norms broadly held by the public, while the latter is an intuitive determination or intuition held by the public. It is somewhat of a leap to conflate the two.

[105] Moreover, based on the objective of obtaining understanding and support though citizen participation in the justice system, it is logically inevitable that trials with *saiban-in* would be those that are major. The interim report states, "in the meantime," so perhaps from a practical perspective major criminal trials, which were seen as having the possibility of expanding, were selected as a matter of policy. The council's position paper notes that the system could begin with certain cases of high public interest to ensure a "smooth implementation" (Justice System Reform Council 2001, p. 106). Accordingly, as with the above art., those writing that the original intent in implementing the system was to bring about some form of change in trials for major cases are encouraging misunderstanding.

at the deliberations of the Justice System Reform Council and the Diet's Justice Committees.[106] This understanding leads us to the issue of the democratic legitimacy of the justice system. The saiban-in system should be explained relating to that principle. Contrary to that, if we understand the purpose of introduction of the system is to reflect the public sentiments to the justice system, legitimacy is not the most critical issue. In that case, the issues should be whether the trials reflect people's emotions or moods.

However, such explanations of the saiban-in system were not broadly reported. Thus discussions of the significance of the fundamentals of the saiban-in system were never broadly promulgated. Because of this, people may think like this: "Why do we need to become saiban-ins? What is the significance of public participation in the justice system? Is there a need to for trials to reflect public sentiment? There is no one to answer these fundamental questions convincingly. They are mysteries!" (Yamamoto et al. 2015). For the public, they are perhaps still mysteries. It is an unhappy situation for the saiban-in system as well as those citizens who serve as saiban-ins. The situation will get better if there is a greater understanding of serving as saiban-ins is to support the foundations of the state in increasing democratic legitimacy in one of the three branches of government.

Saiban-in Selection Process

Overview

Saiban-ins' selection is called "選任 *sen-nin* " in Japanese which means "selection" and "entrusting" as it derives from the meaning of characters. The saiban-in selection process is prescribed in articles from 13 to 40 of the Saiban-in Act concerning criminal trials in which saiban-ins participate.

A person who can become a saiban-in is who is eligible to vote for the House of Representatives.[107] To have a voting right of the House of Representatives, a person needs to be a Japanese citizen.[108] The House of Representatives is one of the two chambers of the National Diet of Japan and consists of parliament members elected for a term of 4 years.[109] If the House of Representatives is dissolved during the official term, they lose their positions without waiting for the expiration of the 4-year term.[110] The other chamber is the House of Councilors. Members of the House of Councilors will not be dismissed in the middle of their six-year office term because the House is never dissolved. Also, since members of the House of Councilors are

[106] See, for example, the House of Councilors Justice Committee discussion quoted in the introduction.

[107] Saiban-in Act, art. 13.

[108] Public Office Election Law (the law no. 100 in 1950), art. 9, para. 1.

[109] The Constitution of Japan, art. 45.

[110] The Constitution art. 54.

reelected in halves,[111] there is no replacement of all members at once. The reason why the House of Councilors exists is considered to ensure continuity of the Diet as a whole.[112] Both draft legislation and budget proposals are deliberated by the House of Representatives and the House of Councilors.[113] In principle, bills and budgets get approved if they gain a majority in both chambers but the House of Representative has more power in case the decision of both Houses is not consistent. The House of Representatives puts more emphasis on representation of the will of the people, and the House of Councilors is called the representative body of good sense that emphasizes continuity. In the Constitution of the Empire of Japan until World War II, there was a two-chamber system consisting of the House of Peers and the House of Representatives. After World War II, the aristocracy system ceased to exist except for the Imperial Family in Japan. After that, the House of Councilors started with elected members.[114] As of March 2018, the quotas of the House of Representative is 465 while the quota of the House of Councilor is 242.[115]

The right to vote for the House of Representatives is granted to Japanese citizens over the age of 18,[116] but to become a saiban-in a person must be over 20 years old.[117] In the past, the voting age for Japanese citizens was over 20 years old for the House of Representatives, but it was changed for the age of 18 and above by the law that revises a part of the Public Offices Election Law in 2015. The qualifications of persons who become saiban-ins do not change accordingly.

There are cases when a person cannot become a saiban-in even if they are over 20 years old and have the right to vote for members of the House of Representatives. There are also cases when a person can become a saiban-in, but he/she can refuse[118] (refusal grounds). For cases when a person cannot become a saiban-in, there may be possible reasons such as the person being considered not appropriate for becoming a saiban-in[119] (disqualification grounds) or it might be undesirable for them to become a saiban-in considering their status, occupation[120] (job-related prohibition grounds).

For disqualification grounds, the following cases are usually considered. Those in adult guardianship or persons under curatorship are not to be saiban-ins. Persons who were sentenced to imprisonment and more severe punishments or those for whom the execution of their sentences is being suspended, those who formed

111 The Constitution art. 46.

112 The Constitution art. 54 para. 2 and 3 prescribes emergency session of the House of Councilors during dissolution of the House of Representative.

113 The Constitution art. 59 and art. 60.

114 The article 102 of the Constitution prescribes the half of the initial members of the House of Councilors have a three-year office term while the rest have a full six year term.

115 Public Office Election Law, art. 4, paras. 1 and 2.

116 Public Office Election Law, art. 9,

117 Supplemental rules art. 10 on June 29, 2015 the law no. 43 in Public Office Election Law.

118 Saiban-in Act, art. 16.

119 Saiban-in Act, art. 14.

120 Saiban-in Act, art. 15.

political parties and other organizations claiming to destroy the government with violence cannot be saiban-is. Persons who had not completed compulsory education,[121] those who have severe obstacles to the performance of duties of a saiban-in due to mental and physical problems cannot be saiban-ins.[122]

Persons who perform following jobs may be under job-related prohibition.[123] They are members of parliament, state ministers, state administrative officials, professional judges, prosecutors, lawyers as well as those who had previously been in these positions. The law also excludes those who have related positions from the service of saiban-ins. They are those qualified for three legal professionals, patent attorneys, judicial scriveners, notaries, full-time employees of courts, employees of the Ministry of Justice and the police,[124] prefectural governors, municipal mayors and self-defense officers. The law excludes those who are engaged as legal officials and in positions related to the power function of the state as well.

The following cases fall under refusal grounds.[125] Persons over 70 years old, members of assemblies of local public organizations, university students or school students can refuse to be saiban-ins. Persons who have served as saiban-ins or reserve saiban-ins within the past 5 years can also refuse to be saiban-ins. Moreover, persons who were planned for appointment as saiban-ins within the past 3 years, those who attended the appointment procedure within a year[126] can avoid becoming saiban-ins. Those who served as prosecution examiners or reservists for that within the past 5 years. Also, those who have critical personal matters such as treatment for diseases, family care, and other similar reasons can file a statement for refusal. In such cases, it is possible to go on and become a saiban-in if the candidate would like to be a saiban-in.

Also, persons involved in the criminal case which is tried by that court are also excluded.[127] Persons accused in that criminal case, victims, their families, proxies and curators, co-dwellers and their employees cannot be saiban-ins for that case. Also, people who made accusations or claims in that criminal cases, those who became witnesses or expert witnesses, those who became proxies, lawyers or curators for the cases, those who became prosecutors and police officers in charge of the

---

[121] The compulsory education in Japan requires nine years attendance in school. Article 16 of School Education Act (the law No. 26 in 1947) prescribes it. Pupils need to be at elementary schools for six years (art. 32), and they need to be at junior high schools for three years (art. 47).

[122] Saiban-in Act, art. 14.

[123] Saiban-in Act, art. 15.

[124] In Japan, the police are under the prefectural governments in general. There are some exceptions like the police in Tokyo Metropolis and the Imperial Guard Headquarters which are governed by the state (the National Police Agency). The Coast Guard is under the Ministry of Land, Infrastructure, Transport and Tourism. None of municipal governments or universities have their police.

[125] Saiban-in Act, art. 16.

[126] The cases where they were not appointed due to illness, family care or essential employment duties are excluded.

[127] Saiban-in Act, art. 17.

investigation, those who served as examiners on prosecution review board for related cases cannot be saiban-ins for the case.

Registration on the List Before Participation in Saiban-in Appointing Proceedings

When a person is registered as a candidate for being a saiban-in, they are informed by receiving notification by mail. Pamphlets explaining what the saiban-in system is are enclosed together with a questionnaire. In the questionnaire, there are questions about whether the applicant is currently in a job corresponding to disqualification grounds (1), or whether they had done the same work in the past, the about right timing for their participation or whether there is any seasonality due to work in agriculture, and other reasons. If a person cannot become a saiban-in due to having a legal qualification, such as a lawyer and they answer like that, they will not be called to the court on the selection date.

The court selects saiban-ins from the lists of candidates. The lists are compiled in the following way.[128] First, a court contacts the municipal election management committee on September 1 of every year. The election management committee that received the contact randomly chooses candidates for saiban-ins from the electoral register of municipalities and compiles a list of prospective candidates for saiban-ins. The list is sent from the election management committee to the court of that year. The list of prospective candidates for saiban-ins is created and updated once a year. The court that received the list of prospective candidates for saiban-ins creates a list of candidates for saiban-ins from that list. When the court finishes compiling the list of candidates for saiban-ins, the court sends the materials, letters, and questionnaires to the candidates.[129]

The court randomly selects saiban-in candidates for each case from the list of candidates for saiban-ins and sends letters of invitation. About 30 to 40 people per case are called to the selection.[130] Even if the person ignores the call from a court, there is no penalty for it.[131]

Procedures for appointing saiban-ins may take over one day or may be performed only within half a day before noon. If done only within half a day before noon, the court will start the first trial date from the afternoon. Below, there will be a description of a typical case based on an educational movie about saiban-ins published by courts and on the Saiban-in Act.[132]

---

[128] Saiban-in Act, art. 21.

[129] Saiban-in Act, art. 25

[130] Initially, 50 to 60 people were planned to be chosen, but since the attendance rate was reasonable, the number was decreased to about 30 to 40 people.

[131] There is no crime category regarding contempt of court in Japan.

[132] The saiban-in movie is available through the internet in Japanese. The practice appeared in the video may be different in some regards from actual practice currently performed, because the mov-

At first, the court sends a letter of invitation to those who did not fall under disqualification grounds or job-related prohibition grounds previously described.[133] Those who have announced resignation based on refusal grounds are excluded from those who receive the letter of invitation. At that time, the court sends questionnaires.[134] Questionnaires include questions on whether they fall under disqualification grounds or job-related prohibition grounds, whether candidates withdraw due to refusal grounds, and other related questions as well as questions concerning whether they possibly can make an unfair decision during the trial. The Supreme Court Regulations determine the content. The court of trial sends a list of those who were called out as candidates for saiban-ins to the prosecutors and the defense lawyers two days before the calling date.[135]

On the calling date, the candidates are gathering together with professional judges, court clerks, prosecutors, defense lawyers[136] at the court. Then the appointment procedures are carried out. The procedure is in private.[137]

Each saiban-in candidate is escorted to a large room as he/she arrives at the court and then gets informed about the saiban-in system. Pamphlets are also handed over. Afterward, they are escorted into a room where professional judges, the prosecutor and the defense lawyer are present, and then an interview is conducted.[138] During the interview, the judgment regarding eligibility of candidates is made based on points such as whether candidates have no obstacles to participate in a trial. For example, in case a candidate finds out there is work he/she must attend to by all means and if they judge that their work will significantly suffer unless they can attend to it, the court will dismiss the candidate. Also, when the court judges that "a candidate for saiban-in a has strong tendency to making a biased judgment," or when the defense lawyers or the prosecutors' request to the court for not appointing the candidate, the candidate will not be appointed. The prosecutors and the defense lawyers can request to remove up to four candidates without explaining the reasons.[139] As a result of the above, six saiban-ins and two reserve saiban-ins are selected by a lottery from the remaining candidates.[140]

The law put on the significance to find the risk of the partial decision making of the saiban-in candidates in the selection process. In the first place, people who are tending to make unfair decisions cannot be saiban-ins.[141] Various factors can be

---

ies were made before the trials by saiban-in started. URL: http://www.saibanin.courts.go.jp/news/flash4.html

[133] Saiban-in Act, art. 27.

[134] Saiban-in Act, art. 30.

[135] Saiban-in Act, art. 31.

[136] Saiban-in Act, art. 32.

[137] Saiban-in Act, art. 33.

[138] Saiban-in Act, art. 34.

[139] Saiban-in Act, art. 36.

[140] Saiban-in Act, art. 37.

[141] Saiban-in Act, art. 18

considered as reasons that may cause a saiban-in to make an unfair decision.[142] However, under the provisions of the Saiban-in Act, it is not stipulated precisely how to handle reports before trial. Professional judges, prosecutors, and lawyers make their judgment based on candidates' responses at the interview.

What happens if pretrial publicity causes all candidates for saiban-ins in a region to have a widespread bias? In such case, the approach similar to the US where it is considered to be better to change the venue of the trial.[143] However, since Japan's territory is not as vast as the US, it is possible that citizens of the newly selected place may know about the incident through the publicity even if the court location was changed. Regarding reports, unlike the United States where there is a large number of independent local newspapers, even though Japan has many different newspapers, most of them tend to report similar information, making it difficult to find regions where the news report does not cover the high-profile cases.

Therefore, it may be considered challenging to change the venue as a way to get "fresh" saiban-ins. Also, recently, as there are no more problems for information distribution and no geographical barriers because of the Internet, information widely spreads to citizens. Even when the court approves a change of the trial venue, it is necessary to consider the influence of diffusion of information on the Internet.

Instead, the media on which the potential saiban-ins rely will be more significant than before because the Internet is prevailing in our society. The content which the potential saiban-ins access may vary according to the media, such as TV, newspapers, or SNS on the Internet. It is necessary to wait for further progress in research on information exposure of Japanese citizens as it will make clear which factor is affecting the process.

The court will pay daily allowances and transportation costs to saiban-ins.[144] The court also pays for saiban-ins' accommodation if necessary.[145] The daily allowance of a saiban-in or a reserve saiban-in is paid as set by the court and is up to 10,000 yen.[146] Saiban-in candidates who were sent back only after the saiban-in appointment procedure are only paid the daily allowance at the amount set by the court up to the maximum of 8000 yen per day.[147] If the appointment procedure ends before noon, half of the daily allowance may be paid with such consideration. In case of a candidate becoming a saiban-in, the amount of daily allowance is the amount

[142] The possible examples of the reasons are personal thoughts, personal opinion about the death penalty issue, tendency for harsh punishment.

[143] Criminal Procedure Act, art. 17. The second petty bench of the Supreme Court denied transferring a criminal case from Naha, Okinawa to Tokyo on the August 1, 2016. In that case, the defense council requested the transfer because of the high publicity in Okinawa prefecture.

[144] Saiban-in Act, art. 11.

[145] The Supreme Court Rule concerning the trials with saiban-in participation (Saiban-in Rule) art. 8.

[146] Saiban-in Rule, art. 7, para. 2.

[147] Saiban-in Rule, art. 7, para. 2.

determined by the court and is up to 10,000 yen. The accommodation fee is 7800 or 8700 yen depending on the area.[148]

In the Diet discussions on the meaning of daily allowance for saiban-ins, at the Legal Committee of the House of Representatives on April 4, 2008, the Supreme Court Representative Shôji Ogawa commented. He said, "A daily allowance for saiban-ins should cover the loss for appearing to the court and miscellaneous expenses within certain limits." The allowance is different from salaries of civil servants.

Also, at the Legal Committee of the House of Representatives on April 3, 2009, the Government spokesperson Kotaro Ôno stated that "we are taking various measures to reduce the burden of citizens by revisions of the Criminal Procedure Act to facilitate prompt trials, by paying transportation costs and daily allowances." This comment is indicating the significance of reducing the burden on citizens who become saiban-ins as well as the meaning of daily allowances.

They also discussed the amounts of the allowance. On October 11, 2005, at the Committee of Legislation of the House of Representatives, Toshimitsu Yamazaki commented on the issue. He was the director-general of personnel management agency at the secretariat-general of the Supreme Court. He replied, "based on thorough consideration of responsibilities fulfilled by saiban-ins, we are providing compensations to people participating in formal affairs of the state as well as in many other departments. We will consider an appropriate amount based on comprehensive analysis of all factors such as the level of compensation, daily allowances paid to jurors in other countries, the circumstances related to the improvement of the environment for ensuring saiban-ins appearing in courts the future".

Besides, at the Legal Committee of the House of Representatives on April 4, 2008, they discussed daily allowance again. That was the time when the implementation of the system was drawing closer. Shôji Ogawa's remarks mentioned the fact of the prosecution review board having a daily allowance of 8000 yen. They took into account it, and they considered that the binding hours of saiban-ins are usually longer than those of prosecution examination board members. There was also an opinion at the Diet that the maximum of 10,000 yen is too low and the upper limit should be about 30,000 yen (Legal Affairs Committee, The House of Representatives, November 14, 2008, remarks of Committee member Hosokawa).

The discussions primarily focused on the meaning of the allowance and the amount of money. In the discussions, there was no opinion insisting that the court should refrain from paying saiban-ins for their duties. The reason for this would be as follows. Japanese people tend to conform social norms (Noriyuki 1985). Even Japanese people do not understand the reason why they have to behave in a specific way or they have to do something in a particular situation; they are convinced if somebody whom they can trust says "that's the way it should be, you know (そういうことになっているから)." In Japan, after the suspension of the saiban-in system in Showa era, the citizens did not participate in the trials at the law courts for more

[148] Please refer to Supreme Court Regulations on criminal trials with saiban-in participation, art. 6 and 7, http://www.saibanin.courts.go.jp/qa/c7_1.html

than 60 years. Consequently, most Japanese citizens did not have chances to think the obligation of being a saiban-ins as a natural obligation. The saiban-in duty was not "the way it should be." In that case, they need another reason or compensation in doing something because that is a newly imposed duty on the people. This consequence may be why there were rarely arguments that insisted citizens should be saiban-ins without any compensation.

The Saiban-in System in Practice

Numbers of Defendants, Length of Trials

Next, here we shall review the operation of the saiban-in system since the system's implementation. The numbers cited here are from the judicial statistics issued by the Supreme Court. The Supreme Court should publish the state of the implementation of the saiban-in system.[149]

According to the Supreme Court (The Secretariat-general of the Supreme Court of Japan 2018), as of the end of 2017, in the approximately 8 years since the system began, there have been 11,612 defendants newly accepted, of which trials 10,732 have been rendered a final judgment, and the cases of 880 defendants have not yet been determined (p.2). In general, an average of approximately 1402 people per year has been tried as defendants in saiban-in trials, with about 1192 had received a final judgment. Of 10,732 defendants, 10,422 were found guilty, and 3780 appealed to the High Courts. The conviction rate in saiban-in trials was 97.11%, and the appeal rate was 36.26% overall.

In the single year of 2017, 1010 defendants were newly accepted, and 1126 got final judgments (p. 1). According to the Criminal Justice Monthly Prompt Report in 2017, 68,830 defendants were newly tried in district courts for criminal ordinal first instance cases (刑事通常第一審事件 *Keiji tsûjô dai-Isshin jiken*). As the cumulative total number of defendants were 1077, based on these figures, saiban-in trials were approximately 1.56% of ordinal first instance cases in district courts. In a total of 10,732 defendants overall, 2445 were tried in murder cases, 2294 were accused of robbery resulting in injury, 1049 were tried as injury resulting in death, and 1022 were charged as arson of domiciles.

Regarding sentencing, 32 defendants got death penalties, 208 sentenced as infinite term penal servitude. Of the defendants who received fixed-term imprisonment with labor, 99 were more than 25 years to 30 years, 135 were more than 20 years to 25 years, 464 were more than 15 years to 20 years, 1103 were more than 10 years to 15 years, 2084 were more than 7 years to 10 years, 2011 were more than 5 years to 7 years, and 1825 were more than 3 years to 5 years. For the defendants who received 3 years or less, 656 were sentenced without stays of execution, while 1794

[149] Saiban-in Act art. 103.

were sentenced to suspension. The rest of defendants convicted imprisonment without labor, fine, and one defendant has exempted the penalty.

Cumulative 2,433,706 individuals have been listed as saiban-in candidates in those 8 years, with 60,502 being selected as saiban-in, and 20,591 as reserve saiban-in (The Secretariat-general of the Supreme Court of Japan 2018, Table 1.4). Averaged out over 8 years, this is 304,213 candidates listed per year, 7563 saiban-in, and 2573 reserve saiban-in. In the single year of 2017, a cumulative 233,600 individuals listed as saiban-in candidates in those 8 years, with 5536 being selected as saiban-in, and 1896 as reserve saiban-in. As of the time of this writing (March 9, 2018), Japan had an estimated population of 126,560,000 ("Jinkô suikei (Heisei 29 nen (2017 nen) 9 gatsu kakutei chi, Heisei 30 nen (2018 nen) 2 gatsu gaisanchi) (2018 nen 2 gatsu 20niti kôhyô) [Population estimation (Fixed numbers in September 2017, estimated numbers in February 2018)," 2018). Thus, 0.18% of the population per year were registered for the candidates' lists, 0.0043% participated in trials as saiban-in, and 0.0015% were reserve saiban-in. The total number of those that have been registered is 1.92% of the population of Japan, and approximately 0.064% have served as either saiban-in or reserve saiban-in.

The Secretariat-general of the Supreme Court of Japan (2018) reported the duration of trials. Through the 8 years, the average length of trials has been 7.7 days, and numbers of court sessions have been 4.4. For the cases in which the defendants acknowledged that they had done crimes, the average duration of trials has been 7.7 days, and average numbers of court sessions have been 4.4. The number of defendants who acknowledged was 5784. Moreover, for the denial cases, the average duration of trials has been 10.6 days, and average numbers of court sessions have been 5.3. The number of defendants who denied was 4730, and 5784 defendants admitted their crimes. The duration of the trials of denial cases has gotten much longer in 2017 (13.5 days) than 2009 (4.7 days) in denial cases. For the acknowledging cases, the duration was 3.9 days in 2017, while 3.2 days in 2009. The numbers are almost the same even a little bit get longer.

Costs of Implementing the Saiban-in System

We need to pay attention to the cost of running the saiban-in system, even the meaning of the system for our society is critical. The best way to find the costs of operating the saiban-in system is to reference balance sheets of the courts. Unfortunately, the courts give the public access to only summaries. According to the summaries, it is unclear what portion of lower court operating expenses on saiban-in trials. However, the courts publish estimates of costs for saiban-in trials. The author attempted to find the general costs incurred for saiban-in trials based on this budget-related information.

Court budgets are published on the court website,[150] as well as in budgetary requests to the Ministry of Finance. These amounts include budgetary requests for the saiban-in trials. Of course, budgeted amounts are not the same as final expenses, but they provide us with an indication of the proxy size of the budgets. Table 1.1 shows this data.

The amount of the budget in 2004 is zero, and the budget requests started in 2005. The saiban-in system went into operation in the summer of 2009, and thus the budgets for 2005 to 2009 would have been for public relations and preparation. The total amount each year was around one billion yen. After 2010, public relations related to the implementation came to an end. Thus the amount budgeted for that area fell dramatically to around 100 million yen, with dropping by half in 2013, and further halving in 2015 to 23 million yen. At the same time, operating expenses between 2007 and 2012 held steady at around 100 million yen, ranging from 90 million yen to 110 million yen, though they did decrease annually from 2013 to 2015, going from 70 million to 40 million, and then to 30 million yen. The movement of the amount of the budget is likely because, while before the initiation of the saiban-in system, the court needed to spend on construction of court buildings, and other related expenses for the infrastructure, later expenses were limited to the running costs of the system. Those may have been saiban-in allowances and other related expenses.

Newly accepted cases for saiban-in trials were 1196 in 2009, and there were between 1300 and 1800 cases afterward (The Secretariat-general of the Supreme Court of Japan 2017). The steady numbers of the cases showing less fluctuation.

Accordingly, if there is no renewal of facilities in saiban-in courtrooms or dramatic fluctuations in the number of cases, we can expect that operating budgets will stay less than 100 million yen, and between 30 million and 90 million yen. When we discuss whether we continue to run the system, we should consider the running cost of the saiban-in system. We would decide the consideration of the balance between the significance of the system and the cost of the system.

Tens of millions of yen are not a small amount of money. However, given that the courts overall had an expenditures budget in 2014 of 309.4 billion yen, the amount spent on the saiban-in system is a small portion of the court budget. If the Government maintain that level of the court budget, it would be worth spending in maintaining the saiban-in system to secure the opportunities of civic involvement in meaningful decision-making for the country. The mass media have focused on the cost imposed on the citizens. We need to consider both sides of the costs in running the saiban-in system.

---

[150] The page of the website which publishes the information on the courts' budget is at http://www.courts.go.jp/about/yosan_kessan/yosan/index.html (in Japanese).

Table 1.1 Amounts budgeted by courts for the saiban-in system (in thousands of yen)

Fiscal year	2005	2006	2007	2008	2009	2010	2011	2012	2013	2014	2015
The annual expenses on the saiban-in system	¥1,043,375	¥1,015,323	¥1,092,865	¥1,376,104	¥1,120,895	¥226,500	¥194,659	¥183,737	¥118,960	¥68,340	¥52,988
Public relation expenses (included above)	¥1,029,160	¥1,001,652	¥1,003,123	¥1,270,710	¥1,030,388	¥126,993	¥97,900	¥71,180	¥49,940	¥29,061	¥23,019
The difference between above two figures	¥14,215	¥13,671	¥89,742	¥105,394	¥90,507	¥99,507	¥96,759	¥112,557	¥69,020	¥39,279	¥29,969

Significant Problems Argued Regarding the Saiban-in System

We here review the purposes of the introducing the saiban-in system, the status of the operation, and the costs concerning the system. In this section, let's look common issues and discussions about the saiban-in system in Japan. Some of these problems are related to the theme of the analysis of newspaper articles in this book. The following list of issues is not exhaustive; here we review the significant points. The issues do not cover the issues concerning the interpretation of legal provisions because the interest here is mainly on the social science facets of the problems.

Concerning the trial jury system regarding the points of issues before its introduction, there is a paper that organizes the problems into the following 10 points mainly from the viewpoint of the criminal legal procedure (Shiibashi 2001). According to the article, the main issues are as follows. "① the necessity of introducing the saiban-in system, ② Constitutional conformity of the saiban-in system, ③ the saiban-in system and litigation structure, ④ saiban-in's authority, ⑤ method of the trial body's composition / method of verdict of the saiban-in, ⑥ obligation of the saiban-in, ⑦ subject matter of the saiban-in system, ⑧ trial procedure in saiban-in system, ⑨ appeal under saiban-in system, ⑩ citizen's understanding and support for the saiban-in system". Ths issues from (3) to (9), the current system already show the realistic answers for them.

Among the remaining issues, the necessity of introducing the saiban-in system of ① is still a significant issue even after 14 years since 2004. This book's "Why was this system introduced?" deals with this issue. Moreover, Chaps. 2 and 4 introduce the findings including empirical data. The Chap. 5 presents results of research on the people's attitude of the people indirectly. The Chaps. 2, 4 and 5 of this book provide data concerning the issues on understanding and support of the people (⑩).

One of the remaining issues is the constitutionality of the saiban-in system (②). Some argued that the saiban-in system may violate the Constitution of Japan. The related articles in the Constitution are as follows. The article 32 stipulates that "No person shall be denied the right of access to the courts." The paragraph one of the article 37 states: "In all criminal cases the accused shall enjoy the right to a speedy and public trial by an impartial tribunal." If we think that the court should consist only of professional judges, the system with civic participation in judicial panels is unconstitutional. Then, the problem is the meaning of the "court." We need to figure out whether the Constitution allows the "court" to involve citizens. Regarding the "Court," the paragraph one of the article 76 stipulates that "The whole judicial power is vested in a Supreme Court and in such inferior courts as are established by law." The paragraph three of the article 76 reads that "All judges shall be independent in the exercise of their conscience and shall be bound only by this Constitution and the laws." The arguments which insist the saiban-in system should be an unconstitutional state that the Constitution excludes the public from the exercise of the authority of judiciary because the paragraph three in the article 76 reads "all judges." The "judges" means professional judges, and it does not include citizens. Consequently, the Constitution entrusts the judicial power only to the professional judges so neither of the "Supreme Court" or "inferior courts" in the article 76 includes civic participants.

Regarding "judges," the paragraph one of the article 80 reads "The judges of the inferior courts shall be appointed by the Cabinet from a list of persons nominated by the Supreme Court. All such judges shall hold office for a term of ten (10) years with privilege of reappointment, provided that they shall be retired upon the attainment of the age as fixed by law." The arguments that the word "judges" does not include the lay participants insisted that judges who are appointed the method other than in the article 80 not be "judges." As a result, the saiban-ins are not "judges" because they are appointed randomly on a case-by-case basis, and they are not at their positions for 10 years as the Constitution prescribes for professional judges. The arguments that the saiban-in system is unconstitutional are not reasonable enough if we take it granted that the Constitution Committee discussed the part of the judiciary in the Constitution of Japan under the possibility of the revival of the jury system in Japan. However, the literary interpretations of the articles in the Constitution are not reaching an impasse, the constitutionality of the saiban-in system was one of the highly disputed issues.

With regards to this issue, the Supreme Court decided on November 16th, 2011. The Full Bench of the Supreme Court which consists of all fifteen judges decided the case. The Full Bench deals with highly essential matters. In this case, the Supreme Court stated that the judicial participation of the citizens conforms to the Constitution of Japan in principle. Moreover, whether the public participation justice system conforms to the Constitution should be decided by the results of examinations of the details of the system. According to the opinion of the Supreme Court, the Bench concluded that the saiban-in system is constitutional. The judgment, in this case, is as follows.

"It is sufficiently possible to harmonize the national participation in the judiciary and the principles for realizing fair criminal trials; there are no reasons that the national participation in the judiciary is constitutionally prohibited, the constitutionality of the system regarding the national participation in the judiciary should be decided by whether the concretely established system infringes the principles for realizing fair criminal trials. In other words, the Constitution tolerates the national participation in the judiciary in general, in case [the Diet] adopt this, it is comprehended that [the Constitution] entrusts the details [of the system] to the legislative policies including that [the Diet] chooses a jury system or a mixed jury system as long as the principles above are secured."[151]

"With [the Court's] considering the setup of the saiban-in system, conducting fair trials based on law and evidence at impartial 'courts' (the articles 31, 32, and paragraph one of the article 37 of the Constitution) is sufficiently guaranteed

[151] The translation from the original Japanese text is composed by the author, this is not official translation by the Supreme Court. The subjects in the squared parentheses are supplemented by the author, as the subjects are omitted in the original text. In Japanese language, sentences do not necessarily have subjects, in case the subjects can be inferred by the context. The round parentheses appeared in the original text.

institutionally. Moreover, it is acknowledged that the professional judges are considered as principal undertakers of the criminal trials, there is no hindrance in securing the principles of criminal trials which the Constitution decrees. Consequently, the appellant's opinion that argues [that the saiban-in system] infringes the articles 31, 32, paragraph 1 of 37, paragraph 1 of 76, and paragraph 1 of 80 has no rationale."

By this decision, the Supreme Court acknowledges the constitutionality of the saiban-in system. Moreover, it is one of the precedents that the public participation in the justice system and the saiban-in system itself are constitutional. Although criticisms still can exist about this, it is reasonable to consider whether the Constitution allows citizens to participate in the justice system is determined (Yanase 2016 for the same argument). As the decision referred in the part which is not cited here, there are records on the discussions at the time of establishment of the Japanese Constitution. In the discussions, it was presupposed that jury system is constitutional in the current Constitution. Also, even the provisions of the Constitution quoted above refers to professional judges, the Constitution does not exclude the citizens from the exercising the authority of the judiciary (Ôishi and Ishikawa 2008, p. 271).

Also, there was a criticism arguing that the citizen's judicial participation system which is different from the jury system is unconstitutional because the jury system conducted in Showa era was supposed at the time of establishment of the Constitution of Japan (e.g., Kaneko 1948). However, the situation in which the Constitution Committee supposed jury system and they did not think about mixed jury system does not mean that the Constitution excludes the citizens from the exercise of the authority of the judiciary (Yomiuri Shimbun Tokyohonsha Chôsakenkyûhonbu 2009, p. 51).

However, it does not necessarily mean that every issue relating to the saiban-in system is constitutional. For example, it is pointed out that the practice in the saiban-in system may violate freedom of conscience when citizens have to answer the questionnaire which is asking whether they would like to join the trial or citizens cannot refuse to show their opinions at the deliberations even they do not like to punish any other persons for personal beliefs (Takeshima 2017). Also, there is a problem over how to deal with religious beliefs of the saiban-ins (Yoshimura 2009). The Constitution of Japan has a provision that stipulates that national institutions are prohibited religious activities.[152] And it guarantees the nationals' freedom of thought and conscience.[153] It is interpreted that the freedom includes religious beliefs. Consequently, there arises a problem of constitutionality if the saiban-in system makes the court impose on citizens the duties which infringe the freedom of thoughts and religion.

From the viewpoint of the persons concerned the trials, we should consider the problem whether the saiban-in system brings any new disadvantages for the accused. We can understand that the saiban-in system utilizes the criminal trials as the place

[152] The Constitution of Japan, art. 20.

[153] The Constitution of Japan, art. 19.

for educating people. This understanding may arise an ethical or political problem that we can utilize the criminal trials at which the defendants' lives are determined. Criminal trials are the places for the discovery of truth and protecting human rights in the first place as the article 1 of the Criminal Procedure Law prescribes.

Regarding the disadvantage of the defendant, it was pointed out before the introduction of the saiban-in system that the fact-finding may become "rough" and the sentence may get heavier (Ida 2010). Moreover, it was claimed that conventional "precise justice 精密司法 *seimitsu shiho*" (Matsuo 2012, p. 30) and "carefully write a judgment" contributed to guarantee the defendant's human rights. The "precise justice" is based on a massive amount of the dossier of the case. The investigation needs to interrogate the suspects intensively and repeatedly to obtain the records possibly including confessions under long detentions, and the investigation uses the record to write the documents. We should think that "precise justice" requires inevitably such human rights violations, even conducting trials with detailed documents looks to realize accurate judgments.

Besides, there were also arguments that the defendants should be able to choose bench trials instead of the saiban-in trials (Shiibashi 2001) and worry concerning whether the saiban-in system can handle denial cases (Ishida 2010). It is also claimed that the procedures should be divided into fact-finding and sentencing (手続二分論 tetsudzuki nibun-ron). Furthermore, there are arguments insisting that the appellate courts might include citizen participants.

There also are the problems of the saiban-in's understanding scientific evidence (Hayashi 2010), and psychiatric evaluations or responsibility evaluations (Juichi 2011; Sugano 2011). These are the same problems found in the countries where the jury or mixed jury system conducted.

Another significant issue was about the schedule of the trials. It was a problem whether legal professionals, especially lawyers, can accommodate themselves to the intensive trial schedule. Once the citizens are called to the court, it is difficult to keep them bound to their duties and the law courts for a long time because citizens have their businesses at the place other than the court. Legal professionals handled criminal trials by a method in which hearings last for several hours in one day, and the trial dates are repeated with intervals of about one month. This custom is called as "Early-summer rain formula 五月雨式 *samidare shiki*" trial. "*Samidare*" means rains lasting for a long time in May. The early summer rainfalls continually drop for an extended period. In the current calendar the rainfall ranges from June to July, but in the lunar sun calendar that was used until the nineteenth century, it corresponded to May. The advantage of conducting trials in this way is that trial procedures proceed in a small step in a single trial date, and there is some time between the trial dates. This situation enables the legal professionals to prepare for work little by little. This method of doing the job is particularly advantageous for attorneys. Attorneys usually take on many civil cases and operate their office based on the revenues earned from the civil cases. It is hard for attorneys to afford to keep their offices by relying only on criminal cases because dealing with criminal cases is not so much profitable. Such situation is typical in Japan. However, because there is no public defender system in Japan, private attorneys should take on the criminal cases.[154]

Since judges and prosecutors are government employees, there is no risk of interruption of income when they concentrate on dealing with criminal cases. Also, saiban-in trial cases require a tremendous amount of time not only for trial but for preparation as well. To complete a trial with saiban-ins within three to 13 days, judges need to make detailed arrangements for the trial before its start. For that reason, it was said that private attorneys are hard to perform the defense service in a saiban-in trial.

However, after the saiban-in system started, lawyers serve as defense councils in saiban-in trials. The reason for this could be that the lawyer's offices in which run by the attorneys more than one are taking the burden of the saiban-in trials. They are less risky to discontinue of incoming when one of the lawyers concentrate on saiban-in trials. Moreover, there are legal offices set up by the legal terrace (法テラス: *hô terasu*), and they are receiving subsidies from the state to run the offices. The lawyers who are in those offices can do defense lawyers' job without worrying about stopping their income. Moreover, the increase of the number of private attorneys after the legal reform in the 2000s contribute to increasing the number of the undertakers as defense attorneys.

Upon introduction of the saiban-in system, one of the issues which the mass media focused upon was the burden on the citizens.[155] As the overall tone of the arguments tended that the citizens regarded the saiban-in duty with disfavor due to the burden. Considering the results of quantitative analyses are presented in the newspaper analyses section of this book, we could not see the arguments like examining the balance between the significance of the saiban-in duty and the burden. Even many newspaper and other articles were published, it looked that the discussion from this viewpoint was not deepened.

The significant burden for citizens should be time and money. The issue of money is the loss of their income if they do not fulfill the duty as saiban-in and expenses to commute the law courts. Citizens are compensated for receiving a daily allowance. The amount is up to 8000 yen for the saiban-in candidates and up to 10,000 yen for the saiban-ins and reserve saiban-ins per day.[156] According to the discussions during the legislative process of the Saiban-in Act cited above, the allowance is not a salary for the saiban-in, but compensation for loss to some extent. Professional judges make efforts to shorten the duration of trials. The average length of trials is 3.9 days in acknowledging cases. The trials for denial cases average more than 13 days.

---

[154] The justice system reform remedied this problem. Lawyers in the office established by the legal terrace (法テラス: *hô terasu*) concentrate on the cases which are not profitable for ordinal private attorneys. Moreover, the number of lawyers increased dramatically after the legal reform, the number of the lawyers who take on criminal cases also increased. Their offices have been emerging in urban areas with criminal cases as the primary handling cases.

[155] This is going to be described in later chapter of this book.

[156] This is prescribed Saiban-in Rule as cited above.

Besides, citizen's "psychological burden"has also been focused. Mass media arose issue the psychological burden before introducing the system, arguing that the citizens will be under much pressure in saiban-in duty. After that, the psychological burden discussion includes the psychological shock of seeing the gruesome evidence. A former saiban-in claiming to have suffered from PTSD (post-traumatic stress disorder) raised a lawsuit against the state for this matter.

The problem of personal dangers is also argued. Notably, in the case that gangsters indicted, saiban-ins may be threatened or harmed. This issue is considered at the time of legislation. The Saiban-in Act prescribes that demanding saiban-in regarding their jobs and threatening saiban-in are punishable acts.[157] However, in general, saiban-ins are not escorted on the way between the court and their homes. After the saiban-in system was implemented, there was a case that some yakuza member spoke to some saiban-ins when they were at a bus stop on the way home. After that case, the judges decide the cases involving yakuza should be tried only by professional judges.

It is also a problem that the attendance rate on the date of saiban-in selection has declined. According to the statistics issued by the Supreme Court, the attendance rate on the selection date was 63.9% in 2017 while the ratio was 83.9% in 2009. It seems necessary to investigate this case,[158] but the burden should be considered as one of the factors the fall of attendance rate.

The duty of confidentiality of saiban-in has also been considered as a burden on citizens before starting the system. The saiban-in shall not talk about who had what kind of opinions during the deliberations even after the trials end.[159] From the viewpoint of establishing the popular base of the justice system, it may be better to share the experience in serving as saiban-in more freely. However, if all saiban-ins can talk or even publish what they know about the case after their saiban-in duty without restrictions, there would be a risk that the secrets of the case can be sold to mass media.

Some argued that false charges and misjudgment would increase with trials by saiban-in (e.g., Kimura 2013; Nishino 2014). But it is not reasonable to assume that a judicial panel consisted of three professional judges makes more mistakes when it adds six saiban-ins. First, a false accusation comes from a mistake of the investigation agency by misidentifying the suspect. That is not a problem of the trial. It is not reasonable to assume that the error rate on identification would be affected by whether the trial procedure involves citizens. Consequently, the argument should be understood as "the court will sentence guilty on the innocence more when citizens take part in trials."

Then, will the probability of mistaking increase when citizens join the trials? Upon the findings of group decision-making research, the probability of achieving

---

157 Saiban-in Act, art. 106 and 107.

158 The court entrusted the survey on this theme to a private research company and made the report public through the Internet. See http://www.saibanin.courts.go.jp/l2/17_05_22_bunsekigyoumu.html

159 Saiban-in Act, art. 108.

the right answer increases as the number of group members increases when there is a correct answer (Steiner 1966). Such task is called "non-additive task." A non-additive task is a task which the group can reach the right answer when one of the members of a group gets to the correct answer. The more member in the group, the higher probability that the group will reach the correct answer in solving a non-additive task. Criminal trials can be understood as non-additive tasks with a correct answer because there exists one single fact from the God's eye. Even if the citizens are not accustomed to law or trial, and the citizens have a low probability of getting to the correct answer than the judges, it would be higher than zero. In that case, the probability of reaching a correct answer will be higher if the judicial panel adds six citizens. Otherwise, if we assume that the likelihood of finding the truth by a trial body with six citizens and three judges should decrease than the panel of three judges, the probability of finding the truth by citizens should always be less than zero. The assumption would not be reasonable if the citizens are reasonable enough as ordinary humans. Not only that, but this assumption does not trust the reasons of the citizen at all, and despising the citizens.

As mentioned above, various issues have been discussed in Japan regarding the saiban-in system. Also, the mass media have closed up related problems of the saiban-in system. Citizens who have formed their views under the effects of the mass media may be inclined to have negative attitudes towards the system without essential arguments on the system. The essential arguments on the saiban-in system are what kind of values the saiban-in system realizes, whether it is worth doing even if we have to pay the cost of implementing the system.

There seemed to be the inclination to label discussants as "proponents" or "opponents" at the start of discussions. During the arguments, discussants are expected to utter their views from the position which are given at the start of the discussing. It is hard to make constructive arguments with starting such labeling, similar to "verdict-driven" type (Hastie et al. 1983) jury deliberations. As a result, it seemed that the arguments in non-essential problems with negative evaluation prevail in the Japanese society. However, we expect to increase the discussions concerning the essential values concerning the saiban-in system along with increasing the number of the citizens who experience saiban-in duty. This may be a process of the system's taking root in the society. Regarding the process of the system's taking root in the society, the decision of the Supreme Court cited above postulated as follows in its final part of the judgment.

"To become the [saiban-in] system established in the society by making the best use of the advantages of the jury system and mixed jury system, it is possible to say that the continuous efforts by all persons concerned in operation are required. Until the saiban-in system was introduced, our country's criminal trials had been undertaken only by the legal professionals including professional judges, and the highly specialized operations had been carried out which had been characterized by the minute fact-finding. As [we] mentioned above, to realize the role of the judiciary, the expertise in law is essential. However, high expertise which is realized only by the legal professionals sometimes makes the national citizens' understanding difficult, and it might turn out to be remote from the nationals' sense."

"The saiban-in system's purpose is to reinforce the national foundation of the judiciary; it is possible to say that [the system] aims to realize criminal trials in which make the best use of the advantages of the viewpoints of the nation and the expertise of the legal professionals with deepening mutual understanding by keeping constant interchange. It is needless to say that reasonable time is required in accomplishing the objective; it seems that the process itself also has significant meaning in realizing the judiciary which has roots in the nationals. It is conceivable that [we] can be realizing the system of the national participation in the judiciary that fits best our country's actual circumstances by accumulating efforts from the long-term viewpoint like mentioned above."

The Impact of Implementing the Saiban-in System

About This Part

In this section, we shall consider the impact of implementing the saiban-in system. The purpose of introduction of the saiban-in system was to establish the popular base of the justice system and to nurture the consciousness of the "subject of governance." Adding to it, the introduction of the system might cause various secondary effects. Let us review both the advantages and the disadvantages introduction of the saiban-in system.

Satoru Shinomiya, who served as one of the members of JSRC, reported the changes after introduction of the saiban-in system (Shinomiya 2012). According to Shinomiya (2012), the saiban-in system has changed (1) the consciousness of experts, (2) legal education, (3) customs about the labor market, (4) the mass media, (5) citizen's awareness and eventually (6) the democracy in the whole state.

(1) Changing the consciousness of experts means the changes in the mentality of judges and court clerks. In Shinomiya (2012), a presiding judge said that he saw the light by the opinions and ideas presented by saiban-in. Another judge said that he could get more matured as a judge through the debates with saiban-ins because saiban-ins presented various viewpoints in their deliberations.

Regarding this point, prominent figures in legal professionals stated that they need to pay attention to the thoughts of citizens. After the saiban-in system started, a former Supreme Court judge Nirô Shimada stated that the citizens always observe the trial procedures after the introduction of the saiban-in system, and he expressed his opinion that the legal professionals should listen to the opinions and criticisms from the nationals (Shimada 2012). It is notable that a former Supreme Court judge gave such opinion when we think about his influence on legal professionals. It had hardly imagined before the introduction of the system such situation has come true. Bringing this situation would be one of the significant secondary effects of the introduction of the saiban-in system. According to the findings of the procedural fairness research, the authority understands genuinely about the differences existing in the heterogeneous society (Tyler 2000, p. 303). If the judges and the citizens are always in contact with each other through the system, professional judges will always be paying attention to citizens' intentions, and the same would be true for vice-versa.

(2) The purpose of legal education is to explain the basics of legal systems to the pupils from elementary school to high school. Traditionally, during the classes of social studies and civics in Japanese schools, pupils have been taught about the division to three branches of power stipulated in the Constitution. However, the pupils had almost no chance to learn the detailed procedures of justice in their classes.

To change the situation, JSRC proposed that legal education should prevail in the country. In reposing the opinion paper and policies determined after that, the Ministry of Education, Culture, Sports, Science, and Technology of Japan decided to include the topics concerning the saiban-in system in the new governmental-led curriculum guidelines in the 2000s. According to this guidance, the government enforced the curriculum for the students who entered the elementary school after 2011, the middle school after 2012 and high school from 2013 respectively.

(3) Concerning the issue of labor, Japanese Labor Standards Act stipulates that "Employer shall not refuse the request of the worker to provide the time necessary to exercising his civilian rights during working hours."[160] Also, the Saiban-in Act stipulates that "A worker may not be dismissed or discriminatively treated by taking days-off to perform or to have performed the duties of a saiban-in, a reserve saiban-in, a scheduled appointment saiban-in or a saiban-in candidate."[161] This provision prevents discriminative treatment of workers by the employers when the worker becomes a saiban-in. "For that reason, the system of paid leave for the duty of saiban-in become prevailing in companies." In the questionnaire conducted by Nippon Keidanren (Japan Business Federation) in 2008, 63% of enterprises have already introduced the saiban-in system, while 37% responded as they were considering introduction.

As shown in the psychological study of media pretrial news reports in the US, there is a concern that the publicity may affect potential jurors. Regarding this point, "court requested for improvement of the way of reporting as there is an undeniable concern of giving unfair prejudice to the saiban-in." Notably, it concerns the issues of mentioning the real name of the suspect and broadcasting it. That way of reporting may let the recipient assume that the suspect has committed the crime.

(4) The Constitution of Japan guarantees freedom of speech.[162] Besides, the state's censorship of expression contents is prohibited.[163] Regulating the press coverage directly by the state is problematic as the regulation may violate the constitution. In this regard, in 2008, the Nippon Shimbun Association announced the "Reporting and Broadcasting Guidelines for the Initiation of the Saiban-in system" as a means of harmonizing between avoiding prejudicing potential saiban-in, freedom of speech and responding to the public's right to know. In the same year, the private broadcasting federation announced, "Regulations regarding the incident

[160] Saiban-in Act, art. 100.

[161] Saiban-in Act, art. 100

[162] The Constitution of Japan, art. 21, para. 1.

[163] The Constitution of Japan, art. 21, para. 2.

reporting under the saiban-in system" from the same point of view. As the mass media associations issued their self-regulatory standards let the government refrain from direct regulation on the content of the mass media coverage.

(5) In the report of the Justice System Reform Council, the council expected the citizens to change their recognition from "governed object" to "the subject of government." Upon observation after the start of the saiban-in system, the civilian's consciousness seemed to change. However, in the previous survey results, there was no survey cast a question to citizens as "Have you changed your mind of being the object to be a subject of that place?". As indirect evidence, there are social surveys conducted before and after the case of serving as saiban-in conducted by the Supreme Court.

On the results of 2010 survey of respondents who have served as saiban-in, the number of response as "Excellent experience" was 55.5% and "Good experience" 39.7% respectively (The Supreme Court of Japan 2011). By combining these number, we could understand that 95.2% of citizens who served as saiban-in evaluated their experience positively. The same inclination also appeared in the latest survey published in 2017. In that survey, the 59.0% of respondents answered, "Excellent experience," and 37.1% of respondents answered, "Good experience" respectively (The Supreme Court of Japan 2017).

To understand what kind of experiences contributed these results, we consider the interviews of the ex-saiban-in and the roundtable discussions after the trials. In the interviews, one ex-saiban-in said that it is essential for individuals to voice to change the society and make the society more livable place. Another ex-saiban-in answered that sentencing in a criminal trial conveys a message that how do the citizens think that the society shall be with using their common sense (Shinomiya 2012). A newspaper reporter observed that it is reasonably conceivable that citizens' consciousness change from "governed objects" to "governing subject" if they disseminate experiences." (Iwata 2010, p. 121).

Considering the voices described above helps us to understand the motivation of the civilians. As it becomes clear, they are not only thinking about the society by participating in a trial as saiban-in but also spreading their views by sending the messages of what kind of community where they want to live. Those citizens' way of thinking is undoubtedly transformation in consciousness towards "the governing subject." Then, if civilians take actions as "the governing subject," we could presume that Japan will transform into society constituted by civilians having a clear understanding of their civil duties, roles and ways of its implementation. This will affect (6) the democracy of the whole state. In part "Considerations on democratic moments of the saiban-in system," we investigate this issue further.

Citizens' Participation in Deliberations

Before the start of the saiban-in system, some believed citizens were used as mere window dressing even they participate in trials (e.g., Mitsui et al. 2004). The courts made efforts so that the citizens' participation has come to be realistic. The results of their effort can be seen from the results of the ex-saiban-ins surveys which are conducted in each year.

According to the survey report which the Supreme Court aggregated the results of the surveys all district courts, 4870 out of 6208 participants (78.4%) responded that the atmosphere of deliberations were discussions comfortable, and as to the level of deliberations, 4718 (76.0%) stated that they were able to "have sufficient discussions" (The Supreme Court of Japan 2017) in 2016. It is impossible to make a snap decision using these questionnaires as to whether the essence of participation has been sufficiently ensured, though the data does allow us to believe that there is enough participation in deliberations to do away with the prior worry about "window dressing."

In this book, the results of social psychological experiments concerning deliberations are presented in the part of "What's in the deliberation." Please refer to the section to think about what the deliberations would be like.

Changes in Criminal Proceedings by Introducing the Saiban-in System

Introduction of the saiban-in system affected the methods of conducting the criminal trial and the investigation of cases involving criminal trials. Other than the citizens have taken part in the court, the problems which had been debated over the years on criminal trial procedures have started to change. The change occurred to accommodate citizens to the courts and criminal procedures.

The Realization of Oralism: From Dead Rituals to Living Exchanges

The legal professionals made much effort in realizing the oralism in criminal trials the introduction of the saiban-in system. Before the introduction of the saiban-in system, it is standard of criminal trial practice that the judges read a massive amount of dossier outside of the court and form their impression on the case.[164] It was natu-

[164] Criminal Procedure Act stipulates the principle of oralism, most of the criminal trials run by prosecutors' submitting dossier and judges' reading the documents outside the court.

This custom was called "精密司法 *seimitsu shihô*: precision justice." This was named by Professor Koya Matsuo. (松尾浩也) In precision justice, legal professionals believe that they can exercise careful trials through judges' examining the massive dossier which are prepared by the police and the prosecution. To compile the massive dossier, the investigation carries out intensive interrogations of the suspects adding to collect objective evidence. To carry out intensive interrogations, the investigation tends to request to keep the suspects into the custody. This custom is one of the factors that the Japanese criminal justice often or usually exercises hostage justice. There are positive opinions on the precision justice arguing that the precision justice realize accurate and minute fact-finding, while negative opinions emphasize the bad effect of hostage justice on the suspects' lives mainly in the cases of miscarriage of justice.

ral for prosecutors to read aloud such documents instead of making some humans understood in the court. Defense attorneys often read aloud their arguments written on paper against prosecutors instead of advocating their theory of the case. Kawai (2011) noted that the efforts of judges focused on prosecutor fact-finding, and defense attorney's attempts to defend by submitting documents. This is so-called "precise justice" practice (Matsuo 2012). Precise justice is not necessarily ideal for maintaining transparency in the courts as judges form their impression outside of the court. Saiban-in trials changed this custom to some extent and contributed realizing the oralism in criminal procedures (Hirayama 2016).

Compared with judges that make careful readings of case records and careful application of the law, saiban-ins are regular citizens chosen on a case-by-case basis. We cannot expect to make careful readings of complicated documents at the same level as a judge. Thus, prosecutors and defense attorneys make explanations of their arguments and evidence in the court as possible as they can. The need for make understood saiban-ins was a high power to motivate oralism in the criminal courts (The Supreme Court Secretary General of Criminal Bureau 2009; Yoshimaru 2006).

In oral presentations of both parties at the courts, the prosecutors and defense attorneys summarize their arguments. And they try to make understood some humans on the court. Judges, prosecutors, and attorneys have pretrial conferences to make detailed plans to conduct trials. The hearing is carried out all at once with saiban-ins in attendance (Ashizawa 2012). This method of running trials has changed the trial schedules significantly, turning them from plodding affairs into something more disciplined.

Further, trials were conducted with enthusiasm and techniques of both prosecutors and defense attorneys to help *saiban-in* understand their assertions and the evidence (Japan Federation of Bar Associations 2009). Also, the presiding judge explains the trial procedure and proof of evidence so that *saiban-in* can make decisions. Judges encourage saiban-in to examine witnesses and the defendants during hearings (Ashizawa 2012).

"Easy-to-Understand Judiciary" (分かりやすい司法 *wakariyasui shihô*)

The legal professionals have made great effort to make saiban-ins understood about trials including the terminology as well as the procedures. One of the typical examples was their explanation of the standard of the proof in criminal trials. The standard is "beyond the reasonable doubt." It is not easy for citizens to understand the exact meaning of the phrase because the phrase is not in the everyday vocabulary, even every word is familiar for the citizens, and it does not make clear sense if we follow the phrase literally. The courts studied how to explain the standard as well as the criminal proceeding itself. This behavior has also appeared in judgments and precedents. After the implementation of the saiban-in system, the lengthy written judgments changed into more short ones which consist of the lists of the necessary factors in straightforward language (Legal Research and Training Institute 2009).

This is much advanced than the proposition of the JRSC opinion paper, as the Council proposed the written judgments to keep the contents as they were.

In the preparation period of the saiban-in system, the notion of "easy-to-understand trial" started to prevail. This notion is found in the opinion paper of the Justice System Reform Council. However, the Council used this phrase in presenting the necessity of changing the provisions of the Civil Law and the Commercial Law Act, which were written in archaic Japanese language into the simple and current language. Other than that, the Council proposed successive trial dates for the saiban-in trials by using the phrase "easy-to-understand judiciary." The Council did not evidently propose using everyday vocabulary in the saiban-in trials. Attempting to realize "easy-to-understand trial" with everyday vocabulary was somewhat radical at that time. Because people thought that legal arguments are difficult to understand in nature, those who concerned the criminal law, including criminal law scholars, did not think their edifying dignifying language to be replaced by normal words. What the lawyer assumed at that time was to explain to the civilians from the viewpoint of experts.

However, at the early stage of preparation period of the saiban-in system, it came to be apparent that the language is one of the significant obstacles to collaborate with citizens in the courtroom. Consequently, the Japan Federation of Bar Associations decided to start a project which aimed to explain or replace words and phrases in "legalese." The next section will deal with the process of how the project went.

Legalese, Simplified

A trial is a place where unique terms are crossing each other. The language used by the legal professionals is called legalese (Hartley 2000). Legalese contains technical terms and abnormal usages of general terms used by legal professionals. Because the legal industry requires particular concepts and arguments which we can never find in everyday life, and the trials are the places for the application of legal norms, it is difficult to eliminate the use of technical terms. Judges, prosecutors, and lawyers are experts in law, who mastered how to operate the language with understandings of the background. The fact that plenty of training is required to master the legalese makes an obstacle when the citizens participate in the judiciary. Not only that, however, there have been unnecessary jargons which are archaic or making just the arguments dignified in the courtroom. If trials are challenging to understand for citizens because of those terms, legal professionals need to explain those terms or stop using some of them if unnecessary. This is the rationale for "easy-to-understand judiciary" in the saiban-in trials. During realizing "easy-to-understand judiciary," the primary activity was to develop a set of explanation of legal language and replacement which can be easily understood by citizens.

Given this situation, the Japan Federation of Bar Associations started a project to convert legalese into everyday vocabulary in 2004. One of the objectives of this project at its conception was to "make the justice system easy to understand." The project was named as "everyday language project for court terms." The initiation of the project was in the early stage of the introductory period of the saiban-in system. This team included attorneys, criminal law scholars, a linguist, a national language specialist, and a social psychologist. The project team involved the author as a member. They gathered to make explanations and invent replacements that civilians understand. They have also prepared the summary of opinions recommending the replacement for the unnecessary words.

The project team first identified the words and phrases to be explained or replaced. To identify the words and phrases, they conducted interviews with citizens and made a ranking the level of difficulty for each word or phrase (Fujita 2005). Then they published the interim report and final report. The reports proposed that the words which were difficult to understand and of little use should be replaced, and the words that were hardly replaced should be well explained. And they proposed possible explanations. One of the explanations which caused controversy was "charged fact 公訴事実." This phrase misleads the citizens because the second word is "fact." (Goto & The Project Team for Altering the Terminology in the Lawcourts into Everyday Vocabulary, 2008). Citizens understand this phrase as the real and objective "facts" that is already proven by evidence. But this is not true because the "charged facts" are presented at the early stage of the criminal trial to clarify the things that the prosecutors intend to prove in the trial. To be precise, that is not a fact, but just an opinion of the prosecutors which explain the whole case. The project team proposed to explain the charged facts as "the story which the prosecutors try to prove by evidence in the trial." At the first time, this explanation was taken as prosecutors saying whatever they wanted rather than stating things based on evidence obtained through investigation because they thought the word "story" implied that prosecutors talk freely even it is nonsense. Also, regarding explaining some specific concepts, such as "self-defense," some criticized that replacing them would destroy the theory of criminal law. The misunderstanding like that criticism disappeared after the true meaning of the project team's opinion got understood. Another prominent example was "dolus eventualis / willful neglect." This is a somewhat unusual phrase used only for criminal legal arguments. The project team proposed that the phrase "willful neglect" should be brought to citizens as "willful neglective intention to kill," and explain in what case such intention will be acknowledged. That was because the most cases in the saiban-in act which deal with willful neglect are murder cases, and it is hard to make citizen understood the whole concept of the willful neglect abstractly. The proposed explanation can be used for only murder or manslaughter cases,[165] and it can convey a lively image to the citizens by using specific examples.

Like above examples, the legal terminology was forced to undergo a major review. Initially, there was a massive accusation from experts, but this project was taken up by the mass media, so at the end of the project explanation and replacement of the words made in this project were accepted for being the commonplace for the

[165] In Japanese criminal law, there is no discrimination between murder and manslaughter. They are considered as one crime category.

public of the world. The words and phrases which the project proposed began to be used by lawyers in the courtroom. Legalese has changed vastly since the start of the saiban-in system.

After the project team issued their interim report, there are similar activities started by other legal professionals. From the first half of the 2000s, the court terminology was simplified by conversion into everyday language. As the project's activities came to be known, it was understood that explaining terms and concepts in the saiban-in system and making the justice system easy to understand was an important issue. At first, achieving "easy to understand trials" began by proposing explanations of terms.

Currently, "achieving easy to understand trials" is reported as the significant purpose of the introduction of the saiban-in system. And the "easy-to-understand" means to explain difficult language, use visual aids, concise material. However, the phrase originally was used in the JSRC report to mean successive trial dates and other similar treatments. The project team and the related events changed the meaning of the phrase "easy-to-understand judiciary."

Related to legalese, the vocal style of prosecutors has been changed (Ito 2012). It is said that prosecutors talk politely compared to the trials before introducing the saiban-in system. Typically, they use the polite language of colloquial Japanese, which every sentence ends with the word "desu" or "masu" after the introduction of the saiban-in system.

The courts make efforts to explain their legalese to civic participants. Those efforts seem to succeed according to their surveys. The Supreme Court has issued the results of surveys for the citizens who have served as saiban-ins. The questionnaire includes the questions concerning instructions. As of this writing, the most recent survey results (The Supreme Court of Japan 2017) had 90.6% (5627) of respondents who answered that the instructions given by judges were "easy to understand." In another question, 66.5% of citizens stated that deliberations were "easy to understand," and 29.3% noted that they were "average," which two responses account for more than 95% of the total.

Visual Aids in the Courtroom

Prosecutors and defense attorneys started to use visual aids in courtrooms to make the saiban-in understood. Before implementing the saiban-in system, there was no PowerPoint nor colossal LCD monitors in Japanese courtrooms. Prosecutors and lawyers started to use PowerPoint in the early stages. They used it most frequently in the early stages. After they get experienced with presentations in the trial, they write a list of discussions on large paper, and they use less often PowerPoint than before (Kawai 2011). Their way of presentation evolves along with their experience. This practice reduces the document to use in the criminal courts (Kawai 2011).

Also, the way of presenting evidence has changed. Prosecutors summarize the outline of the case and the whole claim altogether into one A3 sized sheet. After that, they distribute it to judges and saiban-ins before examining the evidence.

Judges and saiban-ins can take notes on it while hearing the story. Prosecutors sometimes leave the blanks in the material and ask the saiban-ins to fill them. For example, saiban-ins are asked to fill the name of the place where the incident happened; the prosecutor's requested punishment.

The evidence such as a summary of the case, a record of interrogations, the photos of the crime scene is summarized and shown as PowerPoint slides. Basing on it, the prosecutor talks to the judges and the saiban-ins while presenting the slides. The slides are often presented on a large-sized display that can be seen from the observers. In the past, prosecutors and defense lawyers read the records in the court. Of course, they handed the documents to the judges at the court. If the documents are too long to read, prosecutors can inform the judges the summary of the documents. That was no problem because judges read the documents thoroughly after the court session being dismissed. Evidence such as weapons was raised high to be seen in the trial. Compared to the styles found before the saiban-in system, it can be said that the current trial practice is getting overwhelmingly easy to understand when listening from the side. Citizen participation in the judiciary has changed the practice dramatically in the criminal courts.

"Sound Common Sense" in the Trial

It is widely believed in Japan that the purpose of the introduction of the saiban-in system is to infuse sound common sense to criminal trials. Actually, this is not found in official opinions like JSRC opinion paper as the purpose of the introduction of the system. The common sense introduction to the judiciary is a secondary effect or the method of securing the popular base of the justice system, as we reviewed in the sections above. However, reflecting sound common sense would contribute to energizing criminal trials through strengthening citizens' self-efficacy in their participation.

According to the surveys conducted by the Supreme Court, ex-saiban-ins answered that they deliberation reportedly (The Supreme Court of Japan 2017). The results of surveys, even we take it into consideration that the Court itself conducted, the significant part of the ex-saiban-ins felt that they could utter in the deliberations, and the groups deliberated enough the case. Consequently, the citizen participation in the judiciary has achieved satisfactory results as long as we look subjective evaluation of the experience saiban-in duties.

We had expected the saiban-ins put severer punishments for the defendants than professional judges before the introduction of the system. And we had thought that's common sense. The reality was that that's not the case. The results of the sentencing have not so much changed after the introduction of the saiban-in system compared to the bench trials (Kojima 2015). The defendants have got severer sentences for the specific types of crimes, for example, sexual assault with violence. Surprisingly, overall punishments are not getting severer nor more lenient after the introduction of the saiban-in system. There may be criticism that the stableness of the punishments should come from the estrangement of the citizens in the deliberations.

However, it would not be a reasonable assumption because the significant part of the ex-saiban-ins felt that they could talk in the deliberations. The punishments for the defendants are essential but insufficient indicators for measuring the extent of civilian participation to the judiciary. We have to pay attention to other aspects to understand how citizens participate in the trials, and whether the citizens' common sense can be reflected the deliberations. The reflection of citizens' sense would be another factor which is energizing criminal trials.

Made Progress in Visualization (可視化: *Kashi-ka*)

Apart from the introduction of the saiban-in system, the issue of sound and video recording of interrogations in criminal procedure was a long-standing concern in Japan (Ibusuki 2013). Because the criminal investigation institution in Japan can detain suspects for a maximum of 23 days (28 days for some crimes), and investigation agencies can as freely and often interrogate the suspects as they wish. Moreover, the defense councils are not allowed to attend the interrogations, and in principle, the records of the interrogations are kept in the investigation agencies' office. It was rare that the raw record was left.

However, in that situation, it is difficult to judge whether the suspect talked voluntary or he / she talked under the pressure of confinement. It has always been problematic in cases where differences in what the accused says in the trial and what the defendant said during the interrogation, including confessions. The voluntariness of a confession is critical, especially the case in which the rest of evidence is not so strong compared to the case where the investigation agencies collected enough material evidence. In that case, the court has an endless dispute between prosecutors and the lawyers over the credibility of confessions. The judges usually stand by the prosecutors in most of those cases, without objective evidence of the interrogation process.

It is very disadvantageous for the suspect to be put under interrogation violating the human rights where the defendant has no practical way to prove. Defense lawyers and criminal law scholars have requested for many years to make recordings of interrogation at the investigative stage so that lawyers can avoid fruitless dispute in the court and avoid incredibly disadvantageous judgment without evidence on the interrogations. However, the police and prosecutors kept refusing this stubbornly, and interrogations were rarely recorded.

The start of the saiban-in system has had a significant influence and has changed the situation. The saiban-ins (and judges) cannot judge the voluntariness of confessions or other talked contents without the evidence of the process of interrogations. The saiban-ins might complain to the judges if they are requested to judge without evidence. The judges may not be able to tell the saiban-ins to stand by the prosecutor without evidence in that case because it infringes the provision of the Criminal Procedure Law "the fact-finding should be based on evidence."

As a result, the necessity of recording of the interrogation process is insisted more strongly than before. This situation forced the police and the prosecution to start sound and video recording. It has become possible to stop fruitless disputes in the courtroom over the voluntariness of the confession by using the records as evidence of the interrogation process. After that, as the number of recordings increased and coverage for the case raised. The discussion on interrogation recording was dramatically progressing by the introduction of the saiban-in system. Additionally, the word "visualization可視化" has obtained popularity conspicuously around the time of visual and audio recording by the investigation agencies started. The term "visualization" spread rapidly through the mass media, and it has got into every day and businesspersons vocabulary.

The situation has much ameliorated by the introduction of the saiban-in system. Currently, the problems are getting to be what kinds of editing the records of interrogations can be allowed. And the second major issue is that whether judges and the saiban-ins are allowed to form their impressions from the content of video recordings of interrogations. The second issue is called "substantial evidence problem 実質証拠問題." (Jo 2018).

The editing movies can change the impression of the characters' intention and meaning of behavior incredible. In that sense, editing has a great power which influences the impression formation. The substantial evidence problem is whether the video recording can be used as evidence which proves the corpus delicti. If the judges and the saiban-ins use the recordings as the substantial evidence, there occur problems of hearsay evidence because the judge and the saiban-ins may believe that what the defendant talked in the video was true without examining evidence which directly proves the fact. The prosecutors' office once decided to request to the courts to deal the recordings as substantial evidence in 2015. However, at the start, the recording was supposed to be used as just corroborating evidence which proves the sincerity of confessions and other talks in the interrogations. This problem remains unsettled, and the impact of recorded video on impression formation will be required more to make the problem come to an end.

Punishments in the Saiban-in System vs. Bench Trials

In the saiban-in system, the citizens' participants determine the punishment with the judges, if they find the defendant guilty. There is no sentencing officer who is responsible for conducting the investigation and giving necessary advice regarding the punishment in Japan.[166] Consequently, the criteria for punishments are based on the prosecutor's request for the punishment and the sentences for the similar cases in the past. The court prepares a sentencing database and allows judges to refer to them during deliberation. Judges input some significant factors related to criminal cases so that they can collect the case details and punishments for those cases.

[166] In the cases handled by family court among juvenile cases a family court investigator conducts a survey on incidents and give a treatment opinion.

Judges present the data which are showing sentencing distributions to the saiban-ins in their deliberations. The database and data are not disclosed outside the court.

Has there been any disparity in sentences between the bench trials and the trials by the saiban-in system? The mass media tend to report the cases with exceptional disparity sensationally and repeatedly to gather people's attention. However, we overlook the reality of the system operation; we infer just based on the mass media coverage. Here we need to know the facts which the statistics tell us about the issue. The statistics which compare the sentencing bench trials and trials by the saiban-in system are open to the public through the Internet as one of the materials of discussions of the Advisory Panel of Experts of the Operation of the Saiban-in System(裁判員制度の運用等に関する有識者会議)at the Supreme Court. As the materials have been composed for the needs of the discussion of the Advisory Panel, the data are not available for each year. The previous studies on this matter are both based on the data available from the material of the meeting. The latest material available is for the meeting held on November 13, 2014.[167] We examine the data to understand the sentencing disparity with referring the previous studies.

There are two papers regarding the research conducted by Japanese researchers which compare the sentencing distribution after the introduction of the saiban-in system at the time of this writing (Harada 2013; Kojima 2015). Harada (2013) is comparing the distribution until 2011 based on the material which is published concerning the meeting which was held on October 5, 2011. Kojima (2015) reported the distribution the sentence data until 2014, based on the material for the meeting held on November 13, 2014. Our examination in this section is based on the same data as Kojima (2015).

Since only the summarized frequency distribution data is disclosed on the material, we can find the frequencies of the cases for every punishment class in the specific type of crimes. There is no average length of imprisonment nor standard deviations for those data. Because of that, neither Harada (2013) nor Kojima (2015) calculated the average value of imprisonment, standard error or presented the results of statistical tests. In this section, the author will calculate average lengths of imprisonment and standard deviations for every type of crimes and conduct statistical test conduct chi-square tests to examine the difference in the distribution of sentencing.

For each type of crime summarized in the values in the table, mean and standard deviation were calculated concerning the number of years of imprisonment. Then, the confidence intervals of the average values were determined. The 95% confidence interval of the mean value is a continuous interval starting with the mean value minus 1.96 times of the standard error and ending with the mean value plus 1.96 times of the standard error. When there is no overlap between two confidence intervals, it can be said that there is a statistically significant difference between the two average values with 95% probability.

[167] The material is available at http://www.courts.go.jp/saikosai/vcms_lf/80826003.pdf (in Japanese). The data concerning the punishments started from the figure and table 52–1.

Based on the data released by the Supreme Court, the following tables show the results. At this expert opinion meeting, they handled eight types of crimes. Those are murder, attempted murder, injury resulting in death, quasi-rape resulting in injury, quasi-compulsive indecency resulting in injury, robbery resulting in injury, arson of inhabited buildings and violation of Stimulant Control Law. Regarding the violations of Stimulant Control Law, the saiban-in system tries the sort of crimes which can be resulting in severest punishments among the crimes stipulated the Law. The crimes are importing, exporting and manufacturing with intentions of profitmaking. The data included the trials between at the time of start the trials by the saiban-in system until May 2013.

The author conducted chi-square tests to see there was the statistically significant difference between bench trials punishment distributions and the saiban-in trials punishment distributions for the eight crimes above. The data of distributions are shown in from Tables 1.2, 1.3, 1.4, 1.5, 1.6, 1.7, 1.8 and 1.9. The test statistic and significance for each crime type are as follows. The classes in which the frequencies of trials by both of types are zero are deleted from the chi-square test automatically. The degrees of freedom for the chi-square tests for those tables are for those cases were lowered accordingly. Statistics for each type of crimes were as follows. The murder cases' statistics were$\chi^2(17) = 36.41$, $p = .004$, attempted murder cases' statistics were$\chi^2(12) = 14.95$, $p =. 244$, injury resulting in death cases' statistics were $\chi^2(10) = 48.10$, $p = .000$, quasi-rape resulting in injury cases' statistics were$\chi^2(16) = 42.60$, $p = .000$, quasi-compulsive indecency cases' statistics were$\chi^2(9) = 10.88$, $p =. 284$, robbery resulting in injury cases' statistics were$\chi^2(15) = 59.63$, $p = .000$, arson of inhabited buildings cases' statistics were $\chi^2(15) = 19.67$, $p =. 185$, and violations of Stimulant Control Law cases' statistics were$\chi^2(11) = 19.40$, $p =. 054$. Based on the above results, the differences were found in the distributions in attempted murder, injury resulting in death, robbery resulting in injury. The crimes with the marginally significant statistics was a violation of the Stimulant Control Law. Five out of the eight types of crimes sentencing distributions are different between bench trials and the saiban-in trials including two crimes with marginal significance. The sentencing distributions for remaining three types of crime, that is, quasi-rape resulting in injury, quasi-compulsive indecency resulting in injury, and arson of inhabited buildings were not significantly different.

The author accordingly conducted residual analyses to verify which classes in the tables were different between bench trials and the saiban-in trials. The standardized residuals are presented in the cells of the tables. If the absolute value of this number exceeds 1.96, it indicates that the cell differs significantly from the expected frequency at the 5% level. That means there is a distribution difference between bench trials and the saiban-in system in the class.

We see the differences in the following classes. For murder cases, the classes of imprisonment less than 3 years with suspension, imprisonment for not less than 9 years up to 11 years, more than 15 years up to 17 years are different between bench trials and the saiban-in trials. Concerning the average length of imprisonment penalty for murder cases, the average is 12.22 years for bench trials with the standard error 0.27, while the average of 12.08 years and the standard error of 0.24 for

Table 1.2 The distribution of punishment for murder cases

Years	~3, Suspended	~3	3~5	5~7	7~9	9~11	11~13	13~15	15~17	17~19	19~21	21~23	23~25	25~27	27~29	29~30	Infinite	Death penalty
Bench trial	25	7	41	47	47	72	73	63	31	27	21	12	9	7	2	10	31	7
Trial by saiban-in	72	40	59	84	56	75	94	88	78	48	30	18	14	7	5	15	46	8

Table 1.3 The distribution of punishment for attempted murder cases

Years	~3, Suspended	~3	3~5	5~7	7~9	9~11	11~13	13~15	15~17	17~19	19~21	21~23	23~25	25~27	27~29	29~30	Infinite	Death penalty
Bench trial	103	24	88	64	24	20	6	7	3	0	1	0	0	0	0	0	0	0
Trial by saiban-in	219	48	103	113	52	30	16	9	4	1	1	1	0	0	0	1	0	0

Table 1.4 The distribution of punishment for injury resulting in death cases

Years	~3, Suspended	~3	3~5	5~7	7~9	9~11	11~13	13~15	15~17	17~19	19~21	21~23	23~25	25~27	27~29	29~30	Infinite	Death penalty
Bench trial	29	24	123	74	30	18	9	2	1	0	0	0	0	0	0	0	0	0
Trial by saiban-in	74	50	136	156	130	53	25	13	1	0	0	3	1	0	0	0	0	0

Table 1.5 The distribution of punishment for quasi-rape resulting in injury cases

Years	~3, Suspended	~3	3~5	5~7	7~9	9~11	11~13	13~15	15~17	17~19	19~21	21~23	23~25	25~27	27~29	29~30	Infinite	Death penalty
Bench trial	12	9	72	44	19	13	8	7	5	6	4	2	2	0	1	0	2	0
Trial by saiban-in	13	13	68	113	64	43	27	20	7	10	6	4	3	4	3	3	0	0

Table 1.6 The distribution of punishment for quasi-compulsive indecency cases

Years	~3, Suspended	~3	3~5	5~7	7~9	9~11	11~13	13~15	15~17	17~19	19~21	21~23	23~25	25~27	27~29	29~30	Infinite	Death penalty
Bench trial	62	32	26	11	6	3	2	0	0	0	0	0	0	0	0	0	0	0
Trial by saiban-in	141	59	98	44	17	6	2	3	1	1	0	0	0	0	0	0	0	0

Table 1.7 The distribution of punishment for robbery resulting in injury cases

Years	~3, Suspended	~3	3~5	5~7	7~9	9~11	11~13	13~15	15~17	17~19	19~21	21~23	23~25	25~27	27~29	29~30	Infinite	Death penalty
Bench trial	64	34	284	227	95	43	17	9	7	1	7	4	1	0	1	0	2	0
Trial by saiban-in	170	66	358	414	266	86	41	22	8	8	5	1	2	1	0	0	0	0

Table 1.8 The distribution of punishment for arson of inhabited building cases

Years	~3, Suspended	~3	3~5	5~7	7~9	9~11	11~13	13~15	15~17	17~19	19~21	21~23	23~25	25~27	27~29	29~30	Infinite	Death penalty
Bench trial	63	23	96	33	15	9	9	3	2	0	1	0	0	0	1	1	1	0
Trial by saiban-in	163	55	138	77	18	13	11	3	3	3	1	1	1	0	0	1	1	0

Table 1.9 The distribution of punishment for violations of stimulant control law cases

Years	~3, Suspended	~3	3~5	5~7	7~9	9~11	11~13	13~15	15~17	17~19	19~21	21~23	23~25	25~27	27~29	29~30	Infinite	Death penalty
Bench trial	1	2	11	41	65	34	14	2	2	0	1	0	0	0	0	0	3	0
Trial by saiban-in	2	8	14	123	218	104	41	16	9	7	4	0	0	0	0	0	0	0

the saiban-in trials. The bench trials produced more punishments between 7 years and 15 years. The distribution for the bench trials has a mountain-look shape while the distribution for the saiban-in trials has flatter shape than bench trials.

Regarding the cases of the injury resulting in death, the adjusted residuals show that the frequencies of classes of more than 3 years and less than 5 years is significantly larger for judges. However, in the class for more than 7 years for classes of 9 years, the relative frequency of bench trials is significantly less than the frequency of saiban-in trials. This difference contributes the significant difference in average punishment in injury resulting in death cases. The shape of the distribution for bench trials has much sharper mountain shape compared to the shape of the saiban-in cases. The average numbers of the length of imprisonment and standard errors of them are 5. 54 years (0.15) for bench trials and 6. 58 years (0.13) for the saiban-in trials. The confidence intervals for bench trials started from 5.24 years to 5.83 years; while for the saiban-in trials was from 6. 33 years to 6.84 years. There was no overlapping. The punishments in the saiban-in trials are significantly severer than bench trials for this crime.

For quasi-rape resulting in injury, based on the value of the adjusted residuals in the class of the imprisonment more than 3 years and up to 5 years. In the class of imprisonment of more than 7 years and up to 9 years, the bench trials' relative frequencies are significantly less than the saiban-in trials' relative frequencies. The averages and the standard errors of the length of imprisonment are 7.7 years (0.36) for bench trials and 8.69 years (0.27) for saiban-in trials. When calculating the confidence intervals of the average value of both from them, the judges' judgment ranged from 6.76 years to 8.18 years, while the saiban-in trials' judgments ranged from 8.16 years to 9.21 years. There is some extent of overlapping with each other, and the difference is not significant. In the case of a quasi-rape injury crime, it is conceivable that there is a tendency that sentencing in the saiban-in trials is not different from those of the bench trials.

Concerning the robbery resulting in injury, the judge has significantly fewer suspensions of the imprisonment up to 3 years compared to the saiban-in trials. Furthermore, there are significantly more relative frequencies of bench trials in the classes of imprisonment for longer than 7 years and less than 9 years. There are other significant differences over 21 years and up to 23 years. However, this class has very few cases, so we need to refrain from saying something decisive about this. The averages and the standard errors of the length of imprisonment are 6.16 years (0.12) for the bench trials and 6.50 years (0.08) for the saiban-in trials. If we calculate the confidence intervals of the averages, those of bench trials would be from 5.92 to 6.40 years, while those of the saiban-in trials would be from 6.33 years to 6.66 years. There is few overlapping each other. The difference of the averages is highly significant.

Distributions for each type of trial, that is, the saiban-in trials and bench trials is the same as the same type of trials. Looking at the distribution of these types of crime, it seems that the bench trial shows that mountains of distribution are somewhat biased towards less than 5 years. On the other hand, the distribution of the saiban-in trials consisted gentle mountain shape. This result suggests that there would be a mental wall at the 5 years with sentencing in the crime types above.

In the distributions for the violation of the Stimulant Control Law, there found a difference in the class of imprisonment for 3 years up to five years. In that class, the relative frequencies of the saiban-in trials are significantly less than the relative frequencies of the bench trials. The averages and the standard errors of the length of imprisonment are 8.15 years (0.19) for bench trials and 8. 57 years (0.12) for saiban-in trials. The confidence intervals of the average are from 7.77 to 8.33 years for the bench trials and from 8.33 to 8.80 years for the saiban-in trials. The saiban-ins with judges sentenced more extended imprisonment than bench trials. The difference between those two average is marginally significant. The three cases in which the professional judge's sentenced infinite imprisonment are not included the average comparison analysis. The marginal significance came from the difference from other classes of the imprisonment with fixed terms.

In addition to the above, the author conducted F tests to see the statistical differences of whole distributions for each case between bench trials and the trials by saiban-in. The results of the F tests were as follows. F (710, 468) = 1.13, p =. 08 for the murder cases, F (378, 236) = 1.23, p =. 04 for attempted murder cases, F (567, 280) = 1.52, p = .00 for injury resulting in death cases, F (237, 191) = 1.12, p = .20 for quasi-rape resulting in injury cases, F (230, 79) = 1.09, p = .33 for quasi-compulsive indecency resulting in injury cases, F (729, 1277) = 1.19, p = .00 for robbery resulting in injury cases, F (192, 324) = 1.14, p = .15 for arson of inhabited building cases, F (543, 171) = 1.23, p = .05 for violations of the Stimulant Control Act. Based on the above results, statistically significant differences were found in the attempted murder, the injury resulting in death, the robbery resulting in injury cases. The distribution difference for murder cases and the cases of violations of the Stimulant Control Act found significant marginally.

The mass media have frequently reported the "sentencing exceeding requested punishment" cases. In one of the prominent cases, the prosecutor requested 10 years imprisonment for murder, but the judicial panel with saiban-ins sentenced 15 years imprisonment. There rarely found sentencing over "sentencing exceeding requested punishment" cases before the introduction of the saiban-in system. The mass media picked up those cases and insisted that that's the toughening the law by citizens. However, if we saw the whole distribution of murder cases and analyzed statistically, there we not so much differences were found between bench trials and the saiban-in trials in murder cases. The Supreme Court rules out if the sentencing by the judicial panel with saiban-in is too severe or too lenient. There seemed to be not problematic in the sentencing difference between bench trials and the saiban-in trials above crime types.

The mass media tend to focus on exceptional cases with the most substantial difference between professional judges and the saiban-ins. But the reality was presented above. Among the sentencing above, we found statistically different averages in sentencing in three crime types. Two crimes show the marginally significant difference. The average differences in the three types of crimes, 0.30 years for attempted murder, 1.04 years for injury resulting in death, 0.34 years for robbery resulting in injury cases. Certainly, we can find some extent of toughening the law in the saiban-in trials. However, the difference should not worth a turmoil. We have to look into the statistically different crime types above, and figure out the meaning of the difference dispassionately. From such viewpoint, the results suggest that legal professionals' general expectations were less than the citizens about one year on average. We need to think about whether that is a reasonable reflection of citizens' sense.

Public Interest and the Justice System

After the implementation of the saiban-in system, citizens' interest in the justice system has raised considerably. According to a survey administered by the Supreme Court, the average of the responses for the question "Japanese have an interest in public matters such as criminal trials" was 2.92 on a five-point scale before the saiban-in system, and 3.45 after the introduction of the saiban-in system (The Supreme Court of Japan 2013).

The numbers of newspaper articles can also be used as indicators for the public interest (Livingstone and Lunt 1994) because the newspaper companies choose the topics of their articles according to the interest of readers. To obtain the numbers of the articles, the author conducted searches in the database of Asahi Shimbun and Yomiuri Shimbun, which are both major daily newspapers in Japan. The searches were made for the twenty-year period from 1995 to 2015, with articles containing "courts," "saiban-in," "attorneys," "prosecution," "justice system," and related terms. Figs. 1.1 and 1.2 show the results of the searches.

The two figures show a mostly similar trend. These articles began to increase in the latter half of the 1990s, later hitting a high-water mark before the start of the saiban-in system. They peaked in 2009 and 2010, directly after the saiban-in system was implemented, and later gradually decreased as the novelty of the system diminished.

In addition to newspapers, television is a form of mass media that raises topics of everyday concern. Themes in TV dramas are thought to express the interests of people at that time. According to statistics compiled showing justice system-related ideas in TV dramas (Fujita 2010), the numbers of TV dramas in which the legal professionals appear in the title or in the descriptions was less than fifty from the 1950s to the 1970s. However, the number got more than 100 in the 1980s, it increased more than 200 in the 1990s, and finally, it counted more than 300 in the 2000s. Most of these hits were for "bengoshi" (attorneys). From the 1980s on there was a striking increase in the number of titles or synopses with prosecutors.

The number of justice system-related TV drama titles began to increase in the 1980s, continuing into the 1990s and 2000s. The saiban-in system began to be discussed in the 1990s and given that it became a more broadly debated topic at the start of the 2000s thanks to newspapers and other media. This increase could not likely be attributed to the saiban-in system alone. In other words, a general interest in the justice system as reflected in TV dramas began to grow twenty years before the start of the saiban-in system, which system was implemented amidst this wave of interest.

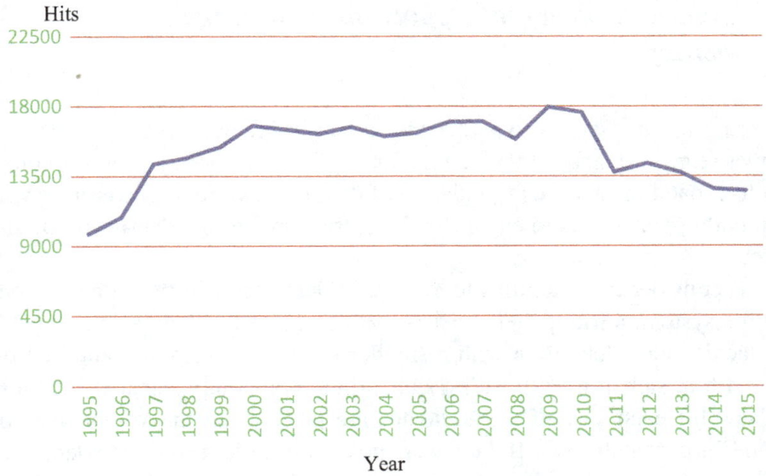

Fig. 1.1 Articles related to the justice system and courts in the Asahi Shimbun

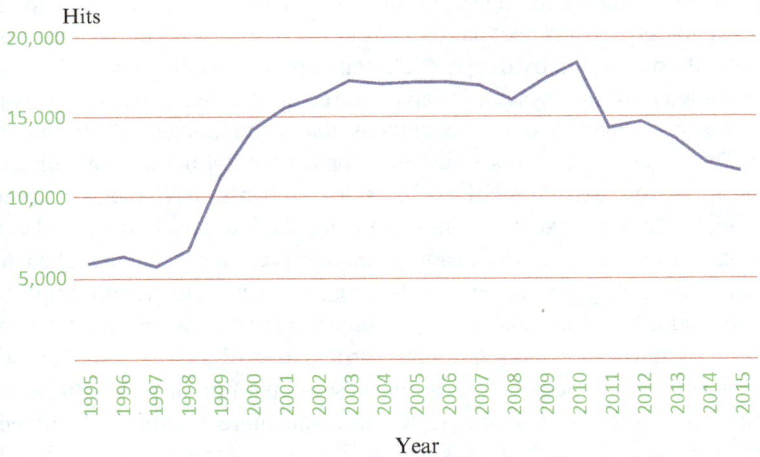

Fig. 1.2 Articles related to the justice system and courts in the Yomiuri Shimbun

Considerations on Democratic Moments of the Saiban-in System: For Future Research

Opportunities to Engage in Democracy

Implementing the saiban-in system is vital for civic participation in the justice system in the justice system reform in 2000s Japan. This section is dedicated to discussing whether the saiban-in system can promote democratic values.

The Saiban-in System and Opportunities to Engage in Democracy

Some bring up the issue of whether the saiban-in system stems from democratic principles (e.g., Watanabe 2005; Yanase 2009). The saiban-in system was conceived in part to expand the national foundation of the justice system. The issue is whether we can find opportunities to engage in democracy in the foundations of the saiban-in system.

Let us consider opportunities to engage in democracy in the saiban-in system. Under the system, a trial panel consists of three judges and six saiban-in.[168] If the judge decides they deliberate with a smaller group, the team is composed of one judge and four saiban-in.[169] Besides, saiban-in are randomly selected from a list of candidates for each case. The candidates are taken from the voters' lists of the House of Representatives.[170] If there were no opportunities promoting democracy in the saiban-in system, then the number of citizens can be fewer. For example, in the discussion of Justice System Reform Council, the fewer number of citizens was preferred by the Supreme Court.

Also, if opportunities to engage in the democracy is not a matter of focus, the system did not require to select participants at random. Moreover, another possibility is that only superior individuals are chosen to participate in "blue-ribbon" juries. The suspended pure jury system in Japan has taxation requirements.[171] This provision allows participation only the citizens that economically contribute to the state.[172] The provision does not select by people's ability, but it is one method for selecting a type of "excellent citizen." Besides, saiban-in have the same power of professional judges to make decisions in applying the law, fact-finding, and sentencing, but saiban-in have authority to apply that interpretation to the fact of each case.

Based on the group size of the saiban-in judicial panels, the random selection in each case, and the fact that there is no requirements citizens' ability, we can consider the system to allow and require the participation of a broad range of citizens. Giving the authority to decide the criminal cases to the full range of citizens should contribute to promoting democracy. Besides, the more numbers of citizens are involved in a judicial panel, the higher likelihood of representation of population will be accomplished from a statistical perspective (Saks and Marti 1997). The current saiban-in system enables more significant opportunities to engage in democracy than a system with deliberation in a small group which was proposed during the discussion of JSRC.

---

[168] Saiban-in Act, art. 2, para. 2.

[169] Saiban-in Act, art. 2, para. 2, provisos para. 3.

[170] Saiban-in Act, art. 13.

[171] Juror Act, art. 12, number 3.

[172] The Juror act prescribed the juror need to pay three yen or more in a year as direct national tax. The three Japanese yen in the early Showa era, around 1925,

Thoughts on Ways to Measure "Popular Foundations"

Given the goal of its implementation set by the Justice System Reform Council, we can evaluate the extent that the saiban-in system has achieved its objective through thinking about whether the saiban-in system has expanded the people's foundation for the justice system. If this is true, then we need to measure and validate whether the saiban-in system has promoted the popular base for the justice system.

How can we measure the impact of the saiban-in system on the popular base of the justice system? As of this writing, a search on CiNii[173] shows that there are no studies that use quantitative data regarding this impact. If a broader range is allowed in searching literature, there are some research deal with the relationship between the saiban-in system and trust in the justice system (e.g., Fujita et al. 2016). However, these studies focus on individual behaviors or social attitudes, not concentrate on a collective action from a more macro perspective.

Based on the state of the research field, we can think that there is room for future research to examine how saiban-in system is affecting the popular base of the justice system. In investigating this topic, the results of the research project from the US (Gastil et al. 2010) is worth paying attention. They reported that jury deliberations have a substantial impact on citizen participation in politics by using data since jury service is thought by researchers to be an essential node connecting civil society, the state, and political society (Gastil et al. 2010, Fig. 2.1).

Just as the subtitle of their document implies, Gastil et al. (2010) examined how jury deliberations and jury service promoted continuous and broad civic engagement and participation in politics. Specifically, they raised two research questions: Is the saiban-in system an engine for promoting involvement in politics? Moreover, does the saiban-in system genuinely have an impact on those serving as jurors?

Gastil et al. (2010) used election turnout data as a metric for participation in politics, as voting in elections is the most general way for citizens to participate in politics. Those that are uninterested in politics are thought to be unlikely to vote. Also, voting costs to some extent to people because people spend their time doing it when they could have spent it elsewhere. What is important to note is that Gastil et al. (2010) used people's behavioral metrics as dependent variables. Survey studies often use questions about people's attitudes towards politics, such as "Do you have confidence in politics?" or "Do you feel a closer connection to politics?" Alternatively, a survey may ask whether a respondent is likely to vote. They used these questions as dependent variables. These social attitudes are suspected to have some level of relevance to actual political behaviors, though the question of what a person did is perhaps more directly relevant. Attitudes and actions are not necessarily equal, and because Gastil et al. (2010) used behavioral metrics directly as dependent variables, their study seems to have a better grasp of peoples' involvement in politics.

---

[173] CiNii is the Japanese academic article bibliographic database provided by the National Institute for Informatics. CiNii is available at http:/ /ci.nii.ac.jp for free of charge.

Gastil et al. (2010) obtained lists of 13,237 people that had both performed jury service and recently voted. By combining the two, they confirmed whether those that had served on a jury had voted in the most recent election. Their results showed that those that had served on a panel but had not voted before that experience were more likely to vote in the next election. Also, their confidence in judges deepened, and the jury service had a positive effect on their political behavior, their confidence in politics, and their sense of responsibility towards public societal systems (Gastil et al. 2010 Table 9.1).

There is likely not a better method to directly validate Gastil et al.'s proposition. Implementing this technique requires cooperation from courts and election committees, as well considerable time and patience to match lists. Those tasks are likely challenging. Gastil et al. (2010)'s study found that it is likely that participating in the justice system through jury service promotes voting behavior. Even we cannot understand the mechanism within the process by their data; the result suggests that jury service and discussing crimes have a positive impact on political attitudes. We can suppose that there is an impact on the transformation of citizens' attitudes.

In examining the issue of how the saiban-in system and participation impact improvements to the national foundation for the justice system, we can investigate by measuring peoples' trust in the justice system after participating in the saiban-in system, or their sense of self-efficacy in societal systems, especially the justice system. If those figures raise after serving as saiban-in, we can take the experience as saiban-in has a positive impact on citizens' sense of democracy. In other words, as we examine changes in these metrics after people serve as saiban-in, we can understand how well the saiban-in system realize the objective of its introduction.

A Count of Studies on Participation in the Courts

Let us briefly look at the number of studies in Japan regarding citizen participation in the courts over time. The number of published papers could be one indicator that shows the level of interest in a civic participation program as a research topic, i.e., how "hot" that research topic is.

CiNii was used for searching literature published in Japan. On November 11, 2016, a query was made to this database for papers that contain both the keywords "law courts (法廷)" and "participation (参加)." Results of the query returned 688 hits. The papers that have the same journal names, volumes and pages are regarded. Fig. 1.3 is presenting the results. The articles were published between 1991 and 2016. Because 2016 was not a full year at the time of the search, numbers for that year were removed from the data.

Among the numbers of publications from 1991 to 1996, there were continually fewer than ten publications per year. This number climbed to almost 20 in 1997, then lowered, increased again with peaking in 2009 and 2010. The numbers are at

Fig. 1.3 Research papers in Japanese regarding "court participation" from 1991 to 2015

their highest in 2010, after the saiban-in system started in 2009, then drop to around twenty articles per year. Upon these numbers, discussions on citizens' participation in the courts increased starting in 2000, and the numbers kept increasing until the saiban-in system began in 2009. The highest amount of publications in 2010, directly after the operation. The number of papers afterward dropped linearly, reaching around twenty per year in 2015. The publication number in 2015 was almost the same level of publications from 1997 to 2000, the period before started justice system reform.

Based on the results above, we can surmise that research interest was low before justice reform taking on a specific form in the 1990s. However, the number started to increase in 1997. In this year, JSRC started its discussion by the initiative of Prime Minister Keizô Obuchi. Moreover, after the Justice System Reform Council published its opinion paper, there was an increase in discussions. The Saiban-in Act was passed the Diet in 2004 and went into effect in 2009. There was an increase the number articles on similar topics in response to a broader interest after the system going into action. This increase in interest crested with the advent of public trials with saiban-in in 2009 and 2010. After that, saiban-in trials became one of the standard topics for specific criminal trials afterward, and excitement dimmed because the system had lost its novelty.

As qualitative results, on a cursory look at the titles in each year shows papers discussing the saiban-in system, there were many articles on commentary and opinions on the Saiban-in Act around the year's implementation of the system. In contrast, around 2015 there were documents which were reporting the results of examining the saiban-in system of its operation, considering behaviors and attitudes of citizens participating in the system, and criminal procedures.

Considerations for Victims and Defendants

When we focus on the national foundation for the justice system and training citizens in discussing citizen participation justice system, we need to consider the protection of defendants' and victims' interest. The Justice System Reform Council has already discussed it.

To sentence punishments to defendants is the primary concern of the criminal court. We never to forget about securing human rights of the defendants in criminal procedures. Also, since the state has the full discretion of indictment, and judges have extensive discretion in criminal sentences, the feelings, and consent of victims as well as precedents.

In that sense, it is worth paying attention to the operation of the victim participation system (cf. Foote 2014; Hans 2013). Ensuring fairness in the courts will likely have a positive effect on hearings in the saiban-in system since it creates opportunities for citizens to hear the voices of victims in person. Of course, the effects of victim impact statement has been highly controversial, so we need to consider negative effects of victim participation with the results of empirical studies (Myers and Greene 2004).

References

Ashizawa, S. (2012). Kôhan jumbi to kôhan tetudzuki no arikata [How the trial preparation and trial procedure should be]. *Quarterly Jurist, 2*, 43–50 [in Japanese].

Foote, D. H. (2014). Citizen participation: Appraising the Saiban'in system. *Michigan State International Law Review, 22*(3), 755–775.

Fujita, M. (2005). Hôtei yôgo ni kansuru mensetsu chôsa: Shimin no goi to kichikan wo shiru tegakari toshite [The interview survey on the terms used in the lawcourts: As a clue to know about citizens' vocabulary and familiarity]. *Jiyû to Seigi [Liberty and Justice], 56*(3), 79–91 [in Japanese].

Fujita, M. (2010). Nihon shakai ni totte no saiban-in seido: Nihon no baishin seido wo sankou ni [The saiban-in system for the Japanese society: With considerations of Japanese petty jury system]. *Hôshakaigaku [Sociology of Law], 72*, 183–192 [in Japanese].

Fujita, M., Hayashi, N., & Hotta, S. (2016). Trust in the justice system: Internet survey after introducing mixed tribunal system in Japan. *Oñati Socio-Legal Series, 6*(2). [Online publication; no pagination specified]. Retrieved from http://ssrn.com/abstract=2769587.

Gastil, J., Deess, E. P., Weiser, P. J., & Simmons, C. (2010). *The jury and democracy : how jury deliberation promotes civic engagement and political participation*. New York: Oxford University Press.

Goto, A., & The Project Team for Altering the Terminology in the Lawcourts into Everyday Vocabulary. (2008). *Saiban-in jidai no hôtei yôgo: Hôtei yôgo no nichijôgo ka ni kansuru PT saishû hôkoku sho [The terminology in the lawcourts in the era of saiban in: The final report of the project team for altering the terminology in the lawcourts into everyday vocabular*]. Tokyo: Sanseidô. [in Japanese].

Hans, V. P. (2013). The impact of victim participation in Saiban-in trials in Japan: Insights from the American jury experience. *International Journal of Law, Crime and Justice*. https://doi.org/10.1016/j.ijlcj.2013.07.002.

Harada, K. (2013). Saiban-in saiban ni okeru ryôkei keikou: Miete kita atarashii sugata [The sentencing tendency in trials by saiban-in: The apperaing new shape]. *Keiô Hôgaku [Keiô Law Journal], 27*, 161–187 [in Japanese].

Hartley, J. (2000). Legal ease and “legalese”. *Psychology, Crime & Law, 6*(1), 1–20. https://doi.org/10.1080/10683160008410828.

Hastie, R., Penrod, S., & Pennington, N. (1983). *Inside the jury*. Oxford: Harvard University Press.

Hayashi, H. (2010). Saiban-in seido no un'yô jittai to mondai ten no kôsatsu: Keihô no shiten kara [Considerations on the state of implementation of the problems of the saiban-in system: From the viewpointo of criminal law]. *Hôsei Ronsô [Law and Politics Bulletin], 47*(1), 185–210 [in Japanese].

Hirayama, M. (2016). Kakenhi kôkai kôza kôenkai Shinomiya Satoru shi kôen: Keiji shihô e no shimin no shinrai wa dou kakuho sareru beki ka [The note on a public lecutre supported by KAKENHI grant Prof. Satoru Shinomiya “How citizens” trust in the criminal justice should be ob]. *Hakuô Hôgaku [Hakuô Law Journal], 22*(2), 151–201 [in Japanese].

Ibusuki, M. (2013). Shiho kaikaku no siten torishirabe “kashika” ron: Keiji shiho kaikaku no kanten kara [Viewpoints on Judicial Reform: Anatomy of Visual Recording Debate : In the View of Criminal Justice Reform]. *Hoshakaigaku [Sociology of Law], 79*, 153–165 [in Japanese]. Retrieved from https://ci.nii.ac.jp/naid/40019868379.

Ichikawa, M., Iwata, K., & En'yo, M. (2008, November 29). Kôhosha Tsûchi ga kitara [In case the letter of candidate notice comes]. *Asahi Shimbun (Morning Edition)*, p. 3 [in Japanese].

Ida, M. (2010). Lay participation in the Japanese criminal justice system. *Gakujutsu No Doko [Trends in the Sciences], 15*(2), 70–75 [in Japanese]. https://doi.org/10.5363/tits.15.2_70.

Ishida, E. (2010). Saiban-in seido no shushi to honshitsu teki na mondai ten ni tsuite: Kenpô no shiten kara [The object and the essential problems of the saiban-in system: From the viewpoint of the constitution]. *Hôsei Ronsô [Law and Politics Bulletin], 47*(1), 238–250 [in Japanese].

Ito, M. (2012). Keiji saiban wa dou kawatta ka [How have the criminal trials changed]. *Toshimondai [Urban Problems], 103*(5), 9–13 [in Japanese].

Iwata, K. (2010). Saiban-in seido: Kono ichi nen wo hurikaeru [The Saiban-in system: Looking back on the past year]. *Sekai [The World], 806*, 114–121 [in Japanese].

Japan Federation of Bar Associations. (2009). *Hôtei bengo gijutsu [The art of trial advocacy]*. Tokyo: Nihon Hyôronsha in Japanese.

Jinkô suikei (Heisei 29 nen (2017 nen) 9 gatsu kakutei chi, Heisei 30 nen (2018 nen) 2 gatsu gaisanchi) (2018 nen 2 gatsu 20niti kôhyô) [Population estimation (Fixed numbers in September 2017, estimated numbers in February 2018). (2018). Retrieved March 9, 2018, from http://www.stat.go.jp/data/jinsui/new.htm [in Japanese].

Jo, Y. (2018). Torishirabe no rokuon rokuga wo jisshitsu shoko toshite mochiiru koto no mondaiten to kentou [The problems and consideration concerning the usage of audio video recording of interrogation as substantial evidence]. *Sosakenkyuu [Research in Investigation], 67*(1), 5–26 [in Japanese]. Retrieved from https://ci.nii.ac.jp/naid/40021445822.

Juichi, G. (2011). Kôhansei hattatsu shôgai ga kan'yo suru jiken no sekinin nôryoku kantei: Shônen jiken keiji jiken wo tsûjite mirareru mondaiten [Liability competence appraisal of the cases which deal with perversive developmental disorder: The problems appear through juv]. *Seishin Igaku [Psychiatry Medicine], 53*(10), 965–971 [in Japanese].

Justice System Reform Council. (2001). *Recommendations of the Justice System Reform Council: For a Justice System to Support Japan in the 21st Century*. Tokyo: Justice System Reform Council. Retrieved from https://japan.kantei.go.jp/judiciary/2001/0612report.html

Kaneko, H. (1948). *Shin kenpô to shihô [The new Constitution and judiciary]*. Tokyo: Kokuritsushoin in Japanese.

Kawai, K. (2011). Gen'eki saibankan ga kataru saiban-in saiban no genjô to bengo katsudô no kadai [The state of the saiban-in system and issues in defense activites which are told by judges on active service]. *Niben Frontier, 102*, 2–11 [in Japanese].

Kimura, R. (2013). Saiban-in seido no tokuchô to mondai ten ni kansuru ichi kôsatsu: Shikô 3 nen go no minaoshi no naka de [A thought on the features and problems of the saiban-in system: In the course of review after three years of the implement]. *Kyûshû Hôgakkai Kaihô [Bulletin of Kyûshû Law Society], 2013*, 23–25 [in Japanese].

Kojima, T. (2015). Saiban-in saiban ni yoru ryôkei no henka [The transition of sentencing by trial by saiban-in]. *Chûkyô Hôgaku [Chûkyô Law Journal], 49*(3), 73–102 [in Japanese].

Legal Research and Training Institute. (2009). *Nankai na hôritsu gainen to saiban-in saiban [The abstruse legal concepts and trial by saiban-in]*. Tokyo: Hôsôkai in Japanese.

Livingstone, S., & Lunt, P. (1994). The mass media, democracy and the public sphere. In *Talk on Television: Audience participation and public debate* (pp. 9–35). London: Routledge Retrieved from http://eprints.lse.ac.uk/48964/1/Amended_Livingstone_Mass_media_democaracy.pdf.

Matsuo, K. (2012). *Keijisosho no riron [The theory of criminal trial]*. Tokyo: Yuhikaku in Japanese.

Mitani, T. (2004). Saiban-in seido no seijishi teki igi [The political historical significance of the saiban-in system]. *Jiyû to Seigi [Liberty and Justice], 55*, 26–34 [in Japanese].

Mitani, T. (2005). Saiban-in seido to Nihon no minshushugi [The saiban-in system and Japanese democracy]. *Hôritsu Jihô [Law Reporter], 77*(4), 52–56 [in Japanese].

Mitsui, M., IIda, H., Inouye, M., Ôkawa, S., Satô, H., & Taguchi, M. (2004). Zadankai: Saiban-in seido wo megutte [Roundtable discussion over the saiban-in system]. *Jurist, 1268*, 6–48 [in Japanese].

Myers, B., & Greene, E. (2004). The prejudicial nature of victim impact statements: Implications for capital sentencing policy. *Psychology, Public Policy, and Law, 10*(4), 492–515. https://doi.org/10.1037/1076-8971.10.4.492.

Naka, M. (2009). Saiban e no higaisha sanka [Victim participation in trials]. In *Saiban-in seido to hoshinrigaku [The saiban-in system and legal psychology]* (pp. 140–148). Tokyo: Gyosei in Japanese.

Nippon Hoso Kyokai. (2011). *Shoko wa dare no mono ka [To whom should the evidence belong?]*. Retrieved January 24, 2018, from http://www.nhk.or.jp/gendai/articles/3127/1.html

Nishino, K. (2014). Shihô seido kaikaku hihan hoi (8): Kimura Shinsuke kanshû "Gekiron! Saiban-in mondai" no hansei [The supplemet of criticizm on justice system reform (8): My reflections on "Heated arguments! The 'saiban-in' problems"]. *Hôsei Riron [Law and Politics Theories: Niigata University], 46*(3), 262–323 [in Japanese]. Retrieved from http://hdl.handle.net/10191/29379.

Noriyuki, M. (1985). Strong, quasi-, and weak conformity among Japanese in the modified Asch procedure. *Journal of Cross-Cultural Psychology, 16*(1), 83–97. https://doi.org/10.1177/0022002185016001007.

Ôishi, M., & Ishikawa, K. (2008). *Kenpô no sôten [Issues in the Constitution]*. Tokyo: Yûhikaku [in Japanese].

Saiban-in hanketsu hakiritsu joushou tudzuku seido shiko 8 nen [Judgments in saiban-in trials overturn rate raises: Eight years after implementation]. (2017, May 21). *Kobe Shimbun*. Retrieved from https://www.kobe-np.co.jp/news/shakai/201705/0010208120.shtml

Saiban-in saiban kyô kaitei [The trial by saiban-in starts today]. (2009, August 3). *Asahi Shimbun (Morning Edition)* (p. 1). [in Japanese].

Saks, M. J., & Marti, M. W. (1997). A meta-analysis of the effects of jury size. *Law and Human Behavior, 21*(5), 451–467. https://doi.org/10.1023/A:1024819605652.

Shiibashi, T. (2001). Sabain-in seido ga kokuhuku subeki mondai [The problem which the saiban-in system should overcome]. In K. Hirose & T. Tada (Eds.), *Collected papers in memory of Dr. Hiroshi Tamiya* (Vol. 1, pp. 119–132). Tokyo: Shinzansha [in Japanese].

Shimada, N. (2012). Keiji saiban ni taisuru kokumin no rikai to shinrai [The nationals' understanding and trust in the criminal justice]. *Quarterly Jurist, 2*, 97 [in Japanese].

Shinomiya, S. (2012). Saiban-in seido wa nani wo kaetsutsu aru ka [What has the saiban-in system been changing]. *Toshimondai [Urban Problems], 103*(5), 4–8 [in Japanese].

Steiner, I. D. (1966). Models for inferring relationships between group size and potential group productivity. *Behavioral Science, 11*(4), 273–283. https://doi.org/10.1002/bs.3830110404.

Sugano, R. (2011). Saiban-in seido ni okeru seishin kantei no mondai ten: Bengoshi no tachiba kara [The problem of psychiatry expert witnesses: From the standpoint of defense council]. *Seishin Igaku [Psychiatry Medicine], 53*(10), 991–996 [in Japanese].

Takeshima, C. (2017). Saiban-in seido ni tsuite no saikô: Ryôshin no jiyû kara no teigen [Reconsideration on the saiban-in system: A proposition from the viewoint of the freedom of conscience]. *Shagakuken Ronshû [Bulletin of the Institution of Social Science Studies: Waseda University], 29*, 56–71 in Japanese.

The Justice System Reform Council. (2000). *Chûkan hôkoku [Interim report]*. Retrieved March 8, 2018, from https://www.kantei.go.jp/jp/sihouseido/report/naka_houkoku.html [in Japanese].

The Secretariat-general of the Supreme Court of Japan. (2017). *Heisei 28 nen ni okeru saiban-in saiban no jisshi jôkyô ni kansuru shiryô [The material for the state of implementaion of saiban-in trials in 2016]*. Tokyo: The Secretariat-general of the Supreme Court of Japan in Japanese]. Retrieved from http://www.saibanin.courts.go.jp/vcms_lf/H28-103-1.pdf.

The Secretariat-general of the Supreme Court of Japan. (2018). *Saiban-in saiban no jisshi jôkyô ni tsuite (Seido shikô- Heisei 29 nen 12 gatsu matsu sokuhô) [On the status of implementation of saiban-in trials (From the initiaion of its operation to the end of* December 2017*; a prompt report)]*. Tokyo: The Secretariat-geneal of the Supreme Court of Japan [in Japanese]. Retrieved from http://www.saibanin.courts.go.jp/vcms_lf/h29_12_saibaninsokuhou.pdf

The Supreme Court of Japan. (2011). *Saiban-in keikensha tou ni taisuru chosa kekka hôkokusho (Heisei 22 nendo) [The report of questionnaire surveys for those who experienced saiban-in or other related roles (FY 2010)]*. Tokyo: The Supreme Court of Japan [in Japanese]. Retrieved from http://www.saibanin.courts.go.jp/vcms_lf/h22_keikensya.pdf

The Supreme Court of Japan. (2013). *Saiban-in seido no unyô ni kansuru ishiki chôsa [The survey on consciousness of the operation of the saiban-in system]*. Tokyo: The Supreme Court of Japan in Japanese.

The Supreme Court of Japan. (2017). *Saiban-in keikensha tou ni taisuru ankêto kekka hôkokusho (Heisei 28 nendo) [The report of questionnaire surveys for those who experienced saiban-in or other related roles (FY 2016)]*. Tokyo: The Supreme Court of Japan. [in Japanese]. Retrieved from http://www.saibanin.courts.go.jp/vcms_lf/h28-a-1.pdf

The Supreme Court Secretary General of Criminal Bureau. (2009). Saiban-in saiban no shinri, hyôgi oyobi hanketsu ni tsuite (shian)(shinban) [The hearing, deliberation, and judgment of the trial by saiban-in (tentative proposal) (new version)]. *Hanrei Taimuzu [The Precedent Times], 60*(7), 53–62 [in Japanese].

Tyler, T. R. (2000). Social justice: Outcome and procedure. *International Journal of Psychology, 35*(2), 117–125. https://doi.org/10.1080/002075900399411.

Watanabe, N. (2005). Saiban-in seido no rinen teki ichidzuke to, kenpô to no kankei oyobi kongo no kentô kadai ni tsuite no ichi kôsatsu [A consideration on the idealistic evaluation, relationship with the constitution and future issues of the saiban-in system]. *Shûdô Hôgaku [Shûdô Law Journal], 28*(1), 551–576 [in Japanese].

Yamamoto, A., Shioiri, A., & Yutaka, H. (2015, November 18). Saiban-in, naze jitai: Hurubira Emi san, Asosan daihunka san, Ii Takayuki san [Saiban-ins, why refuse]. *Asahi Shimbun (Morning Edition)* (p. 19), [in Japanese].

Yanase, N. (2009). Saiban-in seido no kenpô riron [The constitutional theory of the saiban-in system]. *Hôritsu Jihô [Law Reporter], 81*(1), 62–68 [in Japanese].

Yanase, N. (2016). Saiban-in seido no kenpô tekigô sei [The constitutionaliry of the saiban-in system]. *Nihon Hôgaku [Nihon University Law Journal], 82*(3), 1045–1095 [in Japanese].

Yomiuri Shimbun Tokyohonsha Chôsakenkyûhonbu. (2009). *Yomiuri quarterly*. Tokyo: Yomiuri Shimbun sha in Japanese.

Yoshimaru, M. (2006). Saiban-in seido no moto ni okeru kôhan shinri oyobi hyôgi no practice [The practice of tiral and deliberation under the saiban-in system]. *Jurist, 1322*, 108–119 [in Japanese].

Yoshimura, S. (2009). Saiban-in seido to sono mondai ten: Saiban-in saiban in okeru kôheina saiban no jitsugen [The outline and problems of the saiban-in system: Realization of impartial trial by saiban-in]. *Kyûshûkokusai Daigaku Hôgaku Ronshû [Kyûshû International University Law Journal], 15*(3), 1–21 [in Japanese].

Chapter 2
Social Attitudes towards Lay Participation System in Japan

About this Chapter

In this chapter, the author describes Japanese citizens' attitudes towards the saiban-in system. Citizens' attitudes are important because citizens are "popular base" of the justice system. Saiban-in system has been introduced in order to reinforce the base of the justice system (Justice System Reform Council 2001). Researching citizens' attitudes towards the saiban-in system and the justice system is essential in knowing whether the systems would work well or not. If citizens have positive attitudes towards the systems, citizens will make a good base of the justice system, because the citizens are satisfied with how the systems work and the citizens may cooperate in operating the justice system. If otherwise, the opposite will be right and the justice system and saiban-in system will not work well in Japanese society.

There would be two sides of Japanese citizens who could support the justice system. On the first side is within the system. On this side, citizens are selected and behave as saiban-in or possible saiban-in in the criminal trial procedure. The other side is outside of the justice system. Even citizens are not involved as saiban-in, they watch what the justice system does through mass media, their own information sources, or their own experience. Citizens will form their social attitudes towards the justice system and saiban-in system with utilizing the information which has come from those media. The citizens on that side may not affect the justice system directly. But if citizens do not believe that the justice system does its own business right, citizens would not cooperate with the law enforcers, such as professional judges, police officers, prosecutors or other staffs who work for legal institutions.

According to those two sides, this chapter holds two sections. Each section corresponds to each side of the citizens. In the first section, the author is presenting the results of questionnaire survey which have been conducted by the district courts which have held trials by saiban-in. The respondents of the surveys are ex-saiban-in, ex-reserve-saiban-in, and the citizens who were dismissed in the selection procedure as they were not selected. Conducting the questionnaire survey would be

M. Fujita, *Japanese Society and Lay Participation in Criminal Justice*,
https://doi.org/10.1007/978-981-10-0338-7_2

supervised by the Supreme Court of Japan. The Supreme Court prepares the list of questions, gather and analyze the data, and compose the report. In the second section, the author will present research results, which were obtained through my own research. The author planned the research and entrusted carrying out the online research to a researching company. In this research, respondents were general citizens who had volunteered to register themselves to respondents' pool which was maintained by the company. In this research, the author has aimed to describe the relationship between the social attitudes towards the systems and citizens' personality traits. The reason why the author has researched the relationship was that people's attitudes might differ many various factors, and we need to understand them clearly. If we take effect into account, it could be clearer to discuss the influence of the factors other than citizens' own, that is the factors itself. This would help to understand what factors may have an influence on the trust in the justice system, in the later chapter of this book.

On Social Survey Conducted by the Courts, Answered by the Lay Participants

Questionnaire Surveys Conducted by the Supreme Court of Japan

Purpose of this Section

In this section, the author presents the results of the surveys which were conducted by the Supreme Courts of Japan. The Court composed papers and published through the Internet[1] once a year. There are two kinds of surveys conducted by the courts.

The first kind of the surveys aimed to ask how the people who served as saiban-in think about their experience (The Supreme Court of Japan 2017a). The surveys have been conducted on regular bases in the district courts who held the trials by saiban-in. The Supreme Court accumulate the answers which were answered by the ex-saiban-ins. In the first part of this section introduces the report which has been issued in March 2017, which is the newest one as of the time of writing this manuscript. The second kind of surveys concerns the general public's attitudes and opinions on the saiban-in system and the judiciary (The Supreme Court of Japan 2017b). In the latter part of this section, the author will present the critical results on the citizens' attitudes and opinions on the saiban-in system and the justice system, based on the newest results.

[1] The papers can be downloaded at http://www.saibanin.courts.go.jp/topics/09_12_05-10jissi_jyoukyou.html. All papers are written in Japanese.

The First Kind of Surveys: Ex-Saiban-In Surveys[2]

The author will summarize the report and present the remarkable results in the first kind of survey. The courts administer the questionnaire which is standardized by the Supreme Court so that all of the saiban-in answer same questions in the district courts all over Japan. All the citizens who completed their duty as saiban-in are asked to respond the questionnaire, but answering the questions are not part of their saiban-in duty. The report summarizes the results of the surveys which were conducted from April in the last year and March in that year. The reason why the period starts in April is that Japan's every fiscal year starts in April and ends in March.

The statistics about the operation of the saiban-in system are reported by the Supreme Court separately from this survey. The statistics include the information on the numbers of cases tried by saiban-in according to properties of the cases, the average length of trials by saiban-in, and other significant information on the status of the saiban-in system.

The statistics and the results of the questionnaire surveys are made public through the Internet in Japanese. If you are comfortable with reading Japanese, you can easily access the newest information issued by the Court from any part of the world. For the convenience of English readers, the author is presenting the results of the questionnaire survey report by the Court, which was made on the data in 2016 (from January 2016 to December 2016). The following parts of this section in this chapter is based on the report written by the Supreme Court ("the report") unless otherwise specified.

Purpose of the Survey

The purpose of the courts' survey is saliently presented at the first part of the report. The purpose of the courts' survey is to understand the subjective elements held by the citizen participants, and the courts statistically summarize and analyze the results in order to ameliorate the operation of the saiban-in system. The participants can include the citizens who finish their duty as saiban-ins, reserve saiban-ins, and the ex-saiban-in candidates who are dismissed in the saiban-in selection procedure. The "subjective elements" are the opinions and requests held by the citizens.

[2] This part is a partial reproduction of Fujita, M. (2017). Nihon shakai ni okeru saiban-in seido no dônyûno eikyô ni tsuite no ichi kôsatsu: Dônyû nana nen wo humaete [A consideration on effect of introduction of the saiban-in system: Based on seven years after the introduction. In K. Ageishi, H. Ohtsuka, K. Musashi, & M. Hirayama (Eds.), *The Legal Process in Contemporary Japan: A Festschrift in Honor of Professor Setsuo Miyazawa's 70th Birthday, Vol.1* (pp. 231–258). Tokyo, Japan: Shinzansha [in Japanese]. The author thanks Mr. Mamoru Imai at Shinzansha for the prompt permission for this translation.

Method: How the Survey Conducted

The Period and Cases

The report which is presented here is based on the data obtained from January 2016 to December 2016. After gathering information, they compiled the report by March 2017. In all 1039 cases tried by saiban-in were included this survey. If the trial procedure was separated (区分審理),[3] two or more criminal trial panels (the mixed juries which composed of professional judges and saiban-ins) were organized. In that case, the report counted there were two or more trials by saiban-in were conducted.

Respondents

The questionnaires were conducted in district courts in Japan, where trials by saiban-in are conducted. The courts requested all the saiban-ins, reserve saiban-ins and citizens who were dismissed during the saiban-in selection procedure ("saiban-in candidates"). The response rates were 99.5% for those who served as saiban-ins, 96.8% for ex-supplemental saiban-in, and 98.1% for citizens who were saiban-in candidates. The numbers of respondents were 27,763 in total. And the numbers according to respondents' statuses were 6208 for saiban-in, 1952 for supplemental saiban-in. and 19,603 for saiban-in candidates. The 54.7% of the respondents were male, and 44.7% were female (figure/table 3 in the report[4]). There was no information on average ages or standard deviation of ages in the report, but distribution information is provided. According to it, 12.8% of respondents were in their 20's, 18.9% were 30's, 24.6% were 40's, 19.7% were 50's, 20.9% were 60's, 2.5% were 70's or more, and 0.6% were not specified. On their occupation, 55.0% of the respondents were workers for companies or organizations. 6.9% of respondents were self-employed, 16.8% of respondents were part-time workers, 9.2% of them were housewives/househusbands, and 8.2% were in no occupation. 0.6% were students, but the saiban-in act designates that all of the students can be dismissed if they would like to. The reason why students can be dismissed during saiban-in selection procedure is that the legislator thought that students should have a chance to give priority to their study.

---

[3] Saiban-in Act, art. 71.

[4] In the report, all figures and tables are numbered with captions "図表 figure/table." It does not look to be a regular custom in the field of social science, but in this chapter, close translations are adopted in the citations.

Results

The Length of Trials

The report doesn't include the information on average length of trials, (figure/table 2) but the 33.5% of the cases ended in 1 day or 2 days. 29.4% of the cases finished in 3 days, 17.6% of the cases finished in 4 days, 8.5% finished in 5 days, the rest of the cases (11.0% total) ended in 6 days or more.

Comprehensibility

One of the significant issues in operating the saiban-in system is comprehensibility from the viewpoint of citizens. In the report, they asked ex-saiban-ins (6208 responses) the comprehensibility of hearing procedure in trials, prosecutors' activities in the courts, defense attorneys' activities, explanation of the professional judges.

On the comprehensibility overall in the trials, 66.5% of ex-saiban-in answered the contents of trials were easy to understand. 29.3% were answered as "ordinary," and 2.6% of the respondents' answers were "hard to understand."

Concerning prosecutors' activities in the courts, there were five questions which asked ex-saiban-in to answer in dichotomously (yes or no). For the question "there were problems in the way prosecutors talk," 11.5% of respondents answered "yes," while 87.9% answered "no." For the question "the explanation was too difficult," 8.8% of respondents answered "yes," 90.3% of them answered "no." For the question "the contents that prosecutors were talking were hard to understand," 5.9% of respondents answered "yes," 92.9% of them answered "no." For the question "the purposes and the contents of the prosecutors' questions for the witnesses and the accused were too difficult," 13.0% of respondents answered as "yes," 85.6% of them answered as "no." And for the question "(prosecutors') reading aloud written statements were hard to understand (it's too long, monotonous, hard to understand at once, or it made no impression)," 10.9% of respondents answered as "yes," 87.3% of them answered as "no."

The questionnaire also asked about defense attorneys' activities in the courts; there were four questions with dichotomous answer options (yes or no). For the question "there were problems on the way of talking (spoke too fast, hard to hear, attorneys' words were too difficult)," 24.5% of respondents answered "yes," while 74.4% answered "no." For the question "the explanation was too detailed," 6.2% of respondents answered as "yes," 92.9% of them answered "no." For the question "the contents that defense attorneys were talking were hard to understand," 19.5% of respondents answered "yes," 78.8% of them answered "no." And for the question "the purposes and the contents of the defense attorneys' questions cast to the witnesses and the accused were too tricky," 26.9% of respondents answered as "yes," 70.8% of them answered as "no."

On the explanations made by professional judges, 90.6% of the ex-saiban-ins respondents answered: "easy to understand." 8.5% of them answered "ordinary," 0.3% of them answered "hard to understand," and the answers made by the rest 0.5% were unspecified. On those answers, ex-saiban-in evaluated the explanation of professional judges were overwhelmingly natural. The second elements players who provided natural explanations were prosecutors, and the third were defense attorneys. These results were consistent from the first-time survey to the newest one.

On page 21 of the report, the Court reported the ratios of the answers on comprehensibility according to whether the accused admit their charge. When the accused admit the charge, the case is called as "admitting case (自白事件)," while the accused deny the charge, the case is called as "denial case (否認事件)." In admitting cases (3291 responses), 69.5% of ex-saiban-ins answered they easily understood prosecutors' explanations, and 45.8% of ex-saiban-ins answered that they easily understood defense attorneys' explanations. In denial cases, (2917 responses), 63.8% of ex-saiban-ins answered they easily understood prosecutors' explanations, and 29.2% of ex-saiban-ins answered that they easily understood defense attorneys' explanations. In denial cases, the answers that "ex-saiban-ins understood easily legal professionals' explanations" declined when compared to admitting cases. The extent of decline was shaper in the answers for comprehensibility on the explanations of defense attorneys than the prosecutors' explanations.

Deliberation

Deliberation was one of the intensively discussed issues when saiban-in system introduced (e.g., Arakawa and Sugawara 2010; Fujita 2003; Imasaki 2005; Mitsui et al. 2004). How citizens feel or think about deliberations has been considered as cues to understand whether the saiban-in system is workable. On the atmosphere of deliberations, the courts asked ex-saiban-ins how they felt about the atmosphere. The 78.4% of ex-saiban-in answered that they felt comfortable to talk during the sessions. The 19.4% of ex-saiban-in answered "ordinary," 1.5% of them answered that they felt hard to talk during the deliberation. The rest 0.6% of ex-saiban-in's answers were unspecified.

The courts asked whether ex-saiban-in felt they discussed thoroughly through their deliberation experience. The 76.0% of them answered they discussed enough in their deliberations. The 5.8% of them answered "not enough," the 16.5% answered "don't know," and the rest 1.7%'s answers were unspecified.

How Did they Feel about Being Saiban-in

The report figures presented two questions how the citizens feel about being saiban-ins. The first one was the feeling of being selected as saiban-ins. 11.1% of ex-saiban-ins answered that they thought positive about doing duty as saiban-in. 25.6% of ex-saiban-ins answered they felt that they would like to give it a try. 30.9% of ex-saiban-ins were not so like to do the duty as saiban-in, and 16.0% did not like to do it. 15.7% of them did not think about it, and the 0.7% of the answers were not specified.

After completing their duty as saiban-in, 59.9% of ex-saiban-ins evaluate it as outstanding experience; an additional 36.8% answered they felt that it was a good experience. 0.7% of them didn't feel that it was not so good experience, and 0.4% were answered that they didn't feel it was an excellent experience. 0.4% answered they felt nothing about it, and 0.6%'s answers were not specified.

Discussion

Evaluation of the Legal Professionals' Activities

One of the major issues in introducing saiban-in system was whether the civic participants understand the terminology of legal professionals. The terminology is called as legalese (Hartley 2000), which is sometimes hard to be understood by outsiders of the legal community, and that may distract full functionality of the saiban-in system. The legalese sometimes complicated or difficult because it unnecessarily uses archaic words which are discarded away from normal citizens' everyday vocabulary, adding to legal, technical terms or concepts. According to the results of the report, the ex-saiban-ins evaluated the explanations made by professional judges were overwhelmingly understandable. We can think that the first hurdle of operating the saiban-in system was cleared on the fact that civic participants understand what the judges talked. The prosecutors' explanations were next understandable, far more than half of ex-saiban-ins thought their explanations were understandable, and the third was the defense attorneys'. Even the evaluations on the third group were neutral (44.8%) or preferable (38.0%).

According to the responses of ex-saiban-ins, legal professionals' explanations were comprehensive for civic participants. The reasons were not asked in the questionnaire. We can presume that the reasons may be that the legal professionals have made their effort to make their legalese and wordings in their explanation easier (e.g., Kamiyama and Oka 2008; The Supreme Public Prosecutor's Office 2009). Prosecutors prepare explanation materials for trials; defense attorneys have a chance to be trained to present their arguments efficiently without reading their papers that would explain their opinions, as Japan Federation of Bar Associations (日弁連) and local Bar Associations provide training courses which inform and practice about standing at trials by saiban-in (Japan Federation of Bar Associations 2013; Nishimura 2006). Judges find comprehensive ways to explain legal concepts, proof standards to saiban-in (Saito 2007). To date, that instruction and explanation did not look to change any legal, technical concepts or arguments in legal scholarship. We need to watch the situation of legal concepts and legal arguments which often appear at trials by saiban-in because they might be changed according to practicing in trials by saiban-in. Written judgments have looked more natural and shorter than before the introduction of the saiban-in system (The Supreme Court of Japan 2009), and explanations of the standard of proofs have changed easier after civic participants also hear the trials.

The lower evaluations on defense attorneys' activities have been consistent from the time of the introduction of trials by saiban-in. The reasons have been thought that defense attorneys' have not been trained for presentation in trials by saiban-in, because for most of the attorneys, standing at criminal trials is not their primary business ("Bengoshi jiken fairu: Keiji jiken to bengoshi hôshû [Attorney case file: Criminal case and attorney's remuneration]," 2015). They do that as their part-time job, and they have not so much time to be trained for the trials by saiban-in. They gather information on the case and additional evidence on the case and prepare for the trials. Contrary to that, for prosecutors, dealing with criminal cases is their primary business. They have plenty of time to be trained, and they are dividing their work (Johnson 2002). The investigating prosecutors focus investigations, and trial prosecutors stand at trials. Prosecutors specialize in their work, so they are accessible to familiar with how they do at trials.

Adding to it, because only prosecutors can initiate criminal trials, first case theories are always made by prosecutors. Prosecutors deliberately gather information and evidence, and craft case theory, a story which can explain all the evidence which they intend to present at the trial. Defense attorneys are always in the position of defense, as natural, they have to present "another story" which can be elicited from the same pieces of evidence which were gathered by the prosecutors. On this situation which is inevitably the defense attorneys put in, the stories which are presented by the attorneys make less straightforward than those of prosecutors'. We can assume this from the fact that the explanations of the denial cases are more difficult than those of admitting cases. The story which includes denying something or another story which was made from the same evidence would be more difficult to understand because the story may not be straight and complicated. To understand the complicated story requires more resource, the competence of the hearer, and that does not allow processing of information heuristically. This is may be consistent with elaboration likelihood model (Petty and Cacioppo 1986). In that model, the central route requires competence and need for cognition on the matter to which people make their attitudes.

Professional judges are in more advantageous positions than prosecutors and defense attorneys. Professional judges get acquainted at the time of saiban-in selection procedure, and they are at the side of saiban-ins before starting the trial. Judges may have time to explain many things which are difficult to understand for saiban-in. And professional judges can have time to explain and even deliberation at the intermission of the trials (中間評議), in the somewhat relaxing atmosphere compared to the trials. And professional judges can explain many things at the neutral positions, while prosecutors and defense attorneys can only explain and compose their arguments at the positions they stand. Those situations can contribute to elicit high evaluations made by ex-saiban-ins.

Deliberation

On the results of the questionnaire on deliberation, the atmosphere of the deliberations was good for ex-saiban-ins. And in deliberations, the majority of ex-saiban-ins answered they discussed enough during their deliberations. From those results, it suggests that deliberations in the saiban-in system could be meaningful for the majority of saiban-in. One of the major arguments which opposed saiban-in system was that saiban-in system would not be workable because the civic participants, who are not familiar with legal arguments cannot participate in the discussions in deliberations because they are overwhelmed by the specialized knowledge of judges and saiban-in would be just "nominal / ornaments (お飾り)" in criminal trial panels (e.g., Kobayashi 2007; "Okazari ni shitewa naranu: saiban-in (shasetsu) [Don't make them figureheads: Saiban-ins (editorial article)]," 2003).

The data shown here are not based on observation of real deliberations, we cannot be too careful to reach the conclusion that the saiban-in system holds good enough deliberations in the procedure. But the fact that the majority of ex-saiban-ins said that they felt the easy-to-talk atmosphere, and they had enough discussions in the deliberation suggests that saiban-in are not just "decorations" in the system. These suggestions are hopefully and desirably tested empirically by observation of real deliberations.

The Evaluation of Experience as Saiban-in: Citing a General Survey Conducted by the Supreme Court

Overall, almost all ex-saiban-ins (96.7%) positively evaluated their experience as saiban-in. In the questionnaire, the courts did not ask ex-saiban-ins the reasons why they felt the pleasant experience of being saiban-ins. But the Court conducted cross-tabulation analyses on the evaluation of experience, and easy-to-talk atmosphere in the deliberations and the saiban-ins experienced substantial discussions in their deliberations. According to the results of those analyses, when ex-saiban-ins evaluated the deliberations had the easy-to-talk atmosphere, or they felt they had substantial discussions in the deliberations, they evaluated positively on their experience as saiban-in (The Supreme Court of Japan 2017a, p. 52). That's natural that the respondents who evaluated their deliberations were positive thought that their overall experience was positive. Adding to it, we may even hypothesize that there is some construct which has relations to the overall experience as saiban-in, and it affects all of the evaluation of saiban-in related experience held by the respondents.

But the hypothesis above may be modified when we see the results presented on page 52 of the report. On that page, a cross-tabulation analysis of the overall evaluation of the experience as saiban-in and how the ex-saiban-ins felt about being saiban-in before they selected. From this analysis, when the ex-saiban-ins had expected their experience as saiban-in, they evaluated their experience positively after completed their duty as saiban-in. The respondents who had not thought about how they evaluate the experience as saiban-in answered more positively than the respondents who did not so much like to be saiban-ins, and less positively than the answers made by whom the respondents who answered they like to do the jobs of saiban-in.

The results to which we should pay attention is that even the respondents who did not like to do the jobs of saiban-in evaluated the experience positively after finished their duty. 42.3% of them answered they felt it was an excellent experience, and 49.0% of who did not like to be saiban-ins answered they felt it was an excellent experience. The court's questionnaires did not ask the reasons why the ex-saiban-in who did not like to be saiban-ins turned to think their experience after finishing their duty. One explanation which can readily occur is that it is explained by the theory of cognitive dissonance (Festinger and Carlsmith 1959). The theory assumed that humans avoid conflicts of cognitive elements in their minds (cognitive consistency theory: Abelson et al. 1968). The theory hypothesizes that when humans find different cognitive elements in their minds, they may change their cognitive elements if they can do that for pursuing consistency among the cognitive elements in their mind. Applying this theory to the experience of saiban-in, ex-saiban-ins may change their mind to think their experience as saiban-in was more significant than they initially thought after finished their duty, because the cognitive element which holds the idea "the experience was terrible" and the element "I did a job as saiban-in" would occur a serious conflict in their minds. The cognitive element which represents "they finished duty as saiban-in" cannot be changed, because the fact that they did the duty is unchangeable. It would be resulting in changing the evaluation to the more positive direction on the experience as saiban-ins. We should keep the theory in our minds when we interpret the results. But the theory does not explain all of the tendency of our minds and behaviors. We may note that the ratio of the respondents who evaluated their experience positively was the overwhelming majority of the respondents who did not like to be saiban-in. It is reasonable to assume that the experience as saiban-in bears other positive reasons which make reluctant people's attitude positive about civic participation to the justice system.

Opportunities to Educating Citizens

One of the critical issues of civic participation to the justice system is that civic participation can bring chances to general people to be educated as citizens (de Tocqueville and Lawrence 1966). When the saiban-in system was implemented, one point argued by the Justice System Reform Council was that of deepening the citizens' foundation for the justice system. We cannot test whether the aim has accomplished through the implementation of the saiban-in system on the results of the questionnaire survey conducted to ex-saiban-in because the questionnaire does not include questions concerning the civic education.

But in a general survey by the Supreme Court on this subject (The Supreme Court of Japan 2017b), the average response to the question of whether respondents "now thought about problems of the citizenry as one's own because of a heightened interest in them" (p.31) was average of 3.40 on a five-point scale,[5] higher than a response of 3,[6] "neither". Responses by year, starting in 2009, were 3.69, 3.74, 3.51, 3.54, 3.45, 3.40, and 3.40. The saiban-in system was a new topic in 2009 and 2010 when it was most heavily covered by the mass media, and at the time the average value of responses was almost 4. Now that another 5 years have passed since the system's introduction, the responses to this question are not as high and are stable with 3.4 in the last 2 years. That said, in light of the fact that the responses have been higher than 3, we can conjecture that understanding criminal trial has gradually taken hold as a point of public interest. This is consistent with the responses to the question of "Q3 After the saiban-in system began, has your interest in the courts and justice system changed?" In 2010, 48.0% of respondents stated, "There has been no change," while between 2011 and 2017 (the survey is given in January 2017), the percentages gradually grew from 59.8, 61.1, 63.9, 66.8, and 68.6% respectively. Of course, other than that, it is possible to explain this by saying citizens are not thinking as before, though this contradicts the solid average answer of 3. Those in their 60s had the lowest scores, followed by those in their 70s.

In addition, the average responses for each year, on a five-point scale, to the question of whether citizens should voluntarily be involved in criminal trials and the justice system (p.42) were 3.43, 3.43, 3.39, 3.43, 3.35, 3.39, and 3.49 starting in 2009. In general, the responses are right around 3.4 and have gotten somewhat higher only in recent surveys. Only future responses can show us whether this is the start of a new trend or merely annual fluctuation. That said, just as with responses being more positive than "neither" for the question of "Thinking about problems of the citizenry as one's own because of heightened interest in them," these responses are consistently positive, and show a more positive attitude towards involvement in the justice system.

A look at the set of questions that compares impressions before and after the start of the system (p.43), one can see practically the same patterns in responses from 2009 to the latest responses in 2017. In other words, it seems as if there has been a distinct increase in swiftness, understandability, and intimacy compared to before the saiban-in system began. And, there has been somewhat of a more critical feeling that a sense of a nation being reflected, and people are thinking of these issues as their own. In comparing the above, one gets the sense that there have been no sig-

[5]A method for responding wherein responses are number one to five and one response may be selected.

[6]Standard deviations are not shown in the data, and whether this is statically significantly higher than 3 cannot strictly be known with this data.

nificant changes since the system began as to impartiality, trustworthiness, understanding, and clarification of truth in cases.

Limitation of this Data

The author has reviewed the results of the questionnaire surveys conducted by the courts to civic participants. And at the last part, the author referred to the general survey on the saiban-in system. There has been much good news in implementing the saiban-in system on the results of the surveys. The saiban-in have not been just "decorations" at the trials, and they evaluated their experience itself and the activities of the legal professionals positively.

But there are some significant limitations in discussing the results. The survey conducted the district courts under the supervision of the Supreme Court, the operators of the system, themselves. This fact leads us to the assumption that this report cannot tell us that the system does not work well or the saiban-in have severe dissatisfaction with their deliberation, experience as saiban-in, or legal professionals at the courts. This assumption might be to some extent valid, but it may be not wise to assume that all of the results presented here are entirely biased if the responses we have reviewed here are real responses. Maybe we do not need to accept or reject full results; the truth may lay in somewhere between those two views. We need to deliberately find the truth in a saiban-in system with critical reviews on the report and comparing other data of surveys to gather citizens' attitudes on the saiban-in system.

The Second Kind of Surveys: General public's Attitudes and Opinions

The second kind of investigation is a social survey for the general public (The Supreme Court of Japan 2017b). The report is published on the Internet[7] in Japanese. This survey began in FY 2009, and the latest survey result at the time of writing of this manuscript is FY2016. FY2016 is from April 2016 to March 2017. The Supreme Court composes the report after the end of the fiscal year. This series of surveys is valuable data because it is conducted on a regular basis for the general public every year. The content of the questionnaire is not necessarily enough to respond to academic interest, but it is data worth examining. In this section, the author summarizes the results of the latest survey at the time of writing for readers' reference. All information in this section is taken from the report of the results of the survey of the Supreme Court in FY2016.

[7] The URL where the published PDF file is located at http://www.saibanin.courts.go.jp/topics/09_12_05-10jissi_jyoukyou.html

Purpose of this Kind of Surveys:

The Supreme Court carries out a social survey every year to comprehend the evaluation from the general public about the saiban-in system and summarizes the results in a report. The Supreme Court named this survey as "the Consciousness Survey on the Operation of the Saiban-in System." The Supreme Court says about the purpose of this survey as "investigating how the citizens think about and evaluation of the operation of the saiban-in system and examining the results to obtain the guidelines for realizing operation in line with the expectations of citizens." The Supreme Court conducts the series of surveys for the reference to the operating the saiban-in system. The content and design of the questionnaire are created from the viewpoint of collecting information to be helpful for the managing system operation.

Method

The Supreme Court entrusted this investigation to Intage Research Co., Ltd. The period of the survey was January 18, 2017, to February 5. In order to carry out a survey targeting adults throughout Japan, Intage Research has made the population of this survey a person over the age of 20 across Japan. The survey company chose the sample from stratification two-stage random sampling method from all over Japan. The company interviewed the respondents individually in person. The company collected data until the number of responses reached 2000.

The contents of the questionnaire are summarized in following 13 items on the 5th page of the report. The items are translated from the original Japanese text.

(1) Public communication status of the saiban-in system.
(2) The media of publicizing the saiban-in system.
(3) The degree of interest in trials and judiciary.
(4) The impression of criminal trials before the saiban-in system began.
(5) Causes to have an impression of a criminal trial before the saiban-in system began.
(6) What do you expect from implementing the saiban-in system.
(7) The impression of the present saiban-in system.
(8) Cause of having an impression of the saiban-in system.
(9) Worry and troubles in participating in a trial.
(10) On the tendency of judges' judgment (Percentage of probationary observation in a sentence with suspension)
(11) Do you want to participate in a criminal trial as a saiban-in.
(12) Information necessary for enhancing motivation for participation in the saiban-in system.
(13) Whether citizens should voluntarily participate in criminal trials and judiciary.

Other detailed information on this survey is not available in the report.

Results

The breakdown of responses obtained in this survey by gender and age group is as shown in the following table. This table is posted on page 5 of the citation source report. We are examining the results of this survey according to the item in the method section above.

(1) Public communication status of the saiban-in system

The first set of three questions are whether the citizens know the saiban-in system. The 98% of respondents answered "Yes." Regarding the fact that the saiban-in system is a system where citizens participate in criminal trials as saiban-in and decide guiltiness and punishment with professional judges, 97.2% of respondents answered that they know about that. Concerning the fact that any person who is 20 years old or older (who are on voters' list) has the possibility to be chosen as a saiban-in in general, the 93.4% of respondents answered that they know about. Next question was about where the citizens got the information above (The Supreme Court of Japan 2017b, p. 8).

(2) The media of publicizing the saiban-in system

In this question, the Court asked the source of information. According to the answer to that question, the 94.1% of respondents answered TV coverage, 62.0% of them answered newspaper articles, and 18.1% of respondents responded they got the information from the Internet. These three media were the top three media by which citizens got to know about the saiban-in system. From this point, it was the result that television was overwhelmingly the medium to publicize to the public, and the newspaper was second favorite medium.

(3) The degree of interest in trials and judiciary

The third question was "Were there any changes in your interests or concerns in trials and judiciary since the saiban-in system was launched?" For this question, the 69.0% of the 1976 respondents replied that "there was no particular change," 27.8% answered "my interest had increased than before," 3.2% answered " my interest has been decreased. ".

(4) The impression of criminal trials before the saiban-in system began

The fourth part consisted of nine sub-questions. The respondents answered the sub-questions with five-point scales. The instruction for this question was "What impression did you have about criminal trials in Japan before the saiban-in system started? Please choose one of the following that best describes the items (a) to (i) below." The average points were reported. The anchoring stimuli for the five point-scales are "5: agree," "4: somewhat agree," "3: neither agree or disagree," "2: somewhat disagree," "1: disagree."

The subquestion items and average values of the questions and answers of each sub-question are as follows.

a. Fair and neutral 3.48.
b. Trials can be trusted 3.52.
c. Courts and judiciary are not readily accessible 1.90.
d. Trials are conducted in which citizens can be convinced 3.20.
e. The court is reflecting the sense of the nationals 3.06.
f. The truth of the case is discovered 3.16.
g. The procedure and content of the trial are hard to be understood 1.86.
h. Trials take time 1.50.
i. I am interested in trials and think as my own problem 2.91.

According to the report, the scores for the subquestions (c), (g), and (h) are reversed (The Supreme Court of Japan 2017b, p. 10). The scores around 1 or 2 indicate that the respondents agreed with what is written in the subquestions.

(5) Causes to Have Impressions of Criminal Trials before the Saiban-in System Began

This question is similar to (2). According to the answer to that question, the 88.3% of respondents answered TV coverage, 58.9% of them answered newspaper articles, and 19.0% of respondents responded they got the information from the Internet. Other 11 sources are asked and answered, but the percentages of respondents who answered that they got information in these ways are lower than in the above three items.

(6) What Do you Expect from Implementing the Saiban-in System

This question asked the citizens' expectation in implementing the saiban-in system. The question had nine subquestions. The instruction for this question which was presented before the subquestions was "What do you expect from the implementation of the saiban-in system? Please choose one of the following (number) that best describes your opinion for each question of (a) to (i)." The options in answering these subquestions are the same as (4) above. They are "5: agree," "4: somewhat agree," "3: neither agree or disagree," "2: somewhat disagree," "1: disagree."

The subquestions and the average scores for the subquestions were as follows.

a. The trials will be more fair and neutral 3.92.
b. The trials will be more reliable 3.82.
c. Courts and judiciary are felt familiar 3.76.
d. The results of the trials become convincing 3.62.
e. The sense of the citizens is reflected in the results of the trial 3.88.
f. The truth of the case is better discovered 3.52.
g. Procedures and contents of the trials become easy to understand 3.57.
h. The trials will finish quickly 3.30.
i. Citizens' interest grows, and they think the judiciary as their own problem 3.70.

(7) The Impression of the Present Saiban-in System

The next set of questions asked about the impressions on the saiban-in system. The instruction for this question was "What impressions do you have about the current saiban-in system? Please choose one of the following (number) that best describes the items (a) to (i) below." The options for answering the subquestions are same as above (4). They are "5: agree," "4: somewhat agree," "3: neither agree or disagree," "2: somewhat disagree," "1: disagree." The subquestions and the average scores for the subquestions were as follows.

a. The trials have become more fair and neutral 3.25.
b. The judiciary has become trustworthy 3.26.
c. Courts and judiciary can be felt more familiar 3.41.
d. The results of the trial became more convincing 3.10.
e. The sense of the citizens became more reflected the results of the trials 3.52.
f. The truth of cases has become better discovered 3.08.
g. Procedure and contents of the trials became easy to understand 3.02.
h. The trials became to finish quickly 2.90.
i. I became to think the judiciary as my own problem 3.37.

(8) Cause of Having an Impression of the Saiban-in System

This question asked the information source of the question (7). According to the answer to this question, the 87.8% of respondents answered that they formed their impressions base on the TV coverage, 59.1% of them answered newspaper articles, and 20.1% of respondents responded they got the information from the Internet.

(9) Worry and Troubles in Participating in a Trial

This question asked the possible obstacles to participate in the trial. The question was "If you decide to participate in a criminal trial, which is you worried about or obstructed by you? Please indicate all options that apply from the following." The options for answering this question and the percentages of the respondents who answered that the option applied to themselves are as follows.

(1) Because the destiny of the defendant is decided by their judgments, I feel grave responsibility 78.5
(2) I am concerned it is hard to do the laborious task of trials for lay people 63.1
(3) I feel anxious to be threatening my personal security because of the resentments of the defendant or the persons concerned of the defendant 54.9
(4) I am not sure about whether I can give my opinion on an equal footing with an expert judge 52.6
(5) I am not confident in judging calmly 50.2
(6) I am worried about seeing the corpse photos or similar evidence 47.8
(7) Participating in a trial will interfere with work 42.1
(8) I am not sure to keep the secrets which I get to know through jury service 33.8
(9) Participating in a trial will interfere with my duty of nursing care 22.4
(10) Not particularly 2.5
(11) Other 1.2
(12) I do not know 0.5

(10) on the Tendency of the Judgments in the Saiban-in Trials (Percentage of Probationary Observation in a Sentence with Suspension)

Before asking this question, the Court presented some information on the percentage of probationary observation. The presenting sentences were "In case of suspending the execution of sentences in criminal trials, the accused can be in probationary observation. Probationary observation is a system that requires the obligation to receive guidance and supervision by the probation office in order to rehabilitate the defendant. Looking at the proportions of the judgments with probation, the 32.1% cases were put on the probation in bench trials, while the proportions for the saiban-in trials was 54.7%." Then the Court asked, "What do you think about these trends in the saiban-in trials?"

The answering options and the percentages of the respondents who selected the option were "reasonable" 23.3, "rather reasonable" 24.1, "neither reasonable or unreasonable" 39.2, "rather unreasonable" 7.8 and "unreasonable" 5.6. The average score of the answers was 3.52.

(11) Do you Want to Participate in a Criminal Trial as a Saiban-in

The next question asked the volition to participate in the saiban-in trials. The question was "Do you want to participate in a criminal trial as a saiban-in?" The answering options and the percentages of the respondents who selected the option were "I want to participate" 4.1, "I am willing to participate" 10.9, "I do not want to participate so much, but it is inevitable if it is a duty" 42.7, "I do not want to participate even it is a duty" 41.1, and "I do not know" 1.3.

The proportion of the answers are somewhat stable from the year of the start of the series of the survey.

(12) Information Necessary for Enhancing Motivation for Participation in the Saiban-in System

The twelfth question asked the information which enhance the volition in participating in the trials. Before asking the question, the Court presented some information on the thoughts of ex-saiban-ins in participating in the saiban-in trials. That was "Among those who served as saiban-ins, 48.4% of respondents answered that they did not want to do too much or they did not want to do before being chosen as saiban-ins. On the other hand, when asking about the impression of participating in a trial as saiban-ins, 96.1% of respondents said that they felt the service was a good experience or excellent experience. (Questionnaire Survey Results Report 2017)" Then the Court asked "What information do you think is necessary to enhance motivation for participating as saiban-ins? Please give all that apply from among these."

The answering options and the percentage who answered each option applied them were "Support systems for those who participated in the trials and for those who experienced a mental burden" 51.1, "Leave system at work (the system which can be used when appointed as a saiban-in)" 46.2, "A concrete experience story of a person who actually participated in a trial as a saiban-in" 44.0, "Economic compensation which is paid to those appointed as saiban-ins" 42.6, "Temporary nursing care service in the surrounding area" 23.4, and "Other" 7.3.

(13) whether Citizens should Voluntarily Participate in Criminal Trials or Judiciary

The final question of this survey asked whether the nationals should participate in the criminal judiciary voluntarily. The question sentence was "What do you think about the idea 'Regarding public matters such as criminal trials and justice; citizens should voluntarily engage in those matters rather than leave them to the state or experts'?"

The options for answering the question and the percentages of those who selected the options were as follows. The 19.7% of the respondents selected "5: agree," the 32.6% of respondents selected "4: somewhat agree," the 26.5% of respondents selected "3: neither agree or disagree," the 13.9% of respondents selected "2: somewhat disagree," and the 7.4% of the respondents selected "1: disagree." The average score of the answers was 3.43.

Discussion

In this section, we reviewed the results of the survey that was conducted by the Supreme Court that asked the general public. In the survey, the Court found that the saiban-in system is known to almost all citizens. And it was revealed that the information sources were TV, newspaper and the Internet. The sources were the same, and the order of the sources was consistent even when the Court asked the citizens for other kinds information.

About the impression of the criminal trial, before the saiban-in system started, the citizens thought the trials as fair and neutral, and trustworthy. Those answers were somewhat higher than the midpoint. On the other hand, the citizens answered that the trials did not reflect the sense of the people. And they did not think the justice as their own problem. Also, they thought that the court was inaccessible and the trials were time-consuming. After the saiban-in system began, the impression of the people became more favorable.Their impression of the court and judiciary became familiar. And they thought that they came to think of the trials as their own problem.

It seems that something anticipated before the introduction of the saiban-in system is being achieved. It may be presumed that the citizens formed their impressions and attitudes on such issues based on the information obtained from TV or newspaper. However, their familiarity to the judiciary was their own impression, not the speculation on the information obtained from the press. Also, it seems that judging whether the sense of the citizen is reflected in the trial was done by seeing the outline and the judgments on the famous case through the mass media. In that sense, whether the trials reflect the citizens' sense was judged with the information like that.

Regarding the issue whether the citizens would like to participate as saiban-ins, about 80% or more citizens consistently answered negatively. It will be a natural answer if they imagine that their current jobs in their everyday lives are interrupted for about a week by the saiban-in service. It is the same trend as foreign countries. And this is to answer to the experienced judge experts that more than 95% of the respondents said that it was a good experience to participate in the trial as a judge. This is also similar to other countries.

As the question on how to raise motivation for people who will become saiban-ins in the future, the most frequent answers were concerning the mental burden. It is speculated that this may be influenced by having repeatedly taken up on the spiritual burden of judges on TV and news reports.

Whether the citizens voluntarily participate in criminal trials is a slightly positive answer rather than neutral. This answer has not changed from the time immediately after the saiban-in system was implemented. The public's consciousness was not very positive about judicial participation, neither the answer was not negative.

The proportion of probation observation in suspended sentence differs markedly between bench trials and the trials by saiban-ins (Q10). It can be said that as a citizen's consciousness it supports the judgment reflecting the sense of citizens. From this answer, even though results by the trials by saiban-in differ from the results of prior judgments made by bench trials, citizens generally support the judgments made by the citizens.

Trials are not always related to the citizens' life. Also, the proportion of citizens who encounter criminal cases will not be significant. Then, it seems that many of the citizens form the impression about the trial over the imagination from TV coverage. It can be said that it is thoughtfully thinking about the trial as a phenomenon which is basically apart from citizens' own life. In addition, although participating directly by themselves cannot help feeling that it is not comfortable when considering ordinary life being interrupted by participating in a trial. However, the citizens think that the meaning of the participation in the trials and the reflection of their sensitivity to the trials as positive.

Relationships between the People's Attitudes towards Participation into the Justice System and People's Personalities

Problems and Objectives[8]

This chapter's primary purpose is to conduct a questionnaire survey concerning relationships between citizens' social attitude towards citizen participation in the judicial system and personality and to examine the relationships among the

[8]This part of this chapter is an English translation of Fujita, M. (in press). People's social attitude toward a judicial system and personality 2: Examination of relationship with sentencing judgment In D. H. Foote, R. Hamano, S. Ota (eds.) The festschrift honoring the 70th birthday of Professor Masayuki Murayama, Tokyo: Shinzan-sha. The author thanks Mr. Mamoru Imai for permitting

variables based on these data. Regarding this issue, the author has already reported the results of a survey (Fujita et al. 2016) (hereinafter referred to as the "first survey" in this report). In this chapter, the author would like to report regarding the survey conducted based on the same issue. Following the first one, the author gathered new data from another sample and added a question group to observe the relationships between respondents' judgments on sentencing.

Prior to that, we will provide the following explanation regarding the problem consciousness of this series of research. The Japanese justice system reform in Heisei era intended to strengthen the authority of citizens against judicial system. The reform was accompanied by including the introduction of the saiban-in system. The reform also intended to strengthen the authority of prosecution review board. Those measures were already implemented. Such reform was the response to the "fundamental issue" of the Judicial System Reform Council (Justice System Reform Council 2001) in order to deepen the public's understandings of the justice system and to "establish the popular base of the justice system."

As the result of the introduction of a system enabling the citizens' direct participation, the issue of how to make citizens willing to participate became critical. That is because the state could make the people participate in the judiciary by the threat of punishment by law, it will be impossible to convince the citizens unless the people do not participate voluntarily. If the people are not convinced to participate, it will be difficult to make the citizens understood. Making citizens understood on the judiciary and establishing the foundation for the people to support the judiciary are the original purposes of the introduction of the system. And what people think about judiciary will correlate with the matter of whether the judiciary is felt legitimate from the people, and how they feel trusty worthiness in the judiciary (Tyler and Huo 2002).

The citizens' sentiment for participating in criminal trials can be understood as social attitudes in social psychology. It is necessary to consider the individual differences citizens' attitudes systematically, not viewing citizens as a mass. From the psychological point of view, variables of personality should be significant for understanding the individual differences. Personality is stable behavioral tendency existing within an individual. Personality can influence individual behaviors. The author intended to investigate the relationships between personality traits and judgments on judicial participation and attitudes formation.

In the saiban-in system, the saiban-ins are involved in deciding the punishments when they find the defendant guilty. They are considering the key factors influencing the sentencing such as the fact of the case, and what kind of punishment was sentenced in similar cases. However, it will be necessary to consider the factors of

to publish this translation prior to publishing the Japanese version of this manuscript. The two studies presented here were supported by a grant of KAKENHI which was disbursed by Japan Society for Promotion of Science. The grant no. is 20730003.

the saiban-ins' personality as well. Before explaining the details of this research, we would like to review what do "personality" and "social attitude" mean.

About Personality and Social attitudes

What is Personality?

Personality refers to a behavioral tendency that exists stably in a particular person and a reaction tendency to external stimuli (Wiggins and Pincus 1992). This is a general definition in psychology, but may be considered a little bit different from our daily sense since we tend to think that personality is feeling or thinking that it is something inside of the person itself.

However, our awareness about others' personalities is often nothing more than an illusion created by ourselves as a result of the observation of others' (or ourselves') actions. That kind of things often happens in our lives. For example, based on the fact that somebody often does some behaviors that we recognize as expressions of anger (that is characterized by actions like shouting loud, flushing the face), we observe it again in a similar situation, and we find high frequency compared to other people, then we will judge that person has an inclination to be angry. In such case, we feel that there is an "anger" inner substance on the inside of the person, but we can actually observe only the behavior of others, we feel more than that something being done probably contains what our own inference and the illusion caused by fundamental attribution error. Therefore, it is inevitable to define actions as clues about what the personality should be. On that assumption, personality is considered to be a behavioral tendency that each person has stably. These behavior tendencies are considered to be a combination of both the tendency that the person has originally and the behavior pattern acquired by learning. For that reason, it is also defined as "a distinctive thought, emotion, behavioral style that prescribes individual differences in the relationship between individuals and their physical and social environments." (Nolen-Hoeksema et al. 2014).

As we can infer from this definition, the term "personality" is used to describe individual behavior tendencies and individual differences. For this reason, personality has been an essential factor in psychology which has a close interest in individual differences. Personality has also gathered the interest of social scientists who are interested in explaining the behavioral tendency of people.

In the following parts, we will examine authoritarian personality that seems to influence thinking about power decision making. And we will cover Big Five, a widely-supported theory about the basic dimensions of human personality. It will enable us to discuss how authoritarian personality and willingness to participate in the judiciary can be positioned in human personality. In the next section, the author first explains about the authoritarian personality.

What is Authoritarian Personality?

Authoritarian personality is defined as an authority-oriented personality, which is based on traditional value criteria (conventionalism) consisting of nine characteristics (Adorno et al. 1950). The nine characteristics are authoritarian obedience, authoritarian attack, anti-introspection, emphasis on superstition and stereotype, power and rigidity, destructibility and cynicism, a right attitude towards projection, sex (Adorno et al. 1950). This personality theory was developed in search of answering the question about what were the factors familiar to the people who supported the dictatorship in the Second World War. The question was what is familiar to people who followed the dictator in Western Europe. Adorno's research group developed a scale to measure nine characteristics by conducting numerous interview surveys, extracted the nine characteristics from the innate personality tendencies, then conducted questionnaire surveys to develop the scales which can measure the personality tendencies concerning the authoritarian personalities.

Examining the influent of authoritarian personality is thought to be essential for constructing a participatory social system. This is because people with strong authoritarian personality are considered to have negative attitudes towards human freedom and behavior based on it, and also on the belief that a better society will be built based on them. In such case, we will evaluate negatively against participation in social governance mechanisms such as judicial participation and voting behavior. And it is conceivable that the owner of a definite tendency of authoritarian personality shows a robust conservative tendency. Also, as the owners are considered to think there are correlations between social prestige and the strength of power exercise, people with a strong tendency of authoritarian personality are expected to show adverse reaction towards the democratic judicial participation system that general citizens exercise the power of the judiciary. For example, the tendencies have been used to validate the authoritarian personality and the severely punished tendency of the jury (Bray and Noble 1978), the jury bias measure (Juror Bias Scale: Kassin and Wrightsman 1983; revision presented in Myers and Lecci 1998).

There is research studied in relation to the political participation feeling in Japan. Ikeda (2010) conducted studies on trust in the administration, and he suggested that both of trust in the administration and the authoritarian tendencies tend to rise as the respondents' age rises (Ikeda 2010). For another example, the authoritarian personality has an indirect influence on the trust in the judicial system (Fujita et al. 2016).

A person with a strong tendency of authoritarian personality tends to show such a tendency due to his negative evaluation to the belief on a human society's freedom, and behavior based on it for a better society. The persons with authoritarian tendencies will give a negative evaluation on participation in governing social mechanisms such as judicial participation or voting in elections.

It is conceivable that it is the case that those who have authoritarian tendencies show the negative evaluation of the saiban-in system because the system was introduced for the purpose of fostering awareness among citizens. The system also aimed to request the nationals to be involved in the creation of a social order that will become a base of their own society and resulting in fostering the consciousness of the governance entity. However, for that purpose, it is necessary to discuss equally regardless of participants' social statuses, which is inferred to be incompatible with the authoritarian personality tendency.

Difference between Definitions of "authoritarian personality," "authoritarianism" and "conservatism."

The authoritarian personality and authoritarianism are used in different ways in psychological papers. For example, a Japanese dictionary definition of "authoritarianism" will be "Behavior style that brandishes authority and observes others, or following the authority without expressing criticism" (Super Daijirin). The second half of this definition overlaps with authoritarian obedience. However, it becomes narrower than the authoritarian personality defined by Adorno et al. (1950). Also, in the definition of authority in everyday vocabulary, in the above definition, it seems that emphasis is put on actions and ways of wearing the authority in the first half. However, the problems related to the authoritarian personality are specific value criteria and action tendencies that follow dictators. In the context of authoritarian personality, not so much emphasis is placed on setting authority over others.

Also, differences between authoritarian personality and conservatism can be a problem because those two concepts are possibly confused in everyday vocabulary. Conservatism is "a principle that respects old traditions, customs, ways of thinking, etc. and does not prefer abrupt reforms" (Super Daijirin). The definition can be understood as the tendency not to change the conventional way. The authoritarian personality will add to it with the tendency of trying hard to keep the traditional way, and weak flexibility in accepting the changes. Besides, the person with authoritarian personality also values the importance of the traditional ideas themselves. There is a difference in existence together as a result of intertwining with the personality characteristics of others. Indeed, Altemeyer (1990) who developed the Right Wing Authoritarian Scale expressed that conservatism and authoritarianism are different.

Other Personalities Raised up in this Chapter

Big Five is a personality theory which intends to explain human character by the five-dimensional combination (Goldberg 1990). Numerous theories have tried to explain various personalities with some small numbers of fundamental elements. Big Five set five basic dimensions, and it tried to explain the character of a person by combining strengths of each dimension. The five dimensions are openness to experience, conscientiousness, extraversion, agreeableness, and neuroticism.

Nowadays, it has been regarded as the most influential and applicable theory, and the measurement scales have been created on the basis of this theory (e.g., Denissen et al. 2008; Fossati et al. 2011; Schulze and Roberts 2006; Soto and John 2016). The theory has been confirmed by a number of reliable and adequate prior studies (e.g., Fossati et al. 2011; Gosling et al. 2003; Hahn et al. 2012; Hamby et al. 2015; John and Srivastava 1999; Rammstedt and John 2007). It is also recognized as a culturally relevant theory, and it is considered to be valid not only for Western civilization but also for characterization of subjects in other than Western world (e.g., Mastor et al. 2000; Na and Marshall 1999; Robie et al. 2005; Zhai et al. 2013).

Given the significance of Big Five theory, it is a good idea to examine under the light of this theory with new data concerning personality. With Big Five theory, by exploring the relationship between authoritarian personality and attitude towards judicial participation, we will see it can be suggested how to position the two elements with respect to essential personality traits of human beings.

What is the Social Attitude

Social attitude is an evaluative response accompanied by emotional values such as likes/dislikes held among individuals (Cacioppo et al. 1986). Because it seems that it can not be distinguished from mere likes and dislikes, we are quoting a more detailed definition by Allport (1935).

What we can understand from these definitions is that social attitudes have some kind of triggers, which is a psychological state held by a person. And that psychological state is not entirely innate; it is what human beings have acquired through postnatal learning. To acquire by learning suggests that there is a possibility that attitudes towards internalization may differ depending on the culture or community in which the human being was placed. In that respect, the attitude cannot merely judge by likes and dislikes, but it can be said that attitudes are established under the influence of others. In that sense, attitudes are formed socially. And since others are being influenced while being embedded in the community, society, state, and culture, it is assumed that the attitudes that are held by individuals are also affected.

From the above viewpoint, attitudes taken up in social psychology are called as social attitudes. The emotional evaluation response of each individual may be said by paying attention to the point that it is formed under the influence of others. Also, attitudes formation may be affected by the attitudes expressed by the significant others (cf. Heider 1946), attitudes are influenced by the interpersonal relationships.

The willingness to participate in the judiciary is also regarded as a kind of social attitude. We can measure the willingness to participate in the judiciary in the same way of other social attitudes are measured.

The First Paper

The problem in this chapter is to look at the social attitude towards the judicial system in which the citizens participate, the relationship between the personality variables. For this time the purpose is defined as to find the relationship with the tendency of the decision making on sentencing. Prior to present the study that examined the problem, the author is presenting the review of the first paper, since the main report of this chapter is the succeeding research of the first paper.

Method

The survey was entrusted to Nikkei Research Co., Ltd. based in Tokyo. The company constructed a website for this survey. The website was located on a server which was connected to the Internet. The survey began on January 27, 2010, and ended on February 2. The respondents were selected from the company's respondents pool. The respondents resided in Japan. The company randomly sampled recipients from the monitor pool and sent emails which requested the recipients to respond the survey through the Internet. The physical addresses of the monitors were distributed throughout Japan. The age of the respondents ranged from the 20s to 60s. The number of requests was 6502, and the number of responses was 1503. The collection rate was 23.1%. The median of the response time was 17 min 48 s; the average of it was 28 min 40 s.

The questionnaire included Right Wing Authoritarian Scale (RWA) (Altemeyer 1998), 40 items version (Yonamine and Higashie 1965) of Adorno's F scale, the Big Five 60 item version, the Social Dominance Orientation scale (Pratto et al. 1994: preliminary translation into Japanese by the author), a question item group on the participation attitude to the judiciary (original), and a question group on the demographic variables.

Results

The first paper (Fujita et al. 2016) reported the survey as follows. The author conducted factor analyses on the data. In the first paper, three factors were extracted from Adorno's F scale. The factors were named "super-ego directionality," "distrust of others," and "traditional norms." Concerning the Right Wing Authoritarian Scale of Altemeyer (1998), three factors were extracted. These three factors were named "compulsion of norms," "affirmation of freedom," "affirmation of resistance." When looked at the correlation between each factor and the attitude towards participation in the justice system, the author found a correlation between the factor of "enforcement of norms" of F scale and factor of "affirmation of freedom" of RWA. As for

Big Five, another factor analysis revealed five factors which are predicted by the Big Five theory. The factors were extroversion, nervousness tendency, integrity, harmony, and openness to experience.

In the survey, the author put the respondents' answering data for questions of Social Dominance Orientation scale (Pratto et al. 1994) in the questionnaire. The author also conducted factor analysis on the question items on the SDO. The author identified three factors, which were named "importance of equality" "equality of the world" "approval of difference between humans."

After that, the author conducted multiple regression analyses to examine the effects of above personality traits on the citizens' attitudes towards participation in the judicial system. There was a negative effect on participation in the judicial system of "enforcement of norms." The factors "affirmation of freedom," "openness," "approval of the difference between humans" had positive effects (Fujita et al. 2016, Table 9).

Despite the F scale was theoretically designed the scale contains nine personality traits, the results of factor analysis indicated that the scale consisted of three factors. This was partly because the question items contain the elements which have relationships with the multiple theoretical factors. Consequently, when we try to categorize each question item into one of the factors which were identified by the analysis, there were question items which have a significant factor loading on multiple factors. RWA scale was developed with the aim of avoiding this inexpedience, and it was designed to consist of three factors. The three factors are authoritarian obedience, authoritarian aggression, the emblem of traditional value standards (Altemeyer 1988). The three factors in RWA scale were confirmed in the replication of the first paper. In that paper, the author extracted these three factors with the factor analysis. However, the analysis of the reliability of the Altemeyer's RWA scale did not show enough reliability.

Discussion

In the relation between judicial participation and authoritarianism, the normative compulsion tendency was weak, and positive affirmation of freedom, stable tendency turned out to have a positive relationship with the attitudes towards judicial participation. This is considered to be a critical condition for many citizens to actively participate in the social governance mechanism including the judiciary and to construct an open society.

Regarding the relationship with the approval of the difference between humans, it may be related to the judicial system and participation in the judiciary.

More than half a century has passed since the creation of the F scale, and it seems that we need to review the wording or replace the original items. The strangeness of the wording strikes the respondents when they read in today's social context.

New Data in this Article

The author aimed to verify the following with newly obtained data in the second half of this chapter. The aims were (1) to verify the reliability of the scale etc. with different samples, and (2) to analyze the influence of distinctive characteristics such as authoritarian personality, and Big Five on decision making of sentencing. In addition, the author aimed to examine what kind of statistical properties the improved version of the F scale has and whether it is possible to replace the new Japanese translation of the conventional Japanese F scale which was developed in 1965.

Method

The survey was also entrusted to Nikkei Research Co., Ltd. The company constructed a website for gathering responses. The survey was about 1 year after the survey of the first part, the investigation was started on February 24, 2011, and the end was February 28. As in the first part, respondents in this survey were people who answered randomly sampled from the respondent's pool which was held by the company. The respondents resided throughout Japan and age ranged from 20 to 69 years, with an average of 43.71 years (SD 13.40), 894 men and 947 females. The number of inquiries sent was 11,366, and the number of valid responses was 1841. The collection rate was 16.2%. The median response time was 20 min 44 s, and the average value was 32 min 20 s.

The contents of the question items were Adorno's F scale of 40 items edition (Yonamine and Higashie 1965), 32 items improved version of F scale (tentatively), provisional translation of Right Wing Authoritarian Scale (RWA) (Altemeyer 1998), Big Five 60 item version, the Social Dominance Orientation scale (Pratto et al. 1994), a group of questions on the attitudes towards participation in judiciary (original), and a group of questions of demographic variables. For temporary translation, the author had translated these items from 32 item version of F scale. The professional back translation was performed to confirm deviation from the original English version.

In order to see the relationships between judgment tendencies of each personality tendency and sentencing, in this survey, we added a task to read the scenario of the fictitious murder case and decide the length of imprisonment. The outline of the murder case was as follows. In this case perpetrator A stabbed victim B with a knife. A was 78 years old, and B was 49 years old, both were men. B had a mental disorder. For that reason, A had been checking the work performance of B and looking after in his everyday life for decades. However, B started to repeat problematic behaviors in recent years. A was so much worrying about B's behavior which annoyed the surrounding people that A started to think about killing B for stopping annoying people. One day B conducted behaviors which A could not tolerate, and A committed the crime. After the crime, A went to the police before the police acknowledge it. There was no parent-child relationship between A and B. A was self-defeated. The perpetrator A admitted his guilt at the trial and did not contend for the fact.

In the scenario, there were two versions in which prosecutors requested just "severe punishment" and "prison term 15 years". The respondents answered one of the two versions of the scenario in the questionnaire.

The author asked respondents to choose punishment which was appropriate for A. The options were from 3 to 20 years imprisonment.

Results

Results on the Willingness to Participate in the Scale and Justice System

Factor analyses were performed to see the cohesion of each scale obtained. Principal factor analysis and Promax rotation were used for factor analysis. The number of factors was determined by the shape of the Scree plot. The question items with an absolute factor loading amount less than 0.4 were removed. In order to see the reliability of the subscale, the estimated value of α coefficients of each factor was calculated, and then the relevance to other questions was examined. In addition, the author conducted a multiple regression analysis to see the effects of variables appeared in the questionnaire on the attitudes of participating in the judiciary.

Three factors were extracted in Adorno 40 items. Each factor was named superego directionality (.83), traditional norm adherence (.72), distrust in others (.75). In Altemeyer 's RWA, three factors were extracted. This scale was also named as the same as the first half of this chapter. The factors were named as the norm of compulsion (.85), the affirmation of freedom (. 71), the affirmation of resistance (.46). Three factors were extracted for the Social Dominance Orientation scale. The factors were named as the importance of equality (. 81), the equality of the world (.80), the approval of the difference between humans (. 66) (the figures in the parentheses are the estimated values of α coefficients) (Tables 2.1, 2.2 and 2.3).

The author conducted partial correlation analyses with controlling demographic variables. Among the partial correlations between each factor extracted above and the attitudes towards judicial participation, the correlations with the factors in Adorno F scale, "superego directionality" was negative, "adherence to the traditional norm" was positive. A positive relationship was found between RWA's "affirmation of freedom" and judicial participation.

In the general character, the openness of Big Five and the attitude of participation in the judiciary have a negative correlation with positive correlation and emotional instability. Also, among social differences, there was a positive correlation between

Table 2.1 The result of the factor analysis for the 40-item Japanese version of F scale (Yonamine and Higashie 1965)

	Factor		
	1	2	3
Literature and romance make humans weak.	0.79		
Students should devote themselves to study without having cocnern about social or political problems.	0.70		
Every person should have a deep faith in some supernatural force higher than himself to which he gives total allegiance and whose decisions he does not question.	0.62		
The problem of half-blood children which is derived from the war would cause social instability and disarray.	0.56		
Homosexuals are nothing but degenerates and ought to be severely punished.	0.53		
Some day it will probably be shown that astrology can explain a lot of things.	0.52		
Wars and unsightly conflicts could be swiped away by disasters like earthquake or deluges which destroy the entire world.	0.51		
The good part of traditional morals and traditional life styles are being gradually extinguished, so compulsion is needed to keep them.	0.51		
The world should be more livable if people make less their words and labor harder.	0.42		
Human lives are determined by destinies from when they were born.	0.40		
There would probably be nothing more despicable as humans than those who don't feel appreciation and respect to their parents.		0.69	
1The most important things which need to be learned by children are obedient mind and respect for their parents.		0.63	
It is natural to requite other people's facvor.		0.55	
The young in these days are too weak. They need harder discipline and severer regulations.		0.50	
The young tend to be critical; but attitudes like that should be mended as they get older.		0.49	
Sexual offenders who committed rape should be imposed with harsher punishment. Imprisonment is not enough.		0.45	
Anybody cannot be trusted immediately; we have terrible experiences if we trust in others carelessly.			0.73
Other people cannot be depended upon; the only human who can be being counted on is I.			0.55
Familiarity breeds contempt			0.53
Human nature being what it is, there will always be war and conflict.			0.52
To a greater extent than most people realize, our lives are governed by plots hatched in secret by politicians.			0.49
People can be divided into the strong and the weak, the world is running in the form that the strong dominate the weak.			0.48
People put significance more on power or wealth than education or knowledge.			0.42
α	0.83	0.72	0.75

The items which do not have the counterpart of the English version are backtranslated from Japanese version of F scale (Yonamine and Higashie 1965)
The items with factor loading less than .40 were deleted

Table 2.2 The result of the factor analysis for Altemeyer's Right Wing Authoritarian Scale

	Factor		
	1	2	3
There are many radical. immoral people in our country today. who are trying to ruin it for their own godless purposes whom the authorities should put out of action.	0.75		
The situation in our country is getting so serious. The strongest methods would be justified if they eliminated the troublemakers and got us back to our true path.	0.75		
What our country really needs is a strong, determined leader who will crush evil and take us hack to our true path.	0.73		
The facts on crime, sexual immorality, and the recent public disorders all show we have to crack down harder on deviant groups and troublemakers if we are going to save our moral standards and preserve law and order.	0.70		
Our country desperately needs a mighty leader who will do what has to be done to destroy the radical new ways and sinfulness that are ruining us.	0.68		
Our country will be destroyed someday if we do not smash the perversions eating away at our moral fiber and traditional beliefs.	0.62		
The only way our country can get through the crisis ahead is to get back to our traditional values, put some tough leaders in power and silence the troublemakers spreading bad ideas.	0.53		
Once our government leaders give us the "go ahead," it will he the duty of every patriotic citizen to help stomp out the rot that is poisoning our country from within.	0.47		
What our country needs *most* is discipline with everyone following our leaders in unity.	0.45		
The "old-fashioned ways" and "old-fashioned values" still show the best way to live.	0.43		
The established authorities generally turn out to be right about things while the radicals and protectors are usually just "loud mouths" showing off their ignorance.	0.41		
There is no "ONE right way" to live life everybody has to create their own way.		0.77	
It is wonderful that young people today have greater freedom to protest against things they don't like and to make their own "rules" to govern their behavior.		0.62	
Atheists and others who have rebelled agai nst the established religions are no doubt every bit as good and virtuous as those who attend church regularly.		0.59	
There is nothing wrong with premarital sexual intercourse.		0.59	
Gays and lesbians are just as healthy and moral as anybody else.*		0.54	
A lot of our rules regarding modesty and sexual behavior are just customs whIch are not necessarily any better or holier than those which other people follow. *		0.47	
Everyone should have their own lifestyle, religious beliefs and sexual preferences even if it makes them differentfrom everyone else. *		0.44	
It's better to have trashy magazines and radical pamphlets in our communities than to let the government have the power to censor them.		0.43	

(continued)

Table 2.2 (continued)

	Factor		
	1	2	3
People should pay less attention to the Bible and the other old forms of religious guidance and instead develop their own personal standards of what is moral and immoral. *		0.42	
It would be best for everyone if the proper authorities censored magazines so that people could not get their hands on trashy and disgusting material.		-0.40	
Homosexuals and feminists should be praised for being brave enough to defy "traditional family values."			0.52
You have to admire those who challenged the law and the majority's view by protesting for women's abortion rights, for animal rights, or to abolish school prayer.			0.52
There is absolutely nothing wrong with nudist camps. *			0.45
Our country needs free thinkers who will have the courage to defy traditional ways. even if this upsets many people.*			0.45
α	0.85	0.71	0.46

Note: The items with asterisks are reverse items

Table 2.3 The result of the factor analysis for Pratto's SDO scale

	Factor		
	1	2	3
We should try to treat one another as equals as much as possible (All humans should be treated equally)*	0.83		
It is Important that we treat other countries as equals *	0.76		
In an ideal world. all nations would be equal *	0.73		
If people were treated more equally we would have fewer problems in this country*	0.54		
Increased social equality *		0.84	
Increased economic equality*		0.81	
Equality*		0.68	
Some people are just more worthy than others			0.64
Some people are just more deserving than others			0.56
Some groups of people are simply not the equals of others			0.55
Some people are just inferior to others			0.49
It is not a problem if some people have more of a chance in life than others			0.46
α	0.81	0.80	0.66

Note: Items with factor loadings less than .40 were deleted. Items with asterisks are reverse items the perception of the difference between humans and the attitude of participation in the judiciary.

Relationship with Sentencing Judgment: Result of Multiple Regression Analysis

Multiple regression analysis was conducted to investigate factors affecting sentencing undertaken by respondents. In carrying out multiple regression analysis, multiple models were created depending on what type of independent variable was input to the analysis. The model is the following three types. The first model was a model in which demographic variables are introduced for control. And in this model, the scores of the personality scales were included as independent variables (hereinafter, Model 1). In the second model, in addition to Model 1, the model included the variables regarding how respondents felt about the accused or the victim by reading the scenario (hereinafter referred to as Model 2). In addition to Model 2, the third model analyzed six question items that asked about the length of imprisonment.

The difference between these three models is that the model 1 shows the influence of the personality scale on the judgment of the length of imprisonment, the model 2 adds case evaluation, and the model 3 is a model that adds an evaluation of how the judgment of the respondent is seen from other people.

The results of multiple regression analyses of the above three models are shown in Table 2.4. Independent variables that have a significant effect on sentencing are shaded. The darkness of the shade differs according to by the p-value. For demographic variables, the effect of age is consistent. Looking at B (Beta), which is a nonstandardized partial regression coefficient, every time the age raises 1 year, the sentence of imprisonment gets shorter about 0.5 years. "Numeric anchor" is the difference whether the prosecutor asked for "15 years" at the time of the prosecution, or simply said "severe punishment." In reality, it is difficult to think that it does not mention a specific number of years in a request in criminal trials. As a result, the effect that clearly requests leads to heavier punishment.

Looking at the relationships between personality scales and sentencing, in Model 1, if there is "distrust of others" of Adorno F scale, the length of imprisonment gets shorter 0.06 years. When RWA's "positive for resistance" raised one point, the sentence of imprisonment gets 0.14 years longer. However, in both cases, the p-value is 0.05 or more, and the effects are somewhat weak. Meanwhile, when Big Five's "integrity" increased by one point, the sentence of imprisonment gets 0.5 years longer.

Considering Model 2, the effect of "distrust of others" on sentencing disappears, and the effect of "enforcing discipline" in RWA is observed. Also, we could find the weak impact of "openness to experience" in Big Five. On the other hand, "integrity" has the effect of extending imprisonment as well as model 1 although beta is small.

In the question items of the case evaluation added in Model 2, when the respondents evaluated the accused as "unforgivable," "can compassionate," "selfish,"

Table 2.4 The results of regression analyses

		Model 1			Model 2			Model 3		
		B	β	*p*	B	β	*p*	B	β	*p*
Demographics variables	Age	−0.06	−0.15	0.00	−0.05	−0.11	0.00	−0.05	−0.12	0.00
	Sex	0.21	0.02	0.53	0.55	0.05	0.07	0.50	0.04	0.09
	Occuaption	−0.01	−0.01	0.77	−0.06	−0.04	0.13	−0.06	−0.03	0.16
	Household income	−0.10	−0.03	0.34	−0.06	−0.02	0.51	−0.06	−0.02	0.48
Condition	Numeric anchor	1.52	0.13	0.00	1.39	0.12	0.00	1.43	0.12	0.00
	Instruction to ingnore	−0.22	−0.02	0.46	0.01	0.00	0.98	−0.06	−0.01	0.83
AdornoF scale	Enforvement of norms	−0.02	−0.02	0.59	−0.02	−0.03	0.43	−0.03	−0.05	0.20
	Adherence to the traditional norm	0.01	0.01	0.78	0.03	0.03	0.31	0.04	0.04	0.19
	Distrut of others	−0.06	−0.07	0.05	−0.02	−0.02	0.46	−0.01	−0.02	0.59
RWA	Compulsion of norms	0.02	0.03	0.38	0.04	0.07	0.06	0.04	0.06	0.11
	Affirmation of freedom	−0.05	−0.04	0.30	0.01	0.01	0.82	0.00	0.00	0.92
	Affirmation of resistance	0.14	0.06	0.06	0.04	0.02	0.58	0.04	0.02	0.55
SDO	Importance of equality	0.04	0.03	0.31	−0.03	−0.02	0.46	−0.04	−0.03	0.30
	Equality of the world	0.04	0.02	0.44	−0.01	0.00	0.90	−0.03	−0.02	0.45
	Approval of difference between humans	−0.07	−0.04	0.16	−0.07	−0.04	0.12	−0.05	−0.03	0.28
	Participation in judiciary	−0.01	−0.02	0.58	0.02	0.03	0.24	0.02	0.03	0.21
Big Five	Openness	−0.03	−0.05	0.10	−0.03	−0.05	0.07	−0.03	−0.05	0.06
	Neuroticism	0.01	0.02	0.53	0.00	0.01	0.87	0.00	0.01	0.84
	Extraversion	0.02	0.03	0.43	0.01	0.02	0.62	0.01	0.03	0.40
	Conscientiousness	0.05	0.07	0.02	0.03	0.05	0.04	0.04	0.06	0.02
	Agreeableness	0.01	0.02	0.59	−0.01	−0.01	0.63	−0.01	−0.02	0.47

(continued)

Table 2.4 (continued)

		Model 1			Model 2			Model 3		
		B	β	p	B	β	p	B	β	p
Evaluation of the case	1 I cannot forgive the accused				0.90	0.17	0.00	0.79	0.15	0.00
	2*The victim B can be blamed				0.14	0.03	0.30	0.08	0.02	0.53
	3*I can sympathize with the accused				0.57	0.10	0.00	0.46	0.08	0.00
	4 I think the victim B regrets the damage				0.14	0.02	0.40	0.20	0.03	0.21
	5 The motivation of the accused A is irrational				0.06	0.01	0.73	−0.06	−0.01	0.75
	6 The act of the accused A was cruel				0.25	0.05	0.13	0.31	0.06	0.06
	7 The accused A was egocentric				0.53	0.09	0.00	0.62	0.11	0.00
	8 The act of the accused A was pernicious				1.08	0.19	0.00	0.93	0.16	0.00
	9*The apology of the accused A was an expression of reflection				0.49	0.08	0.00	0.38	0.06	0.02
	10 The act of the accused A was persistent				0.05	0.01	0.75	0.05	0.01	0.75
How would the people see your evaluation	1 Others in general							−0.24	−0.04	0.29
	2 Your family							0.10	0.02	0.65
	3 Saiban-ins who heard the case							−0.18	−0.03	0.50
	4 Judges who heard the case							0.30	0.04	0.21
	5 the accused							−0.55	−0.09	0.00
	6 Bereaved familiy of the victim							1.03	0.18	0.00
	(Coefficient)	11.16		0.00	−5.36		0.05	−4.24		0.12
		$F(21, 1391) = 4.49, p < .001$, Adjusted $r^2 = .05$			$F(31, 1354) = 16.78, p < .001$, Adjusted $r^2 = .26$			$F(37, 1326) = 16.38, p < .001$, Adjusted $r^2 = .30$		

Note: * (asterisk) means reverse items. The coefficients in shaded cells are statistically significant. The darkness shows the extent of the significance "malicious," "he admitted his guilt" influence on the length of imprisonment punishment. The asterisk (*) is a reversed item. On the other hand, the length of imprisonment for the factors such as "the victim's fault," "the victim's disappointment," "the motive of the accused is unreasonable," "the action is cruel," "relentless" did not influence the punishment. Those factors are often referred in written criminal judgments. Even in model 3, almost similar results are observed except for cruelty. So the factors such as fault, regret, the unreasonableness of motivation and persistence of victims are not independently evaluated by respondents. They are evaluated on a scale such as "unforgivable" "selfish" "malignant."

In the Model 3, the author asked about how the respondents think when they are viewed their answers by other people. This was a group of questions for asking what criminal trial judgment of the respondents is supported from the viewpoint of others, that is, keeping in mind that it can be shared with any other persons. Among them, the evaluation from the viewpoint of "general public" and the respondent's "family" has no influence, and other "saiban-ins" and "judges" have no effect. On the other hand, when the respondents thought about how their evaluations are viewed from "accused" and "bereaves of the victim" related to the length of imprisonment. When the respondents cared about the evaluation from the accused, the imprisonment gets shorter while the respondents cared about the bereaver the sentence got longer.The former effect had about twice the effect of the latter effect.

In summary, the F scale, RWA scale, Big Five's "openness to experience" had an impact on sentencing, but it was relatively weak. On the other hand, Big Five's "honesty" had the effect of increasing the sentence of imprisonment even if excluding the influence of the evaluation of the respondents' case evaluation and their own judgment from the viewpoint of others. In the assessment of the behavior of the victim / defendant, it was effective in the length of imprisonment for whether the accused could not be forgiven, sympathized, selfish, malignant, or reflective. Finally, in the question asking how the sentencing judgment appears from others, how the judgment of the victim's bereaved family and the accused had significant effects on imprisonment punishment.

Discussion

In the second half of this chapter, the scales for two authoritarian personality tendencies had three-factor structures. The structures were both found in the first half of this chapter and the second half of this chapter. From the fact that the same results were observed in the data of the first half, not only the Altemeyer's RWA which was initially designed in three factors from the beginning but also the Adorno et al.'s F scale also shows a three-factor structure by modern factor analysis technique. Since the F scale is initially designed in such a way that each question affects multiple factors (personality traits), it is not appropriate to merely divide each question item into three factors and interpret each factor. The author found stable factor structures by deleting question items with small factor loading. The nine personality characteristics that Adorno has drawn from their surveys are recognized as three factors by the general people.

As to how to think about this point, we need to decide on it. In other words, whether personality characteristics should be drawn by the property which can be recognized by general citizens or not. If we adopt this way of thinking, it would be overly conceptualization when researchers find other characteristics.

In a way that is similar to that recognition, it is also one way to divide Altemeyer's characteristics of authoritarian personality into three main factors and create and establish a corresponding question scale accordingly. However, the theory of personality traits with nine factors that gained insight from the interviews of a large number of people immediately after the Second World War has been somewhat compelling as a tough sign of conservatism. Therefore, it seems to be premature to throw away the theory of Adorno et al. immediately. The above shows that having the knowledge gained by clinical psychological interviews and qualitative analyses on authoritarian personality may be challenging to capture with behavioral characteristics that appeared on a self-report questionnaire answered by the general public.

The results of the relationship between judicial participation and authoritarian personality showed that the normative compulsion tendency was weak. Positive affirmation of freedom and stable tendency created positive attitudes towards judicial participation. The same results were found in the first half of this chapter. These factors were considered to be essential conditions in order that many citizens actively participate in the social governance mechanism and construct an open society.

In relation to sentencing, it was shown that people with high scores of the F scale tended to sentence severe punishment (Bray and Noble 1978; McCann 2008). In this chapter, there were relationships between factors taken from the scale of F scale and RWA and sentencing. However, the magnitude of the effect was small as compared with the imagination of others evaluation for incident evaluation and sentencing judgment. Given this fact, although the authoritarian personality scale may affect the sentence, the effect looked weak. It is conceivable that it involves complicated influence relations in which we can hardly find particular tendencies. On the other hand, regarding Big Five, the influence of "integrity" was consistently seen in all three models. For this reason, those who are strongly inclined to perform the tasks given to themselves faithfully seriously may tend to make the sentence a little severer to consider the seriousness of criminal cases seriously.

There was a consistently strong influence on the evaluation of the case. From the viewpoint that concern about how sentencing judgment is seen from others influences sentencing to the same extent as the evaluation related to the content of the incident (Model 3), it may be essential to study the impact of concerns about what the saiban-ins may be exposed to the assessment. There was no question about the mass communication, but in the high-profile cases that can be picked up by the mass media, the possibility of being more conscious of the evaluation from others may also increase.

Besides, it was observed that the influence of numerical anchor is significant as a cognitive factor. Although the anchoring and adjustment bias (Epley and Gilovich 2006) is known as a considerably robust bias, it was officially confirmed based on the data of this report. In criminal trials, prosecutors routinely make a requisition referring to the contents of specific punishment, and since it is ahead of the defense side, it shows that it is a very powerful anchor for saiban-ins. And since there is no effect of "instruction ignorance," it was also shown that the effect does not disappear with an instruction of ignorance.

References

Abelson, R. P., Aronson, E., McGuire, W. J., Newcomb, T. M., Rosenberg, M. J., & Tannenbaum, P. H. (Eds.). (1968). *Theories cognitive consistency: A sourcebook*. Chicago: Rand-McNally.

Adorno, T. W., Frenkel-Brunswik, E., & Levinson, D. J. (1950). In R. N. Sanford (Ed.), *The authoritarian personality*. New York: Harper.

Allport, G. W. (1935). Attitudes. In C. Murchison (Ed.), *Handbook of social psychology* (pp. 798–844). Worcester, MA: Clark University Press.

Altemeyer, B. (1988). *Enemies of freedom: Understanding right-wing authoritarianism*. San Francisco: Jossey-Bass.

Altemeyer, B. (1990). Altemeyer replies. *Canadian Psychology, 31*(4), 393–397. https://doi.org/10.1037/h0084416.

Altemeyer, B. (1998). The "other" authoritarian personality. *Advances in Experimental Social Psychology, 30*, 47–92. https://doi.org/10.1016/S0065-2601(08)60382-2.

Arakawa, A., & Sugawara, I. (2010). Communication in a mock mixed court jury trial: Its structure and the satisfaction and understanding of jurors. *Japanese Journal of Social Psychology, 26*(1), 73–88 [in Japanese with English abstract].

Bengoshi jiken fairu: Keiji jiken to bengoshi hôshû [Attorney case file: Criminal case and attorney's remuneration]. (2015). Hôgaku Seminâ *[Legal Seminar], 60*(3), 121.

Bray, R. M., & Noble, A. M. (1978). Authoritarianism and decisions of mock juries: Evidence of jury bias and group polarization. *Journal of Personality and Social Psychology, 36*(12), 1424–1430. https://doi.org/10.1037/0022-3514.36.12.1424.

Cacioppo, J. T., Petty, R. E., Kao, C. F., & Rodriguez, R. (1986). Central and peripheral routes to persuasion: An individual difference perspective. *Journal of Personality and Social Psychology, 51*(5), 1032–1043. https://doi.org/10.1037//0022-3514.51.5.1032.

de Tocqueville, A., & Lawrence, G. (1966). In J. P. Mayer & M. Lerner (Eds.), *Democracy in America*. New York, NY: Harper & Row.

Denissen, J. J. A., Geenen, R., Van Aken, M. A. G., Gosling, S. D., & Potter, J. (2008). Development and validation of a Dutch translation of the big five inventory (BFI). *Journal of Personality Assessment, 90*(2), 152–157. https://doi.org/10.1080/00223890701845229.

Epley, N., & Gilovich, T. (2006). The anchoring-and-adjustment heuristic. *Psychological Science, 17*(4), 311–318. https://doi.org/10.1111/j.1467-9280.2006.01704.x.

Festinger, L., & Carlsmith, J. M. (1959). Cognitive consequences of forced compliance. *The Journal of Abnormal and Social Psychology, 58*(2), 203–210. https://doi.org/10.1037/h0041593.

Fossati, A., Borroni, S., Marchione, D., & Maffei, C. (2011). The big five inventory (BFI). *European Journal of Psychological Assessment, 27*(1), 50–58. https://doi.org/10.1027/1015-5759/a000043.

Fujita, M. (2003). Kinô suru saiban-in seido no tame ni: Chii ni sa no aru shûdan ishi kettei no kansatsu kara [For functionable saiban-in system: From observation of group decision-making with status difference]. *Hôshakaigaku [Sociology of Law], 59*, 209–226 [in Japanese].

Fujita, M., Hayashi, N., & Hotta, S. (2016). Trust in the justice system: Internet survey after introducing mixed tribunal system in Japan. *Oñati Socio-Legal Series, 6*(2). Online publication; no pagination specified]. Retrieved from http://ssrn.com/abstract=2769587.

Goldberg, L. R. (1990). An alternative "description of personality": The big-five factor structure. *Journal of Personality and Social Psychology, 59*(6), 1216–1229. https://doi.org/10.1037/0022-3514.59.6.1216.

Gosling, S. D., Rentfrow, P. J., & Swann, W. B. (2003). A very brief measure of the big-five personality domains. *Journal of Research in Personality, 37*(6), 504–528. https://doi.org/10.1016/S0092-6566(03)00046-1.

Hahn, E., Gottschling, J., & Spinath, F. M. (2012). Short measurements of personality - validity and reliability of the GSOEP big five inventory (BFI-S). *Journal of Research in Personality, 46*(3), 355–359. https://doi.org/10.1016/j.jrp.2012.03.008.

Hamby, T., Taylor, W., Snowden, A. K., & Peterson, R. A. (2015). A meta-analysis of the reliability of free and for-pay big five scales. *Journal of Psychology: Interdisciplinary and Applied, 150*(4), 422–430. https://doi.org/10.1080/00223980.2015.1060186.

Hartley, J. (2000). Legal ease and "Legalese". *Psychology, Crime & Law, 6*(1), 1–20. https://doi.org/10.1080/10683160008410828.

Heider, F. (1946). Attitudes and cognitive organization. *The Journal of Psychology, 21*(1), 107–112. https://doi.org/10.1080/00223980.1946.9917275.

Ikeda, K. (2010). The structure of institutional trust in governmental administration. (Japanese Political Science Association, Ed.), *Annual Review of Political Science 2010-I: Trust and Distrust in Politics and Administration*. Tokyo: Bokutaku-sha.

Imasaki, Y. (2005). Saiban-in seido no moto ni okeru shinri, hyôgi, hanketsu no arikata ni kansuru shian [A tentative proposal on the practices of trials by saiban-in, deliberation, and judgement]. *Hanrei Taimuzu [The Precedent Times], 1188*, 12–19 [in Japanese].

Japan Federation of Bar Associations. (2013). Kenshû e no torikumi/Saiban-in seido/ Nihon Bengoshi Rengôkai [Activities for training/the Saiban-in system/Japan Federation of Bar Associations]. Retrieved 5 Mar, 2018, from https://www.nichibenren.or.jp/ja/citizen_judge/program/training.html

John, O. P., & Srivastava, S. (1999). The big five trait taxonomy: History, measurement, and theoretical perspectives. *Handbook of Personality: Theory and Research, 2*(510), 102–138 https://doi.org/citeulike-article-id:3488537.

Johnson, D. T. (2002). *The Japanese way of justice : prosecuting crime in Japan*. Oxford: Oxford University Press Retrieved from https://global.oup.com/academic/product/the-japanese-way-of-justice-9780195119862?cc=jp&lang=en.

Justice System Reform Council. (2001). *Recommendations of the justice system reform council: For a justice system to support Japan in the 21st century*. Tokyo: Justice System Reform Council. Retrieved from https://japan.kantei.go.jp/judiciary/2001/0612report.html.

Kamiyama, H., & Oka, S. (2008). Saiban-in saiban ni okeru shinri no arikata (2): Wakariyasui shinri to bengonin no kadai [The way of proceedings in trial by saiban-in(2): Understandable trials and problems for defense coulcils]. *Keijihou Jânaru [Criminal Law Journal], 13*, 55–60 in Japanese.

Kassin, S. M., & Wrightsman, L. S. (1983). The construction and validation of a juror bias scale. *Journal of Research in Personality, 17*, 423–442 Retrieved from http://www.sciencedirect.com/science/article/pii/0092656683900703.

Kobayashi, H. (2007). "Okazari saiban-in" wa muyô: "Shihô kaikaku" wo saikentô seyo [Go away with nominal saiban-in: Reconsider the justice system reform]. *Shûkan Hôritsu Shimbun [Weekly Law News], 1742*, 4 [in Japanese].

Mastor, K. A., Jin, P., & Cooper, M. (2000). Malay culture and personality: A big five perspective. *American Behavioral Scientist, 44*(1), 95–111. https://doi.org/10.1177/00027640021956116.

McCann, S. J. H. (2008). Societal threat, authoritarianism, conservatism, and U.S. state death penalty sentencing (1977-2004). *Journal of Personality and Social Psychology, 94*(5), 913–923. https://doi.org/10.1037/0022-3514.94.5.913.

Mitsui, M., IIda, H., Inouye, M., Ôkawa, S., Satô, H., & Taguchi, M. (2004). Zadankai: Saiban-in seido wo megutte [Roundtable discussion over the saiban-in system]. *Jurist, 1268*, 6–48 [in Japanese].

Myers, B., & Lecci, L. (1998). Revising the factor structure of the juror bias scale: A method for the empirical validation of theoretical constructs. *Law and Human Behavior, 22*(2), 239–256 Retrieved from http://psycnet.apa.org/journals/lhb/22/2/239/.

Na, W., & Marshall, R. (1999). Validation of the "Big Five" personality traits in Korea. *Journal of International Consumer Marketing, 12*(1), 5–19. https://doi.org/10.1300/J046v12n01_02.

Nishimura, T. (2006). Saiban-in seido dônyû ni muketa torikumi: Bengoshikai [Activities for introduction of the saiban-in system: Bar associations]. *Hôritsu No Hiroba [Forum of Law], 59*(10), 27–35 [in Japanese].

Nolen-Hoeksema, S., Fredrickson, B., Loftus, G. R., & Lutz, C. (2014). Atkinson & Hilgard's : Introduction to psychology.

Okazari ni shitewa naranu: saiban-in (shasetsu) [Don't make them figureheads: Saiban-ins (editorial article)]. (2003, September 30). Asahi *Shimbun (Morning Edition)*, p. 2 [in Japanese].

Petty, R. E., & Cacioppo, J. T. (1986). The elaboration likelihood model of persuasion. *Advances in Experimental Social Psychology, 19*, 123–205. https://doi.org/10.1016/S0065-2601(08)60214-2.

Pratto, F., Sidanius, J., Stallworth, L. M., & Malle, B. F. (1994). Social dominance orientation: A personality variable predicting social and political attitudes. *Journal of Personality and Social Psychology, 67*(4), 741–763. https://doi.org/10.1037/0022-3514.67.4.741.

Rammstedt, B., & John, O. P. (2007). Measuring personality in one minute or less: A 10-item short version of the big five inventory in English and German. *Journal of Research in Personality, 41*(1), 203–212. https://doi.org/10.1016/j.jrp.2006.02.001.

Robie, C., Brown, D. J., & Bly, P. R. (2005). The big five in the USA and Japan. *Journal of Management Development, 24*(8), 720–736. https://doi.org/10.1108/02621710510613744.

Saito, Y. (2007). Saiban-in seido dônyû ni muketa torikumi no genjô: Saibansho [The status of activities for introduction of the saiban-in system: The Court]. *Hôritsu No Hiroba [Forum of Law], 60*(12), 21–27 [in Japanese].

Schulze, R., & Roberts, R. D. (2006). Assessing the big five. *Zeitschrift für Psychologie, 214*(3), 133–149. https://doi.org/10.1026/0044-3409.214.3.133.

Soto, C. J., & John, O. P. (2016). The next big five inventory (BFI-2): Developing and assessing a hierarchical model with 15 facets to enhance bandwidth, fidelity, and predictive power. *Journal of Personality and Social Psychology*. https://doi.org/10.1037/pspp0000096.

The Supreme Court of Japan. (2009). Saiban-in saiban no shinri, hyôgi oyobi hanketsu ni tsuite (shian)(shin-ban) [Trials, deliberations, and written judgment of trials by saiban-in (tentative proposition)(new version)]. *Hanrei Taimuzu [The Precedent Times], 60*(7), 53–62 [in Japanese].

The Supreme Court of Japan. (2017a). *Saiban-in keikensha tou ni taisuru ankêto kekka hôkokusho (Heisei 28 nendo) [The report of questionnaire surveys for those who experienced saiban-in or other related roles (FY 2016)]*. Tokyo: The Supreme Court of Japan [in Japanese]. Retrieved from http://www.saibanin.courts.go.jp/vcms_lf/h28-a-1.pdf

The Supreme Court of Japan. (2017b). *Saiban-in seido no un'yô ni kansuru ishiki chôsa [The consciousness survey cocerning the operation of the saiban-in system]*. Tokyo: The Supreme Court of Japan [in Japanese]. Retrieved from http://www.saibanin.courts.go.jp/vcms_lf/28-i-1.pdf

The Supreme Public Prosecutor's Office. (2009). *Saiban-in saiban ni okeru kensatsu no kihon hôshin [Basic policies of the proscution in* trial *by saiban-in]*. Tokyo: The Supreme Public Prosecutor's Office [in Japanese].

Tyler, T. R., & Huo, Y. J. (2002). *Trust in the law: Encouraging public cooperation with the police and courts. Russell Sage Foundation series on trust*. New York: Russell Sage Foundation Retrieved from http://search.proquest.com/docview/619994944?accountid=26262.

Wiggins, J. S., & Pincus, A. L. (1992). Personality: Structure and assessment. *Annual Review of Psychology, 43*(1), 473–504.

Yonamine, M., & Higashie, K. (1965). Ken'i shugi shakudo no kôsê ni tsuite [On the construct of the authoritarian scale]. Ryûkyû Daigaku Kyôiku Gakubu Kenkyû Kiyô [Bulletin of Faculty of Education, Ryûkyû University], 8, 197–203 [in Japanese].

Zhai, Q., Willis, M., O'Shea, B., Zhai, Y., & Yang, Y. (2013). Big five personality traits, job satisfaction and subjective wellbeing in China. *International Journal of Psychology, 48*(6), 1099–1108. https://doi.org/10.1080/00207594.2012.732700.

Chapter 3
What's in the Deliberations: Two Deliberation Experiments with Status Differences

Background and Objectives

Justice System Reforms

The Headquarters for the Promotion of Justice System Reform was established in December 2001 following the presentation of the recommendations of the Justice System Reform Council on June 12 of the same year (Justice System Reform Council 2001).The Office was divided into various investigative commissions that are carrying out studies prior to the formation of a bill. It is expected that this will include the introduction of a saiban-in system in an attempt to ensure a judicial "popular base." In this system, citizens will deliberate alongside judges regarding "statutory penalties for serious crimes" (Justice System Reform Council 2001, p. 106 in the Japanese version), so as to determine the guilt or innocence of the defendant. In the case that the defendant is guilty, the citizens will also contribute to the determination of the sentence. Based on the target of this reform to the justice system in terms of "planning the construction of a free and fair society in which each and every citizen autonomously fulfils their social responsibility as a governing body," (Justice System Reform Council 2001, p. 4) the participation of citizens in judicial participation has a major significance. If the saiban-in system that bears such significance is achieved, citizens will be participating centrally in criminal justice for the first time since the suspension of jury law in 1943, more than half a century ago. With the introduction of the saiban-in system, citizens will be expected

---

This chapter was an English translation of Fujita, M. (2003) Kinô suru saiban-in seido no tame ni: Chii ni sa no aru shûdan ishi kettei no kansatsu kara [For functionable saiban-in system: From observation of group decision-making with status difference]. *Hôshakaigaku* [*Sociology of Law*], *59*, 209–226. The author thanks The Japanese Association of Sociology of Law and publisher Yûhikaku for their prompt permissions of translating and reproduction. This study was supported by a grant KAKENHI No. 02 J00538 which was disbursed by the Japan Society for the Promotion of Science

M. Fujita, *Japanese Society and Lay Participation in Criminal Justice*,
https://doi.org/10.1007/978-981-10-0338-7_3

to "make an independent and substantial contribution to court judgments by cooperating with judges while distributing responsibilities." (Justice System Reform Council 2001, p. 102) For the introduction of the saiban-in system to realize above described expectations and to achieve the targets, studies are required to investigate whether it is possible for citizens to collaborate with judges to engage independently and substantially in deliberations during actual deliberations. To that end, the dynamics of the deliberations must also be studied. Given the dynamics of deliberations, the extent to which participants in deliberations are able to speak must be investigated by observing actual deliberation processes. However, such studies have not been sufficiently conducted up to this point. Therefore, in this study, the objective was to obtain fundamental data in order to study the saiban-in system by creating a mock saiban-in system. Also, in order to have a functional saiban-in system, the ideals of deliberations were considered in order for both parties to be able to independently and substantially participate in the deliberations.

Saiban-in System Introduced: Will the Division of Roles Take Place?

In this study, in order for the saiban-in system to correctly function so that citizens can "make an independent and substantial contribution to court judgments by cooperating with judges while distributing responsibilities," an appropriate division of roles was deemed to be necessary in which both the judge and the saiban-in can demonstrate their individual roles and fulfil their duties. That is, in the case of introducing the saiban-in system, during deliberations, it is expected that the role of judges, who are legal professionals, and the role of citizens, who are presumed to be unfamiliar with the law, will be different. In terms of "cooperating with judges while distributing responsibilities," participants can expect at least the following two roles during deliberations. The first is for the judge to take the role of leading the legal discussions and to provide legal knowledge. The other is the role of citizens to present their viewpoints in the deliberation based on their life experiences, that is, to show "healthy social awareness."

If the judge uses his status to make other members involved in the deliberation conform to his opinion, the reflection of a "healthy social awareness" in the deliberation will prove to be difficult, because citizens will struggle to speak in a way that can be incorporated by the judge. Therefore, a study is required in order to find the actual influences exerted by the participants in the deliberation. In order to do this, this study is investigating the contents of utterances during deliberations.

Among the people who exert "social influence" on other people, in the narrow sense of "social influence," there are those who conform to other people and those who make other people conform. Regarding this narrow sense of social influence,

Deutsch and Gerard (1955) classified normative influence and informational influence. Normative influence refers to "the influence from conforming to the normative expectations of other people," and informational influence refers to "the influence of using information acquired from other people as evidence of reality." People familiar with the law may use the status of familiarity to exercise normative influence. However, if it is frequently observed that this status is used to make others conform, it will be difficult for the saiban-in system to achieve its anticipated objectives.

Yet informational influence can be used by both legal professionals and citizens. That is, legal professionals can exercise their influence by speaking of the details of events and through solid legal knowledge and reasoning. On the other hand, it is possible for citizens to exert an influence when their perspective on the event is recognized. Whether this can actually be achieved was a subject for observation in this study.

Study Method and Details

In this study, an experiment of group decision-making was conducted. In this experiment, deliberations were carried out between law department students in the third grades (juniors) or above and students in general education programs in order to observe the deliberation process. The processes in deliberations between students are thought to differ to deliberations between actual judges and citizens. However, there were difference of knowledge between the students groups, and the difference may be a difference of normative influence among the student groups. That is, students with legal knowledge are in a superior position in terms of having the more considerable legal knowledge and being able to promote the deliberation and exercise other influence on the deliberation and members of the group. The form of the deliberations is thus believed to be similar to the saiban-in system, and, in the regard of the differentiation of the amount of legal knowledge, the study can offer significant expertise.

In an effort to consider the aforementioned division of roles, an observation was made as to whether the law students would supply legal knowledge. Regarding the social influences during the deliberation, an observation was made as to the frequency of speech after categorization and the connection between the initial distribution of the verdict and the group verdict. Furthermore, a follow-up survey was conducted into opinions of the trial system. In order to study these opinions, a comparison was made between the behaviors and responses of the participants in the "group condition" and "individual condition." The participants who were assigned to "group condition" were actually discussed among participants while the participants in the "individual condition" did not discuss with other participants.

Method

The experiment was conducted between June 18 and July 9, 2001, at the Faculty of Letters in Hokkaido University.

Participants and Design

1. Group Condition

One hundred and fifty students from Hokkaido University participated in the group condition (100 male, 50 female). Among these, 50 were third or fourth year Department of Law students, or postgraduate students from the Graduate School of Law (referred to hereafter as "law students"), and the remaining 100 students were first or second-year students from other departments (referred to hereafter as "general education students"). In the experiment, there were six people in each group. Of the six group members, two were law students, and four were general education students. There were a total of 25 groups.

Individual Condition

There were 33 first and second-year students from Hokkaido University (21 male, 12 female). Each time, approximately 1–4 people were separately seated so that they could not see each other's replies, and, without speaking, they answered individually as to whether the defendant was guilty or innocent until the end of the experiment.

Procedure

1. Group Condition

After receiving the participants at the meeting place, they were led to a classroom. The classrooms were provided with face-to-face desks numbering from 1 to 6 in order from the far right. The students were seated in order with the law students in seat 1–2 and general education students in seats 3–6. Then, the researcher explained the details of the experiment. The researcher distributed a booklet comprising a paper with the summary of the criminal trial records (referred to hereafter as "court records") and the judgment points (referred to hereafter as "judgment points"), and some blank paper for their notes. The participants read the materials after receiving a simple explanation of the court records. Then, the researcher provided an oral explanation with reference to the "judgment points." With reference to the above materials, each participant then made a judgment of guilty/not guilty on the answer paper without talking to anyone and stated their confidence in their answer. The researcher collected the answer papers and then distributed a single group answer paper. Next, the researcher told the participants that the group included students in their third year or above from the Law Department and first and second-year students from other departments. At that time, it was specified who were law students and who were general education students. After these instructions, the participants engaged in deliberation in order to make a judgment of guilty or not guilty over the case, and they were asked to use the group answer paper to write down the answer and to respond to questions about their level of confidence and the way of proceeding with the deliberation. A "unanimous" verdict was required in order to reach a conclusion in the deliberation. The researchers announced the start of the deliberation and left the students in the classroom. The deliberation was recorded using a video camera with the consent of the participants. The deliberation time was 35 min. An allowance of between five and a maximum of 15 min. was given, and, if there was still no judgment, the group was taken to be undecided (hung). After the participants had filled in the group answer paper, the researcher collected all of the forms and distributed the follow-up survey questionnaires. The main content of the follow-up survey checked the understanding of the details of the case, personal judgments following the group reply, the details of the group deliberation, the prioritization of opinions, specialist evaluations, and knowledge and opinions of the saiban-in system. After all, participants had replied, the researcher told the participants not to disclose the details of the experiment until all the experiments had finished, after which the experiment was brought to an end.

Individual Condition

The procedure was the same as that of the Group Condition up to the reading of court records and the explanation of the judgment points. In the Individual Condition, the replies were made without any discussion. The guilty or not guilty answer paper was distributed and collected for the second time. For the second reply, the participants were told that it was not necessary to change the answer. Later, the participants responded to the follow-up survey, and the experiment was brought to a close after being instructed not to talk about it.

(3) The court records used as the stimuli in this experiment. The "court records" were summaries of courtroom dramas (exchanges between the witness and the prosecutor/defense counsel) based on records from actual criminal case trials, and the issue was whether the defendant was a co-principal in a case of blackmail. The stimulus used in this experiment may differ to those used in the actual saiban-in system, which is expected to be "serious cases," which is thought to be one limit of this study. The reason for this is that the recommendations of the Justice System Reform Council were presented during the implementation period of this study

(June 12, 2001), which stated that the cases handled with the introduction of the saiban-in system would include serious cases. The specific scope of "serious cases" has yet to be discussed, and the situation is still unsettled. Cases handled in "court records" are not cases in which the problem is a conflict over legal interpretation but, rather, are issues on which the conclusion depends on the method of accurate recognition. A plan was made so that the court records used would produce a roughly equal split between judgments of guilty or not guilty regardless of legal knowledge. The objective of the experiment was to observe the division of roles and the cooperative relationship between those with legal knowledge and those without legal knowledge. Issues that produce consistent responses among those with legal knowledge are likely to be resolved through the application of legal expertise; however, cases in which the evidence makes it clear whether the party is guilty or not guilty can be determined on the basis of evidence without relying on a "healthy citizen sensibility." This matter was secured by allowing students from the Department of Law and from the Department of Behavioral System Sciences (social psychology) to read the court records and to make a judgment of guilty or not guilty prior to the experiment after the production of the trial records. In this experiment, the breakdown of the replies of the law students prior to the deliberation was 18 guilty (36.7%), and 31 not guilty (63.3%), while the breakdown of the replies of general education students was 40 guilty (41.7%), and 56 not guilty (58.3%), so, in view of the instruction to "presume innocence," the initial distribution was roughly equal. In this distribution, there was no significant difference between law students and general education students. In the chi-squared test, $\chi^2(1) = 0.33$, *n.s.*, which provided a statistical confirmation of this result.

Results

Speech Analysis

(1) As stated in the overall analysis of the speech count, in order for the "healthy social awareness" of citizens to be reflected in the deliberation, saiban-ins must be able to state their opinions during the deliberation sufficiently. That is, as each saiban-in reflects his or her background in the deliberations, the aim of a functional saiban-in system requires that each saiban-in is given sufficient speech opportunities. Therefore, the frequency of speech was counted in order to measure the opportunities for speech opportunities presented in this study. The speech frequency analytical target was used because this study needs to balance with the analytical targets of speech frequency in past studies in this field including Hastie et al. (1983) and Kaplan and Martin (1999), and also to ensure relative objectivity in terms of the indicators of speech analysis. The total speech count was calculated, as well as the total speech count of both parties among the law students and the general education students, the average speech count per group, and the average speech count per

Table 3.1 Average utterances per group and per capita for law faculty students, freshmen and sophomores and results of t-tests

	Law faculty students	Freshmen and sophomores	t	p
Average utterances per group	50.80 (21.70)	43.16 (24.49)	1.17	*n.s.*
Average utterances per capita	25.40 (10.85)	10.79 (6.12)	5.86	< .01

Note: Figures in parentheses indicates standard deviations. $N = 25$, $df = 48$

Table 3.2 Categories for utterances

1	The utterances concerning the facts in the witness
2	Guess and elaboration based on the witness
3	Referring to social or group norm
4	Referring to personal norm or values
5	Expression of preference for the verdict
6	Pressing to conform to approve the group decision
7	Other pressing utterances
8	Referring to procedure or legal rules
9	Referring to inadmissible evidence
10	Making a story on the case
11	Referring to the evidence from the viewpoint whether it supports his or her opinion on verdict preference
12	Proceeding the deliberation
13	Providing with the legal knowledge
14	Voting (with expression of the verdict preference of all group members)
15	Other

person on the basis of the total speech count. In order to check for any differences in total speech count between law students and general education students, a comparison was made of the average values by means of a *t*-test (Table 3.1). As a result, there was no difference in speech count between law students and general education students. On the other hand, when looking at the speech count per law student and per general education student, the law students had a higher frequency of speech than general education students.

Influences and Division of Roles

Regarding the categorization of speech, based on the categorization table for conversational analysis by Hastie et al. (1983) and Kaplan and Martin (1999), the speech in the deliberation was classified into 15 categories (Table 3.2). The former produces categories for the process of understanding the evidence in the deliberation. The methods of proceeding with deliberations among juries include the "verdict driven" and the "evidence driven." The characteristic of the "verdict driven" is to first vote guilty or not guilty in the process of making a verdict, and then to

Table 3.3 Average utterances concerning normative influence per group

	Normative influence utterances
Law faculty students	1.28 (2.03)
Freshmen and sophomores	0.20 (0.41)

Note: $t(26) = 2.61$, $p = .02$. Figures in parentheses are standard deviations

Table 3.4 Average utterances concerning informational influence per group

	Informational influence utterances
Law faculty students	34.56 (16.18)
Freshmen and sophomores	39.20 (17.94)

Note: $t(48) = -0.96$, *n.s.* Figures in parentheses are standard deviations

consider the evidence appearing in the case from the perspective of whether it supports the assertion of the jurors. On the other hand, in the "evidence driven," voting is not as frequent as in the verdict driven, and the evidence appeared in the case is used to organize the story of the case. The categories of Hastie et al. (1983) are categorized from a perspective that gives consideration to the different varieties of speech in the two styles of deliberation. These categories conform to Categories 10–15 in Table 3.2. On the other hand, the categories of Kaplan and Martin (1999) were produced from a perspective of the influence exerted by the participants during the deliberation. That is, they are categorized from a perspective that divides normative influence and informational influence, which corresponds to Categories 1–9 in Table 3.2. The frequency of speech was counted according to the categories as classified above. Speech that corresponds to multiple categories is counted once for each category. However, the overall speech count prior to categorization was counted only once. The speech was observed entirely by two independent observers. When the categorization of the two observers differed, the most appropriate category was applied through discussions between the two observers. In this way, the speech count of normative influence and informational influence was counted, and a comparison of the average speech count per group of law students and general education students is shown in Tables 3.3 and 3.4. In these results, law students produced significantly greater normative influence speech than general education students. On the other hand, there was no difference between the two parties in terms of the production of speech with informational influence.

Reflecting a "Healthy Social Awareness: Opinions of General Education Students

"Healthy social awareness" is a general term that refers to the thoughts, perspectives and the knowledge of social life that is unique to citizens. Therefore, Categories 2, 3, 10 and 11 shown in Table 3.2 are considered as corresponding to the speech

Table 3.5 Total numbers of utterances and average and standard deviations of utterances per group for categories 2, 3, 10 and 11

	2, 3, 10, 11	Categories other than the left column	Total
Law faculty students	25.96 (12.34) (34.5%)	48.60 (19.50)(65.5%)	74.56(28.17)
Freshmen and sophomores	26.28 (10.08) (42.0%)	38.64 (20.66)(58.0%)	64.92(28.67)
Total	52.24 (15.87) (38.0%)	87.24 (27.62)(62.0%)	139.48(37.89)

Table 3.6 The result of the *t*-test for the utterances concerning categories 2, 3, 10 and 11

	Law faculty students	Freshmen and sophomores	*t*	*p*
Frequencies of utterances in categories 2, 3, 10 and 11	25.96 (12.34)	26.28 (10.08)	0.10	*n.s.*

Table 3.7 Frequencies of utterances concerning category 4

	4	Categories other than the left column	Total
Law faculty students	15 (0.8%)	1849 (99.2%)	1864
Freshmen and sophomores	25 (1.4%)	1598 (98.6%)	1623
Total	40 (1.1%)	3447 (98.9%)	3487

Table 3.8 The result of the *t*-test for the utterances concerning category 4

	Law faculty students	Freshmen and sophomores	*t*	*p*
Frequencies of utterances in category 4	0.60 (1.15)	1.00 (2.27)	0.09	*n.s.*

needed in order to demonstrate a "healthy social awareness," that is, speech that offers one's own ideas and knowledge, and the average frequency of speech per group that corresponds to this category was calculated in order to make a comparison of the average frequency among law students and general education students (Tables 3.5 and 3.6). For general education students, 40% of the total speech count was speech relating to one's own ideas and knowledge. When comparing this speech count to that of law students, the ratio among law students for speech expressing ideas or knowledge is either the same or more. With the introduction of a saiban-in system, the concern is that the subjective speech of citizens will be incorporated into the deliberation, or that much of the speech will not be permissible in the judgment in the trial. It was investigated whether general education students actually produce such speech. Individually, the frequency of Category 4 speech and the count of Category 9 speech were researched (Tables 3.7 and 3.8). For each of these, a comparison was made between the ratio of overall speech and the speech count per group of law students and general education students, which is shown in Tables 3.9

Table 3.9 Frequencies of utterances concerning category 9

	9	Categories other than the left column	Total
Law faculty students	36 (1.9%)	1828 (98.1%)	1864
Freshmen and sophomores	37 (2.3%)	1586 (97.7%)	1623
Total	73 (2.1%)	3414 (97.9%)	3487

Table 3.10 The result of the *t*-test for the utterances concerning category 9

	Law faculty students	Freshmen and sophomores	*t*	*p*
Frequencies of utterances in category 9	1.44 (1.55)	1.48 (1.50)	0.09	*n.s.*

Table 3.11 Frequencies of utterances concerning category 12

	12	Categories other than the left column	Total
Law faculty students	332 (17.8%)	1532 (72.2%)	1864
Freshmen and sophomores	72 (4.4%)	1551 (95.6%)	1623
Total	404 (11.6%)	3083 (88.4%)	3487

Table 3.12 The result of the *t*-test for the utterances concerning category 12

	Law faculty students	Freshmen and sophomores	*t*	*p*
Frequencies of utterances in category 12	13.28 (8.88)	2.88 (3.96)	5.35	< .01

and 3.10. From these results, while subjective speech and speech regarding evidence that cannot be used in the trial was observed among general education students, it was less than 4% of the total. In comparison with law department students, there was no difference in the speech count of this type. In connection to law students, Category 4 and 9 speeches were observed, but such speech was used in order to respond to similar speech from general education students, excluding in Settings 2 and 3, and such speech was not produced spontaneously by the law students.

The Role of Law Students

As to who took the lead in promoting the deliberation, of the above categories, the frequency of Category 12 "Speech to promote discussion" was counted in order to study the frequency of speech during the deliberation. The ratio comprising the overall speech count and a comparison with the speech count of general education students in this category are shown in Tables 3.11 and 3.12. In this way, law students produced significantly more speech for the progress of the deliberation. As to taking

Table 3.13 The responses by law faculty students to questions on legal matters raised by freshmen and sophomores

	Law faculty students	Freshmen and sophomores	Response rate
Frequency	69	62	89.9%

the lead in the deliberation, when general education students produced Category 4 and Category 9 speech, it was observed that law students prevented such speech from entering the judgment of guilty/not guilty in the deliberation, or it just became part of the conversation at that time. Law students took the lead in the deliberation by not proactively raising such speech during the deliberation. Also, one expected role of law students was to supply legal knowledge, but whether this actually took place or not is a subject for a future study. When looking at the speech categories, questions relating to legal matters such as trial procedures and the real approach to trials are classified as Category 8 "References to procedures/references to legal rules." The display of legal knowledge and responses to legal questions by law departments students are classified as Category 13 "Supply of legal knowledge." Speech by general education students classified as Category 8 includes speech in which it is considered that the law students are being questioned, and the responses of law students in this regard are classified as Category 13 (Table 3.13). In summary of the above, law students have a higher speech count per person, a higher count of speech with normative influence per group, and they took the lead in the deliberations. Also, law students provided legal knowledge during the deliberation when necessary.

Influence of Differences in Status on the Verdict

In order to research the effect of social influences on the verdict, an analysis was conducted using Davis (1973)'s Social Decision Scheme. The Social Decision Scheme refers to an analytical framework in which a process of harmonizing the deliberation by the group is simplified into a process that is the same as voting. In this framework, the opinion of each group member prior to the deliberation in contrasted with the group verdict in order to consider how to describe the rules between these two events. In the results of this study, the verdict is frequently described as a majority-led summary. That is, of the total of 25 groups, in 17 groups (68%), the opinions of the majority prior to the start of deliberations became the verdict of the group. This result conforms to the results of prior research into group decision making, in which "the decision of the group regarding issues where the solution is not clear is likely to fall under the main count of the initial majority." (Laughlin 1980; Laughlin and Ellis 1986).

Table 3.14 Question items

1	To what extent do you think it is appropriate to introduce a system like this (1: Not appropriate at all - 7: Highly appropriate)
2	To what extent do you think citizens utter in the deliberations if a system like this was introduced? (1: Not at all - 7: Highly possible)
3	Do you think actual sentencing will reflect citizens' opinions if a system like this was introduced? (1: Not at all - 7: Highly reflected)
4	To what extent do you think judgments under this system would be fair? (1: Not at all - 7: Very fair)
5	To what extent do you think the miscarriage of justice would be reduced if a system like this was introduced? (1: Not at all - 7: It reduces very much)
6	Which rule is do you think fair, the majory rule or unanimity rule? (1: Absolutely majority - 7: Absolutely unanimity)
7	Which rule do you think should be adopted, the majory rule or unanimity rule? (1: Absolutely majority - 7: Absolutely unanimity)

Table 3.15 The result of the *t*-tests for the opinions held by the participants

	Law faculty students	Freshmen and sophomores	*t*	*p*
Introduction is appropriate	3.84 (1.72)	4.67 (1.46)	3.04	< .01
Citizens will utter	4.40 (1.34)	4.79 (1.63)	1.34	*n.s.*
Citizens' opinions will be reflected	3.88 (1.54)	4.03 (1.54)	0.57	*n.s.*
The judgments by the system are fair	3.52 (1.30)	4.13 (1.41)	2.49	< .02
Miscarriage of justice will reduce	2.96 (1.27)	3.65 (1.31)	3.02	< .01
Fair: majority or unanimity	4.38 (1.84)	5.15 (1.38)	2.56	< .02
Adopt: majority or unanimity	4.35 (1.92)	4.63 (1.34)	0.95	*n.s.*

Questionnaire Results

In order to look at the differences in perspectives and opinions between law students and general education students (group condition) in connection to the saiban-in system, a t-test was conducted. The test was performed to calculate the average values for each question regarding the opinions of the saiban-in system in the follow-up survey (Table 3.14). Table 3.15 shows the results. Table 3.16 shows the correlation between each question for law students. There was a correlation between the evaluation of the validity of introducing a saiban-in system and opinions as to the extent to which the opinions of citizens were reflected. With regard to general education students, it was noticed that there was some correlation between the evaluation of the validity of introducing a saiban-in system and opinions about whether citizens were able to produce speech. From this, in the case that a law student highly regards the introduction of a saiban-in system, the reflection of the opinions of citizens in

Table 3.16 The correlation coefficients between opinions and appropriateness

Law faculty students	*r*	*p*
Citizen will utter x Appropriate to introduce	0.14	*n.s.*
It reflects opinions x Appropriate to introduce	0.31	< .05
Freshmen and sophomores	*r*	*p*
Citizen will utter x Appropriate to introduce	0.17	< .1
It reflects opinions x Appropriate to introduce	0.06	*n.s.*

Table 3.17 The correlation coefficients between citizens' possibility of utter in deliberations and citizens' opinion will be reflected

	r	*p*
Law faculty students	0.22	*n.s.*
Freshmen and sophomores	0.33	< .01

Table 3.18 The correlation coefficients between evaluations of the atmosphere of discussion and evaluation of the system

Law faculty students	*r*	*p*
Friendly x Appropriate to introduce	–0.14	*n.s.*
Friendly x the system is fair	–0.12	*n.s.*
Freshmen and sophomores	*r*	*p*
Friendly x Appropriate to introduce	0.21	< .05
Friendly x the system is fair	0.24	< .05

the judgment is emphasized more than the production of speech by citizens. Conversely, general education students are deemed to evaluate the validity of the introduction of a saiban-in system more from the perspective of whether citizens are able to produce speech. Table 3.17 shows the results for general education students. A correlation was observed between opinions about whether citizens were able to produce speech and opinions about whether the opinions of citizens were reflected. From this, it is possible that law students consider the speech of citizens as being separate from the reflection of the opinions of citizens in judgments. On the other hand, general education students either consider that the production of speech by citizens leads to the reflection of opinions of citizens, or they may consider both parties as being equal. Finally, it was investigated as to whether the atmosphere of discussions in the experiment influenced the evaluation of the introduction of the saiban-in system and the justice of a system such as a saiban-in system. The correlation was calculated between questions regarding the atmosphere of discussions between law students and general education students, questions regarding the validity of introducing a system such as a saiban-in system, and questions about the justice of such a system (Table 3.18). From the above results, no correlation was seen among law students for the atmosphere of discussions and the sense of validity and justice of this system, yet a correlation was observed among general education students. Therefore, the atmosphere of the discussions in the experiment had no particular influence on law students with regard to the saiban-in system, and opinions and evaluations of the saiban-in system were made calmly. On the other hand, for general education students, the atmosphere of the deliberations is likely to have had an effect on their opinions and evaluations of the saiban-in system. That is because the discussions were calm, the saiban-in system was felt to be positive, and it is likely that the questions about the saiban-in system were evaluated highly.

Comparison of General Education Students (Group Condition) and General Education Students (Individual Condition)

In the investigation of whether opinions about the saiban-in system were altered (Table 3.19) through the experience of these discussions, in the comparison between general education students in the group condition and the individual condition, a difference was observed only with regard to the extent to which the opinions of citizens were reflected.

Discussion

The Needs of a Functional Saiban-in System

It cannot be said that there is a difference in the average speech count between law students and general education students per group. It suggests that citizens will be able to speak during deliberations and that discussions will arise during deliberations. Indeed, in this study, the average speech count of law students was slightly higher. In this regard, law students took the lead in deliberations and often spoke in order to supply legal knowledge. Therefore, it is believed that speech in connection with the facts of the case and the findings can be inferred thereby do not cause any remarkable disparity due to the presence of legal knowledge.

In this experiment, law students had a significantly higher speech count related to normative influence. That is, law students, as persons with high status, made significantly more speech that had a normative influence. Let us extrapolate this to an actual saiban-in system; when judges and citizens participate together in deliberations, the judge is highly likely to exert a normative influence with his status in comparison to the citizen, which is unrelated to the details of the case. However, only 1/27th of the speech count of law students that had a normative influence was classified as having informational influence. In this way, most of the speech during

Table 3.19 The result of the *t*-tests for the freshmen's and sophomores' opinions by the condition

Freshmen and sophomores	Group	Individual
Introduction is appropriate	4.67 (1.46)	4.64 (1.73)
Citizens will utter	4.79 (1.63)	4.82 (1.65)
Citizens' opinions will be reflected +	4.03 (1.54)	4.55 (1.42)
The judgments by the system are fair	4.13 (1.41)	4.03 (1.31)
Miscarriage of justice will reduce	3.65 (1.31)	3.61 (1.37)
Fair: majority or unanimity	5.15 (1.38)	4.76 (1.38)
Adopt: majority or unanimity	4.63 (1.34)	4.15 (1.72)

Note: + indicates the averages differ at 10% level between the conditions

the deliberation was related to the details of the case, which suggests that there were sufficient discussions in connection with the case.

Division of Roles: Is It Possible to Reflect the Sound Social Awareness of Citizens?

When looking at the overall speech count, general education students as a total group of four persons produced speech to the extent that was in no way inferior to law students. On the other hand, when investigating the categorized speech count, a little over 40% of the speech of general education students was related to one's own ideas and knowledge. In comparison, law students produced approximately 35% of such speech, so general education students spoke more about their own ideas. The speech of general education students that "must not come out in the trial" comprised no more than 4% of the total speech of general education students. With regard to the measures taken by law students in connection with such speech, this speech was not directly excluded. In the study of leadership in the deliberation, from the investigation of the speech count in the 12 categories mentioned above, the law students took on the primary role of promoting the deliberation. When looking at how the verdict was determined, the general tendency for a majority-led verdict was not surpassed by the status difference between law students and general education students. Even in the actual saiban-in system, it is thought that the judge will cooperate to help citizens while offering legal expertise when necessary in order to promote the deliberation.

For a Functional Saiban-in System

In this experiment, it was observed that the law students led the deliberation and provided legal knowledge at appropriate points. That is, the results were positive in the sense that each participant fulfilled his or her role. However, law students had a higher speech count per person, and produced more speech with a normative influence per group, and produced more speech to lead the deliberation. Therefore, in actual saiban-in systems where there is a significant difference in status, it is necessary to consider the distinction between a judge that states his opinion during the deliberation and a judge that acts as a moderator, and that judges are thus aware of consciously encouraging citizens to speak.

Educational Outcomes

We witnessed that no significant statistical difference was seen in opinions regarding saiban-in systems between general education students that participated in deliberations and general education students that did not participate in deliberations. And this may indicate the difficulty of expecting any immediate educational outcomes. However, in order to investigate this point, consideration must be given to the qualitative difference in the experience of imposing an actual punishment on a defendant and the experience of a mock trial situation such as the one used in this study. In order to investigate this matter, this suggests that it is necessary to examine whether the concern for justice is maintained or strengthened after the introduction of a saiban-in system by means of continuous interviews and surveys with deliberation participants.

Features of the Planning of this Experiment

In this study, deliberations were held between two law students and four general education students. Therefore, in these results, the ratio of persons with law knowledge and persons without law knowledge was 1:2. In connection to the fact that the law department students were in their third year or above while the general education students were first or second-year students, the law students had a higher average age (the average age of the law students was 21.2, and the average age of general education students was 19.1). Due to the higher age of law students, the deliberations may have been influenced by both legal knowledge and age. However, in this experiment, participants that were in a superior position in terms of legal knowledge were also in a superior position in terms of age. The difference in status is made more significant in these deliberations among students, although the influence of judges on citizens is believed to be still higher. However, this point must be carefully controlled in a future study in order to consider the effect of status solely.

Another issue is the extent to which an experiment conducted among students can be deemed to be useful to a system that is actually participated in by lawyers and citizens. This is the so-called issue of external validity (Foss 1976). Even in the U.S, where lively research is taking place, most mock jury studies use student participants, and studies that use actual jury candidates as participants comprise no more than 12.5% (Bray and Kerr 1982). Nevertheless, it is well-known that there are systematic disparities to real juries when using students, as they have a strong leniency bias (Sealy and Cornish 1973). Therefore, another issue is how high to regard any study which uses student test subjects. Concerning this point, Hastie et al. (1983, p. 44) stated that (1) mock jury studies conform to reality, (2) the pattern of operational outcomes from experiments are the same as reality, but the quantitative levels of measured values differ from reality, (3) mock jury studies fail to verify effects that actually exist, and (4) the effects are considered from the opposite angle of actual juries in such studies. This study is believed to be valid in terms of (2) because the knowledge gained is from discussions between those with superior legal knowledge and those who do not have legal knowledge. The validity of this evaluation and the existence of the effects advocated by this study are probably issues related to the robustness of the research findings, which must be determined through the accumulation of future experimental studies into saiban-in systems.

Deliberation with Informational Differences

About this Section[1]

The author investigated the effects of information differentials among judicial panel members on group decision-making. Professional judges are exposed to pre-trial information, including inadmissible evidence and testimony. Lay participants, on the other hand, are only allowed to view and evaluate the evidence presented in trials, thereby forming a knowledge gap in regard to evidentiary information and materials. In order to examine the effect of these information gaps on deliberative processes and trial outcomes, a total of 24 civic participants were randomly assigned to three-person groups and deliberated on two false criminal cases. The scenarios that the participants received prior to deliberation varied in the amount of information given. The deliberations were both video-recorded and transcribed. Analysis of the deliberations showed that both shared knowledge among members and unshared knowledge held by the member to whom had been given more information appeared more salient during the deliberative process. Our study suggests that lay participants may be at a disadvantage during deliberation not only because of their lower social influence but also due to their lack of evidentiary information for a given trial.

[1]This section is a reproduction of Fujita, M., & Hotta, S. (2010). The effect of presiding role and information amount differentials among group members on group decision making: Deliberation processes, final decisions, and personality. *International Journal of Law, Crime, and Justice*, *38*, 216–235. The author thanks Elsevier for permitting the reproduction. The author also thanks Professor Hiroshi Fukurai who had greatly assisted at the first time the paper published. This study was supported by a grant KAKENHI no. 2120046 which was disbursed by the Ministry of Education, Culture, Sports, Science and Technology of Japan.

Background and Problems

Information Differentials as a Practical Problem in the Saiban-in System

Japan initiated its newly designed mixed jury system in May 2009 called the saiban-in seido. "Saiban" means a trial or judicial action and "In" (in this context) means members. Thus, "saiban-in" means a judicial panel of civic participants in Japan's justice system. In this adjudicatory system, three professional judges and six lay people participate in judging a criminal case. Many areas of research on problematic issues have also been identified with this new system.

One major problem is the presence of "information differentials" or knowledge gaps among members on the judicial panel. Information differentials refer to the disproportional amount of evidentiary information and legal knowledge between judges on the panel for a criminal case. This discrepancy in legal knowledge and case-specific information constitute one of the difficulties in facilitating an equitable procedural operation of the mixed jury system. Nonetheless, the presence of this problem should not be seen as denying the overall democratic value of the new system.

While we are aware of the apparent differences between professional judges and lay participants in legal knowledge and judicial competence in the interpretation of legal matters, information in regard to the content of a criminal case does not constitute legal knowledge per se. Civic participants are expected to articulate the "common sense judgment of ordinary people" in the deliberation process, so as to make the final outcome of criminal trials to be acceptable by the ordinary people. However, if civic participants are disadvantaged at the outset in the amount of case-specific knowledge and legal expertise, it may be difficult for them to carry out their judicial duties effectively. Despite these differences, serious efforts have been made to accommodate for this shortcoming in order to ensure an equal-footing between both professional judges and civic participants in deliberation (Imasaki 2005a, b).[2]

There has been a lack of recognition of the potential impact of disproportionate amounts of case-specific information between judges on deliberation as one of the most critical issues in the application of the saiban-in system. This may partly be due to the fact that the use of pretrial conference procedures was not critically debated when the saiban-in system was first formally introduced in December 2001. In Japanese criminal trial law, the documentation that professional judges can receive only consist of indictment information prior to the trial date. The dossier of the case is then revealed on the first day of the criminal trial. With the amendment of the criminal procedural law, however, the pretrial conference was introduced before the saiban-in was put into effect.[4] The primary purpose of the pretrial conference was to speed up judicial procedures. This specific policy was declared in the Recommendation of the Justice System Reform Council (Justice System Reform

[2]The saiban-in system is based on saiban-in hô, means "the act related to criminal trials in which saiban-in participate". Articles of saiban-in hô in English can be found in Anderson and Saint (2005).

Council 2001), and a criminal procedural law was amended two years after the Recommendation was issued (Shiibashi 2004). Thus, all saiban-in trials must be accompanied by a pretrial conference, while other types of criminal trials can be conducted without such a conference[3].

Pretrial conferences may create critical information differentials in regard to case-specific information and knowledge between professional judges and saiban-ins due to the fact that the chief judge who also presides over the conference is the same one who also presides over the trial. In drafting the legal framework of the content of the pretrial conference procedures, a proposal was submitted to make the chief judge at the trial different from the presiding judge at the pretrial conference, thereby avoiding the knowledge gap in case-specific information between professional judges and saiban-ins. Policymakers, however, placed a greater emphasis on the need to speed up the trial process, rather than to secure the equality in the amount of information available to judges and lay participants at the trial (Nishimura 2006).[4, 5]

Information Differentials in Group Decision-Making

Problems resulting from information gaps in group decision-making have been addressed by social psychologists specialized in the field of group decision-making studies. They characterize the information differential situation in the saiban-in system as a "hidden profile" situation within their specific discipline.

"Hidden Profile" in Group Decision-Making

Information differentials among group members can be thought as an unequal distribution of information within the group. If the group has some choices from which to pick information and every choice has both advantages and disadvantages, such selective procedures can generate "profiles" of choices for decision-making. We can theoretically assume that there is a profile of choices before the interaction among group members. The profile may not be properly investigated, or the group members may not be aware of it, even after group discussion begins. In this particular situation, the profile is "hidden" for the members of the group. Although members are not aware of the existence of hidden profiles, the distribution of information affects the dynamics of the group decision-making and deliberative processes (Stasser and Stewart 1992).

[3] Criminal Procedural Law, article 316-2, and Saiban-in Act, article 49.

[4] Criminal Procedural Law, article 256, para.6.

[5] The pretrial conference was used in a Japanese criminal trial procedure before WWII, when Japan adopted the inquisitorial system in its criminal procedure. So introducing pretrial conference at his time can be said to be a revival of the pre-war pretrial criminal procedure.

In the hidden profile situation, some pieces of information are held by more than one group member, while others do not. The former is called shared information, while the latter is called unshared information (Stasser 1992, 1999, 2000; Stasser and Stewart 1992; Stasser et al. 1995; Stasser et al. 1989; Stasser et al. 2000; Stasser and Titus 1987). Shared information among group members prior to group discussion and expression of preferences has the power to influence the dynamics of group decision-making (Stasser and Titus 1985).

The reasons that shared information can hold power in the group decision-making process have been previously investigated. In the present research, we are examining the extent of social influence and cognitive centrality from a socio-cognitive network viewpoint. Social influence is one of the major themes in social sciences, and cognitive centrality is examined in the field of network science.

Social Influence in Decision-Making

In decision-making research, two major types of social influence have been identified (Deutsch and Gerard 1955; Kaplan and Miller 1987). One is the informational social influence, and the other is the normative social influence. In short, the former is called informational influence, while the latter is called normative influence.

Informational influence can be described as the influence that comes as an individual seeks information on proper behavior in a specific situation, and the latter is the influence that comes from his or her behavioral conformity "with the positive expectation of another" (Deutsch and Gerard 1955).

In the hidden profile context, the initial preference distribution can be significant sources of normative influence (Henningsen and Henningsen 2003). This is mainly due to the fact that the majority wields social pressure on other group members to conform to its decision. Henningsen and Henningsen (2003) suggested that normative influence is the most potent source of social influence when a clear consensus exists among group members.

In the context of the saiban-in system, there may be two sources of normative influence. One is the power of shared information, as pointed out in Henningsen and Henningsen (2003). The other is the status differences between professional judges and lay participants. Professional judges hold higher status and prestige than most lay participants because of the shared perception that judges possess professional knowledge and skills in the field of law and hold a highly privileged position in society. Lay participants may conform to decisions of professional judges due to their normative influence, especially as the power of normative influence is more significant than informational influence in the hidden profile situation (Cruz et al. 2000).

Cognitive Centrality and Group Decision-Making

Cognitive centrality refers to the extent of information that a select group of members shares with other members. The more information a particular member of a group has, the more "central" that member is regarded within the group. The central member of the group then has more influential power than other members who have less centrality. Kameda et al. (1997) argued that the power is held by the central member regardless of the members' majority/minority status. This is the main reason why cognitive centrality is seen as essential in group decision-making. This is also one of the applications of notions from socio-cognitive network to the group decision-making context (Kameda et al. 1997).

In this part, we decided to focus on the analysis of social influences in group decision-making. We decided not to analyze the effect of the differences in the occupation because we are interested in observing the effect of informational differentials in the deliberation process.

Of course, if we were able to recruit professional judges to participate in this experiment, the external validity would be enhanced, and the generalizability of our research findings can possibly be extended to actual trial settings. Nonetheless, a normative influence which comes from occupational prestige and informational differentials may be confounded in those cross-occupational settings. As we place the greater importance on the analysis of informational differences in this experiment, we did not ask professional judges to participate, nor did we ask participants to reveal their occupation. Thus our mock jury research did not create perceived differentials in social and occupational status among participants, which could possibly jeopardize one of the original purposes of our studies.

Hypotheses

We hypothesized the following outcomes based on the above-cited studies and their socio-psychological considerations. Given that the presiding person has more power in group decision-making, the presiding person will exert more power, even if he or she has less information than other group members.

1. Presiding persons will tend to have more cognitive centrality than other group members.
2. Unshared information held by the chairperson will appear more frequently during the deliberation than unshared information held by the person who does not preside over the deliberation.
3. The effects of discussion in hypothesis 2 will be intensified if the presiding person has high scores on individual personality scales.

Experimental Design

To create a gap in the amount of information obtained among trial participants, we prepared two kinds of scenarios: one was the "complete scenario," and the other which contained two forms of "deleted scenarios." The two "deleted scenarios" were directly extracted from the original "complete scenario." Different points within the two forms of "deleted scenarios" were also deleted without producing logical inconsistency. Each participant was assigned to one of the three scenarios without knowing which type of scenario they were assigned. The deleted points were the "unshared" information on the case, while the other points were the "shared" information on the case.

We made two kinds of "unshared" information through scenario manipulation. The first was shared by two out of three members, while the other was held by only one member of the three-person group.

We analyzed the differences between typical points discussed in deliberation and the frequencies of utterances made by members who had "more" information.

We also paid close attention to the decision of who should preside over the deliberation, which was randomly assigned. If we had left this decision to the participants themselves, the participants likely to choose as chairperson the participants with seniority or higher social status. This randomized assignment of the presiding role was used to eliminate the effect of social status or socio-psychological traits in the allocation of power among group participants.

Method

Overview

This experiment was conducted in March 2010. Twenty-four lay people (11 female and 13 male) were asked to participate in this study. The average age of participants was 45.63 years ($sd = 12.62$). The average age of female participants was 45.64 years ($sd = 12.86$), while for males it was 46.62 years ($sd = 12.95$). There were no statistically significant age differences between male and female participants (F (1, 22) = .00, *n.s.*). The average age of each group varied from 40.6 years to 54.0 years. Again, there were no statistically significant age differences among the groups F (7, 16) = .37, *n.s.*).

This experiment was designed, and all materials were prepared by the author.[6] This experiment was conducted in a group interview room equipped with cameras. In this room, participants discussed two fictitious criminal cases and decided on

[6] Nikkei Research is a research company whose head office is located in Tokyo, Japan. The company is specialized in the field of social survey, group interview, marketing research, and area research. The company has a large pool of survey participants (over 160,000 people). For further information on this company, please visit http://www.nikkei-r.co.jp/english/

guilt or innocence of the defendants. They also decided on appropriate sentencing if they reached a guilty verdict.

Participants also answered survey questionnaires regarding their decisions and completed personality and social attitude scales. All answers were analyzed with the use of statistical software. All procedures of this experiment were video-recorded after the consent of participants was obtained. Discussion processes were analyzed through the use of transcriptions of all utterances of participants during deliberation.

Material

Materials used in this experiment include different scenarios, "points of judgment," and survey questionnaires filled out by research participants.

Scenarios

Participants read two different kinds of scenarios on false criminal cases and deliberated on one at a time. Each scenario was two-pages long, on A4 paper (210 mm × 297 mm per sheet).

One scenario described a blackmail case, in which the accused was charged with helping the principal's act of blackmailing by serving as a watchman. One of the main issues, in this case, is whether or not the individual's act of standing by the door of the room of the crime scene can be construed as him acting as the watchman. If this act is viewed as aiding the principal's criminal act by serving a watchman, the accused would then be convicted as an accessory to blackmail, and the sentence should be less than 5 years of imprisonment. But if the act is not viewed as necessarily aiding in the principal's crime, then the accused should be acquitted.

The other scenario described an attempted murder case, in which the accused arrived at the crime scene, (the victim's home), with a kitchen knife in his possession. He then stabbed the victim with the knife. The wound was 1.26 inches in width and 3.94 inches in depth and reached behind the stomach of the victim. The main issue was the presence of malice in the accused individual's act, i.e., whether or not the wound was made intentionally or happened to be caused accidentally during the struggle between the accused and the victim. If the act was viewed as intentional, the accused should be convicted of attempted murder, and the sentence should be imprisonment of more than 2 years and 6 months but less than life imprisonment. But if the act was viewed as accidental, the accused may be convicted of causing a bodily injury, and the sentence should be imprisonment less than 15 years, or a fine of not more than 500,000 yen (i.e., $5000 U.S. dollars).

Each scenario consisted of a complete summary of the criminal case, with summaries of testimonies by the witnesses. Summaries of opening statements, questions to the accused, and closing arguments were omitted in order to allow for sufficient time for the participants to engage in deliberation and consideration of the cognitive load.

"Points of Judgment" of the Case

As participants were not skilled in the field of law, and time for discussion was restricted to 40 min maximum per case, we prepared extra materials that helped them in arriving at their judgments instead of offering oral explanations that would normally be given by the experimenter. We called this document "points of judgment." It described some critical issues to be considered in the case, including the facts and dependency among the issues. It was printed on one A4 sheet.

The "points of the judgment" on the accessory to blackmail case explained that there were two points to be judged in the case. The first point was whether or not the conspiracy of blackmailing was established between the principal and the accused before the principal proceeded with the commission of the crime. The second point was whether or not the accused was just waiting in front of the door of the crime scene, or aiding the principal's act by being a watchman. These "points" also explained factual information which should be considered in order to declare the accused guilty.

Questionnaires

We prepared the following questionnaires: (1) pre-experimental questionnaire, (2) decision-in-person question sheet, (3) decision-by-group question sheet, and (4) post-discussion questionnaire.

At the beginning of the pre-experimental questionnaire, participants were asked to describe their views and opinions about the merits and shortcomings of the new saiban-in system. The same questionnaire also contained the authoritarian 20-item personality scale items (Adorno et al. 1950; Yonamine 1960). This scale is the so-called "F-scale" (intentionality for force). Also included are 10 items of collectivism scale (Yamaguchi et al. 1988and nine items of social power cognition scale (Imai 1987). This questionnaire was four-pages long, excluding the face sheet.

The second questionnaire of the decision-in-person answer sheet was used after the reading of the scenario and "points of judgment," prior to the start of group deliberations. This questionnaire sheet included participants' opinions on the question of their judgments, sentencing, and the level of their confidence in their decisions. This questionnaire and the next one were both one-page length.

The third questionnaire contained similar items contained in the second survey. The fourth questionnaire included 15 recognition items of the case, the decision of the case at the time, emotional state for the accused, and opinions of the group discussions. This questionnaire was five-pages long, excluding the face sheet.

Procedure

Participants were selected from the pool of applicants for the group-interview. The pool was formed by recruitment through an advertisement to participants in social surveys conducted by Nikkei Research. At the time of recruitment, candidates were told that the methods of the social survey could either be an internet questionnaire survey, mail survey, group interview, or other possible means. The candidates were given a choice to pick the method by which they would like to participate. While candidates were not paid for their registration, some of those who registered received book coupons or other small prizes, drawn by lot.

Selected participants who were willing to participate in this experiment received the pre-experimental questionnaire in advance of the experiment itself. They were asked to fill out this questionnaire before showing up at the conference room where the experiment was conducted. Participants were asked to come to the venue at a specified date and time, and those dates and times vary, according to the group to which the participant was assigned.

Before deliberation, all the members of the group and the experimenter were at the table, and the experimenter explained how the experiment would proceed. The table used in this experiment was an appropriate size for a five-person discussion. The placement of the table then forced the participants to face each other, creating the optimum condition for deliberative discussions. The experimenter asked participants to read the material and the "points of judgment." After reading them, each participant was handed the decision-in-person question sheet to compete. The experimenter collected these sheets and instructed participants to begin deliberation on the case. If they could not decide in 25 min, they would be allowed to extend the deliberation by up to 15 additional minutes. They were then asked to decide whether the accused was guilty or not guilty in the blackmail case, or whether or not the accused should be charged with attempted murder in the second case. If they found the accused guilty, they were also asked to decide the sentence. The experimenter asked participants to make group decisions with unanimity if at all possible.

The experimenter also explained the differences among the materials given to participants. In the instructions, the experimenter referred to the differences between the scenarios, but did not specifically refer to the amount of information given or to whom the case information was given In some limited situations; the experimenter was forced to ask the group to decide who should preside over the deliberation. The participants discussed and decided on the chairperson before starting the deliberation.

In some cases, when no member, even the assigned chairperson, was willing to facilitate the deliberation, the experimenter first facilitated the deliberation instead. Nonetheless, the intervention by the experimenter was kept to a minimum. For most of the cases, there was no need for the experimenter to intervene in the deliberation due to a lack of utterances by participants.

After deliberation, the group filled out the decision-by-group answer sheet to describe their judgment, confidence level, and sentencing (if they found the accused guilty). After completing the question sheet, each participant was asked to fill out a post-discussion questionnaire. After completing the first case, all the materials were collected by the experimenter, and the materials for the next case were distributed.

The order of discussing the two scenarios was randomly assigned to each group to avoid an order effect. Half of all groups (four groups) dealt with the blackmail case first, while the other half (the other four groups) deliberated on the attempted murder case first.

Participants were debriefed and dismissed after discussions of the two scenarios and answering all questionnaires. Participants were paid for their participation some weeks after this experiment, through a banking transfer.

Results

Results from Records of Deliberation Processes

All of the deliberation processes were video-recorded and transcribed after the experiment was completed.

The transcription was analyzed for: (1) total frequency of utterances, (2) utterance frequency distribution among members, and (3) coded-points based on shared or not shared information. The transcription of utterances made during deliberations was content analyzed and examined.

Coding Utterances

To analyze the frequencies of utterances of shared/unshared information, all utterances were carefully coded and computerized. Turns of utterances of every participant were counted, regardless of the length of a turn. The turn was defined as a continuous utterance by one person without interruption by other members of the group.

We prepared the following categories mainly to analyze the third point discussed above. The term "shared" information means that the information was shared by all three members of the group, while "unshared" information means the information was not shared by all of the group members.

The codes for categories were as follows:

1. Shared information
2. Unshared information (total)
3. Unshared information which shared by two out of the three members (hereinafter "Unshared information (majority)")

4. Unshared information which is shared by one out of the three members (hereinafter "Unshared information (minority)")
5. Proceeding with the deliberation
6. Statement of the conclusion of guilt or sentencing
7. Reply (e.g., Yes, uh-uh)
8. Miscellaneous (Including a Statement of Opinion except for Conclusion)

In this analysis, importance was attached to whether the information was shared or not. All the categories appeared above can be exclusive of each other, but many utterances held content related to one or more categories. In coding, one utterance could have two or more codes at the same times. Codes of utterances were counted in order to calculate the frequencies of utterances for those categories.

All eight groups in this experiment deliberated on two cases, so there are 16 sets of deliberation records. Tables 3.20 and 3.21 show the results according to the number of turns, assigned scenario, presiding members, first preference of each member, and final verdict of every group.

The second digit of ID indicates the group that the participant attended.

The same ID number indicated the same person.

The categories except for "total frequency" are not exclusive of each other. Sum of numbers of frequencies in every category may exceed the number of "total frequency."

Relative Frequencies of Utterances: Testing Hypothesis 1

Cognitive centrality can be measured by the participation rate of a targeted group member (Kameda et al. 1997). In this analysis, we observed the extent of participation through relative frequencies of utterances. Although relative frequencies may be a somewhat indirect index of measuring cognitive centrality, it is an explicit index and represents to some extent the centrality of a particular participant through the representation of participation rate.

We calculated relative frequencies and percentage points for each participant. The results of this analysis are shown in Table 3.22.

We also compared the frequencies of presiding participants and other participants. As shown in Table 3.3, presiding participants' relative frequencies of utterances are 41.25% while the average of relative frequencies of other participants is 29.15%. A significant difference is shown by conducting ANOVA, with $F(1, 46) = 40.64$, $p < .01$. Presiding participants made utterances about 1.4 times more often than non-presiding participants. This means that the presiding members participated in the deliberations more actively and the extent may be estimated to be about 1.4 times more than non-presiding participants. This supports hypothesis 1.

Table 3.20 Frequencies of all utterances and deliberation results concerning scenario 1 (Black-mail case)

Group No.	ID	Total Freq.	Shared	Unshared (Total)	Unshared (Majority)	Unshared (Minority)	Proceeding	Conclusion	Reply	Misc.	Scenario[a]	Presiding	Initial preferences[b]	Verdict[b]
1	11	113	20	6	5	1	8	14	49	32	c	a	NG	G
1	12	75	13	1	1	0	3	9	27	31	d1		G	
1	13	87	24	3	3	0	3	14	15	30	d2		G	
2	21	39	4	1	1	0	0	7	26	5	c		G	G
2	22	49	6	1	1	0	1	12	22	9	d		G	
2	23	80	24	5	5	0	23	12	13	15	d2	a	NG	
3	31	78	3	0	0	0	15	7	17	44	c	a	G	G
3	32	24	2	0	0	0	1	6	11	8	d		G	
3	33	72	15	0	0	0	1	4	20	36	d2		G	
4	41	71	10	1	1	0	1	12	28	20	c		G	G
4	42	89	19	2	2	0	7	16	21	29	d1	a	G	
4	43	97	21	0	0	0	3	19	29	37	d2		G	
5	51	87	16	4	4	0	2	9	10	48	c		G	G
5	52	110	26	4	4	0	0	8	18	59	d1		NG	
5	53	147	12	4	4	0	10	11	99	16	d2	a	G	
6	61	61	5	0	0	0	1	9	12	35	c		NG	NG
6	62	73	15	0	0	0	7	13	11	32	d1	a	NG	
6	63	81	13	0	0	0	1	8	34	27	d2		G	
7	71	163	22	14	4	10	6	7	27	93	c		NG	H
7	72	177	19	7	6	1	17	5	108	29	d1	a	G	
7	73	100	13	5	5	0	1	7	66	16	d2		G	
8	82	58	12	0	0	0	0	2	38	9	d1		NG	NG
8	83	90	14	2	2	0	23	7	36	21	d2	a	NG	
8	84	50	13	0	0	0	1	5	14	19	c		G	

[a] *c* Complete, *d1* deleted in some points 1, *d2* deleted in some points 2

[b] *G* guilty, *NG* not guilty, *H* hung jury

Every row corresponds to each participant

Table 3.21 Frequencies of all utterances and deliberation results concerning scenario 2 (Attempted murder/injury case)

Group No.	ID	Total Freq.	Shared	Unshared (Total)	Unshared (Majority)	Unshared (Minority)	Proceeding	Conclusion	Reply	Misc.	Scenario[a]	Presiding	Initial preferences[b]	Verdict[b]
1	11	102	22	6	4	2	5	13	24	41	d2	[a]	I	I
1	12	65	10	7	5	2	2	7	15	27	c		I	
1	13	97	22	2	2	0	0	14	20	40	d1		AM	
2	21	30	8	3	3	1	3	3	12	7	d2		AM	AM
2	22	71	15	4	4	0	2	12	20	22	c	[a]	AM	
2	23	62	7	4	4	1	2	8	34	14	d1		AM	
3	31	65	10	1	1	0	8	7	21	26	d2		I	I
3	32	34	3	0	0	0	3	11	9	11	c		AM	
3	33	95	11	0	0	0	3	14	26	42	d1		I	
4	41	122	6	1	1	0	0	16	46	56	d2		AM	AM
4	42	148	9	4	4	0	5	13	68	54	c	[a]	I	
4	43	100	4	6	6	0	1	10	24	54	d1		AM	
5	51	57	6	0	0	0	23	14	9	12	d2	[a]	I	I
5	52	48	7	0	0	0	3	10	14	16	c		I	
5	53	44	5	0	0	0	3	6	27	7	d1		AM	
6	61	82	9	0	0	0	1	12	11	51	d2		I	I
6	62	79	7	0	0	0	16	13	15	28	c	[a]	I	
6	63	114	18	0	0	0	1	14	39	43	d1		AM	
7	71	180	20	6	4	2	26	16	59	63	d2	[a]	AM	AM
7	72	105	9	7	1	6	4	7	58	26	c		AM	
7	73	102	21	2	2	0	1	11	46	27	d1		AM	
8	82	39	3	0	0	0	1	3	30	4	c		I	I
8	83	25	2	0	0	0	0	6	13	4	d1		I	
8	84	49	5	3	3	0	17	9	5	12	d2	[a]	I	

[a] *c* Complete, *d1* deleted in some points 1, *d2* deleted in some points 2

[b] I injury, *AM* attempted murder

Table 3.22 Relative frequencies of utterances for each participant within the group

ID	Scenario 1	Scenario 2
11	41.09%	38.64%
12	27.27%	24.62%
13	31.64%	36.74%
21	23.21%	18.40%
22	29.17%	43.56%
23	47.62%	38.04%
31	44.83%	33.51%
32	13.79%	17.53%
33	41.38%	48.97%
41	27.63%	32.97%
42	34.63%	40.00%
43	37.74%	27.03%
51	25.29%	38.26%
52	31.98%	32.21%
53	42.73%	29.53%
61	28.37%	29.82%
62	33.95%	28.73%
63	37.67%	41.45%
71	37.05%	46.51%
72	40.23%	27.13%
73	22.73%	26.36%
82	29.29%	34.51%
83	45.45%	22.12%
84	25.25%	43.36%

The second digit of ID indicates the group which the participant attended.

Testing Hypothesis 2: Frequency Differences Between Presiding and Non-presiding Participants

To test hypothesis 2, we compared frequency differences between presiding and non-presiding participants in every category defined. The levels for two scenarios were collapsed before the comparison.

According to the results of ANOVA, total frequencies of utterances were significantly different between presiding and non-presiding participants (F (1, 46) = 6.82, $p < .05$). Frequencies related to conclusion were also significantly different (F (1, 46) = 6.84, $p < .05$). Of course, utterances related to proceeding with the deliberation were significantly different between presiding and non-presiding participants (F (1, 46) = 56.84, $p < .01$).

In relation to hypothesis 2, the frequency of utterances on unshared information in two members (majority) of the group showed a marginal difference (F (1, 46) = 3.74, $p = .06$).

Utterances on shared information, unshared information total, and unshared information held by one member of the group (minority) were not significantly different between presiding and non-presiding members of the group (F (1, 46) = 1.54, *n.s.*; F (1, 46) = .28, *n.s.*; F (1, 46) = .22, *n.s.* respectively).

In relation to hypothesis 2, unshared information (majority) was referred to by presiding participants more than by non-presiding group members. This result supports hypothesis 2.

Testing Hypothesis 3: Conducting Two-Way ANOVAs with Setting Presiding and Personality Scales as Independent Variables

For further investigation of the effects of the relationship between presiding/non-presiding and personality scales on frequency of utterances of unshared information (majority), we conducted 2 × 2 ANOVAs on the utterance frequency of unshared information (majority) with dependent variables "presiding or not" and personality scales—authoritarian personality, collectivism, professional power cognition scale, and legitimacy power cognition scale.

To conduct these analyses, we collapsed scores for each scale to two categories. That is, we divided the participants into two categories, "high-score of the scale" and "low-score of the scale." We used the median of the score to divide the participants. Hereafter we show the results of ANOVAs with setting independent variables as "presiding or not presiding" and the scores of two-categorized personality scales.

In relation to authoritarian personality, the interaction of "presiding or not presiding" and authoritarian personality was not significant (F (1, 44) = .91, *n.s.*). But main effects of presiding and authoritarian personalities were significant (F (1, 44) = 4.96, $p < .05$; F (1, 44) = 5.42 < p.05 respectively).

On the effect of collectivism scale, interaction of "presiding or not presiding" and collectivism was not significant (F (1, 44) = .15, *n.s.*). Main effect of presiding was significant, while main effect of collectivism was not significant (F (1, 44) = 5.25, p < .05; F (1, 44) = .93, *n.s.* respectively).

Regarding social power cognition scales, first, we conducted ANOVA with professional power recognition scale. The interaction of "presiding or not presiding" and authoritarian personality was marginally significant (F (1, 44) = 2.88, $p < .1$). Testing the simple main effect, we found the simple main effect of "presiding or not presiding" was significant in the group with "high-scorers" of professional power cognition scale (F (1, 44) = 6.31, $p < .05$). The average frequencies for "high-scorers" of professional power cognition scale was 3.80 with standard error .86 when they presided over the deliberation, while the average frequency was 1.18 with standard error .58 when they did not preside over the deliberation.

Secondly, on the social power cognition scale, we conducted ANOVA with legitimacy social power cognition scale. The interaction of "presiding or not presiding" and legitimacy power cognition scale was not significant (F (1, 44) = 1.63, *n.s.*). The main effect of presiding was marginally significant, while the main effect of legitimacy power cognition scale was not significant (F (1, 44) = 3.63, $p < .1$; F (1, 44) = .93, *n.s.* respectively).

Overall, the power of presiding in raising the participation rate can be said to be highly salient as indicated by the above analyses.

Hypothesis 3 was partially supported by these results. That is, when the presiding participant scored high on the professional power cognition scale, he or she uttered more in the unshared information (majority) condition.

Frequency Difference with Information differences

To compare frequencies of utterances among members of a group who have informational differentials, three types of scenarios were collapsed into two levels of informational categories. The two new categories were "complete scenario" and "deleted scenario." Deleted scenarios removed some critical points of the scenarios from the complete scenario without leading to inconsistency in their stories.

Comparing frequencies of utterances between those two levels, complete and deleted, marginal differences were found in comparing utterances on shared information of the case (F (1, 46) = 2.88, $p < .1$) and unshared information held by one member of the group (F (1, 46) = 3.60, $p < .1$).

Analysis of Deliberation Processes from the Viewpoint of Deliberation Styles

Hastie et al. (1983) identified two types of typical deliberation processes in jury trials: "verdict-driven" and "evidence-driven." Deliberation in the former process starts with expressing preferences of group members. After initial preferences of each juror are stated, members discuss the evidence from the viewpoint of whether or not every piece of evidence supports their argument. From time to time, balloting is conducted in this deliberation style. Deliberation that is "evidence-driven," starts with a discussion of the credibility of the evidence, and then the preferences of group members are discussed.

Fujita (2010) proposes the notion of "issue-driven" be applied to mixed jury deliberations. In the mixed jury system, professional judges lead the deliberation and set the agenda for deliberation. The agenda is made from the perspective of legal professionals on the points of legal issues and on the points of fact-finding. Every critical point has a connection to other issues identified by legal professionals in advance of deliberation. The issues which should be discussed in deliberation, and the connections among those issues, are identified by legal professionals, like algorithms in computer programs. In discussion with issue-driven processes, deliberation starts with referring to the agenda of the case, and issues are discussed in order of the agenda. Every issue on the agenda is judged whether or not the point is acknowledged in the case. Once decided, the decision cannot be overturned after the deliberation proceeds. The final verdict of the group is the result of the accumulation of every decision on the issue.

Viewing these three kinds of deliberative processes, all of the deliberations can be understood as mainly "verdict-driven" with a mixture of "issue-driven" discussions. As we distributed the "points of judgment" paper, we assumed that most groups were going to deliberate with an "issue-driven" style.

But in observing the records of the deliberations, we found that most of the groups started with the expression of first preferences of group members, although they had "points of judgment" which explained the issues and algorithm of the judgment of the case. This implies that "issue-driven" discussion is not a natural style of deliberation for lay participants. They knew they had to reach the final verdict about 20 or 25 min after the start of the deliberation, and the participants chose the "verdict-driven" style of deliberation. Prior studies such as that of Hastie et al. (1983) argue that a "verdict-driven" style of deliberation consumes less time than does an "evidence-driven" style.

Predicting the Verdict from Initial Preferences

Seen from the perspective of Social Decision Scheme advanced by Davis (1973), many group decisions can be understood as "majority-wins." As shown in Table 3.20, seven out of eight group verdicts are predicted by the majority of initial preferences. In Table 3.21, all of the groups reach the verdicts that the majority had expressed in initial preferences.

The results tend to confirm the robustness of the strength of the initial majority in the situation where one of two options must be chosen, even given the differentiation of information on the case. The second case is conceptually a choice among three options of verdicts: "Guilty of attempted murder," "guilty of injury," and "not guilty by lawful self-defense." The accused in the second case prepared a kitchen knife for making sashimi[7] 2 days before the case. The accused hid it in his jacket until he used it to stab the victim. And the accused prepared an attack with a knife that day, so many participants judged that the illegality of act of the accused was not negated by lawful self-defense in this case. Thus, there was a practical choice between two options: attempted murder and injury. Majority-wins strongly appear when the choice is made between two options, even when unanimity is required in group decision-making because the majority cannot compromise with the minority by meeting each other halfway. That may be one of the reasons why majority-wins apparently appeared in the first case of this experiment.

[7] To make sashimi, bones and skins are removed from fish, and fish is secondly needed to be cut in a long and thin shape. Third, the long-and-thin-shaped fish is sliced by a long and narrow bladed knife. So a kitchen knife for making sashimi is normally long and narrow in blade width.

Table 3.23 Correlations between specialty, legitimacy, collectivism, authoritarian scale and utterance frequencies

	Specialty	Legitimacy	Collectivism	Authoritarian
Total Frequencies	–0.16	–0.04	–0.46[a]	–0.36
Shared information	–0.25	–0.09	–0.33	–0.35
Unshared information (total)	–0.25	–0.14	–0.55[a]	–0.50[a]
Unshared information (majority)	–0.14	–0.04	–0.42[a]	–0.29
Unshared information (minority)	–0.30	–0.23	–0.53[b]	–0.56[b]
Proceeding	–0.53[b]	–0.10	–0.26	–0.32
Conclusion	–0.02	–0.01	–0.20	0.01
Reply	0.24	0.24	–0.20	–0.08

[a]means the correlation coefficient is significant at five percent level
[b]means the correlation coefficient is significant at one percent level

Results of Questionnaires

Authoritarian, Collectivism, and Social Power Cognition Scales

To investigate the reliability of each scale, we calculated Cronbach's alpha for each scale. The results were .84, .56, .91, .63 respectively. Cronbach's alpha for overall social cognition scale was .73. No statistically significant differences were observed between female and male participants in those scales (F values were 1.92, .33, .03, and .07 respectively).

Before calculating correlation, utterance frequencies for two scenarios are added into one number. Those correlations were calculated to investigate the relationship between behavioral indices and personality traits.

As shown in Table 3.23, almost all of the correlations, including statistically significant correlation coefficients, are negative with the personality scale items. Starting with the left column of Table 3.23, the specialty scale in social power cognition item significantly correlated with proceeding utterances, while the legitimacy scale has no significant correlations in frequencies of utterances. The collectivism scale also has a statistically significant relation with total frequencies, unshared information (total), unshared information (total) and unshared information (minority).

Discussion

Importance of Presiding Member on the Deliberation Process

In empirical group decision-making research in Japan's saiban-in system, importance has not always been attached to the status difference between presiding persons and the rest of the group members. But as our results showed, the presence of a presiding individual is critical in influencing the participation rate of the other group members.

In the saiban-in system, the presiding person is usually decided in advance of deliberation. If the social situation is one of "equal-footing," the processes of deciding the chairperson can be understood and studied as a negotiation process. But in the mixed jury system, law or other formal social norm decides who should preside over the deliberations. Therefore, it is essential that the system is designed by a formal social norm to facilitate the deliberation process in order to actualize the aims of the system.

Implications for Designing an Ideal Lay Participation Deliberation

If we had a poorly designed jury system, there would be no problem if the aim of the system is merely the participation of the layperson, regardless of the effectiveness of equitable deliberative processes.

But we believe that many lay participation systems share the goal of realizing democracy, and of continuous legal and political education of civic participants, as de Tocqueville (1835) argued. Therefore, active participation in deliberation should be one of the most critical objectives of creating a participatory lay system.

The findings of this study suggest that an essential factor in determining participation is who will be assigned to the position of chairperson. If the person has social influence, his or her social power will be increased in the deliberative process. This might impair the realization of equal participation of citizens with different social status and backgrounds in society.

In the Japanese saiban-in system, the chief judge at the trial is the same judge who presides over the pretrial conference procedure where all case-specific evidence and information will be presented and discussed. The chief judge also proceeds with the deliberation and the trial procedures as well.[8] The Japanese institution of lay participation systematically concentrates the power of judging the case in the hands of the chief judge, through the processes of entire criminal procedures. This may not be a desirable procedure in order to establish an equal-footing between the professional judges and civic participants.

But the problems are not so simple to solve when we consider the results of our second hypothesis. According to the results, the frequency of utterances of unshared information in two members (majority) of the group showed a marginal difference.

---

[8] Strictly speaking, sometimes the chief judges entrust the role of presiding over the deliberation to one of the associate judges of their team. This is observed in the deliberations of mock trials in preparation period of saiban-in system. After beginning saiban-in system, deliberations are prohibited from being open to the public. So we cannot observe the deliberation processes of saiban-in system. All we can do is to speculate that the role of presiding over the deliberation is entrusted to associate judges in some cases.

The information held by two of three group members was referred to by presiding participants more than the non-presiding group members. And this tendency was greater in experimental situations in which the presiding person was higher on the professional social power cognition scale.

Given these results, it is desirable that the presiding person should have unshared information on the case. In the "hidden-profile" situation, the problem for group decision-making is that unshared information does not become shared through deliberations as the group members exchange the interaction on shared information from the start to the end (Stasser and Stewart 1992). So, most of the deliberation time is consumed for confirmation of what they already knew before the deliberation, not for reaching a new understanding of the case by exchange of unshared information.

If it is the case for the saiban-in, then it is desirable that presiding judges always have "unshared" information on the case prior to the deliberation. If the civic participants are inclined to judge improperly because of the shortage of information, presiding judges can salvage the situation by providing unshared information on the case. This can lead to more proper decisions on the case for the judicial panel.

But this solution for avoiding inappropriate decisions due to a shortage of information can bring a problem to bear on the criminal procedure because "shared information" is information presented and examined at the trial, while "unshared information" is not presented at the trial. In other words, judgments based on "unshared information" are judgments based on the information which is not revealed at the trial. This can be considered illegal in Japan's criminal procedural law if the judgment is based on the information given outside of the trial procedure.

The situation in which the presiding judge has "unshared" information is desirable only from the perspective of facilitating group decision-making processes. But it is not desirable or even legal from the perspective of legal trial procedures. There must be methods to avoid the illegality of allowing "unshared" or inadmissible evidence into the deliberative process. We cannot merely disregard this procedural problem and must find and propose alternative trial procedures.

Deliberation Style

As we saw in Section "Analysis of Deliberation Processes from the Viewpoint of Deliberation Styles", almost all of the groups deliberated in a "verdict-driven" style with some mixture of an "issue-driven" style. It is natural that the groups adopted "issue-driven" styles because we distributed a "points of judgment" sheet and asked the participants to read it before they decided the case.

But more importantly, a "verdict-driven" style appeared more pervasive than an "issue-driven" style of deliberation. One reason may be the restriction of deliberation time imposed on the experiment. As Hastie et al. (1983) pointed out, a "verdict-driven" style can be observed more frequently under strict time conditions. Another reason to consider is that initial preferences of potential verdicts were requested before the deliberations. Although many previous studies on group decision-making requested the participant to declare their initial preferences prior to deliberation, a "verdict-driven" style was not always observed. This point needs further investigation to reveal the processes at work in Japan's mixed trial system.

One of the findings related to deliberation style is that "verdict-driven" and "issue-driven" styles are not exclusive of each other. Although most of the groups started their deliberation with a "verdict-driven" style, many of the groups shifted to an "issue-driven" style after the statement of initial preferences.

Yet this pattern of deliberation may be different from a pure "verdict-driven" style or pure "issue-driven" style. One of the characteristics of "verdict-driven" patterns is that evidence is evaluated from the perspective of whether the evidence is useful for reinforcing initial preferences that were stated in front of other members of the group (Hastie et al. 1983). In this experiment, however, the groups that deliberated with a style that was a mixture of "verdict-driven" and "issue-driven" proceeded in the same way as did "verdict-driven" style groups observed in prior studies, because they started to discuss "issues" that the legal professionals will consider to judge the case under the instruction of "point of judgment".

The relationships between the two types of deliberation and a fuller description of the characteristics of "issue-driven" style should be investigated in future studies.

Limitation and Reservation Regarding this Study

We had only 24 participants in this experiment. This limitation was due to feasibility issues, not theoretical ones. We did not want to make a type II error on the analyses of the data.

Regarding the settings of deliberation, all the participants had the scenarios of the case and "points of discussions" in their hands during deliberations. It might be different in the situation where all the available information is in the minds of participants, and they cannot discuss the difference of the "profiles" with reference to the paper that contains the information on the case.

It may be possible to reveal unshared information more during deliberations, as compared to the situation in which no one has the paper explaining the information on the case. The latter situation is familiar to us because we do not always prepare the materials for discussion in advance. This point should also be investigated further in future research.

Future Direction

Possible Analyses of the Data

Though the size of the dataset obtained from this experiment was small, many analyses were conducted on the data. Besides the analysis reported in this paper, other possible analyses that could be conducted on the data may include social network analysis, as this experiment deals with the socio-cognitive network discussed in Kameda et al. (1997). An instance of social network analyses related to the background problem of the saiban-in system is that of Fujita (2009). The distribution of turn-taking patterns may relate to presiding, informational differentials, or other factors that can be found in the data.

But unlike in Fujita (2009), the data obtained from this experiment are limited by the fact that one group has only three members. It may be not so meaningful to discuss patterns of the shape of the network. In that case, we could conduct more straightforward statistical analyses on the patterns of turn-taking.

Possible Directions for Further Study

Considering that this experiment did not enroll many participants, the first follow-up may be a replication of this experiment with more participants and scrutinize the extent to which a type II error may have been made.

New relationships between those influential factors and strengths on group decision should be further investigated. For example, the sources of normative influence held by professional judges should be identified, as well as the significance of those sources, and their relationships with other factors identified by prior studies. It is especially important to determine whether the normative influence held by professional judges can exceed the robustness of determination by "majority-wins."

Results of verdict prediction from initial preferences confirmed the robustness of "majority-wins." The minority can rarely override the opinions of the initial majority, even if the minority members preside over the discussion. Prior studies cited in this paper argued that normative influence is stronger than informational influence. For ideal fact-finding, it may not be desirable to distort the discussion of fact-finding by including extra-legal factors, or the facts of the case itself. One of the future issues to be investigated would be the sources of the power of the majority and the possibility of distorting group decision-making related to fact-finding under mixed jury settings.

The use of deliberative decision-making and application of the majority rule in the determination of verdict and penalty may constitute the foundation of the democratic institution of the saiban-in system. But the institutional procedure of the participatory lay system should also be questioned empirically, regardless of whether or not it is the ideal (or possibly right) institution in making legally essential decisions, or lay participation is necessary for the administration of the justice system. Future research is needed to improve those democratic dimensions of Japan's lay participatory system.

Deliberation Style in the Deliberations with Status Differences

Issue-Driven Style: The Deliberation Style Particularly Found in Mixed-Jury Systems like "Saiban-in" System[9]

Deliberations in the Saiban-in System

Within civil-participating justice systems like pure jury system or "saiban-in" system, deliberations must be one of the most important issues for social scientists. That is because, the panels evaluate evidence which is presented at the trial, and decisions are made whether the accused should be guilty, through the deliberations. Every technique which is employed by trial lawyers should focus on the decisions which are made in the processes of deliberations.

Of course, the good part of bench trials is accompanied by deliberations. The cases which should be tried by saiban-in should be tried by three judges at the district courts even before the saiban-in act (saiban-in hô)[10] coming into force.[11] Adding to it, in the case that the case is appealed, high courts have three or more judges at one court,[12] and the Supreme Court of Japan has five judges in every minor court and fifteen judges at the major court.[13]

Nonetheless, the reasons why deliberations are focused especially on pure or mixed jury systems would be that people might be concerned about following things:

1. Can citizens understand evidence or law
2. Can citizens make decisions answering law and justice
3. Whether citizens attach greater importance to less relevant information
4. Citizens might ignore evidence or law
5. Can (Japanese) citizens utter in deliberation with professional judges

---

[9]This section is a reproduction of Fujita, M. (2010). Verdict-driven, evidence-driven, and "issue-driven": A proposition of deliberation style particularly found in mixed-jury type deliberations like "Saiban-in seido." *Journal of the Japan-Netherlands Institute*, *10*, 22–34.

The author deeply thanks the Tokyo office of the Leiden University for clarifying the copyrights issues in reproduction of this paper after the dissolution of Japan-Netherland Institute.

[10]Saiban-in no sanka suru keiji-saiban ni kansuru hôritsu [act concerning criminal trials in which saiban-in's participate].

[11]Saiban-sho hô [the Court Act] art. 26 para.2.

[12]Saiban-sho hô art. 18

[13]Saiban-sho hô art. 9 para.2.

Contrary to trials by or with citizens, people in Japan might believe in without firm reasons as they have thought "Because judges are professional, they must be doing very well." This belief would be reasonable to some extent, as professional judges rarely ignore law nor evidence. And public generally doesn't doubt that the judges understand the law well.

In citizens' participating in the justice system, skepticism about citizens competence may raise concern about deliberations in trials, as the civic participant will not experience keen competition to sit at the trial that may be experienced by professional judges.

Even in the United States, where the people are insured the right to trial by jury with their constitution, the competence of civic participants especially jurors have been doubted for years. According to reviews of studies conducted by social psychologists, jurors have enough ability to judge and competence of understanding evidence at least criminal cases (Hans and Vidmar 2001).

Of course, the investigation is needed for the competence of Japanese potential civic participants and to what extent can they make reliable judgments. "Secret of deliberation"[14] in the saiban-in system may harden the examination. But if potential civic participants in Japan have the same level competence of the counterpart of the United States, the civic participants in Japan will have enough competence to decide the cases.

Deliberations and Their Styles

"Deliberation style" is a typical progressing pattern of a deliberation. In relation to jury deliberation, deliberations will be classified with points that when and how many times ballots will be conducted and under what purposes the evidence are referred in deliberation.

The reason why balloting at deliberation thought as important is once people declare their opinion in public, they commit to their opinion through the deliberation. That is "commitment" social psychologists call. Once commitment emerges, people get harder to change their social attitudes. The effect of commitment will affect changing opinion in jury deliberation, and affect the way of progress of deliberation.

In the next section, we would like to show two types of jury deliberations which were found by social psychological studies according to prior studies reported by Hastie et al. (1983), and after that, we would point out the new deliberation style which can be seen particularly mock saiban-in system deliberations.

---

[14] Saiban-in Act, art. 70 para. 1.

Styles in the Pure Jury System

Concerning deliberations in the pure jury system, two typical styles are found with the observation of mock trials (Hastie et al. 1983). We would like to review those styles according to Hastie et al. (1983). One of the two typical deliberations is "verdict-driven" style (Hastie et al. 1983, p.163). This style is featured by following four points:

1. Deliberation begins with a public ballot.
2. Individual jurors advocate only one verdict position.
3. The content of deliberation contains many statements of verdict preferences.
4. Frequent pollings.

The other style is "evidence-driven" style, which is characterized by following four points:

1. Public balloting occurs only late in deliberation, and in extreme cases, only one ballot is taken to validate that a quorum has been reached.
2. Individual jurors are not closely associated with verdict preferences but may cite testimony or instructions with reference to several verdicts.
3. The evidence is reviewed without reference to the verdict categories, in an effort to agree upon the single most credible story that summarizes the events at the time of the alleged crime.
4. The early parts of deliberation are focused on the story construction and the review of the evidence; not until toward the conclusion of deliberation does discussion emphasize the task of verdict classification.

Hastie et al. (1983) pointed out the third style of deliberation as "mixed style," which can be seen the mixture of the two deliberation styles referred above. They made 69 groups of the mock jury, and they had the juries deliberate a case. They classified the juries into three categories. The first category is "verdict-driven." 19 groups are put into this category whose first polling was conducted within first 10 min from the beginning of deliberation. The second category was "mixed style," whose first ballot occurred from 10 to 40 min from the beginning of deliberation. 26 groups were in the second category of the deliberation style. The last was "evidence-driven," whose first ballot was conducted only after 40 min from the start of deliberation. 24 groups of juries were classified into the last category.

From their observation, the verdict-driven style was found more when majority rule was applied than unanimous rule did. The average times for deliberation were 83 min for verdict-driven, 98 min for mixed-style, and 131 min for the evidence-driven style.

Typical verdict-driven style deliberation begins with showing the preferences of jurors, and after that, they go back and forward within the evidence. In consequence, the story was rarely presented at the deliberation in verdict-driven style. (Hastie et al. 1983, p.164) Contrary to that, evidence-driven style juries follow the story model (Hastie et al. 1983, p.22) of individual juror decision-making. That is, deliberation will progress with three stages, (1) story construction, (2) establish verdict categories, and (3) selection of a most fitting category from the categories established in the prior stage. From analyses of contents of deliberation and quantity of utterances, fact-issue pairings were discussed more in evidence-driven style than in verdict-driven style. This implies that verdict-driven style deliberation does not consider testimony-instruction connections well. But there is no relationship found between deliberation styles and final verdict of the jury.

To examine the evaluation of jurors who participated in mock deliberation, answers for questionnaires were analyzed. According to the results of the analyses, there can be observed higher scores in persuasiveness, open-mindedness, seriousness, and pressures to change opinion from other jurors for evidence-driven style deliberation. In consequence, final verdicts formed with evidence-driven were more robust than with verdict-driven.

Based on observation shown above, verdict-driven style deliberation is haste, valued in speed when the jury evaluates the evidence, put less importance on persuasiveness and open-mindedness, and not active in deliberation. In verdict-driven style, a reference to evidence is made mainly from the viewpoint whether the evidence serves to support the opinion of individual jurors, sometimes the evidence is not fully investigated through deliberation (Hastie et al. 1983, p.165).

Style in Saiban-in System

When we observed mock mixed trial, especially real professional judges participated in the deliberation as judges, we found the fairly different type of deliberation style. In the beginning, we thought the new style of deliberation could be understood by regarding as one of the typical deliberation styles pointed by Hastie et al. (1983). And we did not put enough importance on the deliberation style which can be seen especially saiban-in deliberation. Also, we thought it is natural that the deliberation progress "issue-driven" style if the judges took the initiative of the discussion, so we were not aware of potential effects of "issue-driven" on mixed panel deliberation.

But after having repeated several times of observation of mock mixed trials, we understood this style is another deliberation style which is different from pure jury system observed before; we concluded that we need to propose the third style of (mixed) jury deliberation. That is because the third deliberation style has many of characteristics which cannot be attributed the deliberation styles found as of today.

The author named the new deliberation style as "issue-driven." Observed properties of "issue-driven" style can be pointed as follows:

1. Judges present issues which should be discussed in the deliberation.
2. Judges understand the order of the issues, a possible combination of every conclusion of issue and final verdict. On the contrary, civic participants do not understand all of those necessarily.
3. The panel forms a conclusion for every issue, and polling may occur if needed.

4. The conclusion taken in prior issues will constrain possible conclusion which can be taken in posterior issues.
5. The final verdict will be led to one of the possible conclusions necessarily by the composition of conclusions of the issues.
6. Preference for the verdict is asked at the final or later stage of deliberation.
7. It is not put importance on the construction of story which can explain the events which occurred in the case.

Mock Mixed Trials Which Showed "Issue-Driven" Style Deliberation

The deliberation style named "issue-driven" was found in the course of observation of records of mock mixed trials after 2006, which have been conducted by three parties of legal professionals (judges, prosecutors, and attorneys). In those mock mixed trials, judges were real professional judges, and civic participants were real civil participants who were requested to participate in the mock mixed trials by regional legal professional associations. The civic participants were elected with mock jury selection procedures conducted with the same manners of real selection procedures of the saiban-in system.

One of the authors conducted experiments with mock mixed juries at the beginning of studying saiban-in system (Fujita 2003), issue-driven style features were not so noticeable in mock deliberations. That may be because those mock trials were with student participants. This may mean that the manner of thinking and deliberating with "issue-driven" style is acquired through legal education and training. And this may mean that thinking issue-driven way may be a skill which requires expertise.

At the same time, as preparation periods of saiban-in system elapses, the management of procedures of the pretrial conference has been made public. As a result, it has been decided that chief judges who sit at the trial will also preside over the pretrial conference. In relation to that, picking up the issues of the cases in advance of deliberation can be observed more frequently than ever before the management of pretrial conference revealed.

Summing up for "Issue-Driven" Style

Issue-driven style matches very much with the way of decision making by judges in criminal trials. In typical cases, fact-finding in criminal cases is conducted in a manner of requisite-and-effect. In this type of reasoning, a fact finder is required to find some requisites if s/he would like to recognize something happened in the case.[15]

[15] That is some parts of the reasons why some judges say "if we would draft a decision with sufficient reasons, the only style we can take in deliberation should be this style."

But as issue-driven deliberation style lacks the viewpoint of story-construction, civic participants may not feel about enough examination was executed in deliberation.

Especially, this may be found in the item no. 5 of the characteristics of issue-driven deliberation on page 5. The two styles which were found in jury studies conducted by Hastie et al., are found in deliberation whose members are only civics. This may mean that the two styles of deliberation are natural for civic participants – not the third.

Part of the reasons why the evidence-driven is natural for civic participants would be that individual jurors' cognition processes are described with "story model" (Hastie et al. 1983, p.22), and verdict-driven may be explained that the way of progress with final verdict preferences is easy for civic participants. But with issue-driven style, which is fairly different from other two styles, civic participants may think that final verdict appears suddenly. This feeling of suddenness may lead to wonder "can we decide the accused guilty only with this evidence and deliberation?", and may lower satisfaction level for deliberation and final verdict.[16] And, the feature no. 3 on page 5, civic participants may wonder when they fact one of the rules of issue-driven, "conclusion of prior issues will limit possible conclusions of posterior issues." Civic participants may conform to another member of the panel (especially professional judges) because they would like to settle the argument quietly, or inevitably to comply with the results of the majority. In consequence, they may express that they did not fully consent to prior issues in discussion posterior issues. This might overturn the progress of saiban-in deliberation.

If those situations occur repeatedly, civic participants may have an impression on a saiban-in system that deliberation may go ahead without lay participants' full consent, while professional judges may have some sense that deliberation with civic participants is an irritating and laborious task.

To avoid that situation, it cannot be helped professional judges' making mutual connections with civic participants, as they are skillful at legal arguments and they may know about the case during a pretrial conference. That is, professional judges may need to understand the "story model" of juror decision-making and manage deliberation consistently with the model.

When writing a decision, judges have to arrange the contents of deliberation in order of issue-driven way. But in deliberation with civic participants, desirably deliberation goes along with evidence-driven style, and going back and forth among issues should be allowed in the process of deliberation. To ensure that, sufficient time for discussion has to be secured.

Concerning this issue, Ohtsubo (2006) argued that another deliberation style may be assumed in mixed jury system like the saiban-in system, different from the styles. Ohtsubo (2006) showed some examples of breaking down evidence-driven style into two styles. He suggested those two styles should be distinguished with the

[16] In fact, a civic participant said after mock trial and deliberation, expressing his wonder about being able to judge guilty such a "sudden" conclusion which were typically identified by Hastie et al. (1983).

timings of expression of verdict preferences of civic participants. In the first style, civic participants show their views before professional judges reveal theirs. And in the other one, civic participants express their view after professional judges present their thoughts (Ohtsubo 2006, p.208). Difference between the arguments of Ohtsubo (2006) and arguments of this paper is that Ohtsubo (2006) complies with classification by Hastie et al. (1983), and searching for fitting style with breaking down the classification. But in this part, the author would like to propose that legal professionals will set the agenda in advance of deliberation, and deliberation may progress the order of agenda set by professional judges. With this typical issue-driven style deliberation, the nature of this style should be thought entirely different from other two styles which were identified by the prior study.

However, this proposition is just proposition inspired by observation of mock mixed deliberation with real professional judges and civic participants. This proposition needs to be examined by experiments and characteristics should be described with further data. As Ohtsubo (2006) acknowledged, examination of the effects of deliberation styles on content and final verdict of deliberation in mixed jury system are a future problem and still open to us. Not so very different from that argument, characteristics of "issue-driven" style pointed by the author remains to be elucidated. Further experiments and studies are expected.

On the Importance of Identification of "Another" Deliberation Style

Some legal professionals reacted the idea of "issue-driven" style, "it is natural and nothing new for us." This reaction may disregard the context of the argument of deliberation style and undermined their thought by hindsight bias. Being aware of it, we would like to mention the significance of identification of "issue-driven" deliberation style.

In the context of social psychological studies on the jury, many of the studies have been devoted to understanding the mechanisms of the pure jury system; it is rarely assumed that some members of the panel put the issues in order with their knowledge and skill for arguments.

But in mixed jury system like the saiban-in system, there is particular deliberation style which comes from the existence of legal professionals. This proposition may be the basement of posterior studies on mixed jury system in the field of group decision-making and social psychology.

On the other hand, for legal professionals who are natural to establish arguments with "issue-driven" style, it is the efficacy of known as a style of arguments that the issue-driven is one of the possible methods of discussion, and the method is particularly used by legal professionals.

If we comprehend the difference between cognition and argument method between civil participants and legal professionals, we would not be flustered nor having a feeling of futile in deliberation with civic participants.

In the discussion for understandable deliberation in the saiban-in system, it was proposed that flow charts should be used in deliberation to show graphically what should be on agenda and direction of the discussion. Assuredly, flowcharts will allow the lay member of the panel to understand the direction of the discussion easily, and the outlook for deliberation will be easily shared among the members of the panel.

The problem is, however, what should be content of flow charts. If the flowcharts are made under the given conditions of issue-driven style discussion, comprehensive story construction of the case will be moved aside; discussion will focus on just "points" of the issues which are authorized to important issue by legal professionals.

And, if the final verdict is led by the combination of conclusions of every issue, civic participants may have felt that the panel has jumped to a final conclusion. That may be partly because sufficient story construction was not conducted in deliberation. In consequence, some of the civic participants may be not able to understand the case because any story nor image created an image in the mind of civic participants. That may cause unconvinced citizens for a final verdict of the panel.

Therefore, if we draw some flow charts for promoting deliberation, it would be better using charts which show overall story for the case than illustrating issue-and-conclusion relationships.[17]

Of course, this is a proposition led from the discussion of this paper, experiments and other empirical examinations are required for verifying this proposition.

Future Directions

In this part, the author pointed out that "issue-driven" style of deliberation can often be seen in mock saiban-in deliberation. And that style of deliberation has seemed to be rarely identified in prior studies. Some parts of the reason why the issue-driven style has not been specified may be that issue-driven style is not common for civic participants' discussion, nor cognition processes. This would imply issue-driven is not natural for civic participants.

At this point, some questions on jury decision-making may come across us. Which style is the most efficient in jury decision making? In which style, the participants of the deliberations can understand or remember more the facts of the cases?

[17] The nature of flowcharts will be fit for issue-and-conclusion type illustration, so we have to be careful for not making hard-to-understand charts for civic participants. It is vain if we make charts which do not promote civic participants' understandings, as legal professionals do not need flow charts to process cases.

The style used by the legal professionals can lead the decision makers to "just" conclusion of the case?

We have to conduct experiments to examine those questions empirically. At the start point, we need more detailed descriptions of the features of "issue-driven" deliberation style. With those descriptions, we will know whether the features pointed in this paper are generally adopted in mixed jury deliberation or not. After that, we can proceed to investigate whether the style adopted by legal professionals bring about more "just" outcome of the case.

Hopefully, we expect that the style which is employed by legal professionals can lead us to the fair conclusion of each case efficiently. Most of the cases indicted at the District Courts are tried by professional judges even after the introduction of the saiban-in system. But we cannot overlook the possibilities that the "issue-driven" style might twist the fact of the case in order to conform to the framework which is bared in the minds of legal professionals.

Social Network Analyses

Social Network Analyses of Deliberations: An Anecdotal Study on Two Mock Mixed Jury Deliberations[18]

Background

As it may be known, Japan is going to introduce a mixed tribunal system, named "Saiban-in system," to try severe criminal cases on May 21st, 2009. In that system, judicial panels will be composed of three professional judges and six citizen participants, in principle. Contrary to the pure jury system which was implemented in the early Shôwa era (from 1925 to 1989), none of the accused in severe cases can refuse trial by the saiban-in system. In consequence, around 3000 cases per year will be tried by the saiban-in system.

Introducing the saiban-in system has brought a significant impact on the administration of Japanese criminal justice. Especially, administration of deliberation with civic participants is one of the most critical issues. This issue is taken seriously among the three elements of the judicial community (judges, prosecutors, and practicing attorneys at law) in Japan as the implementation of the mixed jury system is approaching.

To try over deliberation of mixed jury panels, mock trials and mock deliberations are being held every corner of Japan in these days. Generally, the initiative is taken

[18] This section is a reproduction of Fujita, M. (2009). Necessary condition of active civic participation: An anecdotal study on communication networks of two mock mixed jury trials. *Zeitschrift für japanisches Recht (Journal of Japanese Law)*, *14*(27), 91–104. The author thanks Professor Harald Baum for quickly and generously permitting reproduction. The author also thanks Professor Dimitri Vanoverbeke to have given the author a chance of publication in that journal.

by a district court, and prosecutors and attorneys participate in a mock trial. Real three judges and six citizens make up a judicial panel, and they sit at and hear the mock trial. After the trial completed, the judicial panel deliberates on the case, decides the case, and sentences if the panel convicts the accused.

Concerning deliberation processes, the law (the act on criminal trials with participating civic members) defines professional judges, and civic members should be on an equal footing with each other. Every member of the judicial panel has same voting power on deciding issues except legal issues. And every member will be given chances to utter during deliberation. But actually, of course, judges and citizens are not equal in regard to their knowledge (concerning legal knowledge and case itself), authority in managing the processes of deliberation, and social power. And even among judges, they are not equal in their career, knowledge, and social power.

In substance, the law itself declares one of the judges should be a chief judge, and "during the deliberation decreed above section 1, the chief judge must carefully explain the laws discussed in deliberation, put the deliberation in order, in order to keep the deliberation understandable for civic participants; and the chief judge must be thought that civic participants perform their duties sufficiently with setting aside times to utter in deliberation" in the article 66, Section "Results". With this article, a chief judge is vested special power in the process of deliberation by law.

As seen in the article 66 cited above, judges are required to explain the law used in the cases of civic participants. This can be thought that judges can always give instructions to lay members of the panel and might lead the deliberation towards the conclusion which he intended. This is very much different from the pure jury system. The panel members are always together as long as the trial and deliberation last. Adding to it, if necessary, the panel will have intermediary deliberations in the course of the trial.

Purpose of this Study

To assess communication patterns of mixed jury panels, the author obtained some records (videos and transcripts) of the mock mixed trial carried out by district courts. The characteristics of data will be described in "data" section in this paper. On those data, the author conducted analyses on communication patterns of mock mixed panels with counting the utterances of members. With assessing communication patterns and qualitative results of those deliberations, the author would like to examine the relationship between the shapes of the networks and results of qualitative aspects of the deliberations.

What Is "Communication Network"?

Prior to promoting to next section, we take a look at the idea of the communication network. A communication network in this regard is a concept used in the field of group decision making. Communication network describes forms of communication patterns within groups in which information is exchanged among members, and resolves a task as a whole group.

Bavelas (1950) proposed that we could know the effects of communication structure of group members with thinking that group members are connected by chains of information exchange.

In the diagrams drawn below Fig. 3.1, a small circle seen like "o" is a "node," which means a person of a group. A line "-" represents communication. If a line is accompanied by an arrowhead, it indicates the direction of the communication. The width of the line reflects frequencies of communication.

Communication Network and Decision Making

According to the studies on a communication network, patterns of communication networks and task complexity affect the performance of group decision making.

For example, groups with communication networks along with centers (centralized network like Fig. 3.2), are fast in decision making, good for resolving simple tasks, taking time for complicated tasks, low-satisfaction level of members, and low morale of each member. Low satisfaction level and low morale cause a low level of performance of the group because individual autonomy is denied by information carrier at the center of the network. And groups with the communication network of this type are not good at complicated tasks due to cognitive overload on the node at the center.

On the contrary, groups with a low-centralized communication network (seen as Fig. 3.3) are taking time for resolving simple tasks, but good for answering complicated tasks because this type of communication network has a high level of information consolidation function. As a result, groups with this type of communication network are faster and more accurate at decision making in complicated tasks accompanied by arithmetic tasks or discussion tasks. And if errors are made in a group with the communication network of this type, the errors are easily remedied in processes of information exchange.

At the same time, satisfaction level and morale of group members are higher than the groups with the centralized communication network.

Directly Related the Prior Study

A study conducted on Korean mock jury by Ms. Min Kim & Prof. Penrod focused on communication patterns of a mock jury (Kim and Penrod 2010). And the study described communication patterns with diagrams. This study was presented at an annual conference of the Law and Society Association.[19]

[19] This study was published in 2010 after this paper had been published.

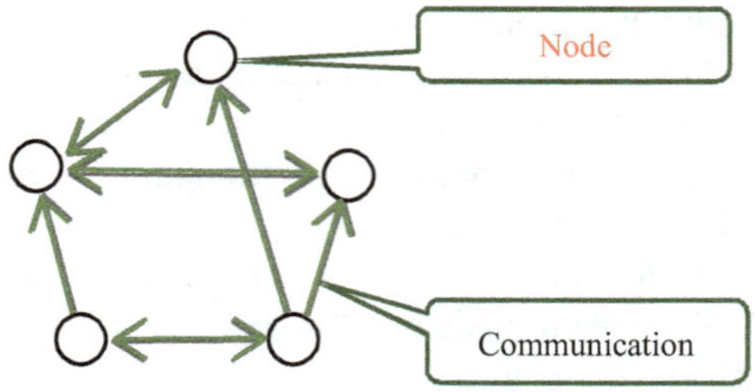

Fig. 3.1 Example of a communication network

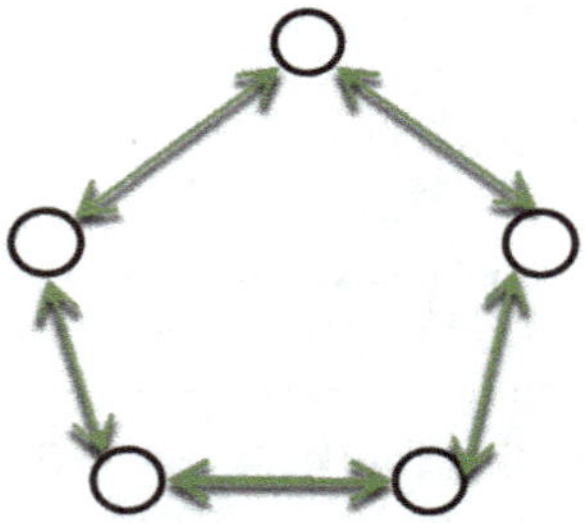

Fig. 3.2 Centralized communication network

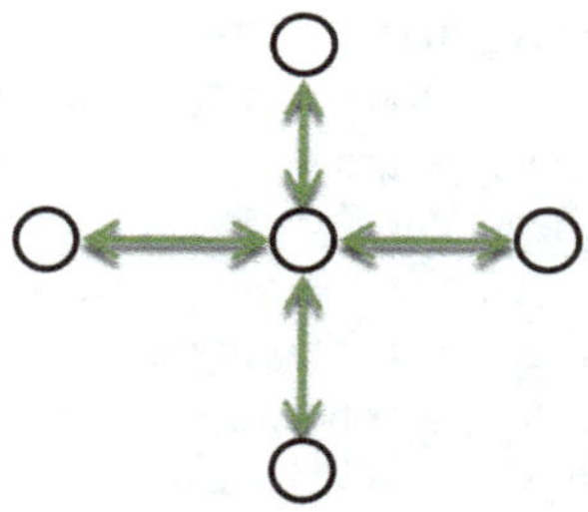

Fig. 3.3 Non-centralized communication network

And this line of study has been developed by Korean researchers. They are Prof. Park and Ms. Lee at Chungbuk University, Korea. They presented lasted results of their study using communication network.

Method

Data

The author used videos and transcripts of mock mixed trials. The mock trials were dealt with almost the same cases whose scenarios were made from a real criminal case. In that case, the accused was charged as an accomplice of a robbery after the fact. The principal of the robbery received some money from the victim, and after that held off the victim's recapturing with force and arms. One of the main issues in the case was whether a concerted action of holding off the recapturing with force and arms was constituted by the principle and the accused.

Those mock trials were hosted by three elements of judicial communities in each district in Japan. As the mock trials were hosted by real legal professionals, real prosecutors acted as prosecutors, real attorneys took roles of defense counsels, and real judges and citizens heard mock trials and deliberated on those criminal cases. Civic participants who sat at the mock trials were selected from pools of employees of private companies who are making common cause with district courts.

The mock trials were videotaped by the secretariat of each district court. Copies of the videos were forwarded to Japan Federation of Bar Associations and were transcribed by the secretariat of JFBA. All of those mock trials were conducted in 2006.

Two mock mixed jury deliberations presented in this paper were selected according to availability and permission. Those two mock mixed trials could be evaluated as quite contrasting in deliberation processes. Although those two judicial panels saw many times of utterances of civic participants, one can be seen less active; in the meanwhile, the other can see active civil participating. Here the author would like to describe the differences among those deliberations and discuss reasonable reasons why the difference emerged.

Venue

The two mock trials from which the data were obtained were held at two district courts. One of the venues was located in Hokkaido island, the northernmost island of four main islands of Japan (hereinafter, the author calls it "venue 1"). The other venue was located in Shikoku island, also one of four main islands of Japan (hereinafter, the author refers to it "venue 2").

To draw diagrams of communication network within mock mixed panels, the author counted the numbers of utterances during deliberations using transcripts. At the same time, the author checked the speakers and listeners of utterances with contents of the transcripts. If the listener of the statement is not clear from the transcript, the author reviewed the videos and decided the direction of the speech.

Results

Venue 1

Here showed below is the result table of venue 1. Table 3.24 is showing the numbers of utterances. The rows indicate the speaker of each utterance, and columns show the listener the utterances. Abbreviation "CJ" means the chief judge, "J2" and "J3" means the second and the third judge, and "Cn" means citizen participant number n.

Table 3.24 Numbers of utterances in the deliberation at venue 1

		From									
		CJ	J2	J3	C1	C2	C3	C4	C5	C6	Total
To	CJ	×	30	18	36	27	29	90	38	48	316
	J2	26	×	1			2				29
	J3	18	2	×			2				22
	C1	33			×	1					34
	C2	26				×					26
	C3	25	3	4			×	1			33
	C4	89					1	×			90
	C5	32		2					×		34
	C6	45	2							×	47
	All	23	2								25
Total		294	37	25	36	28	34	91	38	48	631

Results from which can Be Read by the Diagram

According to the table above, the author drew a diagram of deliberation at venue 1 with Pajek (Batagelj and Mrvar 1998). Pajek is free software for network analyzing which can be run on Windows. Pajek is equipped with functions to draw diagrams with data of nodes and strength of each linkage between nodes. The layout of the diagram can be changed easily after the data were properly read by Pajek, Fig. 3.4.

As seen in the table and figure above, chief judge and each member had frequent exchanges. But members except chief judge had little communication each other Fig. 3.5.

To understand the structure of this diagram more easily, the author changed the layout of the diagram above to have the chief judge centered at the diagram.

With changing the layout of the diagram, it is easy to observe rather a strong centrality. There can be seen many exchanges between the chief judge and another member of the panel, but frequencies of communication among the members except chief judge are rare. We can see it as the chief judge was the center of the communication network, and this diagram can be estimated as communication network with the center.

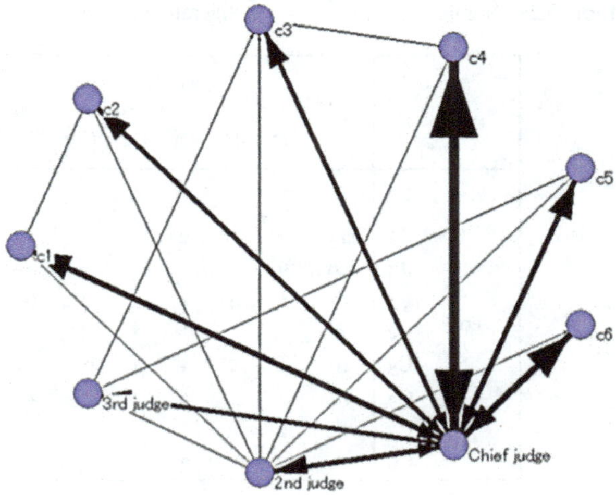

Fig. 3.4 The communication network of the deliberation at venue 1

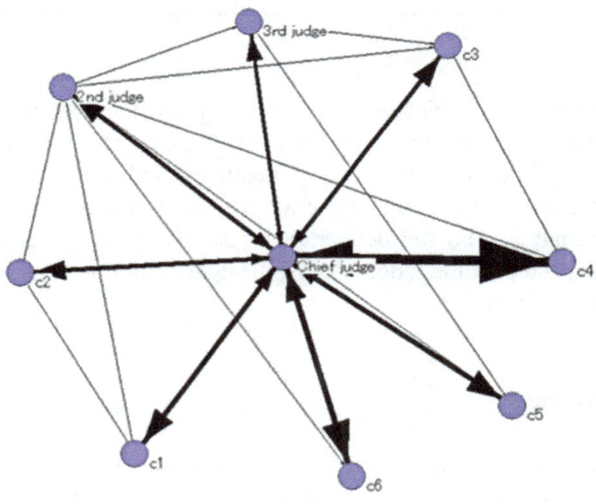

Fig. 3.5 The communication network of the deliberation at venue 1 (the chief judge as a center)

Qualitative Results from Which Can Be Observed from the Transcript and the Video

Communication between the chief judge and civil participant 4 can be seen more action than the exchanges among the other members of the panel. With this figure, we might assume that there may be active participation of civic participant 4 in this deliberation. But looking at the video which record of the deliberation, I found that chief judge often persuaded the civil participant 4, if the civil participant 4 had a different opinion. So, although there could be observed numbers of exchanges

Table 3.25 Numbers of utterances in deliberation at venue 2

		From									
		CJ	J2	J3	C1	C2	C3	C4	C5	C6	Total
To	CJ	×	27	73	18	9	11	22	19	18	197
	J2	23	×	11	2			1	1		38
	J3	69	19	×	1		2		2		93
	C1	17	2	1	×	1	1	6	2	2	32
	C2	6		1	1	×	1	6	1	1	17
	C3	10	1	2	1	1	×		5	2	22
	C4	18	1		5	5		×	1	1	31
	C5	21	2	4	1		5	2	×	3	38
	C6	19			3	1	3	1		×	27
	All	24	1	2	1						28
Total		207	53	94	33	17	23	38	31	27	523

between the chief judge and a civil participant, it was hardly estimated that those exchanges promote civic participant in the sense that the law established.

Though total numbers of utterances can be seen as enough for the time of deliberation, all in all, the deliberation at venue 1 was less active than the deliberation at venue 2. And the deliberation resulted in the conclusion which was somewhat expected by the judge, that is, the deliberation was less emergent than the deliberation at venue 2.

Venue 2

Here showed below is the result table of venue 2. Table 3.25 is showing the numbers of utterances. The rows indicate the speaker of each utterance, and columns show the listener the utterances.

Results from Which Can Be Read by the Diagram

According to the table above, the author drew a diagram of deliberation at venue 2 with Pajek, as the same means used in analyzing the data obtained at venue 1 Fig. 3.6.

As seen in the table and figure above, chief judge and each member had frequent exchanges. Adding to it, the exchanges among the other members were also active. It is showing that interactions between members, even civil participants each other were active Fig. 3.7

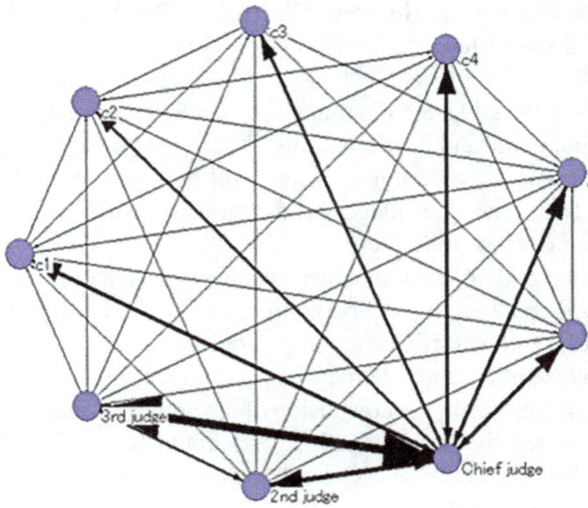

Fig. 3.6 The communication network of the deliberation at venue 2

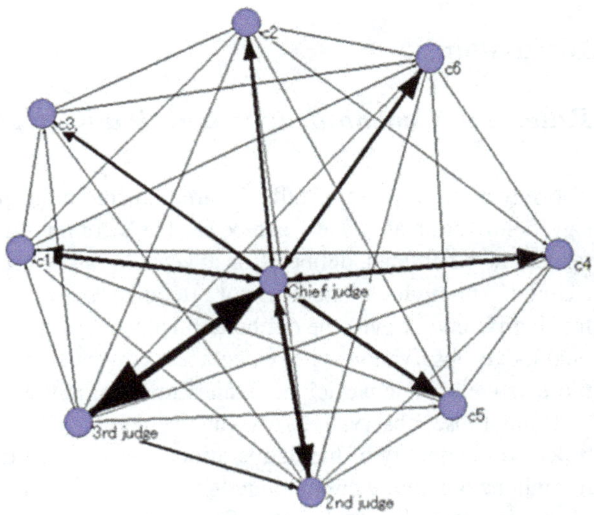

Fig. 3.7 The communication network of the deliberation at venue 2 (the chief judge as a center)

To understand the structure of this diagram more easily, the author changed the layout of the diagram above to have the chief judge centered at the diagram.

With changing the layout of the diagram, it can also be observed the centrality of the chief judge. But compared to venue 1, the centrality is a little bit weaker than the venue 1. There was plenty of communication among the members except the chief judge, adding to exchanges between the chief judge and another member of the panel. We can see it as the chief judge was the center of the communication network, and this diagram can be estimated as a kind of an amalgam of a communication network with center and communication network without a center.

Qualitative Results from Which Can Be Observed from the Transcript and the Video

From the table and diagrams above, we can see numbers of exchanges between the chief judge and the third judge. With reviewing the video recording the deliberation at venue 2, the third judge took a role as a clerk at the discussion. So, the wide arrow between the chief judge and the third judge did not mean the chief judge's persuasion over the third judge.

In general, each member of the panel including every civic participant actively participated in the deliberation. Some of the civic participants stood up from their seats, and walked along and got together to simulate the crime scene. That was episodic evidence of liveliness of the deliberation.

Adding to it, the conclusion of the deliberation was different from what had been expected by the chief judge. This could be confirmed by utterances of the chief judge. That may be collateral evidence of emergent processes had occurred in the process of deliberation.

Discussion

Patterns of Communication and Quality of Deliberation

Those two cases were typically different in communication patterns. As we already saw, deliberation at venue 1 can be seen as a communication network with the center. On the other hand, deliberation at venue 2 can be estimated as a network without a center. Although total numbers of utterances between two deliberations are not so much different, or even the deliberation at venue 1 has more numbers of utterances, qualitative observation with videotapes showed that deliberation at venue 2 was more active in civic participation and emergent in the conclusion of deliberation.

From those observations, it can be concluded that communication patterns reflected the quality of the deliberation process, even in the mock mixed jury. And it might be premature or dare to judge, but the difference may be derived from usage of the power of the chief judge. That is, in deliberation at venue 1, power may be used to inhibit civil participants from unreserved opinions. In the meanwhile, in deliberation on venue 2, power may be used to accept civil participants' unreserved opinions and encourage free discussion.

It is more than probable that the chief judge at venue 1 thoughtful of securing chances of speaking of civic participants, but it would be not enough for raising the numbers of utterances of civic participants.

Effects of Using Dialect in Deliberation

Pondering over another factor which activates deliberation, we might reason that accents used in the verbal deliberation exchanges may be one of the effective factors. At venue 2, almost all of the members of the panels, not only civic participants also judges, used local accents in their verbal exchanges. Those are largely classified in "Kansai" accents, that is rather different from common accents in the Japanese language. Common accents of Japanese language are mainly based on Tokyo accents, classified "Kantô" accents in large. Generally, for native Kansai accents speakers, using Kasai accents in conversation is a comfortable experience not only because they can use their native accents, but Kansai accents itself can be felt like a representation of closer relationships between the speaker and others. Also, they perceive Kansai accent speakers to be warm in their personalities. On the contrary, using common accents or Kantô accents is rather formal, remote in a relationship, cold-hearted. This description may be somewhat stereotypic, but one of the reasons why the deliberation at venue 2 was active may be attributed to their accents used in the deliberation.

At venue 1, accents used in deliberation were near to the common accents in the Japanese language. As many of local people at venue 1 use similar accents to common accents, they may not have negative feelings about using common accents in conversation. So, it is inferable that people at venue 1 did not feel that the members using common accents are remote nor cold-hearted. But also, there may not be observed promoting effects of derived from the accents used in deliberation.

Future Direction

In further research, we need to explore the relationships between communication patterns and qualities of deliberation. In this regard, the author attempted to infer from anecdotal evidence, but firmer theory and demonstration by experiments would be needed.

Also, linguistic aspects of deliberation should be researched. The effects of dialect on deliberation activeness may be one of the examples of this regard. By exploring nature of the deliberation with linguistic methods, we may attain a deeper understanding of the influence of each member of the panel from different viewpoints than network pattern of the communication.

References

Adorno, T. W., Frenkel-Brunswik, E., Levinson, D. J., & Sanford, R. N. (1950). *The authoritarian personality*. New York: Harper.

Anderson, K., & Saint, E. (2005). Japan's Quasi-Jury (Saiban-in) Law: An annotated translation of the act concerning participation of lay assessors in criminal trials. *Asian-Pacific Law & Policy Journal, 6*, 233–283.

Batagelj, V., & Mrvar, A. (1998). Pajek – Program for large network analysis. *Connections, 21*, 47–57 Retrieved from https://s3.amazonaws.com/academia.edu.documents/31188195/pajek.pdf?AWSAccessKeyId=AKIAIWOWYYGZ2Y53UL3A&Expires=1520202902&Signature=Bbt5FFrZ0e%2B1WKgT0F0JBS%2FtgnM%3D&response-content-disposition=inline%3Bfilename%3DPajek_-_Program_for_Large_Network_Anal.

Bavelas, A. (1950). Communication patterns in task-oriented groups. *The Journal of the Acoustical Society of America, 22*(6), 725–730. https://doi.org/10.1121/1.1906679.

Bray, R. M., & Kerr, N. L. (1982). Methodological considerations in the study of the psychology of the courtroom. In N. L. Kerr & R. M. Bray (Eds.), *The psychology of the courtroom* (pp. 287–323). San Diego: Academic Press.

Cruz, M. G., Henningsen, D. D., & Williams, M. L. M. (2000). The presence of norms in the absence of groups? *Human Communication Research, 26*(1), 104–124.

Davis, J. H. (1973). Group decision and social interaction: A theory of social decision schemes. *Psychological Review, 80*(2), 97–125. https://doi.org/10.1037/h0033951.

de Tocqueville, A. (1835). *De La Démocratie en Amérique*. Paris: Michel Lévy.

Deutsch, M., & Gerard, H. B. (1955). A study of normative and informational social influences upon individual judgment. *The Journal of Abnormal and Social Psychology, 51*(3), 629–636. https://doi.org/10.1037/h0046408.

Foss, R. D. (1976). Group decision processes in the simulated trial jury. *Sociometry, 39*(4), 305–316. https://doi.org/10.2307/3033496.

Fujita, M. (2003). Kinô suru saiban-in seido no tame ni: Chii ni sa no aru shûdan ishi kettei no kansatsu kara [For functionable saiban-in system: From observation of group decision-making with status difference]. *Hôshakaigaku [Sociology of Law], 59*, 209–226 [in Japanese].

Fujita, M. (2009). Necessary condition of active civic participation: An anecdotal study on communication networks of two mock mixed jury trials. *Zeitschrift Für Japanisches Recht (Journal of Japanese Law), 14*(27), 91–104.

Fujita, M. (2010). Verdict-driven, evidence-driven, and "issue-driven": A proposition of deliberation style particularly found in mixed-jury type deliberations like "Saiban-in seido". *Journal of the Japan-Netherlands Institute, 10*, 22–34.

Fujita, M., & Hotta, S. (2010). The effect of presiding role and information amount differentials among group members on group decision making: Deliberation processes, final decisions, and personality. *International Journal of Law, Crime, and Justice, 38*, 216–235.

Hans, V. P., & Vidmar, N. (2001). *Judging the jury* (4th ed.). New York: Perseus Books Group.

Hastie, R., Penrod, S., & Pennington, N. (1983). *Inside the jury*. Oxford: Harvard University Press.

Henningsen, D. D., & Henningsen, M. L. M. (2003). Examining social influence in information-sharing contexts. *Small Group Research, 34*(4), 391–412. https://doi.org/10.1177/1046496403251933.

Imai, Y. (1987). Eikyôsha ga hoji suru shakai-teki seiryoku no ninchi to hi-eikyôsha no ninchieikyôsha ni taisuru manzokudo tono kankei (Relationship between cognition of social power held by influential person and satisfaction rate toward cognitive influential person) by. *Janapense Journal of Experiemtnal Social Psychology, 26*, 163–173 [in Japanese].

Imasaki, Y. (2005a). "Saiban-in seido dônyû to keiji saiban" no gaiyô: Saiban-in seido ni husawashii saiban purakutisu wo mezashite [Summary of "Introducing saiban-in system and criminal trials": Aiming at establishing judicial practice suitable for saiban-in system]. *Hanrei Taimuzu [The Precedent Times], 1188*, 4–11 [in Japanese].

Imasaki, Y. (2005b). Saiban-in seido no moto ni okeru shinri, hyôgi, hanketsu no arikata ni kansuru shian [A tentative proposal on the practices of trials by saiban-in, deliberation, and judgement]. *Hanrei Taimuzu [The Precedent Times], 1188*, 12–19 [in Japanese].

Justice System Reform Council. (2001). *Recommendations of the Justice System Reform Council: For a Justice System to Support Japan in the 21st Century*. Tokyo, Japan: Justice System Reform Council. Retrieved from https://japan.kantei.go.jp/judiciary/2001/0612report.html

Kameda, T., Ohtsubo, Y., & Takezawa, M. (1997). Centrality in sociocognitive networks and social influence: An illustration in a group decision-making context. *Journal of Personality and Social Psychology, 73*(2), 296–309.

Kaplan, M. F., & Martin, A. M. (1999). Effects of differential status of group members on process and outcome of deliberation. *Group Processes & Intergroup Relations, 2*(4), 347–364. https://doi.org/10.1177/1368430299024003.

Kaplan, M. F., & Miller, C. E. (1987). Group decision making and normative versus informational influence: Effects of type of issue and assigned decision rule. *Journal of Personality and Social Psychology, 53*(2), 306–313. https://doi.org/10.1037/0022-3514.53.2.306.

Kim, M. C., & Penrod, S. D. (2010). Legal decision making among Korean and American legal professionals and lay people. *International Journal of Law, Crime and Justice, 38*(4), 175–197. https://doi.org/10.1016/j.ijlcj.2011.01.004.

Laughlin, P. R. (1980). Social combination processes of cooperative, problem-solving groups on verbal intellective tasks. In *Progress in social psychology* (pp. 127–155). Mahwah: Lawrence Erlbaum Associates.

Laughlin, P. R., & Ellis, A. L. (1986). Demonstrability and social combination processes on mathematical intellective tasks. *Journal of Experimental Social Psychology, 22*(3), 177–189. https://doi.org/10.1016/0022-1031(86)90022-3.

Nishimura, T. (2006). Saiban-in seido dônyû ni muketa torikumi: Bengoshikai [Activities for introduction of the saiban-in system: Bar Associations]. *Hôritsu No Hiroba [Forum of Law], 59*(10), 27–35 [in Japanese].

Ohtsubo, Y. (2006). On designing a mixed jury system in Japan. In M. F. Kaplan & A. M. Martín (Eds.), *Understanding world Jury systems through social psychological research* (pp. 199–214). New York: Psychology Press.

Sealy, A. P., & Cornish, W. R. (1973). Jurors and their verdicts. *The Modern Law Review, 36*(5), 496–508. https://doi.org/10.1111/j.1468-2230.1973.tb01381.x.

Shiibashi, T. (2004). Kôhanzen-seiri-tetsuzuki to shôko kaiji [Pretrial conference procedure and discovery]. *Gendai Keiji Hô [Contemporary Criminal Law], 6*(12), 17–21 [in Japanese].

Stasser, G. (1992). Information salience and the discovery of hidden profiles by decision-making groups: A thought experiment. *Organizational Behavior and Human Decision Processes, 52*(1), 156–181.

Stasser, G. (1999). The uncertain role of unshared information in collective choice. In L. L. Thompson, J. M. Levine, & D. M. Messick (Eds.), *Shared cognition in organizations : The management of knowledge* (pp. 49–69). Mahwah: Lawrence Erlbaum Associates Retrieved from http://web.a.ebscohost.com/ehost/detail/detail?vid=2&sid=c9fcf7bf-8a3a-4950-9b64-053308a67dea%40sessionmgr4007&bdata=Jmxhbmc9amEmc2l0ZT1laG9zdC1saXZl#AN=1999-02987-003&db=psyh.

Stasser, G. (2000). Information distribution, participation, and group decision: Explorations with the DISCUSS and SPEAK models. In D. R. Ilgen & C. L. Hulin (Eds.), *Computational modeling of behavior in organizations: The third scientific discipline* (pp. 135–161). Washington, DC: American Psychological Association. https://doi.org/10.1037/10375-007.

Stasser, G., & Stewart, D. (1992). Discovery of hidden profiles by decision-making groups: Solving a problem versus making a judgment. *Journal of Personality and Social Psychology, 63*(3), 426–434. https://doi.org/10.1037/0022-3514.63.3.426.

Stasser, G., & Titus, W. (1985). Pooling of unshared information in group decision making: Biased information sampling during discussion. *Journal of Personality and Social Psychology, 48*(6), 1467–1478. https://doi.org/10.1037//0022-3514.48.6.1467.

Stasser, G., & Titus, W. (1987). Effects of information load and percentage of shared information on the dissemination of unshared information during group discussion. *Journal of Personality and Social Psychology, 53*(1), 81–93. https://doi.org/10.1037//0022-3514.53.1.81.

Stasser, G., Taylor, L. a., & Hanna, C. (1989). Information sampling in structured and unstructured discussions of three- and six-person groups. *Journal of Personality and Social Psychology, 57*(1), 67–78. https://doi.org/10.1037//0022-3514.57.1.67.

Stasser, G., Stewart, D. D., & Wittenbaum, G. M. (1995). Expert roles and information exchange during discussion: The importance of knowing who knows what. *Journal of Experimental Social Psychology, 31*(3), 244–265. https://doi.org/10.1006/jesp.1995.1012.

Stasser, G., Vaughan, S. I., & Stewart, D. D. (2000). Pooling unshared information: The benefits of knowing how access to information is distributed among group members. *Organizational Behavior and Human Decision Processes, 82*(1), 102–116. https://doi.org/10.1006/obhd.2000.2890.

Yamaguchi, S., Oka, T., Maruoka, Y., Watanabe, S., & Watanabe, H. (1988). Gôisei no suisoku ni kansuru kenkyû (1): Shûdan-shugi-teki keikô tono kanren ni tsuite [A study on supposition of consensus (1): On relationship with collectivism tendency]. *Nihon-Shakishinrigakkai Dai 29 Kai Taikai Happyou Ronbun Shû [*Japanese Society of Social Psychology proceedings for the 29th annual conference], *29*, 176–177.

Yonamine, M. (1960). Ken'i shugi shakudo ni kansuru ichi kenkyû: F sukêru no kentô [A study on authoritarian personality: Investigation on F-scale]. *Ryûkyû Daigaku Kyôiku Gakubu Kenkyû Kiyô [Bulletin of Faculty of Education, Ryûkyû University], 4*, 43–53.

Chapter 4
Lay Participation System and Trust in the Justice System

Social Survey on the Relationships Between General trust and the Trust in the Justice System[1]

About the First Half of This Chapter

People obey the law because they citizens think it is legitimate (Tyler 2006b), and trust is the key that makes the legal system work (Tyler and Huo 2002). The jury system promotes public trust in the justice system through lay people's participation. In the current study, the authors investigated the relationships between citizens' trust in the social system, general trust, feelings of legitimacy for the justice system, and other social variables. The survey was conducted in March 2013 through the Internet, and 1609 Japanese people responded. With these data, the authors tested relational models of the factors that determine citizens' trust in the legal system and relationships among these factors.

[1] The first half of this chapter is the reproduction of Fujita, M., Hayashi, N., & Hotta, S. (2016). Trust in the justice system: Internet survey after introducing mixed tribunal system in Japan. *Oñati Socio-Legal Series*, *6*(2). This paper is available at http://ssrn.com/abstract=2769587. The author thanks the secretariat of the International Institute for the Sociology of Law for clarifying the copyrights concerning this paper. The text in this chapter is modified to make it more grammatically reasonable.

M. Fujita, *Japanese Society and Lay Participation in Criminal Justice*,
https://doi.org/10.1007/978-981-10-0338-7_4

Background

Trust Is the Key to Society

Increasing trust in the justice system was one of the justifications for the introduction of lay participation in the mixed court system of the saiban-in system in Japan (Justice System Reform Council 2001). Here we explore the factors that influence this important function of trust. Trust[2] is essential for our society[3] (Putnam 2000). Contemporary societies require the trust to allow people to collaborate with others, whom they do not know well through blood relations or regional ties, because the more mobile people are, the harder it is for people to maintain social ties. In societies like these, trust plays an important role, allowing people to connect with each other and to make society work. It is widely acknowledged that general trust is a key to making societies move, businesses succeed, and countries prosper (Fukuyama 1995). Putnam (1993) demonstrated that northern Italy has an efficient social system with high trust, whilst southern Italy has a less efficient social system with lower trust. And Putnam (1993) argued that participation in society promotes general trust.

Trust is the key to making social institutions work. Social institutions refer to formal social systems that which are required to govern society or regulate relationships among people, e.g., national or local governments, the legal system, schools, and monetary systems. Yosano and Hayashi (2005) argued that social systems, in general, are based on citizens' general trust. General trust refers to people's belief in the reliability of others. General trust is measured without specifying the object of trust, especially regarding which people should be trusted, including significant others, family members, relatives, or people with whom a person interacts in everyday life (Yamagishi and Yamagishi 1994). A typical survey question is, "In general, can people be trusted?" This reflects people's trust in others who don't have social ties with them, but who live in the same community or society.

General trust can affect a person's attitudes related to trust. Yosano and Hayashi (2005) developed and tested a model including trust in the social system, general trust, and other social variables. This model is shown in Fig. 4.1.

In that model, Yosano and Hayashi (2005) set "confidence," that is, trust in social institutions, as an independent variable, and general trust as a dependent variable. They confirmed the relationship between these two variables with their data. However, general trust comes before trust in institutions, because we form our thoughts about others before we think about abstract social institutions. Yosano and Hayashi (2005) tested their hypothesis with their data, and the data confirmed their

[2] Trust here means people's positive attitudes toward others and expectation of positive reactions from others. In experimental studies, that is described as "cooperation" among participants (e.g., Yamagishi and Yamagishi 1994)

[3] The term society here is understood to mean an aggregate of persons living together in a more or less ordered community.

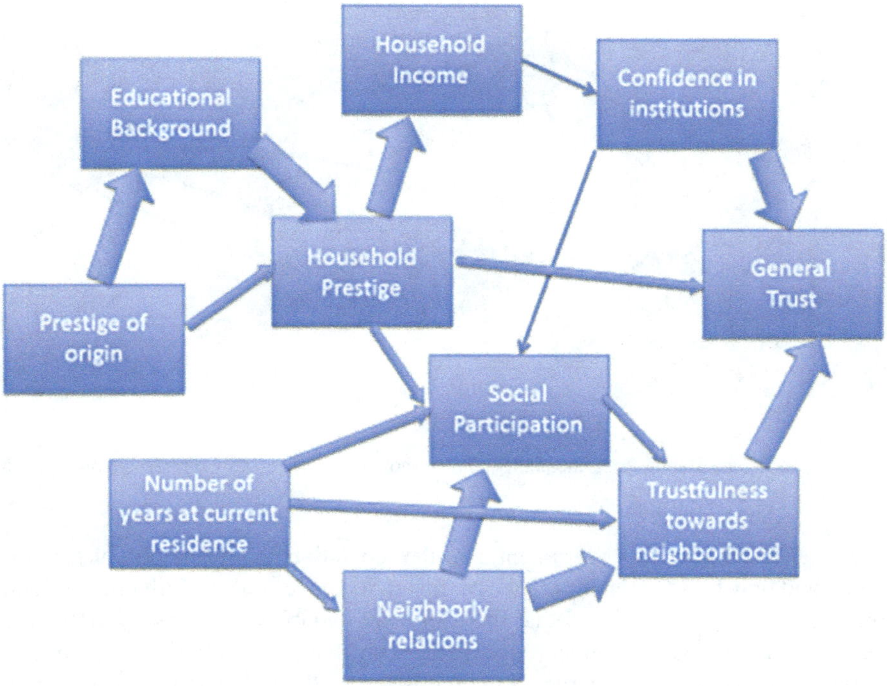

Fig. 4.1 Determinants of general trust. Composed from Yosano and Hayashi (2005). *Thick arrows*, coefficients 0.2 or more; *Medium arrows*, between 0.1 and .2; *Thin arrows*, less than 0.1

hypothesis. It is reasonable that general trust is related to trust in more abstract objects, such as social institutions, as the trust held in the human mind can be derived from the same or similar mechanisms of the mind. In addition, we thought that there should be a path from the general trust to trust in social institutions (Hypothesis 1), which we examine in this paper.

According to Yosano and Hayashi (2007), previous sociological studies have found relationships between trust in the social system and other social variables (see Fig. 4.2). The model shown in this figure was composed of findings from prior studies. Yosano and Hayashi (2007) did not test this model with their data in that paper.

Yosano and Hayashi (2007) concluded from the collected research that social institutions could work when the people who are living in their society trust them.

Trust in Government and Authoritarian Personality

More concretely, trust in government is affected by many social variables. Ikeda (2007) investigated the factors that affect trust in national and local governments with a social survey in Japan. He assessed the effects of demographic variables,

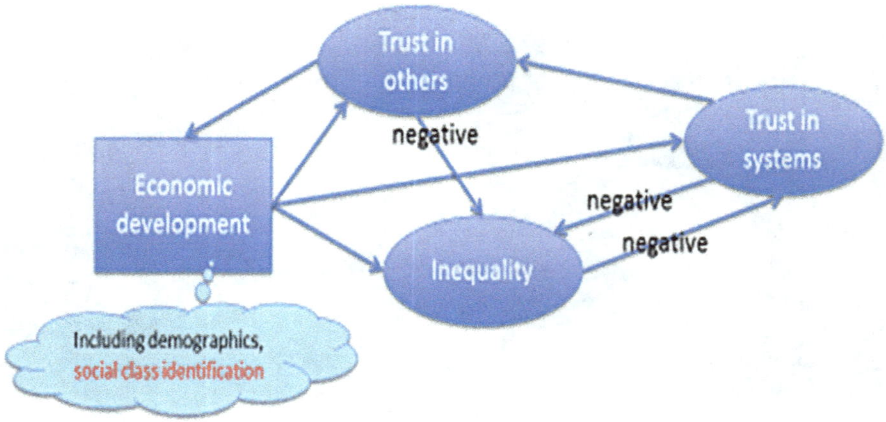

Fig. 4.2 Relations among trust, inequality, and economic development. Composed from Yosano and Hayashi (2007)

social attitudes towards government, and the reputation and evaluation of government, and how these variables related to trust in the government. With ordered logit regression analyses, he found that the following variables significantly affected a person's trust in the government: age, life circumstances, familiarity with government, professional ethics, fairness in administration, the reputation of government, and evaluation of administrative reform. The current study includes the variables of authoritarian personality, life satisfaction, and fairness because these variables are also relevant to a justice system.

Ikeda (2010) discussed that the reason why "age" apparently related to "authoritarian personality." Typically, it can be thought that age itself is not related to personality. Ikeda (2010) speculated that the relationship between age and authoritarian personality suggests that people get positive attitudes towards authorities, as they get old. He thought that people could get develop conservative attitudes as they get old. He did not test this assumption, as he had not asked questions which could provide him the data that could test the assumption. Authoritarian personality refers to personality traits with nine characteristics that generally reflect conservative political and educational attitudes. Those nine characteristics are: (1) sticking to old customs, (2) authoritarian obedience, (3) authoritarian aggressiveness, (4) anti-introspective attitudes, (5) superstition and stereotype, (6) power and integrity, (7) destructiveness and cynicism, (8) projection, and (9) exaggerated interest in sexual issues (Adorno et al. 1950). Adorno et al. (1950) used the term "authoritarian" while they defined the typical characteristics of the authoritarian personality. More properly, (2) and (3) can be paraphrased as "obedience to the people in power" and "aggressiveness with rigid and conservative attitudes.". Sticking to old customs and obedience to seniors and power are especially striking characteristics of the authoritarian personality. In the current study, we assess the effects of an authoritarian personality on trust in the justice system. We hypothesized that an authoritarian personality promotes trust in the justice system, as those who are inclined to an authoritarian personality would have respectful attitudes towards an authoritative social system like justice system (Hypothesis 2).

People in a higher social class would tend to have a more authoritarian personality because they would tend to think to preserve the society as it is, which is the same inclination that the authoritarian personality has. The Authoritarian personality was originally developed as a description of the personality traits of the people who were raised in families in such middle, upper-middle, and upper classes.

As Ikeda (2007) found, life satisfaction and life circumstances may affect trust in a social system. More concretely, as Yosano and Hayashi (2005) wrote, life satisfaction affects general trust. When people are satisfied with their lives, they feel less cautious about their life circumstances (Isen and Means 1983; Schwarz 1990). So, it is reasonable for the people who are satisfied with their lives to be less cautious of others in general, and so they trust more people in general.

Based on these earlier findings, we hypothesized that life satisfaction affects general trust, and via general trust, life satisfaction has an influence on trust in the justice system (Hypothesis 3). People in higher social classes are inclined to be more satisfied with their lives (Hypothesis 4).

We discuss the fairness of trials in the justice system in the next section, with the importance of legitimacy in trust in the justice system.

Trust in the Legal System

Trust in the legal system has been long studied in a sub-discipline of social psychology, the study of procedural justice and legal consciousness (Finkel 1995; Sunshine and Tyler 2003; Tyler 1988, 2001, 2003, 2006a, 2007a, b; Tyler and Bies 1990; Tyler and Fagan 2008). In this field of study, trust in the legal system is associated with people's willingness to accept decisions made by legal authorities and to follow the decisions and rules (Tyler 2006b). Trust in the legal system is an important factor that leads people to accept the law and legal decisions voluntarily. In that sense, what makes the legal system work is the public's trust in the system (Tyler and Huo 2002). It is desirable that people comply voluntarily with the law and decisions made by legal authorities, because if people do not follow the law or accept decisions made by legal authorities voluntarily, legal authorities need to monitor people's behavior more and give sanctions to those who do not obey the law (Tyler and Huo 2002). This increases the costs to legal authorities due to monitoring and sanctioning. It is important for the legal system to be trusted in order for them to function. In much of the literature on trust in the justice system, trust has been treated as an independent variable. Prior studies have investigated factors that affect feelings of fairness, perceptions of outcome favorability, willingness to accept decisions, and procedural justice (Tyler and Huo 2002). Trust in the justice system was treated as an independent variable, not as a dependent variable.

One exception was an analysis of trust in the justice system that treated it as a dependent variable (Tyler and Huo 2002, p. 84). In this analysis, the authors conducted a regression analysis and found that quality of decision making, quality of treatment, outcome favorability, and outcome fairness affected trust in the justice system. Regarding trust in the justice system held by the general public, for the current survey, we considered including question items concerning the quality of decision making, outcome favorability, and outcome fairness, because the quality of treatment cannot be estimated by the people who do not experience legal procedures.

As mentioned above, prior studies have examined factors that affect willingness to accept outcomes and satisfaction with decision making by legal authorities. In those studies, two factors, legitimacy, and fairness, have been thought of as two important determinants. People obey the law not necessarily because of fear of punishment, but because the legal authorities are legitimate (Tyler 2006b; Tyler and Bies 1990). Feelings of fairness promote people's acceptance of legal decision making.

In the next two sections, we deal with those two important factors, legitimacy and fairness.

Fairness and Trust in Social Institutions, and Trust in the Legal System

Fairness is also a significant factor in trust in social institutions, especially legal institutions. Fairness refers to the impartial treatment of people who are involved in important procedures. Procedural justice has been extensively studied, and it was found that fairness in the justice system is one of the important structural elements that influence people to follow the law.

There are two kinds of fairness, procedural fairness and outcome fairness (Tyler and Huo 2002). Procedural fairness refers to whether the people involved in the procedure perceive it as fair. Outcome fairness refers to the conclusion or outcome of the procedure and whether it is regarded as fair.

In this study, we included outcome fairness, because we focused on the general public's sense of the justice system. Many citizens have limited experience in using legal procedures, especially criminal trial procedures. We are interested in the general public's acceptance of and attitudes towards the justice system, as this is one of the "popular bases" (Justice System Reform Council 2001) of the justice system. One major justification for lay participation in the legal system is that it promotes the people's trust in the justice system (Justice System Reform Council 2001).

On the point of the relationship between trust and fairness, one of the factors that affect trust in government, the formal social institutions, is a citizen's feelings of social fairness (Obuchi 2005). Feelings of social fairness are people's subjective evaluation that people they are treated impartially by their government and administrative system (Obuchi 2005). The feelings are sorts of people's heuristic evaluation of public authorities (Lind and van den Bos 2002). When people feel perceive social fairness, they think their government's policies are right on the whole. Obuchi (2005) found that feelings of social fairness promote people's trust in the government. In this study, we expected that sense of fairness would affect trust in the justice system, as the justice system is one of the systems that is operated by state power.

Based on the expectations above, we included questions on the sense of fairness, including outcome fairness from the viewpoint of citizens, and the sense of fairness for the justice system in our questionnaire. We expected that sense of fairness would positively affect trust in the justice system (Hypothesis 5).

Legitimacy and Trust in the Justice System

People follow the law and show their trust in the legal system because they believe the legal system is legitimate (Tyler 2006a, b, 2007a, 2009; Tyler and Bies 1990; Tyler and Jost 2007). Legitimacy is one of the reasons that people obey the law (Tyler and Huo 2002).

Tyler (2006a, p. 375) argued that "Legitimacy is a psychological property of an authority, institution, or social arrangement that leads those connected to it to believe that it is appropriate, proper, and just." According to those arguments and findings, making people feel legitimacy in the legal system is important in operating a justice system. We expected that legitimacy in the legal system would positively influence trust in the legal system (Hypothesis 6). Fairness and legitimacy will be related. Specifically, a feeling of fairness brings about a belief in the feelings of the legitimacy of the legal system (Hypothesis 7).

Equality and Trust

Differentiation among people has the potential to destroy trust among people in the society (Kawachi et al. 1997). There is a correlation between equality and trust; in one study (Uslaner 2002) the correlation coefficient measuring the strength of the relationship between the two variables was .468. This coefficient is rather high as a result of the social survey, and this fact shows there is a strong relationship between equality and trust. Messick and Kramer (2001) argued that inequality in society may destroy people's trust in social institutions, which results in ruining people's general trust for others. Based on these findings, it is likely that when inequality emerges, the trust will be undermined.

In this study, we expected that feelings of equality would have a relationship with trust in others, especially general trust. We thought that a question item that asks respondents about their feelings of inequality would be somewhat counter-intuitive, so we asked respondents in this study about their feelings of equality in the society in which they live. Prior studies found that feelings of inequality or equality were influenced by the general trust. Granted that, we expected that feelings of equality should be affected by the general trust (Hypothesis 8).

Also, people in upper social classes feel that everybody in the society is equal, as they have less of a chance to face inequality in the society and they feel justified for their privileged circumstances. We expected that social class would have a positive effect on feelings of equality (Hypothesis 9).

Interest in the Justice System

Before we trust in something, we have to know what we trust. We cannot trust in something that is out of range of our concern. In a Japanese context, the mixed jury system was introduced in 2004 "for the establishment of the popular base" of the legal system (Justice System Reform Council 2001). In this system, citizens, who are randomly selected and chosen through the jury selection procedure, sit in criminal trials that deal with serious crimes. Citizens decide the cases with professional judges.

With the introduction of this system, civic involvement in the justice system has been much improved. Lay people's interest in the justice system rose dramatically after the mixed jury system was introduced (Matsumura et al. 2012). This was because the mixed jury system was one of the most important issues in the justice system reform in Japan in the 2000's. People began to think that they might be involved in the justice system as jurors. This promoted encouraged people to think that matters of the justice system were their matters, not just other people's matters or remote concerning. This led to provoke the public's general interest in the justice system.

Based on this context, we investigated whether interest in the justice system affects trust in the justice system. We expected that interest in the justice system might promote trust in the justice system (Hypothesis 10).

Current Study

To examine Hypotheses 1 through 10, we gathered data by obtaining the responses of general ordinary citizens. We designed a questionnaire to be able to test these hypotheses, and in response respond to our concerns. In Yosano and Hayashi (2005), legitimacy and trust were not distinguished from each other. The accumulation of findings from prior studies, especially regarding legitimacy and trust in the legal system (e.g., Tyler 2003, 2006a), suggest the value of distinguishing between these two factors. Legitimacy is about the feeling concerning "the manner in which authorities exercise their authorities.". (Tyler 2003, p. 286) And views about legitimacy are rooted in the judgment that the legal authorities are acting fairly when they deal with community residents. While Trust is confidence in the institutions of the legal system, and trust elicits public compliance (Tyler 2003). So, we distinguished these two factors, and we included questions on the legitimacy of social institutions and trust in social institutions in our questionnaire.

Yosano and Hayashi (2005, 2007) did not take personality, traits into account in their studies. As Ikeda (2007) wrote, we could study personality traits, especially the authoritarian personality on trust in social institutions, and we can test the influence of age and authoritarian personality on trust in the legal system In our survey, we could separate the effects of age and authoritarian personality with statistical analysis, and investigate whether the argument by Ikeda is applicable to our data.

On the other hand, the literature on legitimacy and trust in the justice system has examined relationships among legitimacy, justice, fairness, trust in the persons in charge, and outcomes of the procedures in detail. However, there has seldom been an examination of the relationships between legitimacy, fairness, trust in the legal system, general trust, and feelings of equality. We thought that general trust might affect trust in the justice system and trust in the legal system. In this part, "trust in the legal system" refers to people's confidence in the normative system that consists of statutes. This was measured by one question in our questionnaire. And "trust in the justice system" refers to a latent variable which that integrates some sorts of public confidences in the system of statutes and, legal authorities. We distinguish these two variables because we would like to distinguish a single question item from a latent variable, which integrates the results of several questions. So, we included questions on general trust, authoritarian personality, and trust in the justice system, and we examined relationships among those variables with our data.

Method

Overview of the Survey

The author planned an Internet survey in Japan. We had a private research company based in Tokyo, Nikkei Research, Inc., conduct a web-based survey. The survey was conducted in the Tokyo Metropolitan area and the surrounding prefectures. We did sampling and designed the questionnaire. The survey company set up a website that posted the questionnaire and recruited respondents. We received raw data from the survey company and analyzed it.

Sampling Plan

The author carried out quota sampling in order to include samples from cities, suburbs, and the countryside. Without these efforts, major parts of our sample would have come from cities, with few respondents from the countryside, as residents in cities are more responsive to Internet surveys. Also, we made an effort to include samples of all age ranges from 20 to 60 and above.

In our sampling plan, we identified areas of residence as (1) large city area, (2) suburban area, and (3) rural area by respondents' addresses. Ages varied from 20 to 60 and up, divided by every 10 years. At that time, we had a 5 × 3 table for sampling. Every cell of this quota had the same number of male and female samples. We planned each cell to include 40 males and 40 females. In this plan, we expected 1200 people overall in this survey.

Respondents and Procedure

The respondents were Japanese people who lived in the Kanto area. Kanto is located in the middle of Honshu, the main island of Japan. This area consists of the Tokyo metropolitan area and six prefectures: Kanagawa, Chiba, Saitama, Ibaraki, Tochigi, and Gunma. Before the survey, the participants voluntarily registered as respondents. The survey company and its partner companies held and maintained the lots information of respondents. The companies called for responses through the Internet, newspaper ads, advertising flyers posted in train stations, and by direct mail. All respondents were Japanese citizens.

Nikkei Research, Inc. requested that the candidates visit the website and answer the questionnaire posted on the website via email. The respondents voluntarily filled out the web-based questionnaire in response to the email. The respondents who finished the questionnaire were rewarded by a lot. The respondents were informed that the research company would randomly select some of the respondents and give them a monetary award. The survey company waited for the responses to exceed at least 1200 and expected each cell in our sampling plan to be filled by 40 or more respondents. The survey company stopped receiving responses through the website when the number of respondents exceeded 1200.

One thousand six hundred and ten people responded to the survey. Their ages ranged from 20 to 70. The mean age was 44.78, the median age was 45, and the standard deviation for age was 13.98. There were 747 male respondents (46.4%) and 863 female respondents (53.6%).

As a result of quota sampling, the distribution of the prefectures where respondents resided almost resembled the distribution of population among the prefectures. The real population of each prefecture, city, town, and village is recorded by each local government. The numbers of the population are based on the National Census conducted every 5 years, as well as resident registration maintained by the local governments. Maintaining resident registration is required by law.

About half (49.4%) of the respondents graduated from college. This figure is similar to the proportion of college graduates in the Japanese population, which was 46% in 2011 (OECD 2013, p.38). Other respondents' educational backgrounds were elementary school (0.1%), junior high school (1.2%), senior high school

(17.8%), technical college (2.3%), vocational school (10.5%), junior college (10.7%), and graduate school (7.9%).

Respondents' household annual income varied as follows: 0–2 million yen (6.5%), 2–4 million yen (17.9%), 4–6 million yen (20.3%), 6–8 million yen (16.1%), 8–10 million yen (12.0%), 10–15 million yen (10.5%), 15–20 million yen (3.1%), and 20 million and above (1.9%). A total of 11.7% of respondents refused to answer the question on household income. The distribution of answers for social class identification was upper (0.9%), upper-middle (14.5%), middle-middle (43.6%), lower-middle (32.5), lower (8.4%). The respondents identified the class themselves to which class they belong.

Measures

The questionnaire posted on the website included the following measures. All questions were answered on a five-point Likert scale. The scale ranged from 1 (Not at all agree) to 5 (Strongly agree). An option for "I don't know" was added to the Likert scale for each question item.

Trust in social system and persons-in-charge: This set of questions was based on JGSS 2008 (JGSS Research Center at Osaka University of Commerce 2011). The questions asked the extent of trust of respondents have in large companies, scholars and researchers, the legal system, judges, prosecutors, attorneys, police officers, national governments' ministries, law courts, and local governments. We added an explanation of prosecutors to an instruction in the questionnaire, as we thought that general citizens were not familiar with the word "prosecutors."

The sense of legitimacy about system and persons-in-charge: This set of questions asked participants how they felt about the legitimacy of all of the system and the persons-in-charge mentioned above. As we thought that the meaning of the word "legitimacy" might be difficult for general citizens to understand properly, we created the question item, "To what extent do you think below-mentioned items are acting in ways that can be thought as socially right?" We presented the respondents with the specific systems and persons-in-charge, and a five-point Likert scale to assess their responses.

General trust: We assessed respondents' trust in people in general, by asking, "Generally speaking, people can be trusted."

Life satisfaction: We assessed respondents' life-circumstances satisfaction by asking about respondents' satisfaction with their area of residence, household income, relationship with friends, and relationship with the family.

Expectation of trial fairness and quality: To assess respondents' expectations about the fairness and quality of trials, we asked respondents, "Method of trial in law courts is fair", "Punishment which is declared in law courts is fair", "Quality of decision making in law courts is high", and, "People who come to law courts are treated with dignity."

Interest in the justice system: This set of questions included, "I have been interested in the mixed jury system," "My/General public's interest in trials rose after the introduction of the mixed jury system."

Authoritarian personality (3 items): These questions were taken from Adorno et al. (1950). We chose three question items from the California F scale to assess authoritarian personality. See Appendix B for the specific items.

Social Dominance Orientation (SDO, 6 items): To assess a sense of equality, we employed the social dominance orientation measure (Pratto et al. 1994). Due to the length restriction of the questionnaire, we selected six items from this scale, especially regarding the sense of equality, as we expected that feelings of equality would be important in relation to trust in the legal system and general trust. See Appendix B for the specific items.

Demographic variables: This section included questions about respondents' age, sex, educational background, annual household income, social class identification, residence by prefecture, and ZIP codes.

Combine Variables to Make Potential Variables

To identify latent variables within observable variables, we selected appropriate question items, as shown above, and we calculated Cronbach's alpha for each scale. To combine trust in the legal system, we selected responses to questions about trust in the legal system, judges, prosecutors, attorneys, police officers, and law courts. We found an estimation of Cronbach's alpha is very high, so we integrated the score of the sense of legitimacy in the legal system into the scale.

In SDO, the question, "some groups of people are simply not the equals of others," reduces the estimation of Cronbach's alpha of SDO scale. Because of this, this item was removed from the analyses that followed. As a result, three question items, "Increased economic equality," "equality," "If people were treated more equally, we would have fewer problems in this country," were combined into one variable. We called it SDO thereafter.

The estimated alphas are as follows: trust in the legal system (.92), Social Dominance Orientation (Pratto et al. 1994) (.68), interest in the legal system (.84), satisfaction with life circumstances (.74), authoritarian personality (.68), sense of fairness and quality of decision making in trials (.86).

These scales were used as latent variables in the analyses that followed.

Table 4.1 Correlations among combined variables

	Trust in the justice system	Equality	Interest in the justice system	Life satisfaction	Authoritarian personality	Expectation of trial fairness and quality
Trust in the justice system	-					
Equality	.236**	-				
Interest in the justice system	.167**	.150**	-			
Life satisfaction	.318**	.232**	.235**	-		
Authoritarian personality	.180**	.266**	.097**	.141**	-	
Expectation of trial fairness and quality	.457**	.351**	.249**	.277**	.177**	-
General trust	.341**	.274**	.194**	.419**	.195**	.268**

$^{**}p<.01$
$N = 1535$ (Correlations between trust in the justice system and other variables); $N = 1610$ (other correlations)

Results

Correlations among Variables

Table 4.1 shows Pearson's correlation coefficients among the combined variables shown above and the answers for general trust. All coefficients were statistically significant at the .1 percent level.

According to Table 4.1, the highest correlation was found between "trust in the justice system" and "expectation of trial fairness and quality" (.457). The correlation between "trust in the justice system" and "life satisfaction" was the second highest (.318), followed by "equality" (.236), "authoritarian personality" (.180), and "interest in the justice system" (.167).

Concerning "general trust," the second highest correlation in this table was found between "general trust" and "life satisfaction" (.419). "General trust" and "trust in the justice system" were correlated (.341), and moderate correlations were found between "general trust" and "equality" (.274), and "expectation of trial fairness and quality" (.268).

Among other correlations, a relatively high coefficient was found between "equality" and "expectation of trial fairness and quality" (.351). Other coefficients larger than .2 were correlations between "life satisfaction" and "expectation of trial fairness and quality" (.277), "authoritarian personality" and "equality" (.266), "expectation of trial fairness and quality" and "interest in the justice system" (.249), "interest in the justice system" and "life satisfaction" (.235), "equality" and "life satisfaction" (.232).

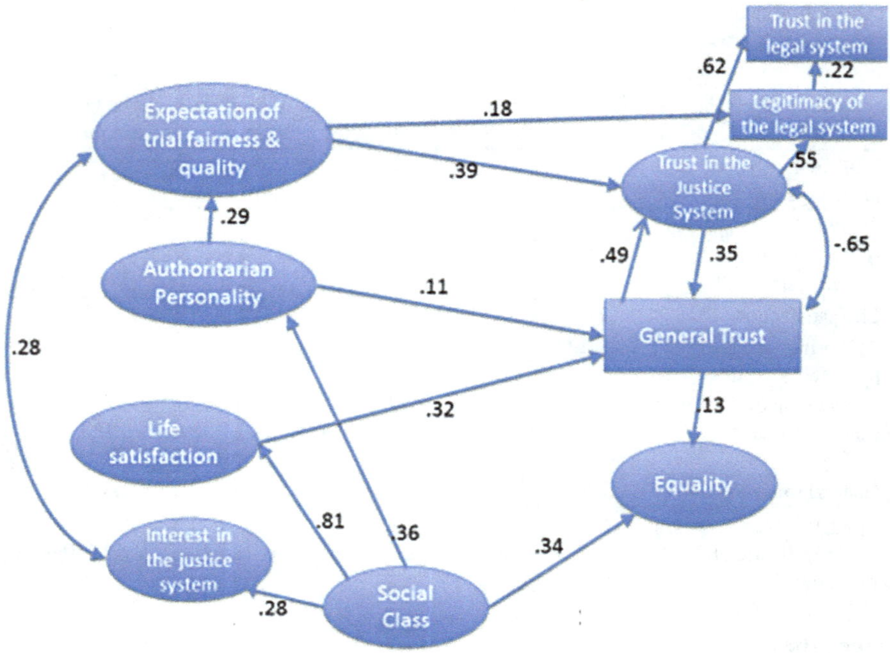

Fig. 4.3 Determinants of trust in the justice system. $\chi^2(447)= 2553.87$, $p < 0.001$. RMSEA = 0.056, CFI = 0.889

Other correlation coefficients were less than .2, but all of them were statistically significant.

Test of Fit of the Model to Data

Under our assumptions, we created and tested our model with Structural Equation Modeling. Fig. 4.1 shows the relationship between latent variables and general trust. All paths and covariances showed in Fig. 4.3 were statistically significant at .1 percent level. The Arabic numerals that were put alongside paths and covariances show standardized coefficients.

In Fig. 4.1, observed variables, standard errors, and paths among those variables were omitted for understandability. But single question items "trust in the legal system," "legitimacy of the legal system," and "general trust" were depicted, as those items have importance in the results and following discussion.

Trust in the justice system affected general trust (.35), and the reverse path was also significant (.49). The general trust had some impact on authoritarian personality (.11) and life satisfaction (.32). These variables had positive effects on equality (.13).

Regarding the expectation of trial fairness and quality, this expectation had positive effects on trust in the justice system (.39) and the legitimacy of the legal system (.18). The legitimacy of the legal system affected the single question item "trust in the legal system" (.22).

Social class widely influenced other variables in this model. Social class positively affected equality, authoritarian personality, life satisfaction, and interest in the justice system. Life satisfaction and authoritarian personality had effects on general trust, and trust in the justice system.

The direct path from an interest in the justice system to trust in the justice system was not significant. In this model, interest in the justice system was an endogenous variable.

Overall, the fitness of this model to our data was acceptable ($\chi^2(417) = 2553.866$, $p < .001$, RMSEA = .056, CFI = .889).

Discussion

What Factors Determine Trust in the Justice System?

General Trust

With a simple correlational analysis, we found that every latent variable and general trust correlated with trust in the justice system. The strongest correlation was found between trust in the justice system and expectation of trial fairness and quality. This confirms Tyler and Huo's (2002) finding that fairness affects trust in the justice system. Adding to it, general trust and life satisfaction had a relatively high correlation. This confirms the prior study (Yosano and Hayashi 2010), which found that trust in the social system is based on a trust in human relationships.

Using Structural Equation Modeling, we confirmed Yosano and Hayashi's (2010) argument that trust in the legal system affects general trust. In addition, our data show a reverse path is significant. That is general trust affect trained trust in the justice system with the coefficient, .49. In this way, our data show trust in the legal system and general trust influence each other.

We expected that trust in the justice system would affect general trust. This expectation was confirmed by our study. The relationship between trust in the justice system and general trust, especially the influence of trust in the justice system to general trust, seems to be robust. Thus, our Hypothesis 1 was supported.

We also found a reverse direction effect of general trust in our work. Thus, general trust has an influence on trust in the legal system, a correlation that was not found in prior studies. General trust and trust in the legal system affect each other. If people think they can trust in other people, they have more trust in the legal system, and if they trust more in the legal system, they have more trust in more in other people. Our data suggest that general trust and trust in the justice system has a circular relationship.

Our study confirmed that life satisfaction affects general trust. This result supports Hypothesis 3. If people are content with their lives, their general trust will increase. This means that if some social circumstances promote satisfaction with their lives, their general trust will increase. For government or policymakers, promoting people's life satisfaction is important not only for the sake of people's welfare but for stabilizing society by making people trust in one another.

But a direct path from life satisfaction to trust in the justice system was not statistically significant. We might expect that increasing life satisfaction would promote trust in the legal system directly. Rather, it increases general trust, and as a part of this, trust in the justice system increases. The indirect effect of raising life satisfaction on promoting general trust is .16 (.32 × .49), according to our data.

Legitimacy and Trust

In this study, the legitimacy of the legal system had such a high correlation with trust in the legal system that those variables could be combined into one latent variable with another trust in legal professionals (judges, prosecutors, and attorneys) and law courts. Combining the legitimacy of the legal system, trust in the legal system, and trust in legal professionals, the estimation of Cronbach's alpha was high (.92).

Given this result, many respondents would think legitimacy and trust are alike. In Tyler and Huo (2002), Chicago data showed that trust in institutions strongly affects legitimacy. This was true on both the occasions when they were measured two times (.85 and .90 respectively). Like the result cited above, essentially, legitimacy and trust are thought of as very similar concepts by the general population. Our study confirmed the similarity between these concepts.

From another standpoint, this result can be interpreted as trust in the justice system overall, as this consists of both trusts in the legal system and trust in other legal professionals and legitimacy of the legal system. Here we need to distinguish "overall trust in the justice system" and "individual trust in the legal system."

With respect to the relationship between authoritarian personality and trust in the justice system, there was a path from authoritarian personality to general trust and expectation of trial fairness and quality. But there was no direct path from authoritarian personality to trust in the justice system. Hence, Hypothesis 2 was not completely supported. However, authoritarian personality had an indirect effect on trust in the justice system via the "expectation of trial fairness and quality" and "general trust."

Fairness and Quality of Decision Making

According to Tyler and Huo (2002), trial procedure and the quality of decision making affect trust in the legal system for those who have experienced treatment by the police and/or by judges. In this study, based on the results of our factor analysis, the fairness and quality of the trial were combined in one scale. Many respondents thought that these two factors were very similar to each other. This is partly because the majority of respondents had not participated in a real trial, while Tyler and Huo's (2002) respondents had experience with legal procedures. Respondents who had not been involved in legal procedures could answer questions using their imagination and their attitudes towards the questions. Thus, those respondents may have thought fairness and quality of trials are similar, based on their attitudes towards trials. As a result, these two variables are considered as one factor in our factor analysis.

To test this assumption, we could compare the answers from those who have experience with court procedures, and those who have not had this experience, ideally comparing SEM analyses among all respondents. However, in our data, only a very small percentage of respondents had been exposed to a trial process. Hence we could not conduct SEM analysis solely with respondents who had experienced trial procedures.

Given that respondents thought that fairness and quality of decision making were very similar, the latent variable "expectation of trial fairness and quality" positively affected trust in the justice system. In that sense, Hypothesis 5 was supported. (Refer to Hypothesis 5 in Appendix A.)

Feelings of fairness will affect feelings of legitimacy in the legal system (Hypothesis 7). In our study, we found that "expectation of trial fairness and quality" had positive effects on trust in the justice system and the legitimacy of the legal system. Our data indicated that "expectation of trial fairness and quality" affected trust in the justice system and trust in the legal system. This was an unexpected result of our study, but the latent variable including respondents' feelings of fairness directly affected legitimacy in the legal system, so Hypothesis 7 was partly supported.

Legitimacy

Based on our factor analysis, almost all of the scores for the legitimacy of social institutions and trust in social institutions consisted of one factor. We selected legitimacy of the legal system, judges, prosecutors, defense counsel, and police officers, and trust in that persons-in-charge for operating the justice system. The results of factor analyses suggested that our respondents thought that trust and legitimacy were very similar factors. So we identified a latent variable "trust in the justice system" overall, and we included all of the variables selected here. The legitimacy of the legal system and trust in the legal system are especially important from the point of view of our study, so we selected these two factors and gave them special attention in our analysis.

Hence, the majority of responses for legitimacy and trust in social institutions are combined and considered as one latent variable in our analysis. In our analysis, the legitimacy of the legal system positively affected trust in the legal system (.22). Hypothesis 6 was supported.

Effects of Social Class

The social class had a broad effect in this model. The latent variable "social class" was combined with the observed variables of gender, age, annual household income, and the five-point scale of social-class identification. Based on the findings of prior studies, we expected that social class would have a positive effect on a sense of equality (Hypothesis 9). This hypothesis was supported by our results, shown in Fig. 4.3.

Overall, in our results, social class positively affected equality, authoritarian personality, life satisfaction, and interest in the justice system.

First, the reason social class affected equality positively is that the higher the social class to which people belong, the more resources people have. Thus, people in upper social classes may feel the need to justify their status. People in upper social classes may tend to perceive society as composed of equals. Also, their resources enable the people in upper social classes to do more things in society when they want to do them, resulting in fewer chances of facing limitations on their actions due to social circumstances. People in upper social classes may be less sensitive about recognizing inequality in the society. And another possibility is that they may be sensitive because they see how much they have then and how little other people have.

Second, social class may have positive influences on life satisfaction, as people in upper social classes experience less emotional distress (Lorant et al. 2003), less psychological disorders (Bradley and Corwyn 2002), less physical illness and experience more psychological well-being (Adler and Snibbe 2003; Seeman et al. 2004). Based on those findings, people in higher classes live physically and psychologically healthy lives. Self-rated health is a predominant variable of life satisfaction, and socioeconomic variables influence life satisfaction (Palmore and Luikart 1972). Our data are consistent with those findings, indicating there is a positive causal relationship between social class and life satisfaction with a rather high coefficient (.81). Hypothesis 4 was supported.

Third, the social class had positive influences on interest in the justice system. This may be because people in upper social classes have more power in social institutions such as in local or national governments, or have connections with members of the Diet, the Japanese legislature, or with other people who have power in the society. Thus, people in upper social classes may have efficacy in social institutions and are hence more interested in those institutions. The Justice system is theoretically, ideally, and constitutionally independent of other governing powers, but the general population may think of the justice system as being only one of the several governing systems.

The Sense of Equality and Trust in the Legal System

According to Messick and Kramer (2001), inequality undermines trust among people. This is because "as the level of economic inequality increases, these bonds are increasingly frayed, and trust in others declines" (Uslaner 2002, p. 4).

In our data, "inequality" is considered the opposite of "equality." Equality was a latent variable combined with the answers from the SDO scale. Equality was affected by general trust and social class. Regarding the relationship between equality and general trust, people in upper social classes tend to feel that people in society are equal, because they may feel the need to justify their status. The relationship that feelings of equality are affected by general trust seems rather robust, based on prior studies and our data. This result supports Hypothesis 8, which argues that the feeling of equality should be affected by general trust.

Interest in the Justice System

We expected that interest in the justice system would promote trust in the justice system (Hypothesis 10). The Justice System Reform Council in Japan expected the same thing in their opinion paper (Justice System Reform Council 2001). According to simple correlation analysis, interest in the justice system and trust in the legal system positively correlated. This result matched our expectation mentioned above. But with SEM analysis, the direct path between those two variables, interest in the justice system and trust in the legal system, was not significant. This means that even though those two variables have a positive relationship, the direct path of interest in the justice system and trust in the legal system, was not found with our data.

Based on the findings shown here, interest in the justice system does not promote trust in the justice system by itself. Hypothesis 10 was not supported by our data. According to our data, interest in the justice system and expectation of trial fairness and quality were positively correlated. But the data did not indicate the direction of the relationship between those two variables.

Limitations

A major limitation of this survey comes from the samples of the study. We made efforts to include respondents from rural areas. However, due to our efforts, we could not have a rigid random sampling. Also, due to our practical restrictions, we just had samples from the metropolitan area of Japan. We think the data from the metropolitan area are more representative of Japan because the population and people's origins vary more in the metropolitan area compared to other parts of Japan. Just 25 of the 1610 respondents participated as saiban-ins in Japan's saiban-in system. Most of 1459 respondents (1459) had no experience with using lawsuits to solve the problems in their lives. The majority of respondents, then, may have based their thoughts about the quality of decision making in trial processes and procedural justice on their imagination, impressions from the media and other sources of information, and their attitudes towards the justice system.

Implications and Future Directions

Social Class

Regarding social class, people in the upper class have more positive attitudes towards life satisfaction, interest in the justice system, equality, and a higher score with respect to authoritarian personality. In recent years, social differentiation keeps expanding; the middle-class is decreasing, while the lower class population is growing. Under these circumstances, a feeling of equality among people may decline, and life satisfaction may become lower. As the number of dissatisfied people increases, general trust and a sense of equality will likely be reduced. Society may become unstable, and there may be less trust in people and in social institutions.

Trust in the Legal System and General Trust

Our data showed that trust in the legal system promoted general trust. This is consistent with prior studies demonstrating that trust in the social system promotes general trust, and general trust increases trust in the justice system. Trust in the justice system was affected by expectations about trial fairness and quality. If we are trying to increase trust in the justice system, raising general trust among people and raising expectations concerning trials could be two good choices for policymakers. In addition, to cultivate general trust among people, our study suggest implies that raising life satisfaction among people would increase general trust, and trust in the justice system.

Interest in the Justice System

Interest in the justice system itself did not promote trust in the legal system. But that does not mean it is useless to promote public interest in the legal system. According to Fig. 4.3, public interest in the legal system positively correlated with the expectation of law courts' fair actions. From this data, we can assume that promoting one of these variables may lead to promoting another. For example, promotion of public interest in the legal system promotes the expectation of law courts' fair actions. People in a society may be expected to have an interest in, monitor, and judge the activities of social institutions that hold state power. Therefore, cultivating interest in the justice system is important, even if this does not have a direct relationship on increasing trust in the justice system, as we had expected before a mixed jury system was initiated.

Equality

Feelings of equality were affected by general trust. This brings about some practical lessons for policymakers. Trust in the justice system positively affects general trust and general trust positively affects feelings of equality. Given this, increasing trust in the justice system may increase the feelings of equality in a society, and make the society more stable.

Future Directions and Implications for Lay Participation

In this study, we investigated the sociological factors that determine trust in the justice system. We identified a circular relationship between general trust and the trust in the legal system. "Trust in the justice system" was determined by "the expectation of trial fairness and quality." These results tell us that we need to enhance people's expectations and their senses that trials are fairly managed if we want to increase people's trust in the justice system.

In a Japanese context, this can be related to the reasons why the Japanese Government introduced the mixed jury system in 2004. The mixed jury system was introduced in order to build a popular base for a justice system (Justice System Reform Council 2001). The Japanese Government thought that introducing the mixed jury system would increase people's trust in the justice system. Recent Japanese history tells us that the more remote the justice system gets, the more the people's trust in the justice system declines. The Japanese pure jury system was suspended in 1943, during the middle of World War II. Since then, for more than a half of a century, the general public in Japan was not allowed to participate in trials. This has kept the people remote from the legal system, and many people may not have had much chance to observe the real processes that are carried out in the law courts. With this situation, people can only imagine what has been done by the law courts and how professional judges handle their jobs. Due to the fact that the trial processes have been isolated from the general public, the judgments shown resulting from the trials and the behaviors of professional judges have gotten become less and less understandable from the public's point of view. To improve this situation, the Japanese Government implemented the Justice System Reform at the beginning of the twenty-first century. It wanted to increase the public's understandings of the justice system.

After introducing the new lay participation system in Japan, the lay participants positively evaluated the system, at least according to the Courts' survey (The Supreme Court of Japan 2014). The general public in Japan feel that the general public are more interested in the justice system than before, as they feel the possibility that they have become more involved in the processes of the trial. With the involvement of ordinary people into the justice system, for example, professional judges seem to be more people-friendly. Increasing people's interest in the justice system may lead to more just support making the criminal procedures more just. It might lead to improvements, such as introducing audiovisual recordings during investigative interviews. If these changes promote people's sense that fairness of criminal trials is fair, these changes can also enhance people's trust in the justice system, as our data showed that people's sense of justice is related to their trust in the justice system.

To enhance people's trust in the justice system, we need to encourage the growth of general trust among people. Putnam (1993) argued that social participation promotes trust. We expect participation in the justice system may promote trust in the justice system, so we should compare the responses between people who have served as jurors and those who have not had such experience. If lay participation in the justice system has the effects that Putnam described, lay participation may increase trust in the justice system. This might affect general trust among people in the society. However, because only a small number of our respondents had been saiban-ins, these relationships are not tested by this study. We need to complete further studies to test these assumptions.

Acknowledgments

This part of the chapter is one of the results of the project on Social Trust and on the Empowerment Process (STEP), based at the Faculty of Sociology, Kansai University, in Osaka, Japan. Project STEP was supported by a Japanese national grant called the Project in Strategic Research to Aid Private Universities (grant code S1001047). This grant has been disbursed by the Japanese Ministry of Education, Culture, Sports, Science, and Technology.

Some parts of the questionnaire used in this study were taken from Japanese General Social Surveys (JGSS) 2008. The following paragraph is an explanation of JGSS, taken from instructions of usage of the JGSS dataset/questionnaire.

> "The Japanese General Social Surveys (JGSS) are designed and carried out by the JGSS Research Center at Osaka University of Commerce (Joint Usage / Research Center for Japanese General Social Surveys accredited by the Minister of Education, Culture, Sports, Science and Technology), in collaboration with the Institute of Social Science at the University of Tokyo."

This study was carried out by the three authors. The analyses were done by Masahiro Fujita during his Foreign Residency Research Program as an Academic Researcher at Kansai University in the academic year 2013–14. Preliminary results of the analyses were discussed at the University of California, Berkeley, USA, where Masahiro Fujita resided as a visiting scholar during the program. Masahiro Fujita deeply appreciates the feedback from the members of the social psychology lab under the supervision of Professor Victoria Plaut. Round trip travel expenses between Berkeley and Oñati, Spain were provided by a grant of the Foreign Residency Research Program. The main conclusions of this paper were also presented in Japanese at the 78th Annual Conference of the Japanese Psychological Association, held at Doshisha University, Kyoto, Japan, in September 2014.

The Changes of the Factors that Determine Trust in the Justice System Before and After the Introduction of the Saiban-in System[4]

About the Second Half of this Chapter

Trust in the legal system is one of the important factors that make the legal system work. The newly introduced mixed jury system (saiban-in system), in which the citizens participate in the criminal trials, in Japan aimed to promote "popular base of the justice system," according to the opinion paper issued by Justice System Reform Council. This aim can be interpreted that the system aimed to promote trust in the justice system of the general public in Japan. The author investigated whether introducing the mixed jury system promoted trust in the justice system of the people in Japan, by secondary analyses of the datasets of Japanese General Social Survey conducted in 2008 and 2010. As the system inaugurated in 2009, those datasets were obtained before and after introducing the system. Compared those two datasets, the author found that "trust in the law courts" of the people increased in 2010 than trust in 2008. With adjusted residual analyses, the author found that in the answers in 2010, the frequencies of "(trust) very much" increased significantly, while the frequencies of answers "seldom (trust)" and "no answer" decreased significantly. Adding to those results, the author conducted multiple regression analyses to specify the magnitude of the introducing jury system on the trust in the justice system. People's trust in the law courts increased after initiation of the trials by saiban-in. And a regression analysis showed that the attitude towards the saiban-in

[4]The second half of this chapter was first appeared in the 2016 annual conference of Law and Society Association. The paper was "Fujita, Masahiro (2016). Does introducing mixed jury system promote trust in justice system in Japan? Discussion based on the secondary analyses of Japanese General Social Surveys and Matsumura et al. (2012)." The paper was presented in the 2016 Annual Meeting of Law and Society Association, held at New Orleans Marriott Hotel, New Orleans, Louisiana, USA, June 3.

system affects positively trust in the law courts. When we compare before and after the introduction of the saiban-in system, we find the people thought that introduction of the saiban-in system does not make the legal system unreliable, and people choose saiban-in system more if they were accused of a crime. The implications and future directions on the results were discussed.

Background

Trust and Justice System

Trust is essential for our society. Contemporary societies require the trust to allow people to collaborate with others, whom they do not know well through blood relations or regional ties, because the more mobile people are, the harder it is for people to maintain social ties (Cook 2001). In societies like these, trust plays an important role, allowing people to connect with each other and make society work. It is widely acknowledged that general trust is a key to make societies move, businesses succeed, and countries prosper (Fukuyama 1995).

Trust is the key to making social institutions work (Dockson and Allen 1993). Social institutions refer to formal social systems which are required to govern society or regulate relationships among people, i.e., national or local governments, legal systems, schools, and monetary systems.

Trust in legal system has been long studied in a sub-discipline of social psychology, the study of procedural justice (Lind and Tyler 1988; MacCoun 2005; Thibaut and Walker 1975) and legal consciousness (Tyler 2007b). In this field of study, trust in legal systems is associated with people's willingness to accept decisions made by legal authorities and to follow the decisions and rules. Trust in the legal system is an important factor that leads people to accept the law and legal decisions voluntarily. In that sense, what makes the legal systems work is the public's trust in the systems. It is desirable that people comply voluntarily with the law and decisions made by legal authorities because if people do not follow the law or accept decisions made by legal authorities voluntarily, legal authorities need to monitor people's behavior more and give sanctions to those who do not obey the law. This increases the costs to legal authorities since monitoring and sanctioning. It is important for legal systems to be trusted in order for them to function. In much of the literature on trust in justice systems, trust has been treated as an independent variable.

Fujita et al. (2016) dealt with those questions and intended answer for that questions with a questionnaire survey taken by the general public residing in Japan.

They conducted a questionnaire survey answered by Japanese people who lived in the Kanto area. Kanto is located in the middle of Honshu, the main island of Japan. This area consists of the Tokyo metropolitan area and six prefectures: Kanagawa, Chiba, Saitama, Ibaraki, Tochigi, and Gunma. Before the survey, the participants voluntarily registered for the lists of respondents held and maintained by the survey company and its partner companies. The companies called for responses through the Internet, newspaper ads, advertising posters posted in train stations, and by direct mail. All respondents were Japanese citizens.

They assessed how the people's perception of Legitimacy of legal systems affects people's trust in the justice systems. They found that many respondents thought legitimacy and trust are alike. In Tyler and Huo (2002), Chicago data showed that institutional trust strongly affects legitimacy. Like those results, legitimacy and trust are thought of as very similar concepts by the general population.

From another standpoint, this result can be interpreted as trust in justice systems overall, as this is composed of both trusts in legal systems and trust in other legal professionals and legitimacy of legal systems.

They also found a circular relationship between general trust and the trust in legal systems. General trust is the extent how the people trust in other people in general. "Trust in the justice systems" was determined by "the expectation of trial fairness and quality." These results tell us that we need to enhance people's expectations and their senses that trials are fairly managed if we want to increase people's trust in the justice systems. The term here used "general trust" means that the extent of trust in others in general, which is measured by the question "in general, what extent do you believe in others?"

Current Study

This study intended to deal with another factor of trust in the justice system — introducing lay participation system.

Given the results are shown above, trust in the justice system is determined by the expectation of trial fairness and its quality. If the introducing lay participation system promotes the expectation of the expectation on trial over fairness and quality, the introduction of lay participation system reinforces the trust in the justice system. So in the current study, the authors cast the question is that "does introduce democratic trial systems like jury systems have an impact on what people think about the society?"

To explore the answers to these questions, the author is conducting secondary analyses on the data of Japanese General Social Surveys. Japanese General Social Surveys have been conducted around every two years, to assess the statuses of Japanese people and their social attitudes and a wide variety of values. The survey includes the questions on how do people trust in social institutions like law courts, police, national Diets, local governments, or other authorities. The author picked up two datasets, which were taken from the JGSS surveys conducted in the years 2008 and 2010. Those are data collected before (in 2008) and after (in 2010) introducing lay participation system (saiban-in system) in Japan.

The Japanese General Social Surveys contains the questions concerning how the people think about social authorities and institutions. Those institutions include law courts, the national government, local governments, police, the officials who are working for national ministries, researchers at universities, mass media, major companies. The questions measure how the people trust in those institutions.

The author is comparing the results of those two datasets and discussing whether there is any impact of introducing lay participation systems in their justice systems. Also, the author is exploring other factors which can affect the social attitudes towards justice systems.

Study 1

In the first study of this paper, the author reanalyzed the datasets of JGSS2008 and JGSS 2010. These two datasets are the first set of data in this paper. In the following section, the outline of the plan of the social surveys is explained.

Method

Method Overview

To conduct a series of secondary analyses, the author received the datasets of Japanese General Social Survey (JGSS) conducted in 2008 and 2010 (hereinafter I call them JGSS 2008 and JGSS 2010 respectively), from the Social Science Japan Data Archive (SSJDA) at the Center for Social Research and Data Archives (CSRDA), Institute of Social Science, The University of Tokyo. The datasets have been entrusted to SSJDA for researchers, graduate students, and undergraduate students with the guidance of university teachers who would like to conduct secondary analyses.[5]

To date, the JGSS's have been conducted almost in every three years by the JGSS Research Center at Osaka University of Commerce. The newest survey conducted in this series is JGSS 2015. But it takes some time that the datasets are cleaned and entrusted to the archive, the newest version of the dataset which is available for researchers who are not members of the JGSS Research Center is JGSS 2010.

Sampling and Respondents

According to the sampling plans of JGSS 2008 (JGSS Research Center at Osaka University of Commerce 2010) and 2010 (JGSS Research Center at Osaka University of Commerce 2011), the respondents were sampled in following plans and procedures.

> **JGSS2008.** JGSS2008 was conducted between October and December 2008. The targeted survey area was all over Japan. The populations of the sampling plans were the residents of Japan who had voting rights, males, and females, from twenty to 89 years old. The sampling

[5] Researchers who are interested in secondary analyses of the datasets of past JGSS's can receive the individual response data which have been collected by the JGSS Research Center in SPSS format upon request. See http://csrda.iss.u-tokyo.ac.jp/en/

size was 8000. They were sampled from the registrants of basic resident registers which were held by the municipalities.[6]

The research project administered two-stage stratified random sampling. At the first stage, the project sampled municipalities according to their locations and populations. The project grouped the prefectures in Japan into six regions, and the project categorized municipalities into four groups by their populations. So they divided municipalities into twenty-four groups. They assigned their planned 8000 samples into those twenty-four groups according to the proportions of the populations (the numbers of the people for the basic resident's registers). Then they sampled spots for administrating their surveys. They picked up around fifteen spots for each group. At the second stage, they sampled respondent candidates randomly from the basic resident's registers. They picked up thirteen to sixteen samples from the registers by equal interval sampling method. Two or more samples must not be picked up within one household.

In JGSS 2008, there were three sets of questionnaires. The first one was that the questionnaire for an interview. In this questionnaire, the interviewer asked the respondents mainly about demographic variables. The second one was form A, and the third one formed B. One of the forms A and B were randomly assigned and left to the respondents and collected after the respondents complete the questionnaire.

According to the project's sampling plan, the samples regarding form A was 3997, and samples for form B was 4003. The numbers which the project targeted at the first time were called as "attack numbers." The survey collectors who were dispatched by the company which was entrusted administering the survey by the project visited the addresses which were registered on the basic resident's registers. The survey collectors attempted to see the sampled respondents at least four times to see the respondents. When surveyors could see the respondents, they tried to administer structured interviews with the interview questionnaire. But the surveyors found a part of the planned samples could not be reached because some parts of respondent candidates had moved, had gotten hospitalized, had had an illness, had been dead or had had other reasons. Those "impossible samples" were 459 for form A and 447 for form B. With subtracting those numbers from the planned samples, the possible samples were 4302 for form A and 4017 for form B.

The project obtained 2060 valid responses for form A, and 2160 for form B. So the response rates were 58.2% for form A, 60.6% for form B. Those two forms had different questions, albeit they have several same questions.

[6]In the English document (JGSS Research Center at Osaka University of Commerce 2010), the "Form of Register" is described as "Register of electors", which seems to mean that they sampled from voter's lists which are held by Election Administration Committees. In the Japanese document (JGSS Research Center at Osaka University of Commerce 2010), they sampled from basic residents registers. Those two kinds of lists cover largely the same populations, among the people who are twenty years or older, as the voters' lists complied based on basic residents registers. The differences between those lists come from whether the people have voting rights in that specific municipalities. For example, every resident can exercise his / her voting right just after three months their moving into the municipalities.

A 500-yen equivalent book coupon was given to each respondent when the research project sent the letters of request to cooperate in answering the survey. When a respondent completes the questionnaire that was assigned to him / her, another 500-yen value book coupon was given to the respondent. Additionally, a set of pens were given to the respondents, when the interviewer thought that it is proper to give the set of pens during the survey.

JGSS2010. JGSS2010 was conducted between February and April 2010. The targeted survey area was all over Japan. The populations of the sampling plans were almost the same as JGSS2008, that is, residents in Japan who are registered on the basic resident's registers, from twenty to 89 years old. The sampling size was 9000, which was 1000 larger than JGSS2008.

Two-stage stratified random sampling was carried out in the same way as JGSS2008. First, the project grouped the prefectures in Japan into six regions, the same way as JGSS2008. Also, the project categorized all municipalities into four groups according to the populations. Then the project selected 600 spots, according to the six regions and size of populations of the municipalities. Secondly, after choosing spots, the project picked up respondents from the basic resident's registers by equal interval sampling method.

JGSS2010 had three sorts of questionnaires, the same as JGSS2008 (the questions which were included in those questionnaires were not necessarily identical with JGSS2008). The first one was the questionnaire for an interview; the second one was questionnaire A, the third one was questionnaire B. The questionnaire A and B were left with respondents and collected after they finish answering by themselves.

According to the project's sampling plan, the samples regarding form A was 4500, and samples for form B was 4500. Like in JGSS2008, there were"impossible samples." Those "impossible samples" were 198 for form A and 394 for form B. With subtracting those numbers from the planned samples, the possible samples were 4302 for form A and 4017 for form B.

The project obtained 2507 valid responses for form A, and 2497 for form B. So the response rates were 62.2% for form A, 62.1% for form B.

Same small rewards for respondents were delivered as the same method which was employed in JGSS2008.

Assessments and Measures

Measures for assessing the extent of trust in the legal system. To assess the extent of the respondent's trust in the legal system, the author picked up the questions on trust in law courts in JGSS 2008 and 2010. Each JGSS questionnaire has a set of questions that ask the trust levels of the respondents about fifteen social institutions. Those institutions are: large companies, religious organizations, newspaper (publishing companies), TV (broadcasting stations), national central governmental agencies / ministries, law courts, schools, labor associations, hospitals, scholars / researchers, national Diet members, local assembly members, Self-Defense Forces, the police, and financial institutions. Adding to the question about the people's trust in the law courts, the author picked up the question on the trust in the police (Tyler 1994). As the police are one of the major social institutes that enforce the law, and conspicuous from the viewpoint of citizens.

The factors that affect people's trust in law courts. In JGSS 2010, there were two questions that referred to the mixed jury system which inaugurated in 2009 (saiban-in system).

Those two questions were as follows: "Do you approve saiban-in system (the system in which general public participate in the trials which try the cases concerning murder, arson, kidnapping, etc.) that was started in May 2009?", and "If you were selected as a saiban-in (juror), do you think you would hesitate to argue for a death penalty, even the case is about a brutal crime?". The former question measured the simple attitude towards the saiban-in system. And the second question was to measure respondents' attitudes towards the death penalty. The second question can be thought to measure the attitude towards death penalty as a personal question, which directly concerns the respondents' life, in the form of asking as if the respondents were selected as saiban-in's.

Unfortunately, JGSS 2008 did not have questions which directly dealt with the saiban-in system, in this paper the author conducted analysis the significance of the only in JGSS 2010 data.

The factors that affect people's trust in law courts for regression (JGSS 2010 dataset). In JGSS 2010, the dataset includes the response data on the answers to the question on the saiban-in system.[7] The question asked the extent of the respondents' support for the saiban-in system. The question was " Do you support saiban-in system (the system that the general public participates in trials which try murder, arson, kidnapping, etc.) which has been started in May 2009?"[8] When we simply read this question sentence, it seems that this question simply asks the social attitudes towards the saiban-in system. But this question includes the words concerning the initiation of the saiban-in system; the author interpreted the responses could include the respondents' evaluation for the introduction of the saiban-in system. In this section, with using the responses to that question, the author analyzed the relationship between people's trust in the law courts and the support for the saiban-in system.

There were four questions which were supposed to relate to the trust in the law courts. The questions are trusted in the police, the evaluation of human nature on the scale that indicates evil to good, the evaluation of recent law courts' judgments, and the attitudes towards (support for) saiban-in system.

The author assumed that the answers to those questions would have some relationships with the trust in the law courts. Because the police are the most popular law enforcement agencies, people think the justice system is legitimate when the police treat people in the communities just (Tyler and Huo 2002). So the police form the base of the people's trust in the legal system. Second, the evaluation of the human nature has relation to how people judge and trust in other people in general. This has a significant relationship with how the people trust in the social systems (Fujita et al. 2016; Yosano and Hayashi 2010). Third, the evaluation of the recent

---

[7] There were no questions concerning saiban-in system in JGSS 2008.

[8] The original question was written in Japanese as: 「2009年5月に開始された裁判員制度(殺人・放火・誘拐などの裁判に一般の人が参加する制度)を、あなたは支持しますか。」

law courts' judgments would have a relationship with the trust in the law courts because this reflects the people's thought about whether the law courts meet people's expectations in the results of the trials. This is about the people's thought about whether the law courts exercise justice. Fourth, the evaluation of saiban-in system can have something to do with the trust in the law courts because the system that requires civic participation would promote trust in the justice system. This is one of the main assumptions that should be tested in this paper, so the author hypothesizes this argument.

> The question sentence for measuring the trust in the law courts and trust in the police was: "To what extent do you trust in the following A ~ O?" The sentence was followed by fifteen social institutions' names under alphabetical letter tags started from "A." The law courts' tag was "I" in the ninth place, and the police's tag was "N" in the fourteenth place.

The question about human nature asked the respondents "what do you think about the human nature? Please pick one of the numbers (1 ~ 7)." Then the respondents answered for this question by picking one of the figures from one (with an anchoring stimulus "the human nature is evil") to seven (the anchoring stimulus for this option was "the human nature is good").

The question asking the evaluation of recent law courts' judgments were "what do you think about law courts' judgments for criminals in recent several years?" The options in answering for this question were "1: too strict", "2: a little strict", "3: proper", "4: should be a little stricter", "5: should be stricter", and "6: I don't know". The author treated the sixth option as a missing value.

Before conducting a multiple regression analysis, the author reversed the answers for the trust in the law courts, the trust in the police, the evaluation of the saiban-in system, and the evaluation of recent law courts' judgments. That's because the answers to those questions were in smaller numbers when the respondents had more positive answers for those questions. On the contrary, the answer to the question of human nature is positive when the answers were in large numbers. Adding to it, the answering options for the question about law courts' judgments are complicated. The option "3: proper" is the most positive attitudes towards law courts' judgments. The options "2: a little strict" and "4: should be a little strict" are a little negative evaluation for law courts' judgments, but the directions of the evaluations are quite the opposite. The last two options that appeared as "1: too strict" and "5: should be stricter" are in the same situation of the options 2 and 4, even 1 and 5 are more extreme in the evaluations. This situation would make the interpretation rather difficult when we throw these variables into a multiple regression analysis. To solve this problem, the author changed the answering categories "1: too strict" and "5: should be stricter" into "1″, "2: a little strict" and "4: should be a little strict" into "2″. The option "3: proper" was kept "3″ as its answering category. This series of changes made the meaning of the answering options for the question. The larger figures mean the respondents evaluated the law courts' judgments positively, while smaller figures showed rather negative evaluations on the law courts' judgments.

After altering the numbers in answers for the four questions quoted above, all the numbers in the answering options are larger when the respondent's evaluations are positive.

Table 4.2 The answers for trust in law courts in 2008 and 2010

	2008	2010	Total
Very much	375	529	904
	18.2%	21.1%	19.8%
Somewhat	1148	1430	2578
	55.7%	57.0%	56.4%
Seldom	137	127	264
	6.7%	5.1%	5.8%
Don't know	374	388	762
	18.2%	15.5%	16.7%
No answer	26	33	59
	1.3%	1.3%	1.3%
Total	2060	2507	4567
	100.0%	100.0%	100.0%

$\chi^2(9) = 14.94$, $p = .005$

Table 4.3 The adjusted residuals of the answers for trust in the law courts in 2008 and 2010

	2008	2010
Very much	−1.98	2.42
Somewhat	−0.53	0.65
Seldom	2.01	−2.45
Don't know	2.00	−2.43
No Answer	−0.15	0.18

Results

The main results of this study are shown in Table 4.2. Table 4.3 is the additional analysis which reveals that where the significant differences between the two distributions of the answers came from.

The Difference of the Answers of "trust in law courts" between before and after Introduction Saiban-in System

The answers in 2008 and 2010 surveys are shown in Table 4.2. In every cell, the figure in upper half shows the numbers of responses, whereas the figures in the lower half show the relative frequencies of the responses in that year.

The options for answers were as shown in Table 4.2, the respondents "trust very much," "trust in somewhat extent," "seldom trust (in the law courts)," "I don't know," and provided with no response. The last row shows the total number of the responses for the specified year.

According to the result of the chi-square test, the distributions of the answers for the question on the trust in law courts are significantly different between the JGSS

Table 4.4 The result of a multiple regression analysis on the trust in the law courts. Dependent variable: trust in the law courts

Independent variables	B	SE	β	*p*
Trust in the police	.40	.02	.44	.00
Human nature is good	.02	.01	.06	.01
Evaluation on recent judgments	.05	.02	.07	.00
Support for saiban-in system	.03	.01	.06	.01
(constant)	1.13	.06	–	.00

F (4, 1691) = 118.05, $p < .001$; adjusted $r^2 = .22$

B means unstandardized coefficients, *SE* means standard errors of the coefficients, β means standardized coefficients, and p means statistical probability when the specified coefficient was assumed to be zero

2008 and 2010. Then the author conducted an analysis on adjusted residuals of the distributions, in order to specify from which answers the significance came from. The result of this analysis is shown in Table 4.3.

In Table 4.3, the figure in every cell represents the standardized differentiation from the expected value, which was calculated based on the total number in the specific year and the specific choice of answer. The figures that are larger than 1.96 or smaller than −1.96 show that the number of the respondents who chose the choice of the answers are significantly different from the expected values.

From the results of Table 4.3, in the answers in 2010, the frequencies of "(trust) very much" increased significantly, while the frequencies of answers "seldom (trust)" and "no answer" decreased significantly.

The Factors that Affect people's Trust in Law Courts (JGSS 2010 Dataset)

The author conducted a multiple regression analysis to test whether the four variables pointed above have a relationship with people's trust in the law courts. The result of multiple regression is shown in Table 4.4. This model was significant (F (4, 1691) = 118.05, $p < .001$) and the adjusted r^2 was .22. The four independent variables are significant in this model.

Because the author changed the answering categories for those questions, all the variables shown in Table 4.4 are getting larger when the respondents evaluated positively. According to Table 4.4, as all the coefficients are positive, all the independent variables affected respondents' trust in the law courts positively.

Focusing on the column β in Table 4.4, we can find that the most significant independent variable was the trust in the police, the second significant variable was the evaluation on the recent law courts' judgments. And the last two independent variables were the attitudes towards human nature and support for the saiban-in system.

All these independent variables were significant in this model according to the p-value in each row.

Discussion

Summary of the Results

In the section of Study 1, the author looked into the frequencies of answers for the trust in the law courts in 2008 and 2010. According to Table 4.2, the distribution of the answers for trust in the law courts significantly differentiated between JGSS 2008 and 2010. Then the author investigated the distributions of the answers in 2008 and 2010 in Table 4.3. We found that the relative frequency of the answer "very much" in 2010 significantly increased compared to the counterpart in 2008. Adding to it, the answers "seldom" and "don't know" significantly decreased in 2010 survey than those in 2008 survey.

According to the results shown in Table 4.4, the support for the saiban-in system had a significantly positive effect on people's trust in the law courts. The most significant variable was the trust in the police. The attitudes towards human nature and recent criminal law courts' judgments also had significant positive effects on people's trust in the law courts.

Interpretation of the Meaning of Trust in the Justice System

Taking the results shown above into consideration, we can understand these results that people's trust in the law courts increased after initiation of the saiban-in system. According to the results shown in Table 4.4, the support for the saiban-in system had a significant effect on people's trust in the law courts. Needless to say, as this analysis was a multiple regression analysis, the effect of the attitude towards a saiban-in system on the people's trust in the law courts is significant even the effects of trust in the police, attitude towards human nature and evaluation of law courts' judgments were removed.

These results support the hypothesis that the initiation of a major lay participation system would promote people's trust in the justice system because the law courts are the central institution for the justice system.

Limitations

As we saw above, the initiation of lay participation system promoted people's trust in the justice system, but there are limitations which derived from the limitation of the dataset.

Regarding Table 4.2, we can apparently see the results that people's trust in the law courts increased after initiation of the saiban-in system, but we can't say that the cause of the increase was coming from the inauguration of the system. That's because there were many social changes between 2008 and 2010 in Japan. The author thinks the starting trials by the saiban-in system is one of the most important issues in the context of Japanese justice system, but we can't argue that only from the Table 4.2. That's the reason why the author conducted a multiple regression analysis with these data, but the analysis had limitations which are being discussed below.

Concerning the multiple regression analysis, strictly speaking, we cannot analyze whether people's trust in the law courts increased by initiation of the saiban-in system because JGSS 2008 didn't have questions on the saiban-in system or another lay participation system to the justice system. This is the largest limitation of this dataset for the arguments of this paper. By this limitation, we cannot compare models before initiation of the saiban-in system.

Regarding the wording of this question, strictly speaking, this question was placed to measure the respondents' attitudes towards saiban-in system themselves, not towards the introduction or initiation of the saiban-in system. This is another limitation of this dataset. But in this paper, the author assumed that this question should include the evaluation of initiation of the saiban-in system because this question was asked just after initiation of trials by saiban-in. Considering the timing of this question asked, the attitudes towards the saiban-in system would inevitably include the evaluation on the inauguration of the system itself.[9]

If we have some data on the relationship between people's trust in the justice system and introducing the saiban-in system, and if these questions are asked before and after introducing the saiban-in system, the problem indicated above would be solved or lightened. So, in the section of study 2, the author is citing some aggregated data concerning trust in the law courts and introducing the saiban-in system.

Study 2

The second sets of data were cited by Matsumura, Ota, Kinoshita, & Yamada, (2008) and Matsumura et al. (2012). The authors of these two papers were a completely different research group from JGSS research center. They are an independent group of law and society researchers. In this part, the author of this paper cites the results from Matsumura et al. (2008) and Matsumura et al. (2012). They conducted two social surveys before and after the initiation of the saiban-in system in order to observe people's attitude changes which may be evoked by the beginning of the trials by the saiban-in system.

[9] This is not shown in results section, in a multiple regression model with independent variables regarding the political attitudes (five-point scale of conservativeness) and stratification belonging consciousness scale (five-point scale from low to upper classes), these two variables were not significant. Both conservativeness and class identification did not have relationships with the trust in the law courts.

Method

Method Overview

Matsumura et al. (2012, 2008) used identical question sets when they conducted those two surveys to assess the citizens' social attitudes towards the saiban-in system, except for their quasi-experiments used several vignettes, after the questions for measuring the attitudes. Matsumura et al. (2012) showed the frequencies of each answering options, the distributions of the answers in the two social surveys which they conducted. In this paper, the author uses chi-square tests and residual analyses to test whether the trust in the justice system has changed after the introduction of the saiban-in system.

Sampling and Respondents

Matsumura et al. (2008) and Matsumura et al. (2012) conducted and chose their respondents almost identical procedures. The author explained here their procedures of the first survey in 2008 and second survey in 2011 respectively.

The first survey (conducted in 2008) Matsumura et al. (2008) carried out a multistage stratified random sampling. They aimed to sample 1800 respondents from all over Japan, according to geographical distributions, generations, and gender. The respondents should be from twenty years to 70 years of age. First, Matsumura et al. (2008) selected 100 spots where they conduct sampling. Then they administered equal interval sampling, to select eighteen respondents for each spot. They conducted sampling from November 2007 to January 2008.

They carried out the survey from February 8 to March 2, 2008. They collected 1160 responses out of 1800 planned samples. The response rate was 64.4%.

The second survey (conducted in 2011) Matsumura et al. (2012) carried out a multistage stratified random sampling. They aimed to sample 1600 respondents from all over Japan, according to geographical distributions, generations, and gender. The respondents should be from twenty years to 70 years of age. First, Matsumura et al. (2012) selected 100 spots where they conduct sampling. Then they administered equal interval sampling, to select sixteen respondents for each spot. They conducted sampling from November 2010 to January 2011.

They carried out the survey from February 4 to February 20 in 2011. They collected 1109 responses out of 1600 planned samples. The response rate was 69.3%.

Assessments and Measures

The two surveys conducted by Matsumura et al. (2008) and Matsumura et al. (2012) had identical question sets because they intended to compare the answers from the respondents, before and after initiating saiban-in system.

Regarding the citizen's trust in the legal system, they had questions as follows:

Q19_4 "An introduction of lay judge system makes trials unreliable."[10]

Q24 "Suppose you are put on a trial for the crime of which you know nothing. If you have a choice, which will choose, a trial by lay judges or a trial by professional judges alone?"[11]

In the following section, the author is going to show the frequencies of the answers for those questions and conduct some statistical analyses on those data.

Results

Table 4.5 is a table which is showing the answer distribution for the question Q19_4 in Matsumura et al. (2008) and Matsumura et al. (2012). In the original article, the answers are presented in two tables, which represent for each survey. Table 4.5 is the results of a combination of those results which were obtained two surveys. This is to make easy to understand the distribution changes between the survey conducted in 2008 and in 2011. In the first row of Table 4.5, "2012" shows that the column shows the frequencies of the answer for the survey in 2011. This is described as "2012". The "2012" are the results published in 2012, in the paper written by Matsumura et al. (2012). The figure located upper half in each cell is frequencies of the answer for a specified option in a specified year, and the figure in the lower half of each cell is the relative frequencies when the number of all responses (the figures are shown in the lowest row) is set to be 100%.

Table 4.6 is a table for residual analysis on Table 4.5. Table 4.6 describes the answers which were shown in Table 4.5. The figure in each cell is the standardized score that shows the difference from the expected value which is calculated from the total numbers of in the far right columns and in the lowest row. The values under −1.96 or above 1.96 in Table 4.6 mean that those variables are statistically significantly different from expected values.

Table 4.7 is the distributions of answers for the question that asked whether the citizens choose trials by saiban-in and professional judges or trials by judges if they had a chance to be accused. We can find the distributions are significantly different between the data obtained in 2008 and 2010 by a chi-square test.

According to Table 4.8 which shows the results of the residual analysis of Table 4.7, the frequencies of answers of choosing trials by saiban-in and judges significantly increased in 2012. Other changes that were observed here were not statistically significant.

[10]The original question is: 「裁判員による裁判の導入によって、裁判が信頼出来ないものになる」.

[11]The original question is: 「あなたが身に覚えのない犯罪を犯したとして、裁判にかけられたとします。もし選べるとしたらあなたは裁判員による裁判と職業裁判官のみの裁判のどちらを選びますか。」

Table 4.5 Trust in trials by saiban-in in Matsumura et al. (2008) and Matsumura et al. (2012)
Q19_4 "An introduction of lay judge system makes trials unreliable"

	2008	2012	Total
Do not think so	113	176	289
	9.81%	15.97%	12.82%
Do not really think so	224	313	537
	19.44%	28.40%	23.82%
Cannot decide	603	475	1078
	52.34%	43.10%	47.83%
Think so a little	156	110	266
	13.54%	9.98%	11.80%
Think so	56	28	84
	4.86%	2.54%	3.73%
Total	1152	1102	2254
	100.0%	100.0%	100.0%

$\chi^2(9) = 59.89, p < 0.01$
The data shown in this table were taken from Matsumura et al. (2012). In that paper, the data in 2008 (which had first appeared in Matsumura et al. (2008)) and 2010 were shown in different tables. The author of this paper combined those data into one table and conducted a chi-square test

Table 4.6 The adjusted residuals of the answers for trust in trials by saiban-in in Matsumura et al. (2008) and Matsumura et al. (2012)

	2008	2012
Do not think so	−4.18	3.99
Do not really think so	−4.45	4.26
Cannot decide	3.24	−3.10
Think so a little	2.51	−2.41
Think so	2.92	−2.79

This table neither appeared in Matsumura et al. (2008) or Matsumura et al. (2012). The author of this paper carried out this analysis based on the data in Table 1.4

Table 4.7 Trust in trials by saiban-in in Matsumura et al. (2008) and Matsumura et al. (2012)
Q24 "Suppose you are put on a trial for the crime of which you know nothing. If you have a choice, which will choose, a trial by lay judges or a trial by professional judges alone?"

	2008	2012	Total
Definitely, choose a lay judge trial	39	63	102
	3.39%	5.70%	4.52%
Would rather choose a lay judge trial	111	168	279
	9.66%	15.19%	12.37%
Do not know	599	528	1127
	52.13%	47.74%	49.98%
Would rather choose a trial by professional judges alone	257	224	481
	22.37%	20.25%	21.33%
Definitely choose a trial by professional judges alone	143	123	266
	12.45%	11.12%	11.80%
Total	1149	1106	2255
	100.0%	100.0%	100.0%

$\chi^2(9) = 24.72, p < 0.01$

Table 4.8 The adjusted residuals of the answers for trust in trials by saiban-in in Matsumura et al. (2008) and Matsumura et al. (2008)

	2008	2012
Definitely choose a lay judge trial	−2.62	2.52
Would rather choose a lay judge trial	−3.80	3.66
Do not know	1.50	−1.45
Would rather choose a trial by professional judges alone	1.11	−1.07
Definitely choose a trial by professional judges alone	0.93	−0.90

Discussion

Summary of the Results

According to Tables 4.5 and 4.6, the answers that saiban-in system does not make the law courts' procedure unreliable increased after the inauguration of the saiban-in system. Distribution of the answers for differentiated between JGSS 2008 and 2010.

And with Tables 4.7 and 4.8, we saw that people chose trials by saiban-in and judges more after initiation of saiban-in trials.

Interpretation of the Meaning of Trust in the Justice System

The results of the first two tables cited above, we can interpret the results as the respondents thought that introduction of the saiban-in system does not make the legal system unreliable. With the wording of the question 19_4, we cannot conclude that people think that introduction of saiban-in system promotes or strengthen the properness of the working of the legal system. But it is conceivable people thought that initiation of trials by saiban-in does not impair the trust in the law courts.

With the results in the last two tables shown above, Tables 4.7 and 4.8, people preferred trials by saiban-in and judges to the trials only by professional judges, if they were accused in a criminal case. This might be collateral evidence that people trust in the legal system more if the saiban-in system initiated.

When we consider those results, it can be inferred that initiation of the saiban-in system had a positive effect on people's trust in the law courts. If the people's trust in the law courts promotes, the trust in the legal system will promote because the law courts can be thought that they are main institutions of the justice system.

Limitations

The same limitations of the Study 1 can be applied to the data interpretation of Study 2 because there have been many changes and factors that might affect people's trust in the law courts between 2008 and 2012.

Another limitation which we can consider is that the respondents answered their preference in a fictitious situation with their imagination in Table 4.7 and 4.8. For ordinal citizens, it is hard to imagine the situation in which they are accused as defendants in criminal trials. In consequence, the answers for the question might have more sampling errors than if the question was not an imaginary case for ordinary citizens.

General Discussion

Summary of the Studies

In Study 1, we've seen that people's trust in the law courts differentiated between JGSS 2008 and 2010, which showed that people's trust in the law courts increased in 2010, after the initiation of the trials by saiban-in. And the regression analysis shown in Table 4.4 showed that the attitude towards the saiban-in system affects positively trust in the law courts. The results supported the hypothesis that introducing saiban-in system promoted people's trust in the legal system.

In Study 2, comparing before and after the introduction of the saiban-in system, the people thought that introduction of the saiban-in system does not make the legal system unreliable, and people choose saiban-in system more if they were accused of a crime.

Introduction of Lay Participation System Promoted Trust in the Justice System

With all the results and interpretation of the results above, we can conclude that initiation of trials by saiban-in increased trust in the legal system. And the introduction of the saiban-in system did not impair the people's trust in the legal system.

Limitations

We cannot test the direct causal relationship between the introduction of the trials by saiban-in and trust in the legal system because we cannot conduct an experimental study about the issue. If we would like to do that, we need to prepare for two societies, or we need to divide one society into two or more, and put the saiban-in system half of the societies and compare the people's trust in the justice system after introduction of the system. That is a kind of real-world experiment. But in reality, there can be ethical problems and governmental policies problems to conduct such kind of experiment.

We've got the datasets before and after the introduction of the system. The authenticity of the data is perfect, as we would like to see the people's attitude change after initiation of the system. But in the real society, there would be many factors that might affect people's trust in the law courts. There might be unknown, but significant factors other than the variables shown above. The adjusted r^2 was .22 in Table 4.4. Consequently, 78% of the variance is not explained by the variables which are used the analyses in this paper.

We have general limitations which have been not pointed above, limitations section in Study 1 and Study 2. Even the datasets are valuable because they were obtained before and after the introduction of the saiban-in system, and some of the answers can be compared to those answers, we have seen just two sets of data. The representativeness of the sample is rather high because these data were obtained by stratified sampling method. But we just saw two sets of data, so we should be careful when we generalize the conclusions which were drawn from these data.

If there is a chance to analyze other datasets, we should analyze those datasets and test whether the findings shown in this paper can be reproduced with the data. But the problem when we do that is that it is impossible to obtain data when the saiban-in system initiated because the system has already started.

Future Directions

One of the significant features of the datasets used here as they are obtained before and after the introduction of the saiban-in system. These datasets perfectly satisfy the feature to know about the impacts of the introduction of the system. But the datasets are getting older as the time passes. Recently, it is said that the public's interest in the justice system has been decreased compared to when the system just started. Whether the argument is true or not should be tested by the data obtained more recently than those of being obtained just after the introduction of the system. The JGSS keep being conducted every several years. If the new data get available, we need to test the notion again with new data. And we need to know the hypothesis that introduction of the lay participation system promotes the people's trust in the justice system can be the truth after substantial years passed after the introduction. But precisely speaking, after substantial years pass, the hypothesis should be changed as the existence of the lay participation in the justice system.

And another possibility to test the hypothesis is to obtain other countries which introduced lay participation to the justice system recently. For example, there are lay participation systems which have been launched recently in Korea, Argentina, Taiwan, and other countries. If we can compare the results of the social surveys on the trust in the justice system and introduction of the lay participation system, we could know more about the relationship between those two variables.

Acknowledgments This study is based on the secondary analyses of Japanese General Social Surveys (JGSS) 2008 and 2010. The author received the datasets which include individual responses with the approval of secondary analyses from

Social Science Japan Data Archive (SSJDA) where the datasets were entrusted with JGSS Research Project at Osaka University of Commerce. The author deeply appreciates that JGSS Research Project at Osaka University of Commerce generously entrust the data to SSJDA and allow to re-analyze the individual response data. The following paragraph is an explanation of JGSS, taken from instructions of usage of the JGSS dataset/questionnaire.

> "The Japanese General Social Surveys (JGSS) are designed and carried out by the JGSS Research Center at Osaka University of Commerce (Joint Usage / Research Center for Japanese General Social Surveys accredited by the Minister of Education, Culture, Sports, Science and Technology), in collaboration with the Institute of Social Science at the University of Tokyo."

Appendices

Appendix A: Hypotheses

- Hypothesis 1: There should be a path from the general trust to trust in social institutions.
- Hypothesis 2: Authoritarian personality promotes trust in the justice system, as those who are inclined to authoritarian personality would have respectful attitudes towards the authoritative social system like justice system.
- Hypothesis 3: Life satisfaction affects general trust, and via general trust, life satisfaction has an influence on trust in the justice system.
- Hypothesis 4: People in higher social class are inclined to be more satisfied with their lives.
- Hypothesis 5: Sense of fairness positively affect trust in the justice system.
- Hypothesis 6: Legitimacy in the legal system positively influences on trust in the legal system.
- Hypothesis 7: Feeling of fairness brings about feeling of legitimacy in the legal system.
- Hypothesis 8: Feeling of equality should be affected by general trust.
- Hypothesis 9: Social class has a positive effect on feelings of equality.
- Hypothesis 10: Interest in the justice system may promote trust in the justice system.

Appendix B: Questions Selected

Three items from California F scale (Adorno et al. 1950)

1. The most important thing to learn for children is obedient attitude toward their parents.

2. The young are too weak in these days. They need more strict discipline and strict regulation.
3. It is polite to be patient to listen to our seniors even they say the things that we don't like. Six items from Social Dominance Orientation scale (Pratto et al. 1994, p. 760) (Words between parentheses are back-translated from paraphrased Japanese items, which are used in our questionnaire)

    1. Some groups of people are simply not the equals of others.
    2. Increased economic equality. (Economic equality in our society is increasing.)
    3. Increased social equality. (All humans should be treated equally.)
    4. Equality. (The world is equal.)
    5. If people were treated more equally, we would have fewer problems in this country.
    6. It is important that we treat other countries equal.

References

Adler, N. E., & Snibbe, A. C. (2003). The role of psychosocial processes in explaining the gradient between socioeconomic status and health. *Current Directions in Psychological Science, 12*(4), 119–123. https://doi.org/10.1111/1467-8721.01245.

Adorno, T. W., Frenkel-Brunswik, E., Levinson, D. J., & Sanford, R. N. (1950). *The authoritarian personality*. New York: Harper.

Bradley, R. H., & Corwyn, R. F. (2002). Socioeconomic status and child development. *Annual Review of Psychology, 53*(1), 371–399. https://doi.org/10.1146/annurev.psych.53.100901.135233.

Cook, K. S. (2001). *Trust in society*. New York: Russell Sage Foundation.

Dockson, R. R., & Allen, H. P. (1993). *Justice in the balance 2020: Report of the commission on the future of the California courts*. San Francisco: Supreme Court of California. Retrieved from http://www.courts.ca.gov/documents/2020.pdf?1512186303858

Finkel, N. J. (1995). Commonsense justice jurors' notions of the law. Cambridge, MA: Harvard University Press.

Fujita, M., Hayashi, N., & Hotta, S. (2016). Trust in the justice system: Internet survey after introducing mixed tribunal system in Japan. *Oñati Socio-Legal Series, 6*(2). [Online publication; no pagination specified]. Retrieved from http://ssrn.com/abstract=2769587.

Fukuyama, F. (1995). *Trust: The social virtues and the creation of prosperity*. New York: Free Press.

Ikeda, K. (2007). Analyses on determining factors on trust in various institutions. *A Report of Studies on Trust in Governmental Administration in Fiscal Year* 2006. Tokyo: Research special committee on measures for securing and improvement of trust in governmental administration.

Ikeda, K. (2010). The structure of institutional trust in governmental administration. (Japanese Political Science Association, Ed.), *Annual Review of Political Science 2010-I: Trust and Distrust in Politics and Administration*. Tokyo, Japan: Bokutaku-sha.

Isen, A. M., & Means, B. (1983). The influence of positive affect on decision-making strategy. *Social Cognition, 2*(1), 18–31.

JGSS Research Center at Osaka University of Commerce. (2010). *Sampling and administration: JGSS-2008*. Osaka: JGSS Research Center.

JGSS Research Center at Osaka University of Commerce. (2011). *Sampling and administration: JGSS-2010*. Osaka: JGSS Research Center.

Justice System Reform Council. (2001). *Recommendations of the Justice System Reform Council: For a Justice System to Support Japan in the 21st Century*. Tokyo, Japan: Justice System Reform Council. Retrieved from https://japan.kantei.go.jp/judiciary/2001/0612report.html

Kawachi, I., Kennedy, B. P., Lochner, K., & Prothrow-Stith, D. (1997). Social capital, income inequality, and mortality. *American Journal of Public Health, 87*(9), 1491–1498 Retrieved from https://www.ncbi.nlm.nih.gov/pmc/articles/PMC1380975/.

Lind, E. A., & Tyler, T. R. (1988). *Social psychology of procedural justice*. New York: Plenum.

Lind, E. A., & van den Bos, K. (2002). When fairness works: Toward a general theory of uncertainty management. *Research in Organizational Behavior, 24*, 181–223. https://doi.org/10.1016/S0191-3085(02)24006-X.

Lorant, V., Deliège, D., Eaton, W., Robert, A., Philippot, P., & Ansseau, M. (2003). Socioeconomic inequalities in depression: A meta-analysis. *American Journal of Epidemiology, 157*(2), 98–112 Retrieved from http://www.ncbi.nlm.nih.gov/pubmed/12522017.

MacCoun, R. J. (2005). Voice, control, and belonging: The double-edged sword of procedural fairness. *Annual Review of Law and Social Science, 1*(1), 171–201. https://doi.org/10.1146/annurev.lawsocsci.1.041604.115958.

Matsumura, Y., Ota, S., Kinoshita, M., & Yamada, H. (2008). Japanese attitudes toward the lay judge system and criminal justice. *Chiba Journal of Law and Politics, 23*(3), 204–284 Retrieved from https://ci.nii.ac.jp/naid/40016452653.

Matsumura, Y., Kinoshita, M., & Ota, S. (2012). Japanese attitudes toward the lay judge system and criminal justice: Based on the second survey conducted in 2011. *Chiba Journal of Law and Politics, 27*(1), 178–282 Retrieved from https://ci.nii.ac.jp/naid/120005939361.

Messick, D. M., & Kramer, R. M. (2001). Trust as a form of shallow morality. In K. S. Cook (Ed.), *Trust in society*. New York: Russell Sage Foundation.

Obuchi, K. (2005). Psychological structure of public evaluation on public enterprise policies: General trust in government and social fairness. *Japanese Journal of Experimental Social Psychology, 45*(1), 65–76. https://doi.org/10.2130/jjesp.45.65.

OECD. (2013). *Education at a Glance 2013: OECD Indicators*. Paris, France: OECD publishing. Retrieved from http://www.oecd.org/education/eag2013(eng)--FINAL 20 June 2013.pdf.

Palmore, E., & Luikart, C. (1972). Health and social factors related to life satisfaction. *Journal of Health and Social Behavior, 13*(1), 68–80.

Pratto, F., Sidanius, J., Stallworth, L. M., & Malle, B. F. (1994). Social dominance orientation: A personality variable predicting social and political attitudes. *Journal of Personality and Social Psychology, 67*(4), 741–763. https://doi.org/10.1037/0022-3514.67.4.741.

Putnam, R. D. (1993). *Making democracy work: Civic traditions in modern Italy*. Princeton: Princeton University Press.

Putnam, R. D. (2000). *Bowling alone: The collapse and revival of American community*. New York: Simon and Schuster. Retrieved from syncii:///Bowling alone The collapse an.pdf.

Schwarz, N. (1990). Feelings as information: Informational and motivational functions of affective states. In E. T. Higgins & R. M. Sorrentino (Eds.), *Handbook of motivation and cognition: Foundations of social behavior*. New York: Guilford Press Retrieved from http://psycnet.apa.org/record/1990-98254-000.

Seeman, T. E., Crimmins, E., Huang, M.-H., Singer, B., Bucur, A., Gruenewald, T., et al. (2004). Cumulative biological risk and socio-economic differences in mortality: MacArthur studies of successful aging. *Social Science & Medicine, 58*(10), 1985–1997. https://doi.org/10.1016/S0277-9536(03)00402-7.

Sunshine, J., & Tyler, T. R. (2003). The role of procedural justice and legitimacy in shaping public support for policing. *Law & Society Review, 37*(3), 513–548 Retrieved from http://www.jstor.org/stable/1555077.

The Supreme Court of Japan. (2014). *Saiban-in seido no un'yô ni kansuru ishiki chôsa [The consciousness survey cocerning the operation of the saiban-in system]*. Tokyo: The Supreme Court of Japan [in Japanese] Retrieved from http://www.saibanin.courts.go.jp/vcms_lf/H25_ishiki_1.pdf.

Thibaut, J. W., & Walker, L. (1975). *Procedural justice: A psychological analysis*. Hillsdale/New York: Lawrence Erlbaum Associates/Distributed by the Halsted Press Division of Wiley Retrieved from https://books.google.co.jp/books/about/Procedural_Justice.html?id=2l5_QgAACAAJ&redir_esc=y.

Tyler, T. R. (1988). What is procedural justice?: Criteria used by citizens to assess the fairness of legal procedures. *Law & Sociey Review, 22*(1), 103–135. https://doi.org/10.2307/3053563.

Tyler, T. R. (1994). Psychological models of the justice motive: Antecedents of distributive and procedural justice. *Journal of Personality and Social Psychology, 67*(5), 850–863. https://doi.org/10.1037/0022-3514.67.5.850.

Tyler, T. R. (2001). Public trust and confidence in legal authorities: What do majority and minority group members want from the law and legal institutions? *Behavioral Sciences & The Law, 19*(2), 215–235. https://doi.org/10.1002/bsl.438.

Tyler, T. R. (2003). Procedural justice, legitimacy, and the effective rule of law. *Crime and Justice, 30*, 283–357 Retrieved from http://www.jstor.org/stable/1147701.

Tyler, T. R. (2006a). Psychological perspectives on legitimacy and legitimation. *Annual Review of Psychology, 57*, 375–400. https://doi.org/10.1146/annurev.psych.57.102904.190038.

Tyler, T. R. (2006b). *Why people obey the law*. Princeton: Princeton University Press.

Tyler, T. R. (2007a). *Legitimacy and criminal justice: International perspectives*. New York: Russell Sage Foundation.

Tyler, T. R. (2007b). *Psychology and the design of legal institutions*. Oisterwijk: Wolf Legal Publishers (WLP).

Tyler, T. R. (2009). Legitimacy and criminal justice: The benefits of self-regulation. *Ohio State Journal of Criminal Law, 7*, 307–359 Retrieved from http://digitalcommons.law.yale.edu/cgi/viewcontent.cgi?article=4026&context=fss_papers.

Tyler, T. R., & Bies, R. J. (1990). Beyond Formal Procedures: The Interpersonal Context of Procedural Justice. In J. S. Carroll (Ed.), *Applied social psychology and organizational settings* (pp. 77–98). Routledge Retrieved from https://books.google.co.jp/books?hl=en&lr=&id=8YvwCQAAQBAJ&oi=fnd&pg=PT71&dq=beyond+formal+procedures+the+interpersonal+context+of+procedural+justice&ots=SmOMlk-NKS&sig=zYL-UemxBSJn8O-8dVmlymxyANI#v=onepage&q=beyond formal procedures the interpers.

Tyler, T. R., & Fagan, J. (2008). Legitimacy and cooperation: Why do people help the police fight crime in their communities. *Ohio State Journal of Criminal Law, 6*, 231–275 Retrieved from http://digitalcommons.law.yale.edu/fss_papers/3037/.

Tyler, T. R., & Huo, Y. J. (2002). *Trust in the law: Encouraging public cooperation with the police and courts, Russell Sage Foundation series on trust*. New York: Russell Sage Foundation Retrieved from http://search.proquest.com/docview/619994944?accountid=26262.

Tyler, T. R., & Jost, J. T. (2007). Psychology and the law: Reconciling normative and descriptive accounts of social justice and system legitimacy. In A. W. Kruglanski & E. T. Higgins (Eds.), *Social psychology: Handbook of basic principles*. New York: Guilford Press.

Uslaner, E. M. (2002). *The moral foundations of trust*. New York: Cambridge University Press Retrieved from http://www.loc.gov/catdir/samples/cam031/2001052721.html.

Yamagishi, T., & Yamagishi, M. (1994). Trust and commitment in the United States and Japan. *Motivation and Emotion, 18*(2), 129–166.

Yosano, A., & Hayashi, N. (2005). Social stratification, intermediary groups and creation of trustfulness. *Sociological Theory and Methods, 20*(1), 27–44 Retrieved from https://www.jstage.jst.go.jp/article/ojjams/20/1/20_1_27/_pdf.

Yosano, A., & Hayashi, N. (2007). Inequality, trust, and cooperation. *Institute of Economic and Political Studies, Kansai University*. Osaka, Japan: Institute of Economic and Political Studies, Kansai University.

Yosano, A., & Hayashi, N. (2010). Social disparity and trust. *Bulletin of Faculty of Sociology, Kansai University, 42*(1), 77–91 [in Japanese with English abstract]. Retrieved from http://hdl.handle.net/10112/4839; http://kuir.jm.kansai-u.ac.jp/dspace/bitstream/10112/4839/1/KU-1100-20101105-04.pdf.

Chapter 5
Lay Participation System in the Society: Newspaper Text Analyses over the Evaluation of the System

The Matters of Interest and their Chronological Changes in Major Newspapers

Overview

In this section, we aim to review the evaluation from the public to the saiban-in system in different periods of time by going through various news articles about the system.

News articles may not be the exact reflection of the public opinion, as they are not based on direct surveys on public opinions or formal statistics. Yet, it is commonly believed that even we are in the era of high penetration of the Internet and overflow of information, mass media, which mirror public concerns and social values (Livingstone and Lunt 1994), are influential to public opinions (Happer and Philo 2013; Sampei and Aoyagi-Usui 2009). Concerning the Japanese justice system, the numbers of the article in the Asahi Shimbun were used as an indicator of public interest in the lay participation system in Japan (Vanoverbeke 2015).

In the past, the news was considered as the reflection of what the public, but not only the media themselves, valued (McCombs and Shaw 1972). Concerning with the relationship between what the mass media report and what the public concern, Higuchi (2004) concludes that the public tends to compare news articles and reports of social surveys, and the extent of being influenced depends on the news topics. For instance, people tend to refer words from news and touch on the topics that are widely reported by the mass media.

However, there are still some hot topics and frequently-used words in news articles that people do not touch on at all, or quickly forget. These topics and words are from specific genres like economics & business, politics, and academic research. According to Higuchi (2004), it is because people cannot relate these abstract topics to their lives as they can do for more comfortable and more relating topics.

M. Fujita, *Japanese Society and Lay Participation in Criminal Justice*,
https://doi.org/10.1007/978-981-10-0338-7_5

On the contrary, topics and words about crimes stay in people's mind (Higuchi 2004). It is because of the anxieties and fears about the unpredictability of city crimes, and people tend to grasp and equip themselves with the necessary information for self-protection. In addition, mass media make use of this kind of information process tendency and draw people's attention to the specific news by using sensational words and stand out specific facts (Richardson 2007, p. 125) as their business strategy. Likewise, the selection of Saiban-in is highly unpredictable because people never know when and at what time they would be appointed to become a saiban-in. As any Japanese citizens over the age of 20 may be randomly selected, people seem to think that the saiban-in system is highly-relating to themselves.

Considering all these, as the saiban-in system is related to crimes and it is highly unpredictable that everyone has the possibility to be appointed. People would pay attention to the related news, and the analysis of that news can be used as an indicator to reflect the public perception of the system.

Based on the above, we aim to see what and how the mass media report about the Saiban-in system, and from the choice of words and focus of the articles, we aim to analyze what and to what extent public concerns are revealed.

Overview of the Data and the Analysis Method

In the following section, we are stating the news data we have used as a reference and the analytical means.

About the News Articles

The 3408 articles from the Nikkei newspaper (Nihon Keizai Shimbun), which were extracted by searching with the keyword "saiban-in" from the database "Nikkei Telecom 21". These articles dated from 30th January 2001 to 30th March 2012. The period included the time before the implementation, the preparation period and 3.5 years after the implementation. The proposal from the Justice System Reform Council was first released in June 2000, and the bill was drafted for the implementation in December of the same year. The Saiban-in Act was established on 21st May 2004 and trials by saiban-in were put effective in May 2009, after a 5-year preparation period. After that, from time to time there were debates asking for the adjustment, and thus we include the news articles from 2000 to 2012, which cover the drafting, preparatory, implementing and a three-year evaluating period as an exact timeline.

All news articles were put in the format of Microsoft Excel files, and all articles come with their publishing date, title, and author name (if there were). The technology of text mining was used for efficient analysis of this massive database with the articles from 13 years. Text mining is extracting meaningful knowledge from the vast amount of text data. In conducting text mining, researchers use computers and software which help to morphologically analyze the numbers and distributions of the usage of different keywords. The software helps to investigate the usage of words and its pattern which matched judging criteria, and that just cannot be done manually considering the massive amount of the data. The result is thus, free of drawbacks of manual processing like judging errors and human errors when dealing with such a significant amount of text.

Software and Computer Used in the Analytical Process

The process of text mining is done in computers installed with exclusive software, which is the KH coder[1] developed by associate professor Koichi Higuchi at the Ritsumeikan University. The KH coder is free and open for the public to download, and it is suitable for Windows, macOS and LINUX users. The coder was initially developed to deal with the textual characteristics of the Japanese language, but now it is able to deal with other languages in its later upgraded versions. For example, in version 2. b27, it became capable of dealing with English, Dutch, French, German, Italian, Portuguese, and Spanish. In version 3, it became useful for simplified Chinese, Korean, Russian and Catalan, and with advanced preparation, it also works for ancient Japanese.[2]

Different from many European languages, there are no spaces between words in the written Japanese language. For this reason, morphological analysis (word unit resolving process from a sequence of characters) is necessary before we look into the number and distribution of our target keywords. The morphological analysis is done by a specific software called morpheme resolver. ChaSen, MeCab, Juman, and KAKASI are the few that commonly used in Japan. The KH coder fits with any morpheme resolvers, while it comes with the default ChaSen (http://chasen-legacy.osdn.jp/). ChaSen is developed by the Nara Institute of Science and Technology, and MeCab is developed by the Graduate school of Informatics of Kyoto University and NTT Communication Science Laboratories in their corroboration research project (http://taku910.github.io/mecab/). Both are, again, free, and open for the public to download for any academic and business purposes. It is an essential tool for the morphological analysis of the Japanese language.

The author used ChaSen as the morpheme analyzer. The author used Lenovo ThinkPad X260 Signature Edition 2016 with the OS Windows 10 Home 64bit operation system version 1607、 CPU Intel® Core™ i7 2.50GHz / 2.59GHz and with 8GB RAM. The author first installed the KH coder on this computer and started the analysis. The analysis result by the coder was shown in graphs, and another data

[1] http://khc.sourceforge.net/en/

[2] http://khc.sourceforge.net/scr_others.html, in Japanese.

processing software R (https://www.r-project.org/) was needed to deal with these graphs. In the download package of the KH coder for Windows comes with R.

Compound Word and Special Technical Words as Necessary Extract Word for Analysis

We specified the compound words for our analysis as a necessary step in the process. 'Specifying compound words' here means the step to name our target compound words that the software shall follow and extract as one single analytical unit. "Compound words" include new words and technical words that are not recognized by ChaSen as the minimal analytical units. For instance, at the time when the software was made, the "Saiban-in system" did not exist and hence in the analytical process, the software automatically chop the compound word "Saiban-in" into two units as "Saiban" (trials, judgment) and "In" (member), and "Saiban-in system" as three units, "Saiban," "In" and "system". Also, the name "Nihon Bengoshi Rengôkai" (Japan Federation of Bar Associations) would be chopped into three segments "Nihon" (Japan), "Bengoshi" (lawyers) and "Rengôkai" (association). Without naming our target words, the software would resolve our target words into small units and thus affect the analysis of the word number and distribution. For example, the term 'Nihon' (Japan) as a general term would be counted even if the original word in the text is "Nihon Bengoshi Rengôkai" (Japan Federation of Bar Associations), and 'Saiban' (trials, judgment) would be counted and extracted by mistake so that we have no ideas whether the original text should be 'judgement', 'court' or 'Saiban-in'.

In our analysis, we have specified and made the software recognize the following compound words as single units.

Saiban-in Seido (Saiban-in system), Saiban-in, Bengoshi (lawyer), Bengo Gawa (defensing side), Kensatsu Kan (prosecutor), Kensatsu Gawa (prosecuting side), Keisatsu Kan (police officer), Saiban kan (judge), Yozai (other crimes), Zaishitsu (nature of crime), Kôhanmae Seiri (pretrial organization), Kôhanmae (pretrial), Kisomae (before indictment), Shihou kaikaku (justice reform), Shikkouyuyo (suspended sentences), Nihon Bengoshi Rengôkai (Japan Federation of Bar Associations), Shihôseido Kaikaku Shingikai (Justice System Reform Council), Shihôseido Kaikaku Shin (a shortened form of Justice System Reform Council), Shihôseido kaikaku (Justice system reform), Shihôseido (Justice system), Baishin Seido (jury system), Sanshin seido (mixed jury system).

The above includes general compound nouns that consist of two nouns, and also technical terms in our analytical area. Since the dictionary inside ChaSen does not include any specific terms and technical terms in the field of laws, we had to pay extra attention to the terms such as "Yozai" (other crimes), "Zaishitsu" (nature of crime) and "Zaishu" (sort of crimes), otherwise they would all be further chopped into small units as they all formed with nouns with the former one 'zai" (crime) in Japanese.

The Overview of the Articles and the Analytical Result

The Overview of the News Paper Articles

Before going deep into the analysis, we can first look at the frequency of the word "Saiban-in system" being mentioned. The result is shown in the following table. As we have extracted the articles with the keyword "Saiban-in," we list up the number of the word "Saiban-in system" for more natural understanding.

As shown in Table 5.1, the number of hits was 14 in the year 2001; then it increased a little to 21 in 2002. There is a sharp increase to 116 in 2003 and a further increase to 145 in 2004, and finally, it exceeded 200 in 2006. From 2007 the total number reaches 300, and from 2008 to 2009 it reaches 400. Yet, in 2010 it halves into 137 and becomes only 42 in the year follows 2011. Then, it further decreases by 21 and returns to the same number as in 2002.

The frequency of the word "Saiban-in system" appear reflects the extent of public concerns. So, we can conclude that the system was rarely known by the public when it was first introduced in 2001, and the concerns increased gradually until the year 2004 when it became effective and went through the preparation period from 2004 to 2009, people started to talk and think about the system more and the attention level reached the peak in around 2008, just before its implementation in 2009. When we look at the algebra square of the numbers, the difference in the frequency becomes more evident and more supportive of our conclusion as the values exceed 1443. However, as the number of the subject grows, its square also increases rapidly that we should think of its reduction.

From the result, we can conclude that in 2001, it's the initial status that the term Saiban-in system is first introduced in governmental documents and proposals, the system was still in its deliberation period that the public could hardly understand its

Table 5.1 The numbers of articles which included "saiban-in system" per year

Year	Frequencies of "saiban-in system"	Total numbers of articles which include "saiban-in"
2001	14 (1.55%)	903
2002	21 (3.15%)	666
2003	116 (17.03%)	681
2004	145 (11.33%)	1280
2005	167 (18.87%)	885
2006	278 (21.00%)	1324
2007	304 (21.17%)	1436
2008	481 (17.53%)	2744
2009	461 (8.72%)	5285
2010	137 (4.48%)	3061
2011	42 (2.00%)	2097
2012	21 (1.61%)	1308
Total	2187 (10.09%)	21670

mechanism and its effect to normal daily lives, and hence the number of articles was somewhat limited. In 2004, the Saiban-in law was established, and the public came to know that the system would be implemented for sure. As a result, the public realized that the system was coming closer to daily lives, and both the mass media and the public started to regard the implementation of the system is a daily life topic to talk about, and the level of understanding increased as well. Together with the budget spent on promotion and campaigns through big advertising agencies, people got increasingly used to the term and increasingly familiar with the system.

Since that time, promotional activities continued to increase, and more Saiban-in courts were put into use in various places in the country. In addition, "mock judge with the three legal bodies," that is the judge, the prosecutor, and the lawyer, also increased and assisted in drawing public attention to the system. And the term "Saiban-in system" became pervasive from around 2008 to May 2009. In 2009, the system was carried out, and thus it becomes a hot topic, or even a social issue, to be discussed. Unsurprisingly there was an enormous number of headlines about the first case of the system in 2010. Under the influence of the first case, the topic was remained popular for a while. Yet, as time went by fast, the topic is no longer new and attention-drawing, and it gradually lost its news value, which shown in the decrease in its news articles. Since then, the focus of attention fell on individual cases, and the concerns about the system itself became less prominent. Considering this, we witness that from 2001 to 2012, the period of 2004–2009 has as a dividing function for the development timeline of the Saiban-in system. And we would further verify through analysis from other angles in the following sections.

Time Phrases as Divided by the Content of News Articles; An Analytical Result

In the previous section, we have divided the development of the Saiban-in system into three phrases with the dividing line 2004 to 2009 based on the frequency that the term Saiban-in system being mentioned in news articles. And now we go one step further and look into the keywords frequently used in the news articles in different periods of time. In order to visualize the distribution and thus the relationship of the public concerns along the timeline, we adopt the method of correspondence analysis.

Correspondence analysis, or analyze factorielle des correspondances, is an analytical method to quantify unmeasurable quality factors by cross tabulation (Benzécri 1969). It was first suggested by P. Benzécri in 1962 (Benzécri 1982; Ohsumi 2000, p. 331) and introduced in English speaking countries in 1974 by M. O. Hill (Hill 1974). Specifically, in the table, the column and row went with two given variables and filled in the table head, and front sider is groups of categories, and the numbers in the cells reveal the frequency of the words belong to the categories of the column and the row. Here, the frequency is either an absolute or a relative value, or in a two values scale as either 0 or 1 for clear illustration. Under the method of correspondence analysis, categories on both the column and row are arranged in their ascending relativity and frequency, and thus the relationship between the variables and the categories can be clearly illustrated. By arranging the relativity of the categories in the table head and front side, a multi-dimensional graph can be plotted while with the purpose to simplify the illustration and to ease understanding; the two-dimensional graph is commonly preferred. Hayashi Chikio from Japan invented mathematically identical statistical analyses method in the 1950s, earlier than Benzécri (Hayashi 1986). The statistical method which corresponds to the correspondence analysis is called Quantification Categorizing III (数量化III類) in Hayashi's theory.

In our analysis, we have chosen to plot a graph with "year of the article" and "frequency of representative keywords" as variables. We first sort all our target articles in different periods accordingly to the year. Then, we picked up the keywords that appear more than 450 times so as to make our analysis both in-depth and easy to understand. As a result, there are 142 keywords fall into our target group. And finally, we further select 100 words to the plot, to make the graph more comprehensible.

Concerning the accounting ratios, 62.42% falls on the first (horizontal) axis, and 16.12% falls into the second (vertical) axis, and the total was 78.54% in these two axes. In the graph, the groups with a healthy relationship between the year and keywords come close, and those without reliable relationship are farther apart. From the categories of the year we see a first distinct group of 2001/2002 & 2003, and another of 2005, 2006, 2007, and 2008. The years 2010, 2011 and 2012 are very close to each other as well. In between these three groups are the isolated year 2004 and 2009. These 2 years can be considered as transitional years while if we try to group them into the former three, 2004 should fall into the group of 2001–2003, and 2009 should be in the group of 2005–2008. Indeed, the years 2004 and 2009 embrace the characteristics from more than one large groups, because of the establishment of the Saiban-in Act law in 21st May 2004 and the implementation of the Saiban-in system in 21st May 2009.

Referring back to the beginning of the section, these are the three main periods of the development of Saiban-in system; period 1, the former half of pre-introduction period from 2001 to 20th May 2004; period 2, the latter half of pre-introduction period from 21st May 2004 to 20th May 2009 and period 3, post-introduction period which is from 21st May 2009 to 2012. We have to clarify that the word "Saiban-in system" is not mentioned in every single day in the respective periods. There are 211 articles collected in period 1, and the publishing dates range from 30th January 2001 to 15th May 2004. From 21st May 2004 to 20th May 2009, 1107 articles are collected as the total in period 2. Finally, in period 3, 2090 articles are collected from 21st May 2009 to 30th March 2012.

In the next section, we are going to look at the characteristics and the representative keywords from the three different periods.

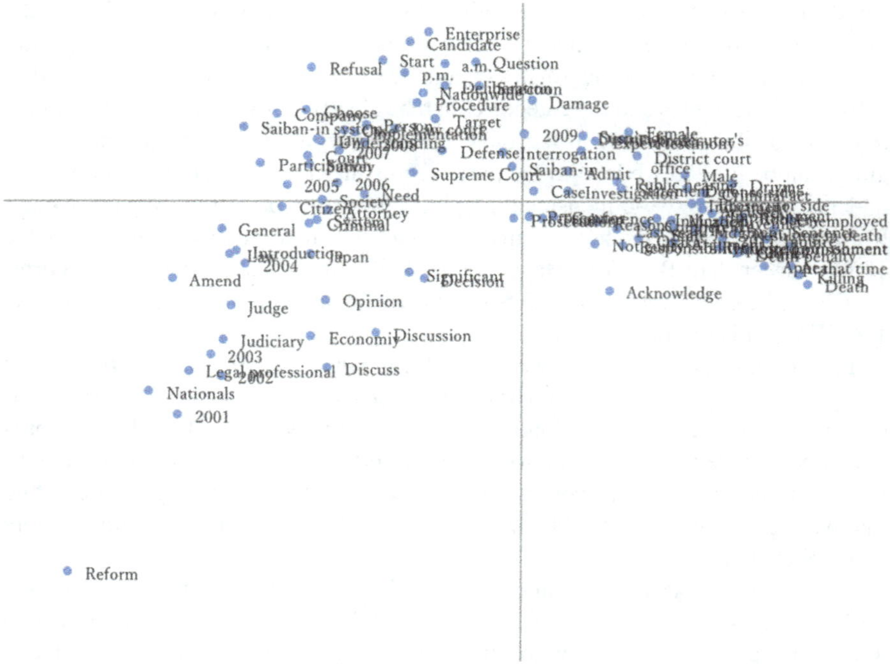

Fig. 5.1 The result of correspondence analysis on newspaper articles

(1) The former Half of Pre-Introduction Period

As shown clearly in Fig.5.1, the years 2001 to 2003 are very much close to each other, and at this time keywords like “kokumin” (nationals), “Housou” (legal professionals), “Kentou” (consideration), “Shihou” (judiciary), “Saibankan” (judge), “Kaisei” (amendment), “Iken” (opinion) and “Giron” (discussion) are frequently used, a little far at the left bottom corner we also see the word “Kaikaku” (reform). From these keywords, we can say that the main concerns are on the background of the system and people talk about the introduction of the system at a very initial status. Especially in 2003, the word “Keizai” (economy) is mentioned, and here we see the public starts to think of the relationship between the introduction of the system and the economic situation in Japan. Similarly, on the right top corner we see the words ‘Jûdai” (important) and “Kettei” (decision), it shows that the public begins to realize that the Saiban-in system are related to important criminal issues and, the randomly selected citizens are involved in these important decision-making processes. When it comes to 2004, words like “Houritsu” (laws), “Dounyu” (introduction), “Keiji” (detective), “Seido” (system), “Ippan” (general), “Nihon” (Japan) and “Bengoshi” (lawyer) appear prominently, and it shows that the public starts to think more in-depth about the introduction process of this system which appointed citizens to involve in the decision-making process of criminal trials.

All in all, the discussion is all about the background and introduction of the system, and the depictions are still instead, abstract.

(2) The Latter Half of Pre-Introduction Period

The years 2005, 2006, 2007 and 2008 make up the second period, which is the latter half of the pre-introduction period. Around these years we see keywords of "Shimin" (citizens), "Shakai" (society), "Hitsuyo" (necessary), "Sanka" (participate), "Rikai" (understand), "Saiban-in seido" (saiban-in system), "erabu" (choose) and "Jisshi" (implement). From them, we see that the focus of the public discussion shifts to the concrete implementation of the system and the preparation of it.

Considering the actual content of the articles, we see a much high degree of understanding and acceptance to the system, as the public starts to believe that the system brings more goods than harms and most importantly the public themselves can get involved in the court system, and they are going to acquire opportunities to understand more about mechanism of the system. At the same time, we see discussions on the concrete problems of the implementation. That is indicated by the appearance of the keyword "Kigyou" (enterprise). It is because of the efforts from court organizations and the Ministry of Justice on explaining to companies about the detailed arrangement of the implementation, such as the arrangement of the working hours of staff and ways to minimize the disturbance to daily work when staff is selected and summoned. Besides, particular topics like the arrangement when the selected saiban-in fail to participate in the intensive schedule of the trial are also being brought out, and there are serious discussions on these particular matters.

(3) The Post-Introduction Period

Afterward, when we focus on the post-introduction period, we can see that the year 2009 is somehow transitional between the second and the third period, while the years 2010 to 2012 are very close to each other. And the keywords in 2009 differ in some way from the ones in the following 3 years; start Looking from the left top corner, we see "Kouhou" (public relations), "Hajimaru" (begin), "Gozen" (a.m.), "Gogo" (p.m.), "Shitsumon Hyo" (questionnaire), "Zenkoku" (nationwide), "Tetsudzuki" (procedure), "Sen'nin" (selection), "Hôtei" (law court), "Saikôsai" (the Supreme Court), "Kensatsu" (the prosecution) and "Saiban-in" appear as the year's keywords. Most probably, in 2009 when time gets closer to the start of the system, accurate reports like the selection of a candidate, results in the questionnaires to selected candidates and the registration situation (happening a.m. or p.m.) throughout the whole country, or other related topics. The contents of articles are factual and concrete, which focus mainly on the procedures.

On the other hand, the keywords in the years 2010 to 2012 are like "Saiketsu" (voting), "Shuchô" (argument), "Gôtô" (robbery), "Kyukei" (requested punishments), "Kouso" (appeal), "Shibou" (death), "Iiwatasu" (sentence), "Hikoku" (defendant), "Shounen" (teenager), "Bengogawa" (defensing side), "Kensatsu Gawa" (prosecuting side), "Hankou" (criminal act),"Unten" (drive), "Mushoku" (jobless), "Satsujin" (murder), "Nintei" (recognition). From these keywords, we witness another shift of the reporting focus in 2010 to 2012 that is to the details in the individual case under the saiban-in system.

The post-introduction period can be further divided into two sub-periods indeed; the former sub-period right after its implementation and the latter sub-period after its stabilization. Undoubtedly as the former post-introduction period, the year 2009 is featured by distinctive keywords such as "Tetsudzuki" (procedure), "Sen'nin" (selection), "Gozen" (a.m.), "Gogo" (p.m.), "Hajimaru" (begin), while later after the year 2010, concrete keywords about the factual contents of the court cases appear, such as "Chiken" (district prosecutor's office), "Jiken" (case / incident), "Mitomeru" (admit). Since then, cases under the Saiban-in system are reported as standard criminal court cases with the focus on the case content but not the system. Hence, news in 2009, the year right after the implementation of the system, are still focusing on the system itself that is very much similar to the ones in the previous years. The year is distinguishing and thus in the following sections, our analytical focus will be on the period of 2009–2012, and about the respective characteristics in different years in the period.

The Summary of the Correspondence Analysis in the Three Periods

To summarize the above three periods, we see abstract and overall discussions nominate the first period, 2001 to 2004. New articles mainly focus on the background information and the meanings of the system. In the next period before the implementation, there are more articles talking about the actual steps and process of the implementation. People express their eagerness to understand how to make good use of the system, as the implementation is by no means avoidable. After that, in 2009 when the system is implemented, people concern how the system function since it becomes something happening at the time. In the years that follow, such as the year 2010 and onward, discussions about tedious details gradually fade out. Instead, we have more attention to the court cases but less on the system itself. So, the articles in these 12 years are all about the Saiban-in system but the focus is very much different from each other, and they can be divided into the above three big groups along the timeline.

Understanding the Central Idea of the Article by the Technology of Text Mining

As illustrated in the previous section, through the method of correspondence analysis we extracted the keywords from the news articles, and we have general ideas about their contents, and we are able to categorize them into three main periods on the timeline. Also, through the distribution of keywords, we can tell the overall message of the articles. And based on the three-period framework as concluded, we aim to look at the contents of these articles in more significant details. That is, still dividing the articles into three-time groups, while through some statistical methods we aim to go more in-depth to the contents.

As our next steps, we first do layer cluster analysis, and then a frequency plot of the keywords and thirdly we construct a network chart. In our first step, we aim to spot out the similarity (cluster) of our data.

With the collected news articles data, we trace the linkage between difference keywords and list up the words with the similarities in their usage and relationships. And the second graph shows the frequency of usage of various keywords in various articles, which can give us an overall idea about the content of the articles. The x-axis is the number of articles, and the y-axis represents the frequency of the keywords. Generally speaking, more frequently appearing words should be found in a broader range of articles. Yet, there are some exceptional cases that they are concentrated within specific article groups. And in these cases, we are convinced that the articles are somewhat particular that deserve separate investigation. And thirdly in the network chart, we aim to visualize by lines the linkage of different morphemes by connecting the ones which appear together within an article unit. All these results provide a fair and thorough computerized analysis, so manual screening and worries about subjective judgment are no longer problems. The statistical result is entirely comprehensible and factual.

First, we go through the result of the cluster analysis.

Layer Cluster and Network Chart in the Three Periods

Cluster analysis, or clustering, refers to the task of grouping a set of data in such a way that data in the same cluster group are more similar, in some sense or another, to each other than to those in other clusters. By looking at the shapes of the clusters, we come to know the relationship between the data (the articles). In clustering, we don't have to sort the data in advance, and the result will show the indiscriminate features directly. And this time, by connecting the similar keywords which appear together within the same piece of article, we aim to have more ideas about their strength of their relationship. The distance illustrated in the image that is the measurement of the relationships of the words is statistical distance. By doing this, we can see the trends of the topics and then come to grasp the overall changes. Cluster layers are illustrated in a tree shape, and this is called dendrogram.

Before the analysis, we first have to fix our target data. It is reasonable to analyze all the data we have while considering the fact that the data are already roughly classified into three main categories according to the change of time, we believe that it would be a better idea to go more in-depth by focusing on the data in a specific period(s). Besides, it would be much easier when we look at the cluster groups if we do the focused analysis. Including all data in one single illustration would be, on the other hand, very much tricky.

Here, we analyze the data with extracted keywords as the basic unit. Sentences in news articles are short, and if we do analysis on the sentence level, it would be hard to see the overall trend. It is common to use sentences as the basic unit for, in fact, the analysis of novels or academic references in where sentences are lengthy. Moreover, it is easier to illustrate the results of clustering by dendrogram instead of plotted graphs or ellipse-shaped diagrams. By doing so, the relationships of our selected keywords and the strength of these relationships are much easier to understand.

While processing the data, we have debates on the calculation of the distance (length), that is the measurement of the strength of the relationships between the keywords. When dealing with sparse data in independent and short articles as in news articles, the Jaccard distance should be the most appropriate. In sparse data, it is still problematic when we try to calculate the average, the distribution, and the Euclidean distance. The Ward method is another possible choice, while in novels sentences are long and they consist a long string of words that the Euclidean distance or cos coefficient shall be, after all, better options. This is from Higuchi (2004, pp. 68–69, 154–155).

When doing clustering, the first thing for the analysts to do is to decide the number of clusters and our decision here is based on the Elbow method. That is to make use of the sum of standard error as the axis as in the scree plotting in factor analysis. Along the axis, there is a largely bent spot when compared with other spots, and the number at the first left position of that spot is the number of clusters. (http://qiita.com/deaikei/items/11a10fde5bb47a2cf2c2).

In the following analysis, the author standardized the number of keywords as 31 words for one period in the Dendrogram as the result of trial and error when making up several dendrograms with different numbers of keywords. For example, the author tried making dendrograms with 75 words while we got unnecessary and unrelated operative words like prepositions in the data that interfere our analysis. Another time we have tried 20, while the result fails to show any notable tendency about the relationships of words. Eventually, after a number of trials, 30 looks the best as it shows the characteristics of the words within the most optimal range. Based on this, we proceed to make up the dendrograms, while the number 31 works the best for the first period (the former period before introduction), so we, again, standardize all three periods with that number.

Cluster Analysis Results

The Former Half of Pre-Introduction Period

This is the dendrogram of the first period. The seven clusters from the top reveal the process of the governmental deliberation of the justice reform, the law-establishment, and the internal evaluation of the justice reform in the council, and also the proposal

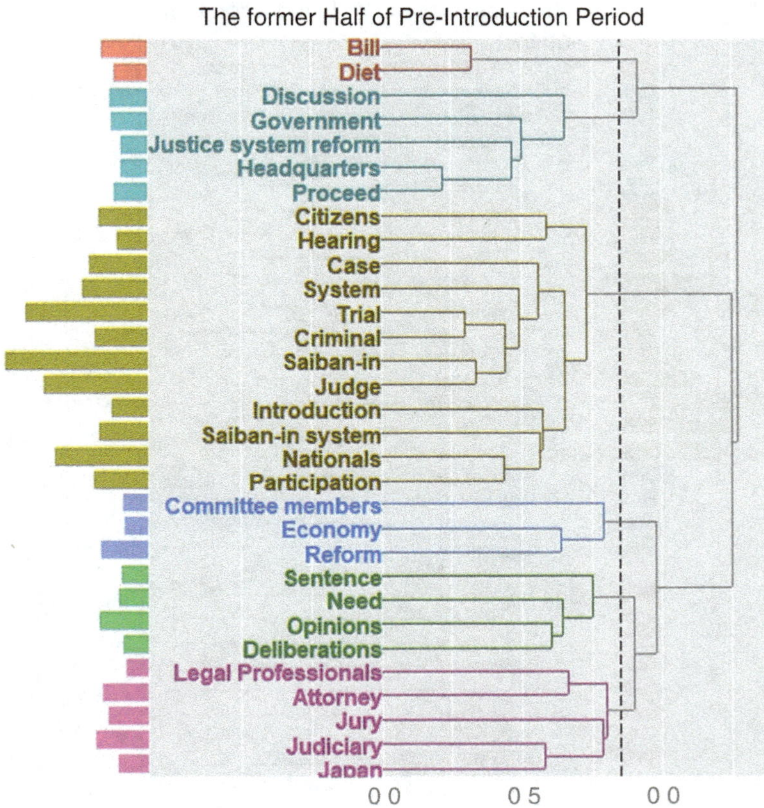

Fig. 5.2 Dendrogram in the first period

of the law in the national assembly. And the 12 clusters follow to explain the content of the saiban-in system- Japanese citizens are randomly selected and get involved in the decision-making process in various court cases, including significant criminal cases. Finally, the last 12 clusters tell the background of the system. Since the abolition of the jury system after WWII, the public starts arousing concerns and suggest citizens should have the right to participate more in the justice system. Going from the period of WWII to the end of the twentieth century, there are rapid development and unprecedented success in Japan's economy, which disclose the loopholes that the development of the justice system is not, sadly, in the same pace of the economic development. A reform in the justice system highly longs, and the Saiban-in system is introduced as one of the significant movements in the reformation process (Fig. 5.2).

As depicted in the dendrograms, articles can be divided along the timeline, and the ideas and directions are different in different periods of time. By conducting the correspondence analysis to the articles accordingly, we shall see the public perception and opinions towards the background and implementation of the saiban-in system, and we could also acquire ideas about the evaluation process carried out in the legal bodies and also related public debates.

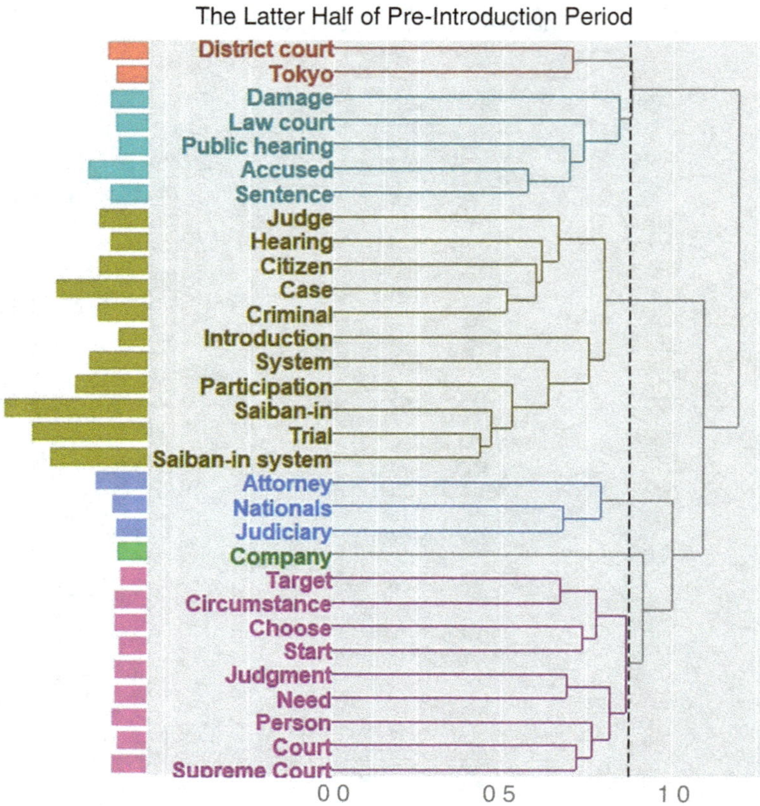

Fig. 5.3 Dendrogram in the second period

The Latter Half of Pre-Introduction Period

Here we have the Dendrogram of the second period. The big cluster in the center explains the mechanism of the system. In the chart on the left, we see the most prolonged bars as saiban-in, saiban (trial) and saiban-in system. As clearly illustrated by the words in the cluster, the Saiban-in system is depicted and perceived as a system that the public can get involved as the saiban-ins in the decision-making process in court trial together with the judge (Fig. 5.3).

The cluster about the implementation process of the system follows. The Supreme Court decides the number of saiban-in needed for the respective cases and appoint them. In this process, cooperation and understanding from employers (companies) come as a determining factor for the successful implementation of the system. Considering the critical meaning of the participation of citizens in the court system, lawyers also play a vitally important role throughout the process.

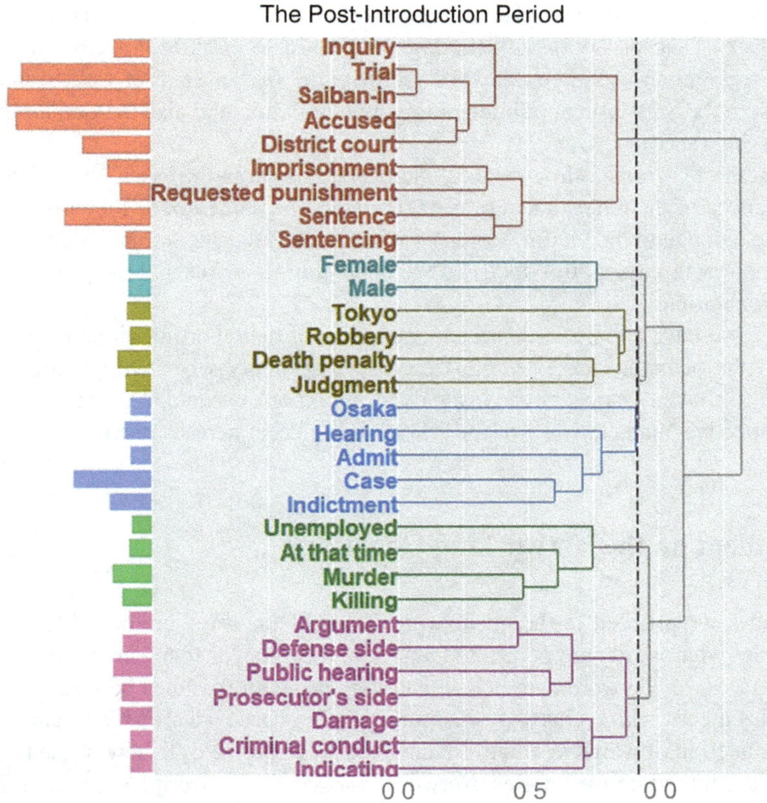

Fig. 5.4 The dendrogram in the third period

Compared with these two significant clusters, we see the reports about the court cases after the implementation of the Saiban-in system come as the seven words from the top. The first case under the saiban-in system was held in Tokyo District Court. The trial, victim and detailed contents were reported as news.

The Post-Introduction Period

Finally, we have the Dendrogram of the third period. The nine words from the top narrate the details of the cases under the Saiban-in system, such as the venue of the trial, the content of the prosecution from prosecutors and also its final judgments (Fig. 5.4).

The 11 words follow the overview of the Saiban-in system, such as the male: female ratio of the saiban-in team, the case when the death penalty decision is made for a robbery which is held in the Tokyo District Court and another case in Osaka

District Court that the defendant admits guilt, the fact that the Tokyo District Court and Osaka District Court rank the highest two in the number of case processed under the Saiban-in system, and the fact that the Osaka District Court ranks the highest in the Saiban-in appointment to population ratio and also the Saiban-in case processing ratio.

And the 11 words follow are the concrete details about the cases, like the respective stances of the defense and prosecuting side, the depiction of the violation acts and the damage to the victim. Here, we witness that after the implementation of the system, new reports mainly focus on the content of the cases and the process of the implementation.

And, we have a more in-depth understanding of the reporting direction and content of the news articles in various periods. Especially when we go through the keywords that only appear once in the dendrogram of a particular period, we can see the respective characteristics of the articles in different periods of time.

Comment on the Networking Chart

And now, we proceed to the networking charts of the three periods. These charts show the what words are connected and how they appear together in our targeted text data. Here, keywords are nodes, and together with the lines between nodes, it becomes a networking chart. By examining these charts, we are able to understand the connection of words in a two-dimensional way and the overview of the targeted text without reading the articles. Networking chart differs from Dendrogram in the way it shows multiple relationships among a large number of words; in Dendrogram, words are arranged in descending order according to their relativeness, and thus only single relationships between words are shown. In networking charts, multiple relationships are shown, and we can investigate them simultaneously. Since we have three networking charts for the three periods, we are able to analyze the respective characteristics of them one by one.

In order to make the comparison of these charts with the previous dendrograms possible, we construct the charts here by using the 31 words in the dendrograms. By doing this, we can also eliminate unmercenary words that would make the charts challenging to understand. Yet, since it is technically challenging to fix the number as 31 when constructing the charts, some of them are made to have 32 words instead. Nonetheless, we believe that absolute accuracy of 31 words is not necessary when we focus on the qualitative characteristics of the data. Down to earth, the number 31 was the best one to work with the Dendrograms, and thus the difference of one word will not be such influential.

Now, we proceed to see the respective characteristics of the discussion in the three different periods.

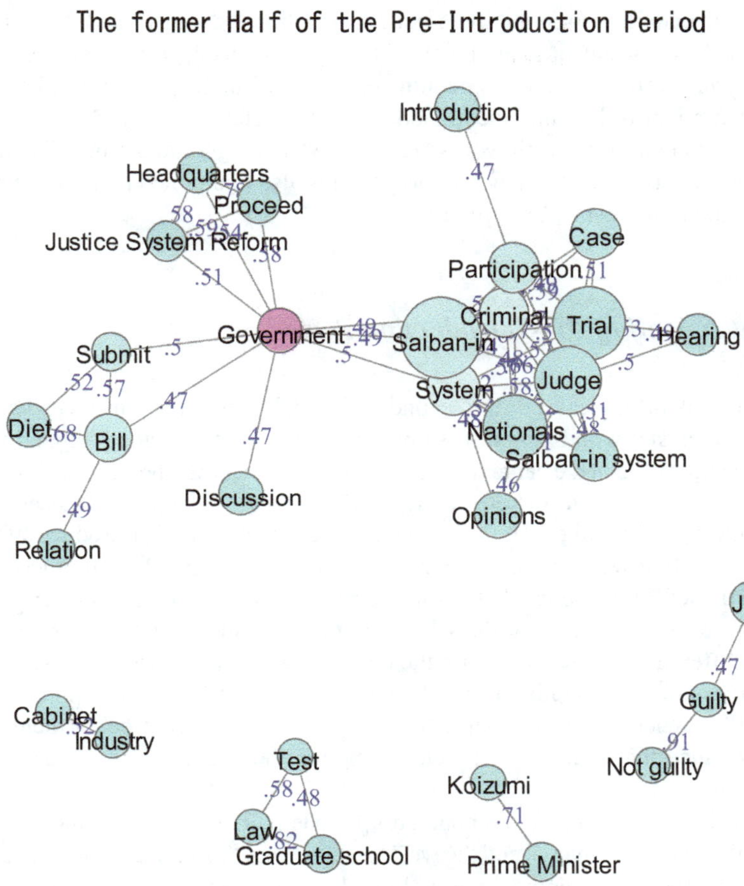

Fig. 5.5 The network in the former half of the pre-introduction period

The Former Half of the Pre-Introduction Period

This is the networking chart of the first period, and there is a significant cluster on the left bottom while all other nodes are somewhat scattered. Every circle (node) represents a word or a phrase. The words and phrases which are connected with lines tend to appear in the same article (concurrent appearance). And in the largest cluster, the central part is the justice system reform, the saiban-in system, and the participation of the saiban-in in the trial of criminal cases. The distribution brings up the idea that citizens' opinions do affect the decision-making process. Besides, extending from the node "Justice System reform," we can see the nodes like "Government" and "Headquarters," so we see that the government and the Reform Council do play essential roles in promoting the Reformation, as that is narrated in the news article (Fig. 5.5).

And in the chart, we see the three-node-group "jury", "guilty" and "not guilty" mirrors the fact that saiban-in are involved in important decision-making processes; the node-pair "Koizumi" and "prime minister" shows that the prime minister at that time, Mr. Jun'ichiro Koizumi, mentioned about the system. At the right bottom, we have another node-group with words "test," "law" and "graduate school," and that shows the establishment of a law school system is also mentioned in the same piece of article about the Justice System reform.

The Latter Half of Pre-Introduction Period

This is the networking chart of the second period; all nodes are connected. There is a significant cluster with big nodes "saiban-in," "participation," and "saiban-in system." The cluster looks the center of the network. The fact that the Saiban-in system involves the participation of citizens is, again, mentioned and emphasized here, while at the right bottom part it is linked with nodes like "May," "introduction" and "start." It simply reveals the timeline that the system is going to be introduced very soon. On the left of the node "Saiban-in" we have "choose" and "circumstances (場合)," and we can conclude that the selection of the saiban-in is being mentioned in the text. Different from the first chart, the node "case" is linked with "accused." The "accused" is connected with "murder," "law court," "district court," "public hearing" and "sentence." It shows that details of a concrete case are being mentioned here. And since that time, news articles depicting the details of court cases keep coming (Fig. 5.6).

And again, we can look at the node group /node pairs in the chart, and we see a group with nodes "company" and "leave," "refusal" and "candidate." Here, detailed arrangement about the appointment and employee's leave application procedures are the topics for people to think and talk.

And, from the nodes "record visually," "interrogation" and "investigation" we see that visualization (可視化) started to be mentioned in the context of saiban-in trials. The visualization was a long history of discussion before the introduction of the saiban-in system, but visualization had scarce possibility to implement before the saiban-in system. But when the law court accommodates citizens who are selected in each case, the introduction of visualization emerged one of the hot issues in the field of criminal procedure.

The Post-Introduction Period

Again, we have the networking chart for the third period. The large cluster remains the same as the other two previous periods with nodes "saiban" and "saiban-in" as the main network. In addition to that, the node "accused" is also centralized. The accused has connections with "sentencing," "imprisonment," "prosecution,"

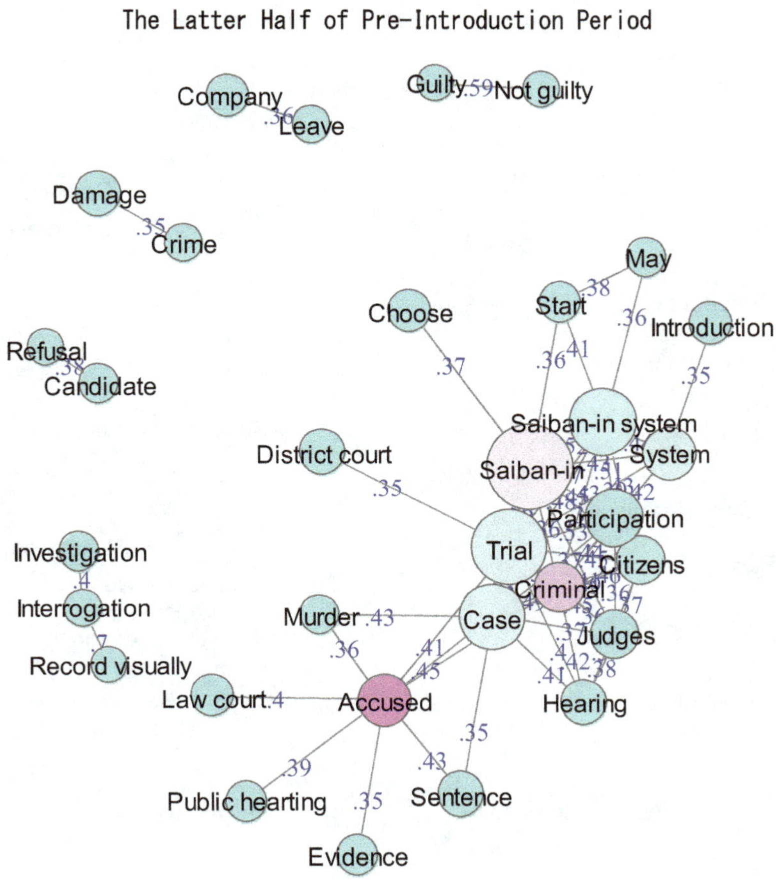

Fig. 5.6 The network in the latter half of the pre-introduction period

"judgment" and "murder." Here, nodes for the detailed depiction of the individual case are slightly cohesive to form a network. And at this point, we can say that details of the court case take over the center of attention from the details of the system itself in this post-introduction period. The shift is especially apparent when we compare this period with the first one, as at this time there are actual court cases to report (Fig. 5.7).

Again, when we look at the smaller node-pairs and groups, we see the pair "reporter" and "media conference." This is the conference in which the selected saiban-in share their personal feelings and comments after the judgment. The pair shows that the conference is reported in a rather large portion at that time. The nodes "smuggling," "stimulant," "violation," "final," "closing argument," "prosecution side," "defense side," "argument," suggest that the content of trials is being reported in detail. Nodes "appeal" and "High Court" is related to the incident that a defendant appeal to High Court and the judgment by saiban-in was overturned.

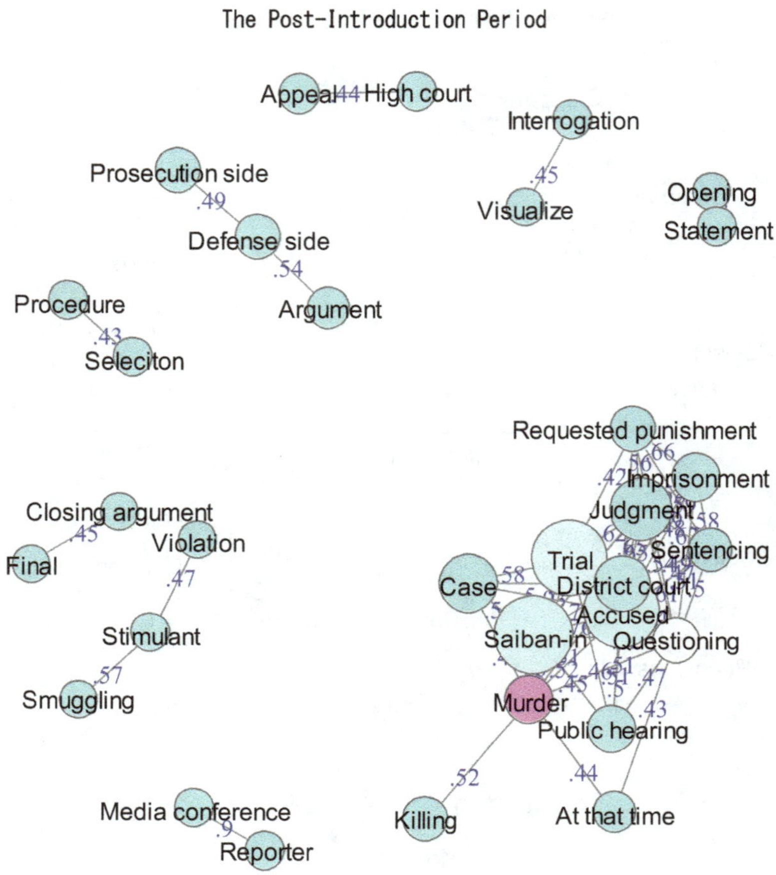

Fig. 5.7 The network in the post-introduction period

"Interrogation" and "visualize" reveal the reports about the controversy on the visualization was still continued from the prior period. The dispute about the use of audio and video recording in the investigation status before prosecution and the also reliability of the judgment from saiban-in are widely and repeatedly stressed in the period.

Public Opinions to the System as Reflected in the News Articles in the Three Periods

In the last section, we have gone through the hot topics and the attention centers in the three different periods, the former pre-introduction period, the latter pre-introduction period, and the post-introduction period. In the first period, reports are abstract like overviews, in the second period, the focus is more on the implementation of the system while in the last, the focus shifts to the concrete details about court cases.

While in this section, what we aim to do is to understand how the public perceives the saiban-in system from the first pre-introduction until the post-introduction period, and, if possible, to visualize the social value about the system through the analysis of news articles. Such a study may be thought as indirect, especially when compared with direct methods like paper-based surveys, while here we firmly believe in the power of mass media -- it's on the same common ground with the public, and it proactively provides the information consciously and unconsciously requested by the public. Moreover, while providing the information, it leads and influences public and mold the social opinions. Higuchi (2004) has also investigated social conception through news articles and acquired a desirable result.

And thus, in this section, based on the overview of the articles extracted by KH coder and further analysis as verification, we aim to study how the public see and deal with the saiban-in system.

Evaluation of News Articles Content by Coding

In order to visualize the concepts in various periods, we adopt the method of coding to evaluate the contents of the news articles. Coding refers to the method to abstractly conceptualize specific target groups of texts. In such method, the concept can be named to a number of word groups, or to different combinations of words. Very much similar to the morphological analysis of general words, once the word undergoes coding, we are able to obtain its frequency of appearance and its co-existing relevant words.

Coding is done to morphologically analyzed articles with its remarkable number of a morpheme. The purpose is to quantify the overall message and the stance of the writer, and also the presentation of these messages and stances. And in the process, we are able to reveal the somewhat abstract, conceptual meaning of the news articles that cannot be done by merely looking at the frequency of the appearance of words and their connected words. Our target is to see what kind of concept is formed in which period of time, whether it's positive or negative and thus to classify the general public opinions towards the saiban-in system.

Coding can also be manually conducted while considering the stability of judging criteria and the large volume of data we have; it seems to be impossible for the analyst to memorize all the requirements and judging details throughout the whole process. Contrasting with this problematic manual way, computerized auto-coding is able to process a massive amount of data by using a set of unchanged, consistent criteria written by the analyst, and thus the extracted concept could be much more objective. As the coding rules and judging criteria are set by the analyst in advance, the correctness may be argued at this point, while undergoing the mechanical analysis, the judgement is steady and consistent, and it also helps to eliminate all other side-arguments and thus stand out the messages and stance directly related to the target topic. Considering all these, we chose to mechanically code the text files by setting rules to the KH coder.

The Coding Method

We first screen through the news articles to grasp the overall meaning, and based on the social arguments about the system in different periods of time, we come to set the coding viewpoints as, 1) the meaning of the saiban-in system 2) the technical challenges of the implementation and 3) the threats and drawbacks when implementing the system. The viewpoint of 1) is about the objective of changing of the Justice system- as with the change, citizens are empowered in a much more significant extent through their participation while at the same time burden is increased. Viewpoint 2) is about the particular technical challenges when introducing and implementing the system, and the whole process bogs down if these problems remain unsolved. And thus, here by "challenges" we also include the articles which criticize the system. As named, viewpoint 3) are threats and drawbacks, which include the public anxiety about the change, uncertainties and also concerns about the increased burden in various aspects. There is an unneglectable number of articles touch on this kind of personal anxiety as criticism, and this is something we have to confront. Thus, we have viewpoint 3).

And based on the above viewpoints we proceed to code with the following concepts; Based on viewpoint 1), the coding categories are set as "the meaning to participate in the saiban-in system", "the opinion reflection of saiban-in", "the reflection of common sense and personal feelings", "reliability and legitimacy of the judgment result" and "improvement in the procedure of prosecution". As for viewpoint 2), the coding categories are "comprehensibility," "feasibility of the implementation of the system," "general burden," "challenges of implementation," "problem of unconstitutionality" and "dysfunction." Finally, in 3), the categories are "physical threats," "psychological burden" and "apprehension."

And in order to classify whether the article is supporting or opposing against the system, we sort the categories into either positive and negative. "The meaning to participate in the saiban-in system", "the reflection of opinion", "the reflection of common sense", "reliability and legitimacy", "understandability", "feasibility of the implementation of the system" and "improvement of procedure of prosecution" belong to the positive category. On the other hand, "general burden," "psychological burden," "issues of implementation," "unconstitutionality," "dysfunction," "threats to the personal safety of saiban-in (in short, physical danger)" and "apprehension" are the negative ones. The categories being neither positive nor negative are regarded as "neutral." The primary analytical unit is a piece of articles. The article includes any keywords that belong to the category would be counted one, and they can be counted multiple times in various categories. The list of the keywords of each category can be found in the appendix.

The Coding Result

Publishing Year and Distribution of the News Articles

In Table 5.2, the coding results in which the numbers of time of the appearance of words in particular categories in each target publishing year are clearly shown together with its percentage (i.e., the relative frequency) of the total number of articles extracted in the year. Since the article numbers are entirely different in different years, (as an intended result of the Chi-square test Content description), it is better to look at the relative frequency rather than the actual number of appearance here. As mentioned, articles can belong to multiple categories, and the list actually does not include all words from the articles, and thus the list does not include all categories that the articles may belong to, and thus the sums here do not count up to 100%. And in the lower table we see the sums exceeding 100%, as, as said, the articles belong to more than one single category. For instance, the stance "the introduction of the saiban-in system puts burden on citizens' shoulders, while it does more goods than harms as it helps to realize the participation of the public in the Justice system" is counted in both "general burden" and "the meaning to participate in the saiban-in system".

When we look at the relationship of the categories and the years, we can see that "meaning to participate" and "the reflection of common sense and personal feelings" frequently appear in the year 2001, with the relative frequency 76.47% and 25.49% respectively. The discussion of the saiban-in system starts around 2000, and in the year 2001 people start to seek for more clue about why the system is introduced, the meaning of participating in it and then in the Justice system. The category "the reflection of common sense and personal feelings" is not about the objective of the implementation, while it also reflects that the public continues to seek for more information from mass media about their rights and roles saiban-in.

The reason is, it is somewhat nonsensical to reach the trial concluded in regardless of the common sense and feelings from the public if there is invited participation of them. This standpoint is repeatedly reported in various articles, and though the primary objective of the introduction of the saiban-in system is not just to include feelings and value standard on the personal level, the public does think judging from their feelings and sense reasonable and essential. Along with the development timeline, the idea remains as the general, universal belief from the public and later, "I judge from my point" is used as a key phrase in a promotional campaign in 2004, in which the public finds somewhat appealing. As for the negative side, the frequently touched on topics are the problems of unconstitutionality (58.82%), worries (54.90%) and burden on the public (45.10%). Trial judgment should be made by legal judges as stated in and guaranteed in the constitution of Japan. It is both literally interpreted and perceived by the public. Thus, the system-opposing critics stress that the judgment from saiban-ins is in violation of the constitution, and the whole introduction of such a system as a return of the lay participation idea around WWII collapses. That is the beginning of the criticism and

Table 5.2 Numbers of articles by coding categories

	Positive							Negative							
	Meaning of participation	Reflection of opinion	Reflection of commonsense	Trust and legitimacy	Understand-ableness	Feasible	Improvement of cirminal procedure	General burden	Psychological burden	Issues until introduction	Unconsti-tutionality	Dysfunction	Physical danger	Apprehen-tion	Total numbers of articles
2001	39 (76.47%)	7 (13.73%)	13 (25.49%)	1 (1.96%)	3 (5.88%)	0 (0.00%)	0 (0.00%)	23 (45.10%)	3 (5.88%)	1 (1.96%)	30 (58.82%)	9 (17.65%)	0 (0.00%)	28 (54.90%)	51
2002	11 (42.31%)	2 (7.69%)	1 (3.85%)	0 (0.00%)	0 (0.00%)	0 (0.00%)	0 (0.00%)	5 (19.23%)	1 (3.85%)	1 (3.85%)	9 (34.62%)	0 (0.00%)	1 (3.85%)	10 (38.46%)	26
2003	29 (43.94%)	0 (0.00%)	6 (9.09%)	2 (3.03%)	3 (4.55%)	1 (1.52%)	0 (0.00%)	26 (39.39%)	6 (9.09%)	1 (1.52%)	45 (68.18%)	4 (6.06%)	0 (0.00%)	34 (51.52%)	66
2004	51 (43.97%)	2 (1.72%)	12 (10.34%)	2 (1.72%)	3 (2.59%)	1 (0.86%)	1 (0.86%)	48 (41.38%)	5 (4.31%)	6 (5.17%)	78 (67.24%)	14 (12.07%)	2 (1.72%)	50 (43.10%)	116
2005	48 (38.40%)	1 (0.80%)	5 (4.00%)	0 (0.00%)	6 (4.80%)	0 (0.00%)	0 (0.00%)	27 (21.60%)	7 (5.60%)	0 (0.00%)	66 (52.80%)	8 (6.40%)	0 (0.00%)	33 (26.40%)	125
2006	67 (36.81%)	1 (0.55%)	12 (6.59%)	6 (3.30%)	10 (5.49%)	0 (0.00%)	0 (0.00%)	47 (25.82%)	11 (6.04%)	0 (0.00%)	103 (56.59%)	17 (9.34%)	1 (0.55%)	59 (32.42%)	182
2007	48 (22.75%)	2 (0.95%)	9 (4.27%)	3 (1.42%)	2 (0.95%)	0 (0.00%)	1 (0.47%)	66 (31.28%)	17 (8.06%)	0 (0.00%)	126 (59.72%)	10 (4.74%)	6 (2.84%)	83 (39.34%)	211
2008	96 (26.45%)	3 (0.83%)	20 (5.51%)	11 (3.03%)	13 (3.58%)	3 (0.83%)	1 (0.28%)	90 (24.79%)	20 (5.51%)	0 (0.00%)	221 (60.88%)	22 (6.06%)	8 (2.20%)	149 (41.05%)	363
2009	104 (12.47%)	12 (1.44%)	59 (7.07%)	12 (1.44%)	26 (3.12%)	2 (0.24%)	2 (0.24%)	202 (24.22%)	71 (8.51%)	0 (0.00%)	488 (58.51%)	20 (2.40%)	7 (0.84%)	303 (36.33%)	834
2010	33 (4.44%)	3 (0.40%)	35 (4.71%)	0 (0.00%)	4 (0.54%)	0 (0.00%)	1 (0.13%)	142 (19.11%)	44 (5.92%)	2 (0.27%)	344 (46.30%)	14 (1.88%)	2 (0.27%)	278 (37.42%)	743
2011	14 (3.02%)	2 (0.43%)	8 (1.73%)	1 (0.22%)	0 (0.00%)	0 (0.00%)	0 (0.00%)	62 (13.39%)	13 (2.81%)	0 (0.00%)	186 (40.17%)	12 (2.59%)	2 (0.43%)	129 (27.86%)	463
2012	3 (1.32%)	3 (1.32%)	8 (3.52%)	0 (0.00%)	0 (0.00%)	0 (0.00%)	0 (0.00%)	24 (10.57%)	4 (1.76%)	0 (0.00%)	97 (42.73%)	2 (0.88%)	1 (0.44%)	59 (25.99%)	227
Sum	543 (15.94%)	38 (1.12%)	188 (5.52%)	38 (1.12%)	70 (2.05%)	7 (0.21%)	6 (0.18%)	762 (22.37%)	202 (5.93%)	11 (0.32%)	1793 (52.63%)	132 (3.87%)	30 (0.88%)	1215 (35.66%)	3407
Chi-square	577.730**	92.082**	66.842**	39.847**	54.973**	19.011	6.65	108.526**	28.926**	109.823**	97.082**	90.900**	27.313**	52.373**	

controversies about the unconstitutionality of the system. Worries and burden are familiar topics to be brought out when there is a new social change or any new governmental movement are introduced, while we do not see any notable features in the depiction herein at this time.

Moving to 2002 we see that the news articles talk about the meaning of participation halve into 42.31%, and the actual number decrease by eleven. And, there are only two articles talk about the reflection of public opinions. The article number on the positive side sharply decreases. Meanwhile, the same decrease is also found on the negative side, with a decrease of 26 in the total number of articles. News about worries, unconstitutionality, and burden are still the nominating topics on this side, while we see a decline in the relative frequency here as well.

The total number of articles increased in 2003 when compared with that in 2001. We have a steady number of 43.94% pro articles that remains more or less the same as 2002, while the numbers in all other categories become much less notable. On the contrary, on the con side, there are 68.18% of articles talk about the unconstitutionality, and 51.52% about public worries, on a comparable level with 2001 in their relative frequencies. Articles about the overall burden drop a little to 39.39%.

The year 2004 was the significant year as the system was officially put forward and introduced, and articles about the meaning of participation remain stable at 43.97%. And in this year articles about common sense/personal feelings have the relative frequency as 10.34% and actual number as twelve. The reason here is because the saiban-in act is established in the year, and there is a rebound in the number of articles talking about the meaning of the participation. On the other hand, as a notable change, articles about the unconstitutionality, worries, and burden are no longer the top three topics on the negative side. The number of articles about unconstitutionality remains high as 78, and also the relative frequency does not drop significantly. It could be believed that because of the formation of the saiban-in law, people still concern about the unconstitutionality here.

Moving one more year to 2005, which is the year promotional activities flourish, technical terms about the system go pervasive through the continuous exposure to the public in news articles. As a result, the number of articles talks about the comprehensibility of the system triples from 2 to 6, with the relative frequency of 4.8%. The actual number of articles about the participation meaning remains high as 48, while the relative frequency drops to 38.40%. There are 5 articles about common sense and personal feeling, with the relative frequency of 4%, while it is just on the same level of that one about comprehensibility. It is the same result on the negative side with unconstitutionality as the highest and followed by worries and overall burden.

In 2006, the articles about the participation meaning remained steady at 38.61% when compared with 2005, and there are 6 articles about the reliability and political parties which make up the relative frequency of 4.8%. Comprehensibility increases to 5.49%. It reflected the positive influence of the "Promotion of Legal Terms to Common Lives Project" from the "Nihon Bengoshi Rengôkai" (Japan Federation of Bar Associations) in 2005, and the result is also seen in the coming year of 2006. On the contrary side, on the contrary, we see the nominating numbers of unconstitutionality (56.59%), worries (32.42%) and global burden (25.82%). The number of psychological burden increases to 11, a two-digit number for the first time with the relative frequency of 6.04%, and it is a slight but notable increase from 2005.

In 2007, we witnessed the beginning of the decline to 22.75% in the number of articles about participation meaning on the positive side. While on the negative side, the number of unconstitutionality remain as high as 59.72%, that is almost six-tenths of the total. Articles about worries (39.34%) and global burden (31.28%) again, follow, and these three make up the top three of the rank.

In 2008, there is a rebound in the participation meaning to 26.45%. Comprehensibility is 3.58%, and reliability/legitimacy is 3.03%. A very much similar result is noted on the negative side with over 60%, which is 60.88% articles about unconstitutionality, 41.05% in worries and 24.79% in overall burden. Psychological burden is 5.51% in the year.

In 2009, we saw a sharp decrease in the number of articles talks about the meaning of participation to only 12.47%, on the positive side. Articles about common sense/personal feeling go to 7.07%, which is a slight increase when compared with the previous years from 2005 to 2008. And, the 26 articles about the comprehensibility make up 3.12%, which is not really a unique number. On the contrary side, again we see the same distribution that the unconstitutionality remains the highest at 58.51%, and then followed by worries (36.33%) and overall burden (24.22%). The article number about the psychological burden goes up to 71 and make up 8.51%, which is the highest since it appears. The increases incomprehensibility and psychological burden are brought by the actual trial happen in this year.

The year 2010 is the second year of the post-introduction period, while the articles talk about the participation meaning drops sharply to only 4.44% when compared with the large numbers in the past. And, the portion of articles about common sense/feelings becomes 4.04%, which is nearly a halved number when compared with the previous years. In this year, articles about the comprehensibility of the system also severely drop to 0.54%. When we look at the negative side, articles about the unconstitutionality also decreases around 15% to 46.30%. Again, it is followed by worries (37.42%), overall burden (19.11%) and psychological burden (5.92%). The structure of the distribution remains the same, while all the relative frequency of all these categories decrease.

In the two following years of 2011 and 2012, we see the change continues in the same direction. On the positive side, the participation meaning, which was somewhat a hot topic in the previous years as illustrated, drops considerably to 3.02% and 1.32%. And we are convinced by this fact that at the time, the meaning to participate in the system needs not to be emphasized anymore. The numbers of articles about common sense/feelings are 8 in both years, and the relative frequency is 1.73% and 3.52%. And on the negative side, the highest remains as the unconstitutionality, which is around 40% in both years as 40.17% and 42.73%. There is also a decrease in the number of articles about worries, and the frequencies are only 27.86% and 25.99% in the respective two years. Yet, it still makes up a quarter of the total. The number of articles about overall burden is around 10%, as 13.39% in 2011 and 10.57% in 2012. A similar sharp decrease can also be found in the category psychological burden, which has the relative frequency of 2.81% and 1.76% as the result of the stability of the system and also efforts from the court to deal with the problem. While later in the incident in which a PTSD complainant sue the government, the related news is believed to increase significantly while since the year 2014 does not fall into our analytical target, we leave the discussion untouched here.

We have a unique category "dysfunction" through its relative frequency is low when compared with the categories above. It refers mostly to the articles which predict potential problems before they actually happen. When we check the relative frequency of its appearance, we see there are 9 articles as 17.65% in 2001, which is a unique number right after the introduction but it continues to drop until 2004 when the saiban-in law is established, and the actual number and frequency is 14 and 12.07% respectively. In this year, the public pays much more attention to the practice of the system and criticizing opinions also increase. After that, we see there are 2 to 22 articles each year. The discussion remains here throughout the process, while it only makes up a small portion (less than 10%) and the number is insignificant when we compared it with other negative categories like the unconstitutionality, overall burden, and worries.

The discussion about the unconstitutionality of the system is around from a very early stage till 2012. In accordance with the national constitution, only judges are empowered with jurisdiction, and the ideas to include saiban-ins who are ordinary citizens being randomly selected for one single time in the decision-making process remains controversial. On November 16, 2011, the Supreme Court eventually confirmed the constitutionality of the system, and since then the discussion sharply drops and fades out.

As an index of the analysis of the article number throughout the year, we can look into the chi-square test value at the bottom. It shows the difference of the article number (as in relative percentage of its frequency) in different years. We have more ideas about the changes of the reporting trends when we look at the difference in the number of percentage in various years, and when the test value gets more significant, we see more asterisk attached. Yet, only large values and thus the categories with the large values should be taken as a reference here as small values are considered less referential.

With the above idea in our minds, we look at the numbers, and we come to realize that all categories are here with a referential value except "the possibility of implementation" and "improvement of the prosecution process." In other words, it shows that discussion under these two categories is not continuously around throughout the 12 years. The article number in this category is different from those of hot categories like "meaning of the participation," "reflection of common sense and general feelings" that the number changes according to the updates of the system. Especially like after the first trial case under the saiban-in system, the focus of news articles shifted to the details of the case instead of the meaning to participate. Therefore, there is a relatively low number of news articles on the topics, which are constant and independent of the timeline.

Concerning the valence of the newspaper articles, we need focus on the positiveness of the categories. The number of articles about each conceptual category is illustrated in the table, this time, we see that there are some categories appearing multiple times within one single year while there are also categories appearing insufficient times only. By investigating the distribution of the categories, we have more definite ideas about the characteristics of the news articles in our target years, as in how is the distance between the categories and the year change so which categories are close to or far from the year. By looking statistically at the distributions of the categories, we are able to compare the coding categories in various years, and the result is shown in the table.

In this table, we have the categories with different concepts and in different publishing years. Again, the concept here is divided into either positive or negative, and we conduct analysis on both sides. Here, we see that positive articles are all concentrated on the left-hand side in the year 2001 to 2006. Negative articles, on the other hand, are concentrated on the right-hand side, and they appear from 2007 onward. We continue to analyze the valence of the newspaper articles with analyzing by calculating odds ratios in the years.

Positive & Negative Analysis

As illustrated we have divided the article categories into positive or negative, and here we can compare their numbers of articles. To do this, we have to make up another table to show the comparison of a total number of articles on both sides. Since articles can belong to multiple categories as explained, the total number of our two tables do not match with each other.

In order to have a better understanding of the positive and negative ratio, we calculate the odds ratios in different years, which is a single value that reveal the ratio in a highly direct way. In this table, we see the values {positive articles / (total number of articles - positive articles)} / {negative articles / (total number of articles - positive articles)}. The values here are always larger than zero, while whether they are larger than one indicate the relationship of the positive articles and the negative articles (Table 5.3).

Here we see that contrary articles are below the value 1 while definite articles are substantial than one. The odds ratio is, as we see, simple straightforward and useful for illustration. The logarithm base can be any numbers, here we adopt the number from natural logarithm so that definite articles are concentrated on the plus side, and negative articles are on the minus side. And, with the odds ratio, we can compare their values and relationship in a straight line.

Also, we regard the data in the table as sampling data with the standard error of 5%. Since our analysis entirely bases on news articles, the size and choice of the sampling significantly affect the statistics and thus the result. Yet, we adopt the odds ratios to reveal any notable differences in the ratio of positive and negative articles as a useful aid here.

Based on the above design, we calculate the odds ratio and together with the natural logarithm we see the relative proportion of the positive and negative articles,

Table 5.3 Odds ratio on the numbers of positive-negative articles

	Positive	Negative	Number of total articles	Odds ratio p(1−p)/n(1−n)	Standard error (ln(Odds ratio))	Lower limit of 95% CI	Upper limit of 95% CI	ln(Odds ratio)
2001	41	39	51	1.26	0.48	0.31	1.74	0.23
2002	13	14	26	0.86	0.56	−0.23	1.41	−0.15
2003	33	53	66	0.25	0.40	−0.53	0.64	−1.41
2004	58	91	116	0.27	0.29	−0.30	0.57	−1.29
2005	54	81	125	0.41	0.26	−0.10	0.67	−0.88
2006	82	117	182	0.46	0.21	0.03	0.67	−0.79
2007	53	150	211	0.14	0.22	−0.29	0.36	−1.99
2008	115	262	363	0.18	0.16	−0.14	0.34	−1.72
2009	172	595	834	0.10	0.11	−0.12	0.22	−2.26
2010	63	471	743	0.05	0.15	−0.24	0.21	−2.93
2011	21	259	463	0.04	0.24	−0.44	0.28	−3.29
2012	13	129	227	0.05	0.32	−0.57	0.36	−3.08
Total	718	2261	3407	0.14	0.06	0.03	0.19	−2.00

and within the confidence interval of the odds ratio we check whether we can find any value "one." The value "one" means there are no differences between the positive and negative article numbers, and the appearance of the value "one" in the confidence interval of odds ratio means that there is no notable and thus analysis-worthy difference between the positive and negative article numbers.

However, the lower limit of the confidence interval is calculated mechanically by deducting "standard error x 1.96" from the odd ratio, and thus the value may be a seemingly problematic negative value.

So, when we look into the values, we saw the odds ratio 1.26 in 2001, and we can conclude that there are quite a massive number of definite articles in the year. While since there is a valuable one in the confidence interval, so the statistical result is insignificant. In 2002 there are many negative articles, and the odds ratio is lower than one. And similarly, we have a value one in the confidence interval, and thus the number is again insignificant. Yet, from 2003 onward we see the odds values are all lower than one, and there is no value one within the upper limit of the confidence interval. Statistically, the numbers are then referential to conclude that the news reporting direction in the years tends to be negative. The trend remains unchanged until 2012.

When we look at the individual values of different years, we see that both positive and negative articles make up around 80% in the year 2001, and in 2002 they make up around half the number. Then, from 2003 to 2006, we see definite articles make up around or slightly less than 50% of the total while negative articles make up 60% to 80%. The gradual change continues in the years 20,067 to 2009, with definite articles further drops to 20–30%, while the negative ones make up consistently around 70%. And, since the years the saiban-in system is implemented, from 2010 to 2012, there are only around 10% positive articles but around 55–60% negative articles.

We expect articles are touching on positive elements after the introduction and implementation of the system while the truth is just the opposite- there is an increasing number of negative articles (with the odds ratio getting closer to zero).

Therefore, we witness the fact that the number of articles on the positive and negative sides is slightly comparable in the first 2 years, while in the decade after that, there are more negative articles and more important the value is statistically significant. It can be argued that there are political intentions behind, while the undoubted fact is, the public continues to receive more negative information about the system, and generally, the impression should also be harmful, mainly when the individuals rely heavily on or even thoroughly on newspapers for information acquisition.

After all, it is commonly considered that journalists play a role to criticize the governmental powers. And, the saiban-in system, which is introduced and implemented by the country is here for them to criticize and that is the reason the number of adverse reports never decrease.

Analysis of the Networking Chart

Besides the morphological analysis, we have also constructed networking charts for the categories, while unlike the previous analysis, there are a massive number of fixed nodes in the networking charts. Hence, the charts here look very much alike, which is preferably different from the straightforward and direct illustration in the morphological analysis. Networking chart is used to reveal overall concepts hidden in texts, and thus by constructing charts for the three periods, the former pre-introduction period, the latter pre-introduction period, and the post-introduction period, we aim to visualize characteristics and thus the differences of them. By doing this, we can also see the cohesiveness of various concepts, and also the inter-relationships and their changes throughout the periods. Nodes are fixed and universal in all charts, as it carries no meaning to compare charts with different kinds of nodes, and we believe that these networking charts can bring us insight from another angle of the morphological analysis.

Before we go to look at the networking chart of the first period, it should be mentioned that these charts are constructed by a number of steps; it is first filtered and counted by the KH coder, node-connected and plotted as networking data. The result is then analyzed, exported, and screened by a free text-analyzing software called "Pajek.[3]" All analysis on the plotted charts is done through Pajek because of its natural and comprehensible connection-formation function. It is just much more efficient than just analyzing through the statistics software R.

Also, since the concepts in these periods are similar, the outcome would be hard to compare if we export them through KH coder. The advantages of using Pajek

[3] Pajek is available at http://vlado.fmf.uni-lj.si/pub/networks/pajek/. "Pajek" means a spider in Slovenian.

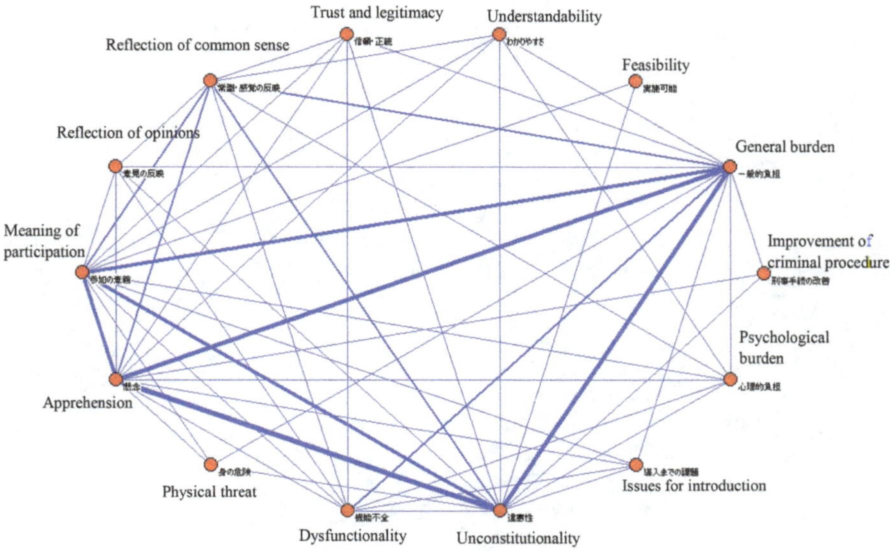

Fig. 5.8 The network of categories in the first half of pre-introduction period

include the thick connection lines and the ellipse-shaped concepts, and they contribute to our easy comparison. This is the bmp file exported by Pajek.

Here we have the networking chart of the former pre-introduction period. The thickness of the lines clearly shows the strength of the relationship of the nodes, while the thickness here is based on the value form the export result of the KH coder and the small values cannot bring any notable difference in its thickness. Thus, we multiply the value by ten before inputting to Pajek and ensure the thickness are easy to compare (Fig. 5.8).

From the chart, we see that the relationships between "meaning of participation," "worries" and "constitutionality" are closely linked with each other. The node "common sense and personal feelings" is, though a bit weaker, closely linked and these four nodes make up the center of the chart. Besides, there are 12 lines from the node "general burden" which makes the highest number in the chart and show that the node is both frequently mentioned and strongly linked with other nodes. As an obvious contrast, the nodes "possibility of implementation" and "improvement of the prosecution process" are marginalized and weakly linked with others, mainly because of its rareness of appearance in the news articles. The same also applies to personal threats. On the contrary, "trust and legitimacy," "dysfunctions," "psychological burden" are weakly linked with other categories but contribute together to make up ideas and concepts here.

And, this is the chart for the second period, the later pre-introduction period. There is a difference in the vertex (category) here because previously there was an insignificant vertex plotted when we construct the chart. That means, in other words, the vertex "challenges before implementation" in the first chart forms a strong network with other nodes in the first period, but it becomes unimportant in this period.

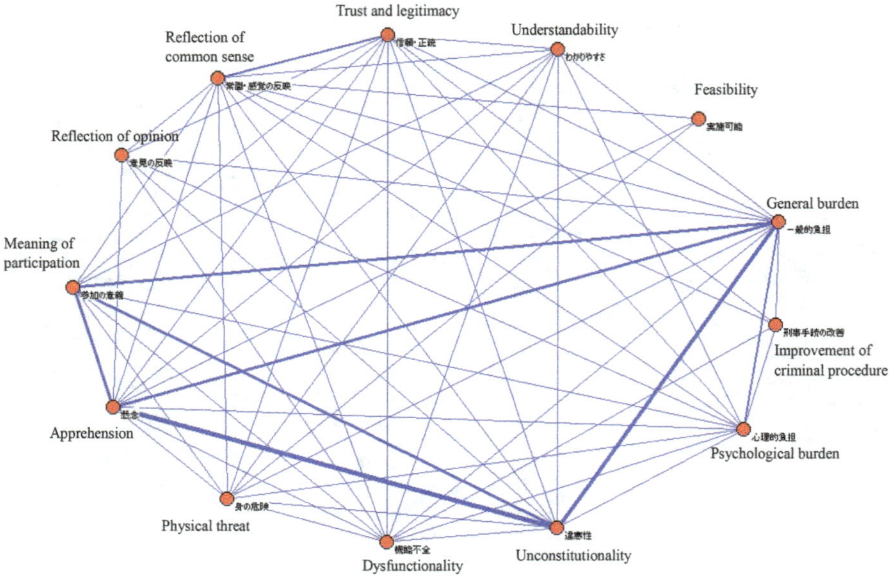

Fig. 5.9 The network of categories in the second half of pre-introduction period

"General burden," "meaning of participation," "worries" and "constitutionality" form a strong network together as in the first chart. And there are eleven lines emitting from the node "general burden" which reveals the strong concept formed. Different from the first period, we see the connection between "improvement of the prosecution process" and "reliability & legitimacy" in this chart. And at this point, the nodes "reflection of opinions" and "meaning of participation" lose their connection. Also, the lines of the node "psychological burden" increases from seven to eleven when going from the first to the second period, which exemplifies the increase of its relativeness with other concepts (Fig. 5.9).

Lastly, we have the chart for the post-introduction period. In the chart, the vertex "feasibility" becomes less important, loses its significance, and drops out from the chart. Also, the node "meaning of participation" becomes less connected with others through the previous strengths were prominent. Following that, in descending connectedness, we have "general burden," "apprehension" and "unconstitutionality." Moreover, the connection between "general burden" and "psychological burden" becomes stronger. The number of lines from the node "general burden" is twelve, as a V-shaped rebound, i.e., it changes back to roughly the same as the first period. The most connected node in this period is "unconstitutionality," while as for the node "psychological burden" the number of lines decreases by 9, but when compared with other nodes, the number is still a high one. Last but not least, we see that the nodes "reflection of opinions" and "meaning of participation" is re-connected here in this chart (Fig. 5.10).

We have gone through the characteristics and differences of the charts in the three periods. And here at this time, we make use of a command from Pajek and

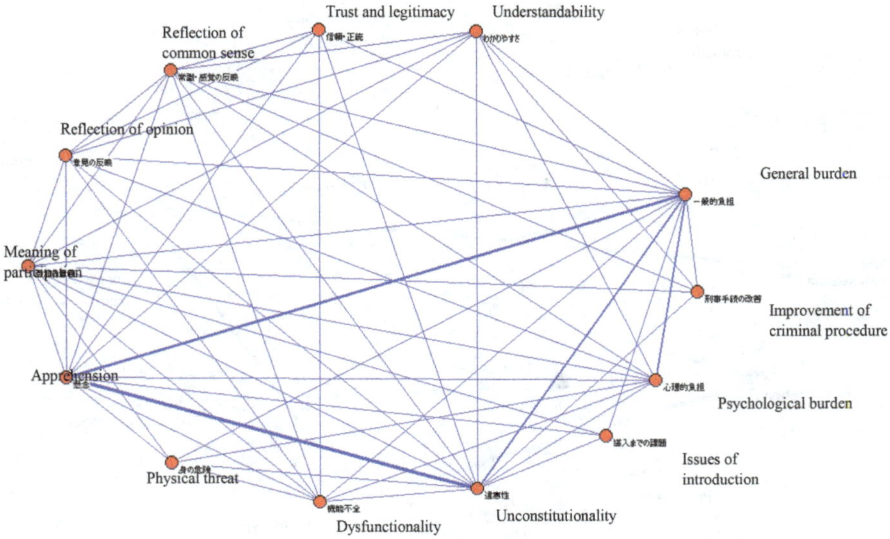

Fig. 5.10 The network of categories in the post-introduction period

visualize the specific difference between the two post-introduction periods, and also between the last pre-introduction and post-introduction period.

The difference between the two-pre-introduction period is illustrated in this image and thicker the lines, more significant the difference it is revealing. Here, we witness that the links between "general burden," "unconstitutionality" and "worries" are stronger in the former period but becomes weakened in the latter, the decline is also found in their connectedness. A similar weakening phenomenon is also found in the connection between "general burden" and "meaning of participation." Quite the opposite, the connection between "trust and legitimacy" and "reflection of common sense" is strengthened when going from the former to the latter period (Fig. 5.11).

Then, we have the image showing the difference between the last pre-introduction and post-introduction period, while this time the difference is less notable. The big difference between the two pre-introduction periods is due to the two solid years 2004 and 2009. 2004 is the year in which the saiban-in law established, and it is the beginning of the actual and full-scale previous period. 2009 is the year the system comes to real practice and thus it is a year when all the reporting directions and styles are great changes. Here between the pre and post introduction period, a notable change is the connection between "general burden" and "psychological burden"; it is connected to the implementation of the system. It is commonly believed that these two terms are used as a single set after the first trial. In addition, the number of connection lines from "psychological burden" increases probably as a result that the invisible worries are becoming visible and close to the concrete facts and result about the first trial. Also, there are many lines from "physical threat." Articles related to the physical safety of saiban-in are rather prominent before the

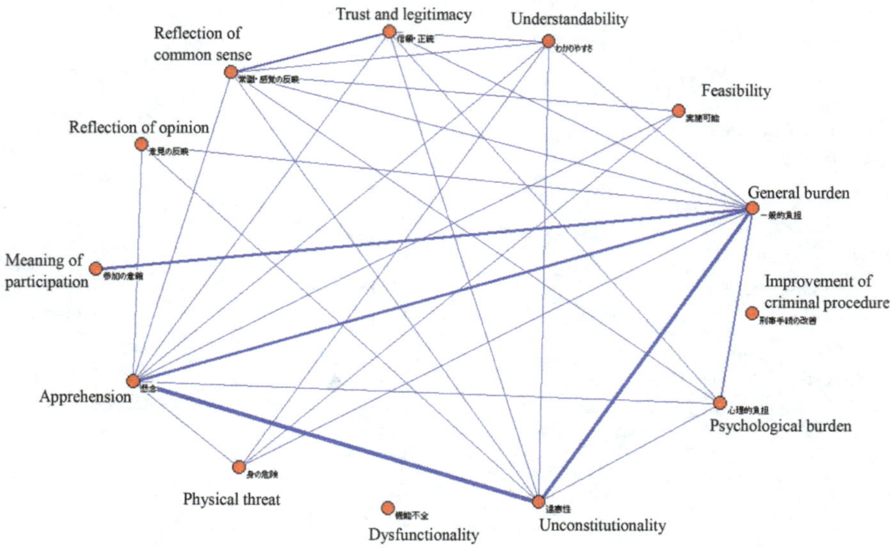

Fig. 5.11 The difference between the two pre-introduction period

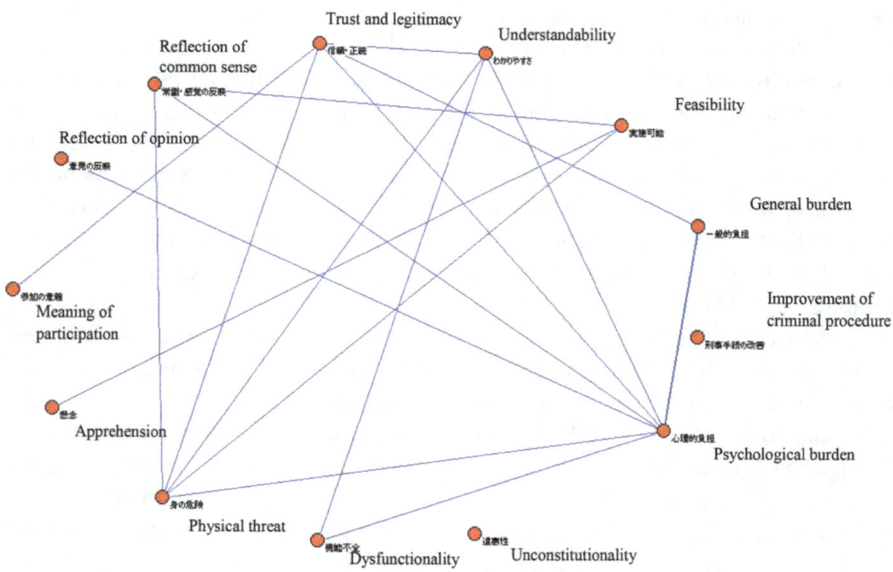

Fig. 5.12 The network of difference between the second half of pre-introduction period and post-introduction period

implementation, that is in the latter pre-introduction period, while later, until the actual case that a saiban-in is bodily approached on streets there are no notable incidents and thus no related reports on this topic (Fig. 5.12).

Correspondence Analysis; Respective Contents in Various Years

In this section, the author first conducts a correspondence analysis on the relationship between morphemes (keywords) and the publishing year, and we also do the same on the conceptual categories of the articles. Through such an analysis, we are able to visualize how the article categories change the timeline and its penetration (Fig. 5.13).

When we focus on the distribution of the categories, we see that the category "issues of implementation" is positioned at the left bottom corner, which is a bit far from other categories. It simply illustrates that the category is frequently mentioned in the previous pre-introduction period. And, before the year 2006, we see that "meaning of participation," "reflection of opinions," "understandability," "trust and legitimacy," "feasibility" and "reflection of common sense" are all at the center of attention on the positive side. As for the negative side, we have "dysfunction" and

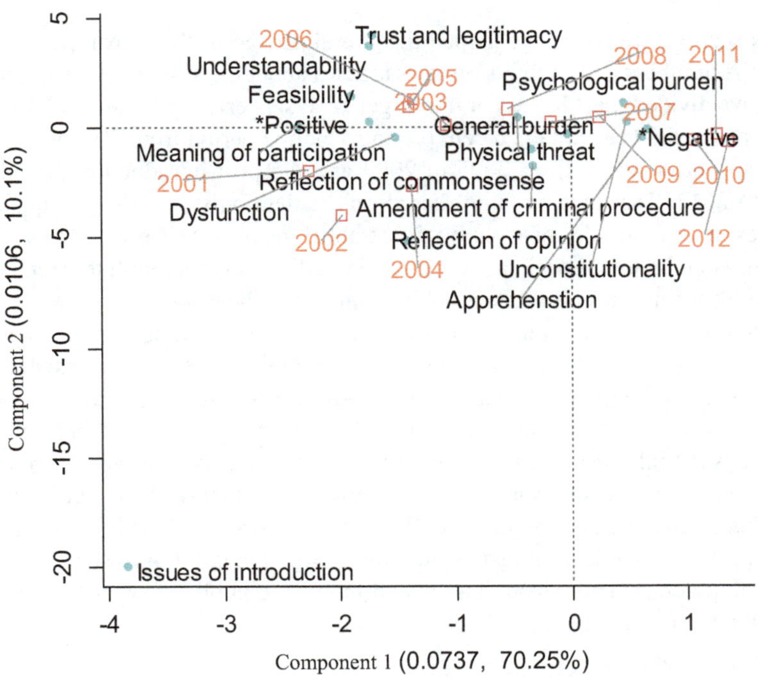

Fig. 5.13 The result of a correspondence analysis of categories, year and positivity

"physical threat." The saiban-in system is entirely new in Japan in 60 years' time since the abolition of the petty jury system. We reasonably believe that the saiban-ins who presented themselves in court under the former jury system, and the persons related such as the lawyers, may have already passed away.[4]

When we look at the right-hand side of the table, we see "unconstitutionality," "psychological burden," "general burden" and "apprehension" are the major negative categories in the latter pre-introduction period. As noted earlier, "unconstitutionality" is a frequently mentioned issue throughout the whole timeline, while the discussion is especially hot after the implementation and the first trial. The same pattern is also found in the category "psychological burden." On the contrary, "amendment (improvement) of criminal procedure" concentrates on the latter period, and it is positioned slightly closer to the positive side. Nonetheless, as illustrated previously, the number of articles under this category is insufficient to support the analysis.

From the above, we come to understand that the general reporting direction about the system tends to be negative at all times. It is both illustrated by the fact that the meaning of participation is repeatedly emphasized right from the beginning, and also the anxiety that saiban-ins has to present themselves in court.

Looking Back to the Overview

In this section, we have first shaped the overall image of the saiban-in system by using the numbers and contents of news articles about the system. By using the KH coder, we divided the 12 years of our target analysis period 2001 to 2012 into three smaller periods. They are the recent pre-introduction period from 2001 to 2004, the latter pre-introduction from 2005 to 2009 and the post-introduction period from 2009 to 2012. The division is not based on the data only, but also the qualitative changes in news articles brought by the establishment of the saiban-in law on 21st May 2004 and the first trial case on 21st May 2009. Together with the content, the number of the articles also reflect public opinions to the system.

When we look at the number of articles, we see low numbers in the year 2001 and 2002, while the number is unprecedentedly high in 2004, which exceeds 100, and also in 2009 and 2010 (around 800 in both years). At this point, we witness a tenfold when we compare the lowest and the highest. As mentioned before, in earlier stages, people just don't pay much attention to the system while through the continuous promotional events, they gradually realize that they can get involved in the decision-making process in the trial through the system. 2004 is a breakthrough as the saiban-in law is established. 2009 is another breakthrough when the system comes to practice. The impact here is enormous; the public is eager to learn more about the vital system,

[4]Considering the time of implementation, we believe that citizens who experienced the saiban-in system in the era of Okinawa under American occupation were still alive.

Later, when the system is no longer new, and people start to lose their interest in that, which causes a sharp decrease in the number of articles.

The Content of the News Articles in the Three Periods

And now, we move one step further for a more detailed analysis. Here we first go back to the relationship between the keywords and the publishing year as analyzed by correspondence analysis and also the Dendrograms in the three periods. Until 2003, the reporting focus is on the background of the system, such as the topics about the Justice System Reform Council, general ideas about the saiban-in system and cause of the introduction of a such a new system. Around the preparatory period when the system is about to be implemented, people pay more attention to the meaning of participation as well.

In the latter pre-introduction period, the public pays much attention to the establishment of the saiban-in act. From the Dendrograms, we see that people are very much interested to know what the system is formed under the newly established saiban-in law. As an indication of the actual progress and newest situations of the system, court activities are also widely reported. Also, people are interested to read how enterprises cooperate with the court by making the leave application procedures more accessible for their employees for supreme trial cases. Last but not least, there are also a vast number of news articles about the first trial case in 2009.

After the implementation in 2010, the focus shifts to talk about the details of individual cases, such as the venue in where the trial is held and the statements from defendants. As illustrated above, the system is no longer new after the first trial and news articles tend to report about the cases but not the system itself.

To sum up, news reports are more like an introduction to the systems at the initial states, as the public find the system unfamiliar. Then, more and more articles touch on the relativeness of the system to daily lives while eventually, the focus is on the case details. Court cases always draw attention from the public, and thus here we can conclude that the whole reporting direction returns to normal.

In order to have a thorough understanding of the contents of the article, we construct networking charts for the three periods from 2001 to 2012. And from the result, we come to know that "saiban-in," "system," "saiban," "judge," "saiban-in system," "participation" and "prosecutor" are the keywords which make up the necessary infrastructure of the charts.

Interesting we also find a change in the word used for "saiban-in," the randomly selected public. In the former pre-introduction period with articles talking about the system background as the introduction of the system, the word "kokumin" (nationals) is used like in phrases like "people participate in the justice system." Later in the latter pre-introduction period, the term 'Shimin" (citizens) is used instead, and phrases become "citizens participate in the justice system." In Japanese, the word "kokumin" (nationals) is coherent to the word "Kuni" (nation/state), and the "people" here refer to the Japanese people (people with nationality of Japan); on the other hand, "Shimin" (citizens) are more associated with the image of an independent individuals regardless of the nationality. The change in the term reflects the shift in the reporting direction. The saiban-in system is first perceived as something ascended from the nation while as time goes by, the sense of confrontation fades out gradually. The public sees equality and sees the system on the same level as theirs, and start to have an expectation on the system to bring actual social changes.

As a notable characteristic of the networking chart, we see the distance between the centers and their neighboring concept groups. In the first chart, we see that the concepts "government," "promotion," "headquarters," "opinions," "incident" and "deliberation" are around the center, and "reform" is also linked as an illustration of the justice system reform. The focus of the attention is on how the government move and act; for "kokumin" (nationals, as demonstrated above), the system is something from the government, and people grasp information for their reaction to the action from the government. In contrast to this, in the latter pre-introduction period we also see "defendant" (most probably referring to the defendants in criminal cases) are connected, though in the distance. Following that we have crimes-related concepts such as "incident," "murder," "judgment," "court," and "evidence" are all linked. The illustration here is that people start to pay attention to the concrete potential cases details under the saiban-in system as side topics. However, in this period, since there is still not an actual trial so the public is showing interested in the functions and practice of the system but not any real cases.

In the same chart as we see "candidate," "withdrawal," "enterprise" and "employee leave." They show that the public start to grasp information as accurate preparation for participating in the system, and thus they want to read more about the system details and its selection procedures.

Lastly, in the chart of the post-introduction period, we have the words "prosecution," "sentence," "penalty" and "murder" in the form of intensive network, and this reveals that public concerns about the trial. We should also note that neighboring we have "killing," "at that time" and "trial" connected, and this group of terms reveals the related concepts and keywords mentioned together with the central ones. In this chart, we see 2 to 3 words come together to form a group that is also linked together, but the bonding is not as strong as the central ones. This can also be found in the previous two charts while it becomes prominent here in this new chart. Especially we see crimes-related words, and these words are connected rather in a disseminated way. It shows that there are multiple focuses on the public concerns. These words are "selection," "procedure," "beginning," "statement," "prosecuting side," "defensive side," "argument," "eventually," and "closing argument," and, they are all related to the flow of trial. Besides murdering and damaging, there are many cases of "stimulant," "violation" and "smuggling" and hence, these words also appear in the chart. Post-trial words like "journalist" and "press conference" also appear. The wide range of words here construct a conclusion here that people concern about the process and everything little small steps about the saiban-in system.

Positive & Negative Articles about the Saiban-in System

During the first half of this section, the change of the focus of the public attention was presented in a neutral way. Yet, another actual picture displayed by the method of coding is how the readers of these articles that is the acceptant of the saiban-in system and the public perceive the new system. Through coding, we aim to reveal the changes in the positivity or negativity of the public opinions and the frequency of their appearance. Here, we witness that there are more positive articles about the systems in the first 2 years, though the number may not be adequate for statistical analysis. Negative articles start nominating from 2003, and importantly the number is right for statistics. The result of the correspondence analysis about the text concepts and their publishing year demonstrate this result clearly, as definite articles are found mostly from the former half, from 2001 to 2006 while negative articles are found mainly from the latter one, from 2007 to 2012.

The center of the negative side is "unconstitutionality," "worries" and "general burdens" while once the Supreme Court confirmed the constitutionality of the system, articles uphold the idea of unconstitutionality are eliminated immediately. The picture posted by this is the resolve of the biggest negative issue. While we should also note that the second biggest negative issue is "worries." A conventional approach for news articles to emphasize on changes and future matters is, as mentioned, stress on the dark side. To see this convention in a positive way, the subject could be understood in both the positive and negative side at the end but down to earth, the nature of exaggerating mere prediction of the bad side is just a common practice Thus, an important issue we have to confront is, negative prediction without any support of evidence is unfair to the issue, saiban-in system, and it leads the public with an intention. As a big negative issue continuously mentioned in the related articles, "worries" is a significant element but some of them remain inconclusively unproved. The overall adverse impression generated by the news articles can be quantitatively measured in a statistical approach by the high ratio of the negative articles, we are thus able to conclude that news articles have an adverse effect on the acceptance of the system and it leads people to think about the wrong side of the system, it modes the public attitude, as claimed in socio-linguistic theories.

On the positive side, "meaning of participation" and "reflection of common sense, and personal feeling" are the main keywords, which are followed by the less frequent ones "reflection of opinions" and "reliability & legitimacy." Such a constant tendency can rightly carry weights to emphasize the participation of the public. The saiban-in system is put forward to gain public trust on the civil law (As stated in Saiban-in act article 1 in the proposal of Justice System Reform Council (2001)). So, articles should carry positive images like trust and legitimacy but they did not, and they fail to clear the air and provide a satisfying answer to the question on the public's mind- "Why the government did the saiban-in act?" Instead, there are so many harmful elements included in the articles that cast the system and also the participation to the system in shadow, the grand vision of making a new system to ensure public participation and the separation of powers is, sadly, not efficiently explained.

It may be argued that newspaper articles are not the one should function that, but books are. However, when we consider the number of copies, the newspaper merely is much more influential as it continuously, steadily sends out messages about the system to the public over a decade. The fact also displays that it entirely takes control of the perception of the people who think about the form and the structure of the nation.

To see the concepts and the linkages of the concepts on both the positive and negative sides we have constructed the above networking charts. The charts do not reveal only the linkages among the concepts but also the writing intention of the authors.

A common characteristic throughout all three charts is the prominence of the three categories "general burden," "unconstitutionality" and "worries." On top of that, we also witness the eminence of "meaning of participation" in the pre-introduction periods. The linkage between these three negative categories is represented as a negative triangle, and the cast of this triangle is associated strongly with the saiban-in system to the public. Since the Supreme Court confirmed the constitutionality of the system, we see a notable change in the public perception.

And, as mentioned, the category "meaning of participation" is also closely linked with the attention center in the two pre-introduction periods. While the system is associated with a negative impression, the public has no ways out but to dig out meaning to participate in this system. Later after the implementation, the strong connection of the negative triangle remains and the "meaning of participation" fades out, and it merely tells the truth that saiban-in system is, from the beginning to the end, something harmful and somewhat undesirable.

The reasons that the public thinks that "the saiban-in system is difficult to understand" and "the saiban-in system does more harms than goods" are naturally revealed. An intriguing conclusion we can draw is, the confirmation from the Supreme Court about the constitutionality of the system comes as merely a piece of information to the public, while the native impression about the system is what the public perceive or experience every day. There isn't any shadow of a doubt that in person experience comes much stronger than something comes from words and news. Moreover, from the viewpoint of the persuasion process model from social psychology (Cacioppo et al. 1986) we can also conclude that when news reporting something does not match with one's own belief, the words come no more than just words but not persuading words.

Limitation of the Analysis

Use of Nikkei News Articles as Analytical Data

As a caution of the analysis above, we should note that our analysis target is the Nikkei Newspaper only. One of the reasons is because articles from Nikkei is the only clean data source we can access, process, and analyze at this time. This remains as a limitation to the analysis indeed.

Nikkei is a national newspaper, and its readers are located throughout the country. In this sense, we can believe that the information presented is not area-biased at all (though there is a page about the "regional economy" in the paper every day). Yet, Nikkei is an economical and financial paper that the majority of its readers is enterprises, employees, CEOs, self-employees and most of them are on the management level ("Nikkei media data," 2018). And, Nikkei is rather pro-governmental in its political stance. For instance, in the social statistics about the supporting index to the government, we see an error of 7% and Nikkei tends to show the higher numbers when compared with other newspapers and when reporting the decline of the supporting index, Nikkei never use sensational headlines like "THE END OF ABE'S POWER." So, we are convinced that when reporting about the Saiban-in system, Nikkei similarly uses a rather confirmative approach. Thus, we should note that Nikkei's articles are more favorable when compared with other major newspapers and thus our analysis, may be more on the positive side as well. Also, newspapers tend to create a shared enemy with the public, and they keep criticizing that enemy as a mean to better the number of sales. In Japan, the hypothetical enemy is usually the government, self-governing bodies (like the one in Tokyo) and specific national associations (Like the city officials in the centralized government). As the saiban-in system is brought by the government to gain public trust on the Civil law, it also becomes the object to be criticized and negatively reported through the system here is brought to include the participation of the public. Mass media, with business concerns and some other intentions, tend to dig out and amplify every little loophole as much as they can. The seeming discussion or arguments, in fact, come with a lousy intention for criticism only. Nonetheless, are they critical to the issue itself? Do they criticize just for the sake of criticism? Are the news articles just the self-confirmatory of the authors to reveal personal feelings and comments with a particular stance but not objectively deepens any understanding and leads the public to think? If the news articles remain on this level of self-confirmatory, no matter how many pieces of articles the public receive and how much information they acquire, understanding to the saiban-in system, the society, and the whole country is still superficial. Down to earth, mass media are also business organization needs to have readers as their customers and to make a profit. In this sense, their harmful and destructive articles are merely necessary evils, and the mass media itself is not the only one to be blamed.

Periodical & Incidental Influences

Our analysis focuses on the year 2001 to 2012 only. One of the reasons for that is the limitation on the time we conduct it, and because of this limitation, we are not able to reveal potential influences and changes after 2012. As a very concrete example, the constitutionality of the saiban-in system is confirmed by the Supreme Court on 16th November 2011, and all problems and arguments about the unconstitutionality come to a conclusion. So, as previously illustrated, the number of unconstitutionality-related articles started to decrease in the year 2012, and the number dropped only to 40% of that in 2010. The decrease is a gradual one, so we expect it goes on even after 2012. While no doubt that the confirmation of the constitutionality comes as a fact that no matter what intentions newspapers have and what approach mass media use, articles about the topic will continue to drop.

Also, as reported by the Asahi Newspaper, a saiban-in is intimidated by a member of a gang as a violation act in mid-May 2016 ("Saiban-in koekake, baiku de surechigai zama [Saiban-in being called: When passed by a motorbike]," 2016). Later the intimidator is convicted in the first court trial in January 2017.

As a result, the news articles about the physical threat of saiban-in should go up tremendously in that period, as safety is always an important issue that draws attention, and the concrete case attracts merely more and more discussion about the problem. As a follow-up action, the Supreme Court has sent a checklist memo to the regional courts as a precaution to prevent it from happening again. Since then, exclusive coaches are used to sending the saiban-ins to the courts.

When we try to search news articles in the Nikkei news database "Nikkei Telecom" by the keywords "saiban-in" and "iken" (unconstitutional), there are much fewer criteria than that set in our KH coder, and thus the number of articles hit is low. Hence, if a comparative analysis with another analytical period of time is needed, the same condition has to be applied that the KH coder analysis is needed as well.

As told by its name, Nikkei focuses on economic and financial facts and issues that the number of additional criticisms or claims of protections is relatively low when compared with other newspapers. If we had chosen another newspaper with another reporting focus for our analysis, more articles might be found on the topics that the public are obliged to know. For instance, topics like the improvement of the prosecution procedures, personal experience sharing from the saiban-ins might be presented in greater detail and higher frequency. All in all, all ideas and findings from our analysis should be taken together with these limitations and concerns.

Appendix: Coding Rules

Below are the actual coding rules the author inputed to the KH coder for our analysis. Refer to the KH coder manual and Higuchi's paper for the presentation of the rules and their respective meanings (Higuchi 2004).

```
*参加の意義
seq(役割-果たす)
| seq(重要-役割)
| seq(参加-意義)[3]
| 主役
| seq(直接-参加)
| seq(国民-参加)
| seq(市民-参加)
```

| seq(意義-深い)
| seq(国民-(意思 | 意志)-問う)
| seq(発言-できる)

*意見の反映
seq(意見-反映)

*常識・感覚の反映
seq((常識 | 感覚 | 社会常識 | 市民感覚)-反映-(する | される))[3]
| seq(常識-反映)
| seq(感覚-反映)
| seq(社会常識-反映)
| seq(市民感覚-反映)

*信頼・正統
seq(裁判-信頼)
| seq(信頼-高める)
| seq(信頼-高まる)
| seq(信頼-向上)
| seq(理解-増進)
| 正当性
| 正統性

*わかりやすさ
seq(わかる-やすい)
| わかりやすい

*実施可能
seq(実施-できる)

*刑事手続の改善
seq(司法-良い-する)
| seq(審理-短い-する)

*一般的負担
(

    負担
    | 義務
    | 守秘義務
    | seq(仕事-休む)
    | 長期
    | 長引く
    | 長びく
    | 長期化
    | seq(審理-日数-(増加 | 増える))
    | seq(責任-重い)

)
&! (心理 | 心理的 | 感情 | 感情的 | seq(負担-軽減) | seq(負担-ない) | 減らす)

```
*心理的負担
(
    seq((心理 | 心理的 | 感情 | 感情的)-負担)
    | seq(人-裁く)
    | seq(精神-圧力)
    | 重圧
    | seq((遺体 | 死体)-写真)
)
&! 軽減

*導入までの課題
seq(運用-詰める)
| seq(大論議-なる)
| seq(調整-難航)
| seq(休暇-取得-保障)
| seq(乗り越える-課題)
| seq(解決-課題)

*違憲性
seq(憲法-違反-(する | あたる | なる | だ | である))[3]
| seq(違憲-(あたる | なる | だ | である))[3]

*機能不全
seq(裁判官-(主導 | 誘導 | リード | 支配))
| 形式的
| お飾り
| 飾り物
| 飾りもの
| seq(発言-できる-ない)
| seq(感情-流れる)
| seq(感情-先走る)
| seq(準備-ない)[3]
| seq(裁判員-知る-ない)
| seq(法廷-パフォーマンス)
| seq((裁判員制度 | 制度)-('知らない' | '知られていない'))
| seq(素人-裁く)
| seq(量刑-崩れる)
| 行き詰まる
| seq(誤判-多い)
| seq(誤判-増える)
| 頓挫
| seq(辞退-(出る | 続出))
| seq(欠席-増加)
| seq(出席-低下)
| '参加したくない'
```

|'なりたくない'
| seq(評議 | 不十分)

*身の危険
seq(身-危険)
| お礼参り
| 報復
| 声掛け
| 声かけ
| 仕返し

*懸念
不安
| 懸念
| seq(慎重-(審議 | 判断 | 議論 | 論議))
| seq(弊害-もたらす)
| seq(問題-指摘)

*ポジティブ
<*参加の意義>
| <*意見の反映>
| <*実施可能>
| <*刑事手続の改善>
| <*常識・感覚の反映>
| <*信頼・正統>
| <*わかりやすさ>

*ネガティブ
<*導入までの課題>
| <*一般的負担>
| <*心理的負担>
| <*違憲性>
| <*機能不全>
| <*身の危険>
| <*懸念>

References

Benzécri, J.-P. (1969). Statistical analysis as a tool to make patterns emerge from data. In S. Watanabe (Ed.), *Methodologies Of pattern recognition* (pp. 35–74). New York: Academic Press. https://doi.org/10.1016/B978-1-4832-3093-1.50009-2.

Benzécri, J.-P. (1982). *Histoire et préhistoire de l'analyse des données*. Malakoff, France: Dunod.

Cacioppo, J. T., Petty, R. E., Kao, C. F., & Rodriguez, R. (1986). Central and peripheral routes to persuasion: An individual difference perspective. *Journal of Personality and Social Psychology, 51*(5), 1032–1043. https://doi.org/10.1037//0022-3514.51.5.1032.

Happer, C., & Philo, G. (2013). The role of the media in the construction of public belief and social change. *Journal of Social and Political Psychology, 1*(1), 321–336. https://doi.org/10.5964/jspp.v1i1.96.

Hayashi, C. (1986). Sûryôka riron no dekiru made [The process of making the quantification theories]. *Operations Research, 31*(12), 728–734 [in Japanese]. Retrieved from https://ci.nii.ac.jp/naid/110001187298

Higuchi, K. (2004). *Shakai chôsa no tame no keiryô tekisuto bunseki: Naiyô bunseki no keishô to hatten wo mezashite [The quantitative text analysis for social survey: Aiming for succession and development of the content analysis]*. Kyoto: Nakanishiya Shuppan [in Japanese].

Hill, M. O. (1974). Correspondence analysis: A neglected multivariate method. *Applied Statistics, 23*(3), 340. https://doi.org/10.2307/2347127.

Justice System Reform Council. (2001). *Recommendations of the justice system reform council: For a justice system to support Japan in the 21st century*. Tokyo, Japan: Justice system reform council. Retrieved from https://japan.kantei.go.jp/judiciary/2001/0612report.html

Livingstone, S., & Lunt, P. (1994). The mass media, democracy and the public sphere. In *Talk on television: Audience participation and public debate* (pp. 9–35). London: Routledge Retrieved from http://eprints.lse.ac.uk/48964/1/Amended_Livingstone_Mass_media_democaracy.pdf.

McCombs, M. E., & Shaw, D. L. (1972). The agenda-setting function of mass media. *Public Opinion Quarterly, 36*(2), 176–187 Retrieved from http://www.jstor.org/stable/2747787.

Nikkei media data. (2018). Retrieved 6 Mar 2018, from https://adweb.nikkei.co.jp/paper/data/pdf/nikkeimediadata.pdf [in Japanese].

Ohsumi, N. (2000). From data analysis to data science. In A. L. Henk, J.-P. Kiers, P. J. F. Rasson, & M. S. Groenen (Eds.), *Data analysis, classification, and related methods* (pp. 329–334). Berlin: Springer Retrieved from https://books.google.co.jp/books?id=ilDxCAAAQBAJ&pg=PA331&lpg=PA331&dq=Benzécri+1962&source=bl&ots=Fwso5qsX5N&sig=1uQNUGDFVi8e-bwqU3gW2r1BFgw&hl=en&sa=X&ved=0ahUKEwiCwaS-mtfZAhVGErwKHfHnDhcQ6AEIMDAB#v=onepage&q=Benzécri 1962&f=false.

Richardson, J. E. (2007). *Analysing newspapers*. London: Macmillan Education. https://doi.org/10.1007/978-0-230-20968-8.

Saiban-in koekake, baiku de surechigai zama [Saiban-in being called When passed by a motorbike]: (2016, June 29). Asahi Shimbun *(Morning Edition)*, p. 32.

Sampei, Y., & Aoyagi-Usui, M. (2009). Mass-media coverage, its influence on public awareness of climate-change issues, and implications for Japan's national campaign to reduce greenhouse gas emissions. *Global Environmental Change, 19*(2), 203–212. https://doi.org/10.1016/j.gloenvcha.2008.10.005.

Vanoverbeke, D. (2015). *Juries in the Japanese Legal System: The continuing struggle for citizen participation and democracy*. Abingdon/New York: Routledge.

Chapter 6
General Discussion Over How the Japanese Society Thinks About the Lay Participation System

In this final part, the author would like to review what we found in the research presented in this book. Then the author discusses the evaluation how Japanese people and society think about the lay participation system. This is one of the purposes of this book. Also, another purpose of this book was to introduce ideas about the relationship between general trust and trust in the justice system. And the third purpose of this book was to examine whether the introduction of the saiban-in system has had an impact on trust in the justice system. Before starting reviewing and discussion, we briefly go over again the purpose of the introduction of the system and the state of the saiban-in system. If you are familiar with these issues, please skip to the next section.

The Purpose of Introduction and the State of the Saiban-in System

In the first section of this chapter, we briefly remind the official purposes of introduction of the system. Unless otherwise noted, the opinions on the saiban-in system are taken from "official" materials, such as Opinion Paper of JSRC (Justice System Reform Council, 2001), the minutes of the JSRC, or statutes of the saiban-in act.

Purpose of the Introduction of the Saiban-in System

As we saw in the first chapter, the purpose of introduction of the system is to establish the "popular base of the justice system" (Justice System Reform Council 2001, Chap. 4). According to the opinion paper of JSRC, in the twenty-first century, people

M. Fujita, *Japanese Society and Lay Participation in Criminal Justice*,
https://doi.org/10.1007/978-981-10-0338-7_6

in Japan need to "break out of the excessive dependency on the state," and "develop public consciousness within themselves, and become more actively involved in public affairs." To attain these purposes, the JSRC argued that Japanese society needs civic participation in the justice system. The civic participation systems will be the saiban-in system, strengthening the power of the Committee for Inquest of Prosecution, and involvement in professional judges' selection processes in inferior courts. To substantialize the civic participation, lay participants need to participate in the criminal procedure substantially, and they need to speak out in the deliberations. If we would like to accomplish those requirements to citizen participants, the circumstances should be altered to lay-friendly. The legalese in the courts needed to be explained, or replaced, and the sense of ordinary people needed to be taken account into deliberations. Note that the last two features related to the saiban-in system were not the purpose of introduction of the system, but the methods of substantialize participation of the civic participants. This seems to be widely misunderstood in Japanese society, and it was supposed to be due to reports on mass media.

The State of the Saiban-in System

According to statistics published by the Supreme Court (The Secretariat-general of the Supreme Court of Japan, 2017), 6363 were selected as saiban-in, and 2140 were selected as reserve saiban-in. The cumulative number of saiban-in is 56,747, and the total number of reserve saiban-in is 19,308 as of the end of April 2017. Total summoned citizens were 384,898. Out of them, 282,380 citizens were present at the selection procedure as of April 2017. The total attendance rate is 73.4% while the rate in 2016 was 64.8%. Attendance rate keeps decreasing from at the time of the start of the saiban-in system.

Concerning the numbers of cases which they have dealt with, the published statistics represent the amount of the criminal cases according to the numbers of the accused. If one criminal case has two or more accused persons, the numbers of the accused exceed the numbers of the cases. The number of new incoming accused persons in criminal cases which brought to the district courts as ordinary trials (通常第一審) was 75,563 in 2016. Out of those cases, 1302 accused persons were tried by the saiban-in system. About 1.7% of the accused were tried by the saiban-in system. The number of the cumulative total of the accused who have been tried by the saiban-in system is 10,864 until the end of April 2017.

Social Attitudes Towards the Saiban-in System

The general public's interest in the saiban-in system has been surveyed continually by the Supreme Court. According to the survey conducted by the Supreme Court (The Supreme Court of Japan 2017), the answers for the question "after the saiban-in system initiated, have you ever experienced any change in your interest or concern in the justice system?" have changed. The answers obtained just after the system started 1 year, the 50.4% of responses were "my interested has raised compared before," and the 48.0% of them were "I experienced no change." The Court has conducted the surveys annually, the ratio of the answer of "my interested has raised compared before" has gradually decreased while the ratio of the answer "I experienced no change" has increased. The newest available results, which has been conducted in January 2016, the 28.8% of responses were "my interest has raised compared before," and the 68.8% of them were "I experienced no change." The percentage of the answer "my interest has reduced compared before" has been from 1.1% to 2.5%, it has kept around 2% throughout the survey periods.

These results suggest that the introduction of trial by saiban-in revoked general public's interest in the justice system, especially right after in the year started. After 2 years passed, the percentage of the answer was 38.5, and the percentage has kept decreased gradually in every year, we can think that the effect of raising the interest in the justice system remained for one or two years. After that period, the saiban-in system has become ordinary to exist. In this sense, citizens thought that their interest has not raised after it became natural for them that the saiban-in system is a part of criminal justice. The saiban-in system arose public interest in the justice system, and the arisen interest has not decreased after once elevated by the initiation of the system. Starting saiban-in system would have had a particular impact on citizens' interest in the justice system.

The Courts asked the citizens overall impressions on the saiban-in system. The results were on the 22nd page of the report in 2016. The detailed results were reported in Chap. 2 in this book. Let us review some significant results here. The Court presented nine questions on the impressions on the circumstances after the introduction of the saiban-in system, and they requested respondents to answer those questions in five-point scales. The respondents picked one of the answering options from "1" which was least extent of agreeing to the answer "5" which was the extreme extent of agreeing. From the results presented, the average for the question "the sense of nationals are reflected the results of trials more than before" was 3.53, the figure for the question "I feel more familiar with the courts and the justice than before" was 3.47, and the figure for the question "I have become thinking (the matter of justice) as the problems of my own" was 3.40. The Court's paper does not report standard deviations or standard errors for the answers, so we cannot calculate and test whether those answers are different from the midpoint "3". But the number of the respondents were 2000. According to the number of the respondents and the formula for calculating standard errors, those answers may be different from "3". For example, if the average number of responses was 3.53, if this answer was not significantly different from the answer "3" in 95% confidence level, the standard deviation must at least be 12.09. But it would be hard to possible that the standard deviation is 12.09 for the answers in five-point scales. We can conclude that the answer 3.53 must be significantly different from the answer "3". Adding to that, the responses by the citizens evaluated that the trials have got more impartial after the introduction of the saiban-in system. These results suggest that the saiban-in system affect general citizens' impressions of the justice system positively.

And concerning the citizens who completed duty as saiban-in, their answers showed positive attitudes towards the experience as saiban-in, according to the survey conducted by the district courts, 96.7% of ex-saiban-in evaluated the experience as saiban-in was right for them.

Those results cited here above were all reported by the Courts. So, we should keep in our minds that we might need to discount to some extent to interpret those results. But similar results have been reported in the jury study which was conducted in the U.S. (Bornstein et al. 2005); we don't need to think all the results presented here have been distorted by the Court.

The issues whether those attitudes towards civic participation may have relationships with personalities, if so, how are the relationships between a particular type of personalities and social attitudes? On the results of relationships between authoritarian personality and trials presented in Chap. 2 in this book, the personality tendencies that imposes norms to others, be positive about freedom, and stable tendency bear positive attitudes towards civic participation to the trials. In other words, the people who have open and flexible personalities to social norms have positive attitudes in civic participation to the justice system.

It may be hard to assume that the number of people with such personalities has increased just after the introduction of the system. Instead, we can interpret these results as the initiation of the trials by the saiban-in system may have had a positive impact on the citizens' social attitudes towards the justice system and the trials in which citizens participate.

Deliberations in the Saiban-in System

In deliberations, it is essential to secure lay participants' meaningful and active participation. JSRC requested the public generally "to participate autonomously and meaningfully in deciding trials." (Justice System Reform Council 2001, Chap. 4, Part 1) At the first time of the decision of the introduction of the system, it was said that "the Japanese have such reserved attitudes towards in public especially in front of experts that lay participants in the saiban-in system will be just 'ornaments' in criminal trial courts."(e.g. Kobayashi, 2007; "Okazari ni shitewa naranu: saiban-in (shasetsu) [Don't make them figureheads: Saiban-ins (editorial article)]," 2003) Some critics said that the saiban-in system was introducing because the courts would like to evade criticism to their judges' decisions by making general public participate in the trials (e.g. Ishimatsu et al. 2007, p. 5; Uozumi and Saito 2003, p. 69). If the saiban-in system shows the signs of empty civic participation in the trials, at least one of the meanings of the introduction of the system will be eroded.

We need to know how the things are going in the deliberations to discuss the issue above. According to the results of the questionnaire surveys report by the Supreme Court (The Supreme Court of Japan, 2017), the 78.4% of ex-saiban-ins answered that they felt comfortable to talk during the sessions. The 19.4% of ex-saiban-ins answered "ordinary." And the 76.0% of them answered they discussed enough in their deliberations (Chap. 2). Frankly speaking, the courts need to publish information which tells us the saiban-in system goes well because they are in the position which they have to take responsibility to manage the system. So, we have to consider the possibility of the report includes information which is inclined to show that the system is successful. But it seems to reason that we think that significant part of the ex-saiban-in is evaluated their experience positively as saiban-in and their deliberations.

According to the data presented in Chap. 3 this book, deliberations had occurred among the participants who were the students from the faculty of law in their third and fourth years and the students from other faculties in their first or second years in their university (the first sect. in Chap. 3). In that study, the author found that the law students tended to utter to advance the deliberations. The same results were also found in the studies in deliberations on status differences.

Based on the above data, it is presumed that although the external validity problem exists, the statement that "Japanese cannot speak when talking with people who are more knowledgeable than himself from the beginning" will be different from the fact. The circumstances can be guessed similarly by looking at the results of the deliberations in simulated trials conducted between real judges and citizens. Let us look back the social network analyses of the mock trials.

In the mock jury data with real judges and civic participants, we saw social networks among participants in the deliberations. In that study, we saw different types of deliberation communications. Usually, the presiding judges will take a central role to preside the deliberations. They are in the center of the network, and they communicate with all other participants. If the centrality is too high, it would be assumed that each civic participant (and other judges) just talk with the presiding judges in the deliberations. In a pattern of networks where citizens discuss each other, the conclusion appears to emerge. On the other hand, the discussion was not very active in the pattern that the presiding judge and other members are exchanging on a one-on-one basis. Although it cannot say decisively based only on two cases, discussions will be more active when the participants other than the presiding judge talk each other and smoothly. And in that case, citizens will get the high participation feeling.

Adding to it, we saw the two significant factors in deliberations. One was the deliberation style, and another was the informational difference. Professional judges in the saiban-in system are usually present at the pretrial conference with prosecutors and defense councils. They have chances to know about the case during the conference, and they have much more information on the case when the trials start. The persons who have more information, especially standard pieces of information tend to speak more often in deliberations. And professional judges who participate in the pretrial conference know the critical issues in the trial. In the trials by the saiban-in system, professional judges who know the construct of the issues lead the processes of the deliberations; even the conclusions may keep open when the professional judges. We saw this phenomenon through the results of the studies presented in Chap. 3. It is inevitable that the professional judges speak more than the civic participants, as they know about the law, the case, and the critical issues of the case. To share that knowledge and lead the deliberations properly are the expected roles of professional judges in the deliberations. Based on the findings, to be realistic, it is not necessary for all the civic participants to speak as many times as professional judges. More than that, we would expect professional judges to draw the opinions of the civic participants and accept their wisdom to the deliberations. This may bring the well-functioning the saiban-in system, and civic participants think that they can participate in the deliberations meaningfully and positive about their experience as saiban-in. This could promote "popular base" of the justice system and sense of self-efficacy of lay participants.

Impact on Trust in the Justice System

The results of social surveys on general public's trust in the justice system were presented in Chap. 4. In these surveys, the responses obtained before initiating the saiban-in system and the responses obtained after initiating the system were compared. In Japanese General Social Surveys, the project asked public general's opinions on the saiban-in system. The most responses to the trust in the justice system of the general public in JGSS were "somewhat." The extent of the general public's trust in the justice system was somewhat stable at the time before having started the saiban-in system started. And just after started trials by saiban-in, in other words, just after the people's interest in the justice system rose, the percent point of the people's responses to this question increased three. This change was statistically significant.

Then, how about the people's attitudes towards the saiban-in system? We reviewed Matsumura et al. (2012) and their studies before and after implementation of the saiban-in system. Matsumura and his colleagues showed people's attitudes towards saiban-in system after having started trials by saiban-in, were positive and the differences were statistically significant.

From those results, we can conclude that the people's trust in the justice system itself and trust in trials by saiban-in raised after trials by saiban-in started. But note that those results are obtained from the comparison of responses between just two times of the points. There were many significant events in Japanese society other than initiation of trials by saiban-in between those two-time points; we seem to reserve to conclude that those increases in trust in the justice system and trials by saiban-in can be attributed to the saiban-in system. At least it is certain that people's attitudes towards the justice system and trials by the saiban-in system after initiation of the trials saiban-in got better.

According to the results shown in the first half of Chap. 4, the trust in the justice system was affected by respondents' perceptions of trial fairness and trial quality. On the results shown above and the responses in Chap. 4, we can think that there were changes in the attitudes of the general public towards the justice system, and their trust in the justice system has moderately raised after implementation of trials by saiban-in. Adding to it, the citizens' perceptions of the impartiality of criminal trials, the starting trials by saiban-in reinforced the trust in the justice system.

The findings shown in the second half of Chap. 4 reported that the trust in the justice system affected general trust. When we consider this finding with the results shown in 04–01, the introduction trials saiban-in system raised the trust in the trials by saiban-in and citizens' positive evaluations in the system; we could conclude that those changes would have positive effects on Japanese people's general trust in the long run. This is, and the fact that the results from the Supreme Courts' general survey showed that the responses to the question "(I became to think the matters of the justice as) problem my own" positively shifted after introduction, we could think that the purpose of introduction of the system which was stated by the JSRC has been fulfilling, even some parts of them.

But we can't tell how large the magnitude of the effects of the saiban-in system on the evaluations on those changes, we cannot say that Japanese society's integrity and mutual trust are going to be much developed when we keep bearing the saiban-in system in operation in the society.

Foci of Media Coverage

In the above parts, we have seen the impact of the saiban-in system on the general public's trust and interest in the justice system. Then how about the mass media coverage of the saiban-in system? According to the newspaper article analyses in Chap. 5 in this book, they discussed the saiban-in system in the relationship with nationals' participation to the justice system at the time of its birth. After that, they reported the specific procedures of the saiban-in system, the practical problems of civic participation, then the focus of issues moved on to the criminal cases themselves which were tried by the saiban-in system. Around 2012, the end of the period in which our data are available, most of their report covered the content the criminal cases which were dealt with the saiban-in system, and the frequency of referring the system itself decreased. This may have been one of the reflections of movement of social interest in the system. This change was consistent with the rise of people's interest in the justice system, which was shown in the survey conducted by the Supreme Court. The survey started at the same time of the initiation of the trials by saiban-in. People may have thought the matter of criminal justice as the problem of their own because the possibilities of being involved got much realistic at that time.

The analyses on coding results of the contents of the newspaper articles showed that they reported the meanings of public participation to the justice system, for the positive facet of their content. It was in 2009, at the time of having started the trials by saiban-in started that they most frequently refer the meaning of the participation. This may have had an inevitable impact on the general public's positive responses to the questions on interest in the justice system. Their responses were mostly positive just after the media most frequently published newspaper articles on the meanings of civic participation to the justice system.

And contrary contents of media reports argued the unconstitutionality of saiban-in system and general anxiety over implementing the saiban-in system. The Japanese petty jury system has been suspended since the wartime of WWII. At that time, Japanese constitution was Imperial Constitution, which was so-called Meiji Constitution. At the time the petty jury system was in operation, the entirely different constitution was in force. Japanese petty jury system has kept being suspended after the WWII ended, and no single case was tried by the petty jury system under the current constitution. Because no jury system was operated under the current constitution, the saiban-in system was haunted by the problem of unconstitutionality since the birth of the system. The Supreme Court apparently judged saiban-in system is constitutional in its judgment made on November 16, 2011, this issue is already not so hot as to attract the interest of reporters and readers as social or practical issue apart from pure academic interest.

The anxiety in general, ambiguous worry about being involved in the saiban-in system. This kind of articles or referring are prevalent in newspaper articles. They often show their worry about something if the thing does not have specific future. Among those negative issues, they like to refer the burden of civic participants. Even the participation is a duty for citizens, in reality, people usually have their own business, and they are engaged in the business (even the business is not paid one). In that circumstances, time- and economic burden for the participants would naturally matter. Saiban-in receives up to ¥10,000[1] per day for their compensation. Given that average minimum wage per one hour is ¥823[2] in 2016, saiban-in' compensation is much better to pay than the wage, and the compensation is almost the same as about 7.5 hour-work of the average wage for legal office work (¥1328).[3] The "pay" of saiban-in is not so sick in the circumstances that average annual pay for company employees is ¥4,200,000 in 2015.[4] But it is hard to take some days off for people who are in unstable employment, the self-employed, or people who have family members who need continuous care. District courts have made an effort to treat reasonably those who are in the circumstances like that; they would need to keep that effort in accordance with changes in the circumstances of Japanese society. Also, the courts and Japanese Government need to inform the nationals of the meaning of civic participation to the justice system in order to compensate the burden of the civic participants, which cannot be compensated for a certain amount of money.

[1] http://www.saibanin.courts.go.jp/qa/c10_7.html

[2] http://www.mhlw.go.jp/stf/seisakunitsuite/bunya/koyou_roudou/roudoukijun/minimumichiran/

[3] http://salarymap.jp/occ_a

[4] https://www.nta.go.jp/kohyo/tokei/kokuzeicho/minkan/gaiyou/2015.htm#a-01

Democratic Values and "Popular Base" of the Justice System

On the quantitative analyses on the contents of the newspaper articles, they rarely referred the legitimacy of the justice or the relationships between the legitimacy and civic participation to the trials. They didn't discuss the purpose of the introduction of the system, that is, to "break out of the excessive dependency on the state that accompanies the traditional consciousness of being governed objects" within the article data analyzed. It would have been hard to find a chance to see discussions of the purposes of introduction of the saiban-in system for citizens, because they make uses of newspaper to obtain information of justice system, according to the Supreme Courts' general surveys. Under the circumstances, it could assume that the meaning of introduction the saiban-in system and civic participation to the justice system have rarely been understood or prevailed among the citizens.

Apart from quantitative analyses of whole contents of the newspaper articles, other than the Nihon Keizai Shimbun, the author could find issues and themes concerning the saiban-in system which has not emerged with quantitative analyses above. The issues may include the stories of ex-saiban-ins who were worried about the experience of judging people, psychological burden of being saiban-in, security of saiban-in to whom gangster spoke outside of the law court during trial period, some stories ex-saiban-ins who became to think about their communities through hearing at the trials, ex-saiban-ins who started community service. Those cases may show that the situation has moved ahead toward realizing the purpose of introduction of the saiban-in system.

The findings above suggest that the effect of media reports on the saiban-in system on the trust in the justice system evoked interest in the justice system to a great extent, and the interest has become established.

There seldom appeared the topics concerning legal education (法教育). It has seemed to assume an essential role in conveying the information on civic participation to the justice system and meaning of the participation. Legal education is an activity to educate students and inform them of legal systems, trail systems, and first legal thinking in the course in high school or elementary school. It is often reported by the mass media that schools carry out mock trials with students. But not limited to do mock trials, teachers including legal professionals educate students other aspects of the legal field. It might come from legal education in some extent that the results of the survey conducted by the Supreme Court showed that respondents in 20's and 30's were more positive about trial participation compared to 50's or older respondents. The people who were in the age of eighteen in 2004, the year started legal reform, are 31 years old in 2017. All respondents under 20's graduated from high schools in the era of "after saiban-in."

Getting out of "excessive dependency to the state" (Justice System Reform Council, 2001) and nurture autonomous, it would be important to develop democratic values among the citizens. Concerning this issue, the Supreme Court's general survey has had a question in its questionnaire. The question states that "what do you think about the notion that we should not let public matters like criminal trials or justice be left to the nation or professionals?" The responses were on a five-point scale. The anchoring stimuli and answering options are "1: disagree", "2: moderately disagree", "3: neither agree or disagree", "4: moderately agree", and "5: "agree." The average of responses from 2009 to 2015 were 3.43, 3.43, 3.39, 3.43, 3.35, 3.39, 3.49. Those responses are slightly more positive than the middle point "3: neither agree or disagree". The standard errors for those answers are not included in the report published by the Supreme Court. However, when we take the sampling size into account, the extent of positive from the middle point would be significant. From the time of the started the trials by saiban-in in recent years, people's attitudes on the extent public matters should not be left to the nation or legal professionals can be thought as positive. It would be interesting if we could know how ex-saiban-ins think about this issue after completed their duty.

Then, what about whether the system promotes democratic values in Japan? There were no questions which directly ask respondents about democratic values in the surveys conducted by the Supreme Court, JGSS, or Matsumura et al. (2012). The results of the quantitative analyses of newspaper articles in this book did not clearly show the evidence that they discussed democratic values which could be realized by introducing lay participation system. Unfortunately, we cannot argue something whether implementation of the saiban-in system has promoted democratic values in Japanese society, based on data shown in this book. This issue would be reserved for future research. The fact that significant surveys which were cited in this book have not dealt with the relationships between implementation of saiban-in system and promotion of democratic values might show that this issue has not been given high priority at least as issues of social surveys. Of course, there has been literature on realizing democratic values by implementing jury system in Japan by Japanese researchers (Mitani, 2013; Yanase, 2016). Those researchers have published their papers on this issue. The opinion paper of JSRC did not explicitly refer democratic values in initiating saiban-in system (Justice System Reform Council, 2001). JSRC requested the presence of one of the famous researchers in Japanese jury system, and they heard the history of the introduction of Japanese petty jury system during Taisho and Showa eras, and they were aware of the ordinary meaning of introduction of the saiban-in system. It would be conceivable that JSRC did not refer democratic values in introducing the saiban-in system[5] would be that JSRC started their arguments from how Japanese society should be in the twenty-first century ("The Shape of Japanese Society in the twenty-first Century"). The argument was followed by their request for the nationals how the nationals should be, and JSRC's focus was on "The Shape of the Justice System," and how the justice system should be in the century. This narrows down the issues in the report and made their arguments clear and robust over the reform of justice system. On the other side of this policy of writing the paper, many issues seemed to be excluded. For example, the effect of promoting democratic values in implementing the saiban-in system. The author assumes that JSRC was aware of this issue, but their strategy

[5] In the opinion paper of the JSRC, democracy (民主主義) was referred once in the section of support for development of legal system.

of writing paper excluded the issue as a result. This might be a reason that the issues concerning democratic values have not emerged as one of the often-discussed significant issues. Of course, researchers in this field understand the importance of the issue, and Japanese translation of Gastil et al. (2010) was published in 2016, the circumstances allow to develop the discussion of the meaning or effect of implementing the saiban-in system on promoting democratic values in Japan.

Overall Evaluation of the Saiban-in System

On the findings and discussions above, we think over again how we evaluate the saiban-in system.

From the numbers of the cases (precisely speaking, the numbers of the accused) which tried by the saiban-in system, the system seems to have had a small impact on the overall criminal trials in Japan. It tried about 1.7% of the criminal accused in which indicted as the usual first instance criminal case at district courts in 1 year. But from the viewpoints of the numbers of potential saiban-in, involved citizens in the selection process, selected as saiban-ins and selected as reserve saiban-ins, the impact would not be seen as small as the system really has tried in the years during the system has been in use.

In the newspaper articles, this system has been referred as many times either in pro or con or neutral ways. This may have evoked people's interest in the justice system, as well as the saiban-in system itself. The problem seems how the courts keep asking proper participation in the system, as the attendance rate has to keep decrease from the time of the start of the system. Maybe part of the reason would be the enthusiasm at the start of the system has cooled as the system gets not new in the society.

According to the general survey conducted by the Supreme Court cited above, the general public thought that after implementation of the saiban-in system, the trials have got familiar and reflected their thoughts on the trials. The Court itself has carried out the survey, so we need to caution that those results might be exaggerated in a positive way. But on that data, we can think that Japanese people are positive about implementing the saiban-in system, on the issues concerning ameliorating criminal trials and their thinking the criminal trials as the issues of themselves.

One of the important things which we need to keep in mind would be that the significant part of the evaluation issues on the saiban-in system have been discussed from the viewpoint of participating citizens. That is natural in a certain sense because the policymakers and the mass media have discussed from the viewpoints of the designer of social systems, professional judges, and the general public who may be involved as saiban-ins. In the literature which discussed the saiban-in system, the small numbers of papers have discussed from the viewpoint of the accused. We may need not to forget that we might "utilize" the chances in which the accused tried at the courts as the chances to establish a popular base of the justice system and to develop ourselves to more matured citizens. If Japanese society thinks this is not the way they should take in order to make social solidarity and matured citizens, they need to stop the system and seek another way to nurture society and citizens.

Remaining Issues

In this book, the author tried to make it clear that some facets of the saiban-in system. Of course, the findings presented in this book do not represent all features of the system. Ideally, we would like to know whether the system has promoted popular base of the justice system, make the people more mature than before. Because "popular base of the justice system" is somewhat ambiguous and hard to measure because the concept allows many possible ways to define operationally. And concerning the issue, we need to consider whether Japanese people have been more independent, autonomous, and responsible in social matters and getting out from their "excessive dependency to the state" or "the consciousness of being governed objects" (Justice System Reform Council 2001). It may be good to conduct social surveys on such attitudes held by Japanese people to assess the second issue. The measure of those attitudes is ideal if the attitudes are measured in their behaviors. In that sense, research like Gastil (2010) needs to be also done in Japan, in which Gastil and the colleagues conducted the survey whether the people once completed their jury duty will vote more in elections. The thing we should keep in our minds is that it is hard to prove that the changes undoubtedly come from the saiban-in system, even we could find the change in people' attitudes in accordance with the JSRC's opinion papers because there could be so many variables which could affect people's attitudes.

Intuitively and desirably, direct participation in the justice system will promote mutual understanding, consent and the sense of supporting the society, and keep building trust among people in society with diversity. Even racial diversity looks to be fewer in Japan compared to other societies in the world, but it would not be negligible. And economic, political, digital, generation, cultural and other divides in Japanese society demand a new way of social integration, while classical methods of social integration were undermined after industrialization and urbanization in the twenty century. In the twenty-first century, Japan gets to be an aging society and shrinking society in which hamlets in rural areas have disappeared. Even in that situation, the Japanese society keeps integrated, and if the saiban-in system promotes it, we can find some hope for the future in the society and the system itself.

Satsuki Eda, Reprise

"I believe that the fact that all parties have agreed in this manner is extraordinarily important in our legislative process…though in the process various issues pop up, and each time there is further discussion, with everyone coming to an agreement, that is very precious." (comment continued from Satsuki Eda's quote in the introduction).

References

Bornstein, B. H., Miller, M., Nemeth, R. J., Page, G. L., Musil, S., Lincoln Bornstein, N., & Miller, M. K. (2005). Juror reactions to Jury duty: Perceptions of the system and potential stressors, *Behavioral Sciences & The Law, 23*, 321–346. Retrieved from http://digitalcommons.unl.edu/psychfacpub.

Gastil, J., Deess, E. P., Weiser, P. J., & Simmons, C. (2010). *The jury and democracy : How jury deliberation promotes civic engagement and political participation*. Oxford/New York: Oxford University Press.

Ishimatsu, T., Tsuchiya, K., & Isa, C. (2007). *Enzai wo umu saiban-in seido: Baishin saiban no hukkatsu ni mukete [The saiban-in system generates false charges: Toward revival of the trial by jury]*. Tokyo: Gendaijinbunsha [in Japanese].

Justice System Reform Council. (2001). *Recommendations of the Justice System Reform Council: For a Justice System to Support Japan in the 21st Century*. Tokyo, Japan: Justice System Reform Council. Retrieved from https://japan.kantei.go.jp/judiciary/2001/0612report.html

Kobayashi, H. (2007). "Okazari saiban-in" wa muyô: "Shihô kaikaku" wo saikentô seyo [Go away with nominal saiban-in: Reconsider the justice system reform]. *Shûkan Hôritsu Shimbun [Weekly Law News], 1742*, 4 [in Japanese].

Matsumura, Y., Kinoshita, M., & Ota, S. (2012). Japanese attitudes toward the lay judge system and criminal justice: Based on the second survey conducted in 2011. *Chiba Journal of Law and Politics, 27*(1), 178–282 Retrieved from https://ci.nii.ac.jp/naid/120005939361.

Mitani, T. (2013). *Seiji seido toshiteno baishin sei: Kindai nihon no shihôken [The jury system as a political system: Judiciary and politics in modern Japan]*. Tokyo: University of Tokyo Press in Japanese.

Okazari ni shitewa naranu: saiban-in (shasetsu) [Don't make them figureheads: Saiban-ins (editorial article)]. (2003, September 30). *Asahi Shimbun (Morning Edition)*, p. 2 [in Japanese].

The Secretariat-general of the Supreme Court of Japan. (2017). *Heisei 28 nen ni okeru saiban-in saiban no jisshi jôkyô ni kansuru shiryô [The material for the state of implementaion of saiban-in trials in* 2016*]*. Tokyo: The Secretariat-general of the Supreme Court of Japan [in Japanese]. Retrieved from http://www.saibanin.courts.go.jp/vcms_lf/H28-103-1.pdf

The Supreme Court of Japan. (2017). *Saiban-in seido no un'yô ni kansuru ishiki chôsa [The consciousness survey cocerning the operation of the saiban-in system]*. Tokyo: The Supreme Court of Japan in Japanese]. Retrieved from http://www.saibanin.courts.go.jp/vcms_lf/28-i-1.pdf.

Uozumi, A., & Saito, T. (2003). *Ittai, kono kuni wa dou natte shimatta no ka! [What in the world happened to the state!]*. Tokyo: Nippon Hôsôkyôkai Shuppan [in Japanese].

Yanase, N. (2016). Deliberative democracy and the Japanese Saiban-in (Lay Judge) Trial system. *Asian Journal of Law and Society, 3*, 1–23. https://doi.org/10.1017/als.2016.52.

Index

M. Fujita, *Japanese Society and Lay Participation in Criminal Justice*,
https://doi.org/10.1007/978-981-10-0338-7

CPSIA information can be obtained
at www.ICGtesting.com
Printed in the USA
LVHW06*1920190918
590426LV00008B/1/P

9 789811 003370